Insubordination

Trends in Linguistics Studies and Monographs

Volume 326

Insubordination

Theoretical and Empirical Issues

Edited by
Karin Beijering, Gunther Kaltenböck,
María Sol Sansiñena

DE GRUYTER
MOUTON

ISBN 978-3-11-076435-2
e-ISBN (PDF) 978-3-11-063828-8
e-ISBN (EPUB) 978-3-11-063420-4

Library of Congress Control Number: 2019937535

Bibliographic information published by the Deutsche Nationalbibliothek
The Deutsche Nationalbibliothek lists this publication in the Deutsche Nationalbibliografie;
detailed bibliographic data are available on the Internet at http://dnb.dnb.de.

Typesetting: Integra Software Services Pvt. Ltd.
Printing and binding: CPI books GmbH, Leck

www.degruyter.com

Preface

This volume has its origin in a workshop on *(Semi-)independent subordinate constructions*, held at the Annual Meeting of the Societas Linguistica Europaea (SLE) in Leiden, 2-5 September, 2015. The aim of the workshop was to bring together linguists working on different types of (semi-)independent constructions in a range of languages to deepen our understanding of this somewhat peculiar phenomenon by combining theoretical and empirical perspectives. We are greatly indebted to all the participants of this workshop, both the speakers for their presentations and the members of the audience for the stimulating and constructive discussions.

The written versions of the papers have gone through a selective peer-reviewing process with each chapter having been reviewed anonymously by two to four referees as well as the editors. We would like to thank the contributors for their patience and excellent cooperation in the reviewing process. We are extremely grateful to all the external reviewers for their time and expertise, namely Peter Arkadiev, Dagmar Barth-Weingarten, Giulia Bossaglia, Laurel Brinton, Bert Cornillie, Hendrik De Smet, María Estellés, Nicholas Evans, Werner Frey, Pedro Gras, Martin Hilpert, Ritva Laury, Beatriz Mato-Míguez, Heiko Narrog, Adeline Patard, Nikolaus Ritt, Daniela Schröder, Elizabeth Traugott, Freek van de Velde, Johan van der Auwera, An Van linden, Anne Wichmann and Camilla Wide.

We also wish to thank Volker Gast and De Gruyter for their support and the opportunity to publish this book in the Trends in Linguistics Series, and to Julie Miess for the editorial assistance. Finally, our particular gratitude goes to Sebastian Haas for his invaluable help with formatting and proof-reading of the manuscript.

Oslo (Norway), Graz (Austria), Leuven (Belgium), November 2018

Karin Beijering, Gunther Kaltenböck, María Sol Sansiñena

https://doi.org/10.1515/9783110638288-201

Contents

Karin Beijering, Gunther Kaltenböck and María Sol Sansiñena

Insubordination:
Central issues and open questions

1 Introduction: A brief history of insubordination

The past decade has witnessed an ever-increasing interest in insubordination and related phenomena, particularly since the appearance of Evans' (2007) seminal paper 'Insubordination and its uses'. Since then, numerous studies have been published on various types of insubordinate constructions in a wide variety of typologically different languages from different analytical perspectives (see especially Evans and Watanabe 2016a and references therein).

What makes insubordination so intriguing is that it presents a challenge for traditional grammatical frameworks owing to its ambivalent, Janus-like appearance, which combines subordinate structure with main clause function. This dual nature is neatly summarized in Evans' definition, which has by now become accepted currency in the field: "the conventionalized main clause use of what, on prima facie grounds, appear to be formally subordinate clauses" (Evans 2007: 367).[1] An insubordinate clause thus has the appearance of a subordinate clause, but has been reanalysed as a main clause. It is in this subordinate form that insubordination differs from nonsubordination (de Vries e.g. 2007), which is described as a strategy of paratactic text planning that includes parenthesis, apposition, coordination, juxtaposition and hedging.[2] Some illustrative examples of insubordination are given in (1) to (4).

(1)   ENGLISH (ICE-GB:s1a-089-159)
      If you'll just come next door.

(2)   SWEDISH (D'Hertefelt 2015: 23, ːC)
      https://issuu.com/danielheiniemi/docs/o4u05_tr/19)
      Att   du   aldrig   kan   passa   tider!
      COMP   you   never   can.PRS   watch.INF times

---

1 This is a refined version of an earlier definition given in Evans (1988: 255), which identified insubordination as "the use of a formally subordinate clause type as a main clause".

2 De Vries defines nonsubordination as "parataxis in the broad sense. It means the equipollent ranking of clauses or constituents: if β is paratactically construed with respect to α, β is not subordinated to α, and β does not restrict the meaning of α; rather it adds information to α." (de Vries 2007: 203; n.d.); cf. in this context also Heine et al.'s (2016) notion of "theticals".

https://doi.org/10.1515/9783110638288-001

'Why can't you ever keep track of the time!'
(lit.: That you never can watch the time!)

(3) SPANISH (MABPE2-01b, COLA M)
Juan (.) que   v-a   a llov-er
VOC   COMP go-PRS.IND.3SG to rain-INF
'John, [QUE] it's going to rain. (..) [. . .]'

(4) JAPANESE (Evans 2009: 1)
あれを見て！
Are wo   mi-te !
that ACC look-CNJ
'Look at that!'

As can be seen from the examples, insubordinate clauses have all the formal
cues of subordinate clauses. These are, for instance, subordinators, infinitive,
participal or subjunctive inflections on the verbs, subordinate clause word order,
depending on the language-specific markers of subordination. What is absent,
however, is a matrix clause. Instead, they are – at least in their prototypical forms – stand-alone structures as a result of their reanalysis over time
as conventionalized independent constructions. Insubordination thus has
an inherent diachronic side to it. Insubordinate clauses may look like subordinate clauses but to the extent that they adopt main clause use "the
term 'subordinate' means, at best, 'having diachronic origins as a subordinate clause'" (Evans 2007: 370). As such, they straddle the boundary between syntactic structure (mental representation) and actual language use
(see Section 2).

The motivation for subordinate clauses becoming conventionalized as independent structures lies in their adoption of specialized discourse functions.
A number of different functions have been identified for insubordinate clauses,
for instance the expression of requests, epistemic, evidential and deontic
meanings, exclamations, evaluations, and contrastive focus (e.g. Evans 2007;
see Section 4 for further discussion). In the examples above, for instance, (1)
expresses a request, (2) an evaluation, (3) a warning, and (4) a command/
request. Despite the range of different pragmatic possibilities, the functions
of insubordination are still relatively constrained in that they typically involve
interpersonal relations such as the expression of speaker attitudes and the
management of speaker-hearer interactions (e.g. Van linden and Van de Velde
2014: 228; Sansiñena, De Smet and Cornillie 2015a: 16; Heine, Kaltenböck and
Kuteva 2016).

Although the interest in insubordination has been sparked only recently, mainly by Evans' (2007) first systematic study, the phenomenon did not go completely unnoticed before. Some of these notable exceptions include Buscha's (1976) study of *isolierte Nebensätze* 'isolated subordinate clauses' and Weuster's (1983) study of *nicht-eingebettete Nebensätze* 'non-embedded subordinate clauses' for German, and Ohcri's (1996, 2000) study of *chuudansetsu* 'suspended clauses' for Japanese. It was particularly in the Romance languages that insubordination has received some attention, for instance Schwenter's (e.g. 1996, 1999) investigation of independent *si*-clauses in Spanish (cf. also Almela Perez 1985; Montolío 1999; Gras 2011), Lombardi Vallauri's (2003, 2004) study of *ipotetiche sospese* 'suspended hypotheticals' and 'free conditionals' in Italian, and Debaisieux's (2006) discussion of *subordonées sans principales* 'subordinates without main clauses' in French (cf. also Deulofeu 1988, 1999).[3] In English, the focus has been mainly on what Stirling (1998) calls "isolated *if*-clauses" (cf. also Ford and Thompson 1986; Ford 1997; Declerck and Reed 2001). Other studies relate to smaller languages such as Evans' (e.g. 1988) earlier work on the Australian Kayardild language and Mithun's (2008) work on the North American languages Yu'pik and Navajo.

As can be seen from the brief overview above, the phenomenon of insubordination has been discussed under various different guises. Other terms used to refer to it include, for instance, "independent conditional clause" (e.g. D'Hertefelt 2013), "free conditional" (e.g. Lombardi Vallauri 2004, 2010), "suspended clause" (e.g. Ohori 1996), "stand-alone nominalization" (e.g. Yap et al. 2011), and "de-subordination" (Givón 2015: 661–691). Although some of these terms may be more accurate, the present volume has adopted Evans' "insubordination" as it has by now become the most established term. It also conveniently highlights the process nature of the phenomenon and captures its 'unruliness' in terms of fitting into traditional grammatical frameworks.

It is precisely this 'unruliness' which makes it fall outside the moulds of traditional grammar that can be seen as responsible for the lack of attention insubordination has received in grammatical descriptions. This is true even for the reference grammars of well-described languages such as Latin, Classical Greek and English (as noted by Evans and Watanabe 2016b: 19). As a clause type which does not meet the criteria of completeness of written syntax, insubordinate clauses were either ignored in earlier linguistic work or marginalized as anomalies (see Section 2).

---

3 For Spanish Evans (2007: footnote 3) also notes an early mention of insubordination in Bello (1847).

In recent years, however, insubordination has moved more centre stage. This is in no small amount due to Evans (2007), who has shown insubordination to be far from exceptional but widely attested cross-linguistically. His work has led to a spate of studies which have identified the phenomenon in ever more languages, providing more and more fine-grained descriptions: for instance for Spanish (e.g. Gras 2011, 2013, 2016; Sansiñena, De Smet and Cornillie 2015a, 2015b; Gras and Sansiñena 2015, 2017; Sansiñena 2015, 2017; Elvira-García 2016; Elvira-García et al. 2017), English (e.g. Mato-Míguez 2014a, 2014b, 2014c, 2016; Brinton 2014a, 2014b; Schröder 2016; Kaltenböck 2016), Dutch (e.g. Verstraete, D'Hertefelt and Van linden 2012; Boogaart and Verheij 2013; Boogaart 2015; Beijering 2017), Swedish (e.g. Laury, Lindholm and Lindström 2013; D'Hertefelt and Verstraete 2014; Lindström, Lindholm and Laury 2016), Danish (e.g. D'Hertefelt and Verstraete 2014), Norwegian (e.g. Beijering 2016), Finnish (e.g. Laury 2012; Laury, Lindholm and Lindström 2013; Lindström, Lindholm and Laury 2016), Italian (e.g. Lombardi Vallauri 2010), French (e.g. Patard 2014; Debaisieux, Deulofeu and Martin 2008), German (e.g. Kaiser 2014), Germanic languages more generally (e.g. D'Hertefelt 2018) and various non-Indo European languages (e.g. Cable 2011). This surge of interest in insubordination can, no doubt, also be attributed to the availability of large spoken corpora, which allow for the investigation of low-frequency phenomena, as well as the development and coming of age of new theoretical frameworks which take into account the emergent and interactional nature of language (see Section 2).

The most comprehensive book-length treatment of insubordination to date is Evans and Watanabe (2016a), which offers a timely overview of the advances in the field since the publication of Evans (2007) and Mithun (2008). The contributions span a wide range of different topics from detailed descriptions of (language-specific) structural and semantic correlates of insubordination (e.g. Mithun [Mohawk], Schwenter [Spanish], Gras [Spanish], Lombardi Vallauri [Italian], Narrog [Japanese], Watanabe [Sliammon Salish]) to insights from discourse and interactional linguistic approaches (e.g. Heine et al. [English], Dwyer [Inner Asian Turko-Mongolic languages], Floyd [Cha'palaa language of Ecuador]) and typological overviews of insubordination phenomena (e.g. Evans and Watanabe [Kayardild], Verstraete and D'Hertefelt [Germanic languages], Berge [Aleut], Comrie et al. [Tsezic languages], Robbeets [Transeurasian languages], Cristofaro [cross-linguistic perspective]).

The present volume complements Evans and Watanabe (2016a), in particular with regard to the delimitation of the concept by extending the scope to semi-insubordination and other related constructions. Based on a selection of studies presented in the workshop '(Semi-)independent subordinate constructions' at the 48th SLE conference in Leiden, the volume provides an up-to-date overview of current research on the topic. The perspective adopted is a cross-linguistic one which covers a range of different languages (viz. English, Finnish, French, German, Mohawk, Navajo, Old Church Slavonic, Polish, Russian, Spanish, Swedish) and various forms of (semi-)insubordination. By bringing together contributions from different perspectives and theoretical backgrounds, this volume hopes to deepen our understanding not only of individual instances of insubordination, but also of the category as a whole. More specifically, the volume has the following three aims:

(i)   To explore how the category of insubordination can be delimited and which different levels of (in)dependence should be distinguished (e.g. syntactic, semantic/pragmatic, dyadic)

(ii) To investigate the grammatical status of insubordinate constructions and how they can be accounted for in a grammatical analysis/model.

(iii) To describe the formal and functional characteristics of specific instances of insubordination, both synchronic and diachronic.

In the remainder of this chapter we will give a brief overview of some of the pertinent topics in the research on insubordination and related structures. Section 2 looks at the question of the grammatical status of insubordinate constructions. Section 3 discusses different possible types of this phenomenon. Section 4 outlines their functional versatility and Section 5 highlights the challenge of insubordination from a diachronic perspective. Section 6, finally, provides an overview of the individual contributions to the volume.

2 What is their grammatical status?

As noted above, insubordinate clauses represent a challenge for grammatical representation. They are clearly subordinate in terms of their structure; in terms of their use, however, they are like independent main clauses. This combination of syntactic independence on the one hand, and formal signs of subordination (e.g. subordinator, subordinate-clause word order, etc.) on the other, is difficult to account for in a grammar. In this sense insubordinate clauses live up to the double-meaning of the term 'insubordination' as highly 'unruly' constructions.

Various attempts have been made in the grammatical literature to come to terms with their ambivalent nature. One approach is to deal with them simply as performance features which involve ellipsis.[4] The problem with ellipsis-based

---

4 Ellipsis-based accounts have also been applied in the domain of generative semantics (e.g. Lakoff 1968).

accounts is, however, that the missing matrix clause is not always fully and unambiguously recoverable from the context (as shown e.g. for *if*-clauses by Stirling 1998; Lombardi Vallauri 2004; Mato-Míguez 2014a, b). Compare, for instance, the following example, where there is a wide range of possibilities for the reconstruction of a matrix clause (e.g. *I'd be grateful, feel free to do so*, etc.).

(5)   *If you'd like to say a few words.*

Moreover, an ellipsis approach may be problematic as it fails to account for cases where the subordinate clause i) has a complete (i.e. terminal) prosodic contour (e.g. Schwenter 2016; Elvira-García, this volume; cf. also Kaiser and Struckmeier, this volume), ii) has its own illocutionary force, and iii) shows structural signs typical of a main clause such as the ability to coordinate with another main clause or the ability to take a subordinate clause as its dependent (e.g. Mato-Míguez 2014a, b). Features such as these suggest that we are not dealing with incomplete structures which are the result of performance 'accidents', but rather with deliberately produced and complete constructions.

When insubordinate clauses are treated as part of the grammar, they are often relegated to its margins and classified as unsystematic, non-canonical patterns, which are somehow incomplete. Quirk et al. (1985: 838ff), for instance, subsume them under so-called "irregular sentences" on account of their "not conform[ing] to the regular patterns of clause structures". Similarly, Huddleston and Pullum (2002: 944) take insubordinate clauses to belong to the category of "minor clause types", which subsumes "a number of main clause constructions that do not belong to any of the major clause types".[5] However, the notion of incompleteness is tied to our concept of grammar and can be seen as an artefact of grammatical tradition (see Debaisieux et al., this volume; Struckmeier and Kaiser, this volume; Wiemer, this volume; Bergs 2017; Traugott 2017: 294).

The reason why insubordinate clauses have for a long time either been ignored or marginalised by grammatical description is to a large extent rooted in our understanding of grammar itself. Clearly, a phenomenon such as insubordination is difficult to accommodate in a view of grammar which builds on a relatively stative model of competence divorced from performance and which has written language as its main object of interest. Instead, insubordination requires us to rethink certain grammatical assumptions and adopt a more

---

5 In a similar vein, Stirling (1998: 289) identifies insubordinate *if*-clauses as "minor sentence types".

dynamic view of grammar which takes into account spoken interaction in equal measure. More specifically, insubordination is particularly compatible with grammatical models that embrace positions such as the following:

(a) *A dynamic link between usage and structure (parole and langue, performance and competence)*: This is of course the view adopted by the paradigm of usage-based grammar (e.g. Langacker 2000; Haiman 1994; Bybee 2010), which sees linguistic structure as emerging out of actual language usage with constant interaction between these two levels. As a theory of grammar which has gained momentum in recent decades it has undoubtedly provided fertile ground for the investigation of phenomena such as insubordination (see also Kaltenböck, this volume). Evans and Watanabe (2016b: 1) even identify insubordination as "a key site for understanding the dynamic and constant interplay of parole and langue, i.e. of actual spoken data in discourse on the one hand, and grammatical models used by speakers (or grammarians) on the other". This interplay is particularly obvious in the presumed emergence and diachronic development of insubordination (see Section 5), but also synchronically, in the use of insubordinate clauses in interaction (see next point).

(b) *The adoption of an interactional perspective:* With the rise of corpus linguistics, the focus in grammatical investigation has increasingly shifted to spoken language, particularly to its interactional use, which is generally seen as the most natural 'habitat' of spoken language. Speech in interaction is, in fact, at the core of many more recent approaches to language, such as Conversation Analysis, Emergent Grammar and Interactional Linguistics, which focus on how utterances are being co-constructed by the participants. In these frameworks insubordination no longer has to be conceptualized in terms of complete complex sentences, as demonstrated for instance by Couper-Kuhlen's (1996) interactional discussion of independent *because*-clauses in conversation. Such an interactional perspective is particularly relevant for the analysis of dyadic insubordinations or "collaborative insubordinations" (Hilpert 2015), as in (6), and can provide vital clues for explaining the emergence of the construction, both synchronically and diachronically (e.g. Sansiñena 2015; Sansiñena, De Smet and Cornillie 2015a; Lindström et al., this volume).

(6) SPANISH (YCCQA, Sansiñena et al. 2015a: 4)
A: *¿Qué significa ser racional?*
'What does it mean to be rational?'
B: *Que distingues entre el bien y el mal creados por un precepto social.*
'That you distinguish among good and evil created by a social precept.'

(c) ***The inclusion of prosody in grammatical description:*** An extension of grammar to account also for all types of spoken language, including its interactional forms, naturally entails a foregrounding of the role of prosody. All too often, however, prosody is still seen as a mere appendage to grammatical description, rather than one of the formal means that signals meaning as an integral part of grammatical constructions. The study of insubordination thus serves as an important reminder of the role of prosody for a comprehensive grammatical description. In fact, prosody has been shown to be a crucial factor in distinguishing insubordinate clauses from regular subordinate clauses (e.g. Gras 2011, 2016; Schwenter 1996, 1999, 2016; Debaisieux 2006; Debaisieux, Deulofeu and Martin 2008; Lombardi Vallauri 2016; Kaltenböck 2016; Elvira-García, this volume), with cases of prosodic ambiguity being centrally involved in the emergence of insubordination.

The concept of insubordination thus challenges our understanding of grammar on a number of different levels. It reminds us, in particular, of the necessity to conceptualize grammar not only as an inventory of stored, more or less conventionalized linguistic units, but also as an activity, used for designing utterances in a given situation. As noted by Evans and Watanabe (2016b: 2), insubordinate clauses "lie at the threshold of process and product, or energeia and ergon". To capture this dual process-product nature, certain concepts and frameworks seem to be particularly helpful. One such concept is 'constructionalization' (Traugott and Trousdale 2013: e.g. 22), which refers to the creation of new mental representations (form-meaning pairs) in the grammar of a speaker and has been applied for the process of conventionalization involved in the development of insubordinate clauses (e.g. Evans 2007: 374; Heine et al. 2016). Another concept that has been proposed for the creation of insubordination is that of 'cooptation' (Kaltenböck et al. 2011; Heine et al. 2017). It denotes a cognitive operation which is supposed to precede the constructionalization of insubordinate clauses (Heine et al. 2016), and so-called 'theticals' more generally (for further discussion of the diachrony of insubordination see Section 5). Finally, one framework that seems to be particularly suited to accommodating a phenomenon such as insubordination is that of Construction Grammar (e.g. Goldberg 2006), which sees constructions as conventionalised form-meaning pairings with some idiosyncrasy, where meaning may be attached to the construction as a whole (as discussed in Section 4). It can also account for the close link to related constructions (e.g. subordinate clauses with explicit matrix clause) by its network concept, where constructions are seen as independent, but not isolated entities and as such are linked to other formally or functionally related constructions in a taxonomic network of constructions (e.g. Kaltenböck 2016).

3 How many types of insubordination are there?

As a typologically wide-spread phenomenon which potentially involves the whole gamut of subordinate clause types available in a particular language, the phenomenon of insubordination not surprisingly encompasses a considerable number of different forms as well as functions. In terms of form, it is possible to distinguish different types of subordinate characteristics, such as infinitive, participial, or subjunctive inflections of the verb, subordinate word order, and different types of subordinators. In terms of function, Evans (2007), for instance, has identified a wide range of different types which include interpersonal control (e.g. warnings, requests), modal meaning (e.g. epistemic, evidential, deontic, exclamation, evaluation), and signalling presupposed material (e.g. negation, contrast, reiteration) (see Section 4 for discussion). Insubordination is thus marked by considerable variation in both its structure and discourse function.

A further criterion for distinguishing different types of insubordination is its degree of autonomy or independence from the preceding co-text. This question is particularly interesting as it interacts with the scope of dependency and also impinges on the issue of category delimitation more generally (see Kaltenböck, this volume). The insubordinate constructions originally discussed by Evans are typically fully autonomous or self-contained, as illustrated by the example in (7).

(7)   ENGLISH (Evans 2007: 380)
      If you could give me a couple of 39c stamps please.

However, Evans' account already incorporates different degrees of insubordination by virtue of its diachronic perspective, which proposes a historical trajectory from ordinary subordinate clauses with an overt main clause to fully reanalysed and conventionalised main clause structures via two intermediary stages: (i) ellipsis of a fully recoverable main clause, (ii) conventionalized ellipsis with restrictions on permitted reconstructions (see Section 5). Although Evans' definition of insubordination focuses on fully conventionalised main clause uses of formally subordinate clauses, the boundary between conventionalised and non-conventionalised is clearly a fluid one. While thus acknowledging different *degrees* of dependency in the development of insubordinate constructions, the *scope* of these dependency relations is generally confined to the domain of the sentence and its missing matrix clause.

By contrast, a wider scope of dependency relations is noted by D'Hertefelt and Verstraete (2014), who distinguish two types of Swedish and Danish *at(t)* constructions: (i) expressives, which have scope over the sentence as in Evans' account and (ii) elaboratives, which elaborate on something that was said before by the same speaker or a different one. This latter type, illustrated in (8), is thus pragmatically dependent on the preceding co-text. As such, it is seen as falling outside insubordination proper and is attributed to a different mechanism, viz. that of dependency shift (Günthner 1999; Verstraete 2007).

(8) SWEDISH (GSLC, D'Hertefelt and Verstraete 2014: 92)
     A: *om vi skulle fråga våra eh förstaklassare här om dom vill ha betyg eller*
         inte skulle dom inte fatta vad det handlade om vet inte hur vad betyg
         eller vad det e (. . .) så det ju nånting som / andra lägger på
     B: *ja*
     A: **att   det det kommer   ju   sen   atomatist   i**
         COMP   it   it   come.PRS PART   afterwards automatically in
         skolan   att   man får   betyg *å då kommer den här /*
         school.DEF COMP one   get:PRS   grades
         konkurrensen ännu mera in tror jag va
     'A: if we were to ask our first-graders here if they want to have a diploma
         or not they wouldn't understand what it was about don't know how
         what grades or what it is (. . .) so it's something that / others impose
     B: yes
     A: **that it it then comes automatically in school that one gets grades**
         and then this competition starts even more I think right'

An even wider scope of dependency has been observed by Mithun (2008) in her study of Navajo and Yup'ik markers, which operate over larger stretches of discourse, rather than over the sentence concerned. Mithun (2008: 108) analyses these data in terms of what she calls (functional) extension, whereby patterns of grammatical dependency can be extended from the sentence into larger discourse and pragmatic domains.

Another type of dependency beyond the sentence has been identified in dyadically-dependent clauses, i.e. clauses in spontaneous interaction which can be construed as projections of a complement-taking predicate in a previous turn (Gras 2011, 2013, 2016; Sansiñena 2015; Sansiñena, De Smet, and Cornillie 2015a; Gras and Sansiñena 2015). A typical example are question-answer pairs as in (9), where the complementizer-initial answer can be construed as depending on the matrix clause *it means* in the preceding question. The scope of the insubordinate clause thus extends over two sentences.

(9)   ENGLISH (YCCQA, Sansiñena et al. 2015a: 5)
      A: *What does it mean if you're getting white hair before 20?*
      B: ***That you are the next messiah.***

Dyadically dependent clauses such as these are seen as providing a functional motivation for the ellipsis of the main clause, as proposed by Evans' (2007) account (Sansiñena, De Smet, and Cornillie 2015a: 17).[6] In a similar vein, various other studies have identified the mechanism of co-construction in interactive discourse as a major factor in the emergence of insubordination in a range of different languages (e.g. Dwyer 2016; Floyd 2016; Evans and Watanabe 2016; Heine et al. 2016; Hilpert 2015).

The typology of semi-autonomous subordination has been further expanded by Van linden and Van de Velde (2014), who draw attention to subordinate *dat*-clauses in Dutch which are preceded by a single matrix element. Constructions such as these with an incomplete matrix clause are referred to as semi-insubordination. The matrix element may be a noun, as in the example below, or an adjective or an adverb.

(10) DUTCH (CONDIV, Van linden and Van de Velde 2014: 231)
      chance   ***dat***   ***mijne radio hier nog opstaat***
      good.luck COMP   my   radio here PRT be.on.PRS
      'Luckily my radio is still on (here).'

To conclude, formally dependent clauses used as independent sentences do not represent a uniform, monolithic category. Various types of autonomous and semi-autonomous insubordinate clauses have been identified, in addition to different formal and functional types. This variety raises a number interesting research questions, some of which will be addressed in this volume. First, do all of these types necessarily have to be subsumed under insubordination or can some of them be included in a separate category (see e.g. Mithun, this volume; Kaltenböck, this volume; Sansiñena, this volume). Second, is the relationship between the different types of autonomy a gradient one and how can we best account for such a cline? Third, to what extent is the degree of autonomy

---

6 Although Evans (2007: e.g. 418) does not seem to include dyadically construed examples in his category of insubordination, he does acknowledge that "independent clauses may also be a powerful device for integrating successive conversational turns: 'a participant in a conversation may interject, add to, or question the statement of another participant, by using a sentence that is a clause morphologically subordinated [...] to a sentence uttered by another participant.'" (Evans 2007: 418).

linked to different forms and discourse functions? Fourth, have the different types emerged from different source constructions and do they all follow the same pathways of development? (see e.g. Mithun, this volume).

4 Functions of insubordination

Evans (2007: 387–423, 2009) sets out heuristically to explore the full functional range of insubordination. As was mentioned in Section 3, he proposes three high-level functions of insubordination cross-linguistically: (i) indirection and interpersonal control, which is found in orders, commands, hints, requests, permissives, warnings and threats, as in (11), (ii) modal insubordination, which expresses epistemic, evidential and deontic meanings, as well as evaluation, as in (12), and (iii) the marking of various discourse contexts which involve a high degree of presuppositionality such as negation, contrastive focus constructions, trans-sentential contrast and switch-reference, discourse contrast, reiteration, disagreement with assertions by the previous speaker, and conditions on preceding assertions in interaction, as in (13). This third function, Evans (2007: 368) points out, is related to the adjustment of certain devices which express inter-clausal relations "to the expression of discourse relations more generally".

(11) ENGLISH (Evans 2007: 393)
   If you (dare) touch my car!

(12) ENGLISH (Evans 2007: 403)
   That I should live to see such ingratitude!

(13) ENGLISH (Evans 2007: 418)
   A: *Is it practically impossible to have that [a certain demand curve]?*
   B: ***If you have this base.***

Let us briefly look at each of the three functions in turn. The first function is related to so-called 'face-threatening acts' (Brown and Levinson 1987), i.e. acts which challenge the face wants of an interlocutor. Evans (2007) argues that insubordinating ellipsis puts the face-threatening act 'off the record' by leaving the implication suspended. He illustrates this first function by providing examples of ellipsed requests and desire predicates, such as the Latin independent subjunctive in (14): This example – originally discussed in Lakoff (1968) – may express an imperative, a wish or a possibility.

(14) LATIN (Lakoff 1968: 158, cited in Evans 2007: 388)
Ven-ias
come-PRS.SUBJ.2SG
'Come!/May you come!'

Other structures discussed by Evans in this category include ellipsed enabling predicates, result clauses, and free-standing infinitives.

According to Evans (2007: 393–4), the threatening nature of directive speech acts forces speakers to come up with alternative formulations whose pragmatic force does not carry the negative connotations of existing formulas. However, he also concedes that in certain cases the pragmatic value of the insubordinate request might not be more polite than that of a more direct form. Similarly, Gras (2011) points out that it is not clear, on the basis of the diachronic motivation proposed by Evans, whether certain insubordinate structures expressing the first function of Evans' typology actually operate as strategies to achieve indirectness.

As for the second function, i.e. modal insubordination, Evans (2007: 394) discusses (i) epistemic and evidential insubordination, involving ellipsed main clauses of reporting, thinking, perceiving and asserting, (ii) deontic insubordination, typically involving complementizers with "additional semantic content, such as showing tense/mood relations between clauses", and (iii) evaluative insubordination, in which the omission of the matrix clause implies amazement or shock. An example of deontic insubordination is given in (15), where the Italian independent subjunctive is used to express hortative meaning:

(15) ITALIAN (Moretti and Ovieto 1979, cited in Evans 2007: 401)
Si   aggiunga   poi   che   l'uomo   è   pedante
3REFL add.SUBJ.3SG then that DEF.man is pedant
'And then may it be added that the man is a pedant.'

The third function, finally, implies high levels of presupposed material about the discourse context in which the sentence can occur (Evans 2007: 401). As was mentioned above, there are various types of this use of insubordination, such as the expression of negation, contrastive focus, and reiteration. For negation, Evans (2007: 410–13) proposes that independent negative clauses used to be subordinated to main clauses which carried the assertion, while contrastive focus constructions presuppose a clause that is similar but predicated of another referent. The use of reiteration implies ellipsis of a main clause which reports the speech act of saying or asking. This is illustrated in (16), where the declarative subjunctive in Basque is used to signal a reiterated statement:

(16) BASQUE (Evans 2007: 419)
    A: *Jon   d-a-tor*
       John 3SG.ABS-PRS-come
    B: *Zer?*
       what
    A: **Jon   d-a-tor-ela**
       John 3SG.ABS-PRS-come-SBJV
    A: 'John's coming. B: What? A: [I said] That John's coming.'

Evans (2007: 422) explains this third function of insubordination by arguing that "grammatical machinery that originally developed around overt relations between a main and subordinate clause [. . .] is subsequently generalized to encode similar relations between the insubordinated clause and some other part of the discourse".

The three different functions are, however, not always clear-cut categories. Gras (2011: 352–3), for instance, points out an overlap of the first and second functions of insubordination. Evans himself acknowledges that cases of multifunctionality are common and that, despite his distinction of three higher-level functions, in many languages, such as Gooniyandi and Kayardild, one single insubordinate type can take on diverse functions (Evans 2007: 423). Similarly, Sansiñena (2015: 204) shows that the parameters that define Evans' (2007) three higher-level functions are not mutually exclusive and, for Spanish, multipurpose insubordination is plausible.

Evans' functional classification has been extended in subsequent work on related and unrelated languages from diverse language families. Verstraete, D'Hertefelt and Van linden (2012: 142–143), for instance, discuss the functions of *dat*-constructions in Dutch which expand on – and explain – preceding discourse and establish the functional category of "discursive" insubordination. On the basis of formal and semantic-pragmatic criteria, Sansiñena (2015) identifies three broad construction types for complement insubordination in Spanish: (i) displaced directives, i.e. clauses that express various kinds of deontic meanings, (ii) evaluatives, i.e. clauses that express the speakers' evaluation of a certain state of affairs, and (iii) connectives, i.e. clauses that refer to previous discourse within the same communicative event or in a previous communicative event, and clauses that point to an event that can be directly observed or inferred from the situational context (cf. Gras 2011, 2016).

A number of contributions in Evans and Watanabe (2016) also add functions to the originally proposed list by Evans. Lombardi Vallauri (2016), for instance, argues that Italian 'suspended' or 'free' conditionals can endorse a number of different pragmatic functions ranging from an invitation, an offer and a request, to a protest or refutation of the preceding turn (17) (see also Schwenter 2016 for Spanish and Floyd 2016 for Cha'palaa).

(17) ITALIAN (LIP – *Lessico di frequenza dell'italiano parlato*, Re11)
    D: *signor giudice io ci ho sessantasei anni so' più vecchio pure de lui*
       'your honour I'm sixty-six I'm even older than him'
    E: **se ci   hai   un anno più de me**
       if there have:2sg one year more of me
       'if you are one year older than me'

Gras (2016: 139–140) argues for the necessity to distinguish between sentence-type, modal and discourse insubordination in order to have a better understanding of the functional range of the phenomenon cross-linguistically. He proposes that sentence-type insubordination "codifies a speaker position towards the proposition", while modal insubordination "expresses a modal evaluation [...] without assigning the speaker a modal position" (Gras 2016: 139–140).

Kaltenböck (this volume) argues that insubordinate clauses share many discourse functions with theticals, which relate "to the immediate Situation of Discourse, more specifically the components of Speaker-Hearer Interaction, Speaker Attitude, and Text Organisation", and that semi-insubordination shares with insubordination a similar subjectivising function.

Several authors, including Malčukov (2013) and Mithun (this volume), have argued against there being any functional unity to insubordination, in spite of there being recurring macro-functions, such as context dependency and non-declarative sentence modality, across diverse languages (see D'Hertefelt and Verstraete 2014; D'Hertefelt 2018; Mithun, this volume). Interestingly, within the insubordination literature, there has been a growing interest in exploring the relation between the range of functions and the sources and mechanisms of development of insubordinate constructions. Cristofaro (2016: 14), for instance, has argued against there being a single diachronic source. She posits that an insubordinate clause can have a variety of possible source constructions even if it is related to only one developmental mechanism. However, in many cases, when the discourse function of the construction is ambiguous, it may not be possible to establish which is the mechanism followed. Mithun (this volume) argues that the opposite is also possible, i.e. that only one source construction can be the starting point for the development of different insubordinate constructions with diverse functions, via different developmental processes. We can thus argue that insubordination is an umbrella term for a formally-defined phenomenon which encompasses a wide range of constructions with different formal realizations – which have emerged via different mechanisms – and whose functions can be mapped cross-linguistically but with different sets of functions for individual languages.

5 A challenge for models of diachronic change

Not only does the grammatical status of contemporary (semi-)insubordinate constructions pose problems for its structural representation, it also challenges extant diachronic hypotheses on the grammaticalization of clause combining (e.g. Beijering and Norde, this volume). That is, insubordination seems to run counter to observed unidirectional tendencies in the domain of grammaticalization and clause combining, according to which looser pragmatic elements become more tightly integrated into syntactic structure. Insubordination, by contrast, concerns developments from subordinate clause to main clause, from morphosyntax to discourse, and (in its initial stage) from grammar to pragmatics (Evans 2007: 429).

According to Evans (2007: 370–5) the diachronic path to insubordination consists of four successive stages from subordinate to insubordinate constructions (see Table 1). The first stage, subordination, includes full constructions with an overt main clause. At the second stage, the overt main clause is ellipsed, but any grammatically compatible main clause can be 'reconstructed' by the hearer. The reconstruction of syntactically permitted main clauses becomes restricted by convention at the third stage. At the fourth stage, the construction acquires a specific meaning of its own, and it may not be possible to restore any ellipsed material.

Table 1: A diachronic model of insubordination (Evans and Watanabe 2016b: 3).

Subordination	Ellipsis	Conventionalized ellipsis	Reanalysis as main clause structure
A	B	C	D
Biclausal construction, with subordinate clause	Ellipsis of main clause, any contextually appropriate material can be recovered	Restriction on interpretation of ellipsed material	Conventionalized main clause use of formerly subordinate clause

From this diachronic model, Evans (2007: 386–423) derives a corresponding functional typology of insubordination on the basis of three main types of elided matrix clauses (see Section 4). On this account, insubordinate constructions are the result of ellipsis of (i) predicates of ordering, enablement, permission, desire, etc. (indirection and interpersonal control), (ii) predicates of reporting, thinking, perceiving, asserting, emotion, evaluation (modality), and (iii) markers of cleft constructions, from complex bi-clausal constructions (presupposition) (see Mithun 2008: 105–106).

Recently, several studies (see chapters in Evans and Watanabe 2016a) have pointed out a number of problems with respect to the application of the (synchronic) definition and diachronic model of insubordination as represented in Table 1. These observations also touch upon questions of delimitation (see Section 2): how to analyse 'lookalike' constructions with either too much or too little elided material (e.g. pseudo-insubordination or semi-insubordinate constructions), or which do not result from main clause ellipsis in a complex clause (e.g. ellipsis of a copula/auxiliary, or no ellipsis)?

Narrog (2016: 278) introduces the notion of 'pseudo-insubordination' to refer to "constructions where the former main clause has already grammaticalized (auxiliarized)". Note that this definition also captures instances of 'semi-insubordination' (see Section 2), which concerns formally subordinate clauses introduced by a single matrix element. The main difference between these pseudo-insubordinates and genuine cases of insubordination is their diachronic development: (gradual) condensation/fusion of the main and subordinate clause in case of the former versus (abrupt) omission of the main clause for the latter (see Table 1).

Another scenario applies to 'lookalike' constructions which fulfill the criteria for synchronic insubordination, but do not meet the diachronic prerequisites. This concerns constructions that derive from ellipsis of a copula or auxiliary instead of ellipsis of a main clause (see Comrie et al. 2016). These lookalike insubordinates may also follow an 'indirect' developmental path with intermediate stages. An example of this is the attested path from "subordinate > periphrastic > independent" in the Tzecic languages (Comrie et al. 2016: 179–81). This group of related constructions also includes cases of 'direct insubordination', which do not involve ellipsis of a matrix verb. Instead, nominalized forms are directly reanalyzed as finite forms (see Robbeets 2016: 240).

Thus, especially the role of ellipsis as the main mechanism leading to insubordinate constructions has been questioned in recent studies. A number of alternative mechanisms through which insubordinate constructions come into being have been identified in the past decade: extension of dependency markers beyond the sentence level (Mithun 2008), cooptation (Heine et al. 2016), hypoanalysis (Van linden and Van de Velde 2014), dependency shift (D'Hertefelt and Verstraete 2014), and clausal disengagement (Cristofaro 2016). Likewise, it has been argued that insubordinate constructions may derive from multiple source constructions (cf. Cristofaro 2016) or that one source construction may yield multiple insubordinate constructions (see Mithun, this volume).

6 The present volume

This volume contains eleven contributions dealing with various aspects of insubordination and related phenomena, as outlined in Section 1. The individual contributions are loosely arranged in three groups, each centering around a general topic. The first group (Mithun, Lindström et al., Beijering and Norde, Wiemer) addresses in particular the question of the emergence of insubordination on the basis of diachronic and interactional data. The second group of chapters (Kaltenböck, Sansiñena, Elvira-García) is concerned particularly with questions of delimitation, viz. how to distinguish insubordination from other, related and/or lookalike constructions. The third group of chapters (Von Wietersheim and Featherston, Sánchez López, Struckmeier and Kaiser, Debaisieux, Martin and Deulofeu) addresses a number of issues pertaining to the question of how to account for the peculiar structural features and the special grammatical status of (semi-)insubordinate constructions. The individual contributions are briefly outlined in the remainder of this section.

In her chapter *Sources and Mechanisms*, **Mithun** explores the relations between the diversity of functions of insubordination and the diversity of sources and mechanisms of development. The main argument put forward is that the functions of insubordinate clauses are shaped by their structure of origin and the processes they undergo in their historical development. More specifically, the chapter argues that a single source construction can serve as the starting point for the development of different insubordination constructions, via various developmental processes. Mithun analyzes the Mohawk *tsi* construction and the Navajo *=go* construction, which are formally dependent clauses that are now used as independent sentences. She shows that they originate in adverbial clauses from which they developed via different mechanisms, viz. matrix erosion and extension, with their different paths of development leading to different results regarding function and scope.

Lindström, Laury and Lindholm's chapter *Insubordination and the contextually sensitive emergence of 'if' requests in Swedish and Finnish institutional talk-in-interaction* reports on a synchronic study of Swedish and Finnish insubordinate *om* and *jos* 'if' clauses. These constructions may be used as directives (requests) without any main clause. On the basis of a multimodal analysis of data from service encounters and medical consultations, they demonstrate that these insubordinate *if*-requests are the product of the interaction between participants in a conversation. That is, insubordinate conditional requests emerge on-line in response to verbal and non-verbal actions carried out by the addressees of the requests. Their study takes a critical stance towards Evans' (2007) diachronic pathway of insubordination, in particular the role of ellipsis in this model. The data show that *if*-requests are clearly treated as directives, even in cases without ellipsis when the main clause is subsequently produced. Moreover, insights from language acquisition indicate that insubordinate *jos* 'if' requests emerge prior to the embedded use of 'if' clauses. On this assumption, it would be odd to argue that a main clause is elided, since the child has not acquired the clause combination yet. These two observations call into question whether the ellipsis hypothesis can adequately account for the insubordinate *if*-requests in Finnish and Swedish conversation.

In their chapter *Adverbial semi-insubordination in Swedish: synchrony and diachrony*, **Beijering and Norde** address the problems that semi-insubordinate constructions pose for traditional syntactic analysis and unidirectionality issues in the domain of clause combining and grammaticalization. They show that, although semi-insubordinate constructions are syntactically independent, they are always bound to a preceding proposition in discourse. As such, they occur discourse-internally and function as additional comments or continuations to prior statements and questions. Because of this, semi-insubordinate constructions reflect a sequential/incremental dependency at the discourse level. It is precisely these discursive properties of semi-insubordinate constructions that cannot be accounted for within previous sentence-based accounts that assume a hierarchical/grammatical dependency between the 'minimal matrix' and the subordinate clause. Moreover, it is argued that contemporary semi-insubordinate constructions can only be fully understood in light of their diachronic development. This is illustrated by means of two corpus studies of a particular subtype of semi-insubordination: constructions with subordinate word order introduced by an epistemic adverb. The data support a developmental path in terms of (further) reduction of complex sentence constructions, accompanied by a functional shift of the minimal matrix and subordinate clause, as well as an extension of dependencies at the discourse level.

In his chapter *On illusory insubordination and semi-insubordination in Slavic: putting independent infinitives, clause-initial particles and predicatives to the test*, **Wiemer** presents a critical assessment of the notions of insubordination and semi-insubordination and extant hypotheses on the diachrony of these constructions. On the basis of diachronic data, he shows that three apparent '(semi-)insubordinate' constructions in the Slavic languages (independent clauses with infinitival predicates, *da*-headed finite clauses, and predicatives with clausal complements) cannot be regarded as instances of (semi-)insubordination because their development differs from the explanations in Evans (2007) and Van linden and Van de Velde (2014). For these constructions it is shown that they were not derived from more complex structures, but that these structures are diachronically primary to their complex counterparts which have emerged through analogical expansion, syntactic reanalysis and categorial differentiation.

In his chapter *Delimiting the class: A typology of English insubordination*, **Kaltenböck** proposes a heuristic for delimiting the class of insubordination and identifying its different subtypes in English. He takes a usage-based approach which involves two interrelated levels of analysis, language usage and syntactic structure, to examine the form-function mismatch typical of insubordinate constructions. Both levels are defined in terms of (in)dependency: syntactic dependence vs. independence on the level of syntactic structure, and pragmatic dependence vs. independence on the usage level. It is argued that the criterion of syntactic independence is crucial in distinguishing insubordination from the category of subordination. In addition, the criterion of syntactic independence emphasizes the commonalities that insubordination shares with a number of other extra-clausal structures (e.g. parenthetical uses of subordinate clauses). The larger category of syntactically independent constructions includes instances of semi-insubordination. Application of the criterion of pragmatic (in)dependence results in a twofold division for subtypes of insubordination: stand-alone insubordination and elaborative insubordination.

The chapter *Patterns of (in)dependence* by **Sansiñena** investigates the phenomena of insubordination, semi-insubordination (Van linden and Van de Velde 2014) and causal *que* in Spanish from an interactional-constructional perspective based on conversational data. The chapter describes in detail the pragmatic, speaker-related functions developed by the Spanish complementizer *que* when used without a matrix clause, but also delimits the concepts 'subordination' and 'insubordination' when applied to this phenomenon. In doing so, Sansiñena addresses a number of important aspects in the study of (semi-)insubordination, such as the degrees of (in)dependence of these constructions, the distinction of (semi-)insubordination from lookalike structures, as well as the types of possible elements immediately preceding a *que*-clause and types of relations established between the *que*-clause and its preceding element. The analysis in terms of turn-constructional units (TCUs) which takes into account the structure of the turn-intervention offers a new perspective and an alternative to prior sentence-based analyses of these constructions.

In her chapter *Two constructions, one syntactic form: Perceptual prosodic differences between elliptical and independent <si + V indicative> clauses in Spanish*, **Elvira-García** presents the results of two perceptual forced-choice discrimination experiments aimed at testing whether listeners' disambiguation of two apparently identical utterances depends on the intonational realization. The results clearly reflect how speakers perceive the grammatical construction <*si* + V indicative> as either elliptical or insubordinate depending on its intonation contour: continuation rise contours are preferably selected for elliptical contexts while rising falling contours are preferably selected for insubordinate refutative contexts. The two experiments were carried out using first original recordings and then synthetically manipulated recordings and efforts were made to consider different varieties of Peninsular Spanish in the design of both tests. In line with Elvira-García, Roseano and Fernández-Planas (2017), who show that the distinction between elliptical and insubordinate clauses can be made on the basis of the acoustic prosodic features of the constructions, this chapter demonstrates that the same distinction can be detected perceptually. It is further argued that prosody cannot be considered as a mere reflection of a pragmatic function but rather as a means to convey it and that prosody can provide evidence for assigning constructional status to a given structure.

The chapter *Does structural binding correlate with degrees of functional dependence?* exemplifies how experimental methodology can help improve argumentation in a theoretical debate. **Von Wietersheim and Featherston** present the results of a series of experiments aimed at finding empirical support for certain theoretically predicted differences in binding behaviour between formally identical but functionally different adverbial clauses introduced by German *während* 'while', viz. central adverbial clauses (CACs) and peripheral adverbial clauses (PACs). The authors discuss how CACs show formal and functional dependence on their matrix clause being structurally fully integrated into it, while PACs are functionally more independent of their matrix clause and less integrated. By testing the variable 'binding' in a range of adverbial clauses with different degrees of structural integration, such as temporal and adversative clauses with *während*, it is shown that binding between a main clause and a subordinate clause varies in acceptability, depending on several parameters. The authors compare the binding behaviour of CACs and PACs focusing particularly on the linear order of matrix clause as well as adverbial clause and the relative position of the universal quantifier expression *jede NP* 'every NP' as binder in either the matrix clause or in the adverbial clause.

In her chapter *Optative and Evaluative* que *'that' sentences in Spanish*, **Sánchez López** discusses 'exclamative' and 'optative' readings of Spanish main sentences introduced by *que* 'that' with a subjunctive verb (<*que* + VSUBJ>) and argues that the main differentiating factor between them is intonation. It follows that prosody has a semantic effect: while the optative reading is marked with a downward final intonation, the evaluative reading has an upward final intonation. The two readings also differ in the presuppositions they carry: anti-factive for the optative reading and factive for the evaluative reading. The study proposes that the speaker's emotion is evaluated with respect to a bouletic scale related to the desires of the speaker. In this sense, it is argued that intonation marks the orientation of the bouletic scale. Sánchez López proposes that these *que*-sentences are expressive utterances containing an expressive operator *EX* with a complex left periphery. In line with the proposal by Rodríguez Ramalle (2008a, 2008b), it is argued that *que* is located in the Force Phrase in subjunctive sentences.

Struckmeier and Kaiser take a critical stance towards the concept of insubordination in their theoretically-oriented chapter *When insubordination is an artefact (of sentence type theories)*. They question the basic foundation of research on insubordination which is often rooted in generally accepted – but incomplete or empirically inadequate – assumptions about subordination. By putting various sentence types to the test, they show that an illusion of subordination may be created by sentence type theories that define subordination on too narrow an empirical basis. That is, syntactic theories may mislabel sentences as subordinate clauses, which, upon closer inspection, turn out to be not subordinated at all. Subsequently, these mislabelled subordinated clauses (i.e. non-subordinated clauses) may consecutively be mislabelled as *in*subordinated. The contentious issues with insubordination raised in their chapter are illustrated by means of insubordinate sentences in German as discussed in Evans (2007). They contest Evans' analysis by showing that the alleged subordination of the sentence types in question is an artefact of sentence types theories, and not a property of the clauses themselves. However, they do not claim that insubordination does not exist. Rather they wish to point out that research on insubordination must be carried out with empirical caution and should involve careful analyses of individual languages instead of reference to descriptive grammars.

In their chapter *Apparent insubordination as discourse patterns in French*, **Debaisieux, Martin and Deulofeu** treat the concept of insubordination as an artefact of sentence type theories (similar to Struckmeier and Kaiser's contribution). This claim concerns two empirical situations in French: formally subordinate clauses functioning as independent discourse units (Evans 2007) and peripheral subordinate clauses which display 'main clause features' (Debaisieux 2013). Their analysis is not confined to the level of syntax (unlike Struckmeier and Kaiser's), but extends to the level of discourse. Their approach is based on the fundamental distinction between grammatical syntax and discourse syntax (cf. Blanche-Benveniste 1990). They argue that, by extending syntactic dependency to the level of discourse, candidates for 'insubordination' represent instances of regular syntactic patterns. Their findings are supported by two corpus-based studies on the prosodic, syntactic, semantic, and pragmatic properties of apparent exclamative insubordinates introduced by the subordinating conjunctions *si* and *quand*.

References

Almela Pérez, Ramón. 1985. El *si* introductor de oraciones independientes en español. *LEA: Lingüística española actual* 7(1). 5–13.

Beijering, Karin. 2016. Semi-insubordinate *at*-constructions in Norwegian: formal, semantic and functional properties. *Norsk Lingvistisk Tidsskrift* 34(2). 161–182.

Beijering, Karin. 2017. Semi-insubordinate *dat*-constructions in Dutch: formal, semantic and functional properties. *Nederlandse Taalkunde* 22(3). 333–357.

Bello, Andrés. 1847. *Gramática de la lengua castellana destinada al uso de los americanos*. Madrid: EDAF.

Bergs, Alexander. 2017. The myth of the complete sentence – a response to Traugott. *English Language and Linguistics* 21(2). 311–316.

Blanche-Benveniste, Claire. 1990. *Le français parlé: Etudes grammaticales*. Paris: CNRS.

Boogaart, Ronny. 2015. *Een sprinter is een stoptrein zonder wc. De sturende kracht van taal*. Amsterdam: Amsterdam University Press.

Boogaart, Ronny & Kim Verheij. 2013. Als dát geen insubordinatie is! De pragmatiek van zelfstandige conditionele zinnen. In Theo Janssen & Jan Noordegraaf (eds.), *Honderd jaar taalwetenschap. Artikelen aangeboden aan Saskia Daalder bij haar afscheid van de Vrije Universiteit*, 13–28. Amsterdam/Münster: Stichting Neerlandistiek VU/Nodus Publikationen.

Brinton, Laurel J. 2014a. The extremes of insubordination. Exclamatory *as if!*. *Journal of English Linguistics* 42(2). 93–113.

Brinton, Laurel J. 2014b. If you choose/like/prefer/want/wish: The origin of metalinguistic and politeness functions. In Marianne Hundt (ed.), *Late Modern English Syntax*, 271–290. Cambridge: Cambridge University Press.

Brown, Penelope & Stephen Levinson. 1987. *Politeness: Some universals in language usage*. Cambridge: Cambridge University Press.

Buscha, Annerose. 1976. Isolierte Nebensätze im dialogischen Text. *Deutsch als Fremdsprache* 13. 274–79.

Bybee, Joan. 2010. *Language, usage and cognition*. Cambridge: Cambridge University Press.

Cable, Seth. 2011. Insubordination in Tlingit: An areal effect? *Northwest Journal of Linguistics* 5(1). 1–38.

Cristofaro, Sonia. 2016. Routes to insubordination: A cross-linguistic perspective. In Nicholas Evans & Honoré Watanabe (eds.), *Insubordination*, 393–422. Amsterdam: John Benjamins.

Comrie, Bernard, Diana Forker & Zaira Khalilova. 2016. Insubordination in the Tsezic languages. In Nicholas Evans & Honoré Watanabe (eds.), *Insubordination*, 171–182. Amsterdam: John Benjamins.

Couper-Kuhlen, Elizabeth. 1996. Intonation and clause combining in discourse: The case of 'because'. *Pragmatics* 6(3). 389–426.

D'Hertefelt, Sarah. 2013. Independent conditional clauses in Germanic languages. Paper given at Complex Sentences International Workshop, Leuven, 16 Nov. 2013

D'Hertefelt, Sarah. 2015. *Insubordination in Germanic: A typology of complement and conditional constructions*. Leuven: University of Leuven dissertation.

D'Hertefelt, Sarah. 2018. *Insubordination in Germanic. A Typology of Complement and Conditional Constructions*. Trends in Linguistics. Studies and Monographs [TiLSM] 318. Berlin/Boston: De Gruyter Mouton.

D'Hertefelt, Sarah & Jean-Christophe Verstraete. 2014. Independent complement constructions in Swedish and Danish: Insubordination or dependency shift? *Journal of Pragmatics* 60. 89–102.

Debaisieux, Jeanne-Marie, Henri-José Deulofeu & Philippe Martin. 2008. Pour une syntaxe sans ellipse. In Jean-Christope Pitavy & Michèle Bigot (eds.), *Ellipse et effacement: Du schème de phrase aux règles discursives*, 225–246. Saint-Étienne: Publications de l'Université de Saint-Étienne.

Debaisieux, Jeanne-Marie. 2006. La distinction entre dépendence grammaticale et dependence macrosyntaxique comme moyen de résoudre les paradoxes de la subordination. *Faits de Langue* 28. 119–132.

Declerck, Renaat & Susan Reed. 2001. *Conditionals. A comprehensive empirical analysis*. Berlin: Mouton de Gruyter.

Deulofeu, Henri-José. 1988. La syntaxe de *que* en français parlé et le problème de la subordination. *Recherches sur le Français parlé* 8. 79–104.

Deulofeu, Henri-José. 1999. Problèmes méthodologiques de l'analyse morphosyntaxique de *que* en français contemporain. *Recherches sur le Français parlé* 15. 163–198.

Dwyer, Arienne. 2016. Ordinary insubordination as transient discourse. In Nicholas Evans & Honoré Watanabe (eds.), *Insubordination*, 183–208. Amsterdam: John Benjamins.

Elvira-García, Wendy. 2016. La prosodia de las construcciones insubordinadas conectivo-argumentativas en español. Barcelona: University of Barcelona dissertation.

Elvira-García, Wendy, Paolo Roseano & Ana María Fernández Planas. A. M. 2017. Prosody as a cue for syntactic dependency. Evidence from dependent and independent clauses with subordination marks in Spanish. *Journal of Pragmatics* 109. 29–46.

Evans, Nicholas. 2007. Insubordination and its uses. In Nicolaeva, Irina (ed.), *Finiteness: Theoretical and Empirical Foundations*, 366–431. Oxford: Oxford University Press.

Evans, Nicholas. 2009. *Insubordination and the grammaticalisation of interactive presuppositions*. Methodologies in Determining Morphosyntactic Change Conference, Museum of Ethnography, Osaka.<http://www.r.minpaku.ac.jp/ritsuko/english/sympo sium/pdf/symposium_0903/Evans_handout.pdf>.

Evans, Nicholas & Honoré Watanabe (eds.). 2016a. *Insubordination*. [Typological Studies in Language, 115]. Amsterdam: John Benjamins.

Evans, Nicholas & Honoré Watanabe. 2016b. The dynamics of insubordination: An overview. In Nicholas Evans & Honoré Watanabe (eds.), *Insubordination*, 1–38. Amsterdam: John Benjamins.

Evans, Nicholas. 1988. Odd topic marking in Kayardild. In Peter Austin (ed.), *Complex sentences in Australian languages*, 219–266. Amsterdam: John Benjamins.

Floyd, Simeon. 2016. Insubordination in interaction: The Cha'palaa counter-assertive. In Nicholas Evans & Honoré Watanabe (eds.), *Insubordination*, 341–666. Amsterdam: John Benjamins.

Ford, Cecilia E. & Sandra A. Thompson. 1986. Conditionals in discourse: A text-based study from English. In Elizabeth Traugott et a. (eds.), *On conditionals*, 353–372. Cambridge: Cambridge University Press.

Ford, Cecilia E. 1997. Speaking conditionally: Some contexts for *if*-clauses in conversation. In Angeliki Athanasiadou & René Dirven (eds.), *On conditionals again*, 387–413. Amsterdam: John Benjamins.

Givón, Tom. 2015. *The diachrony of grammar*, Vol. 2. Amsterdam: John Benjamins.

Goldberg, Adele E. 2006. *Constructions at work: The nature of generalization in language.* Oxford: Oxford University Press.

Gras, Pedro. 2011. *Gramática de construcciones en interacción. Propuesta de un modelo y aplicación al análisis de estructuras independientes con marcas de subordinación en español.* Barcelona: University of Barcelona dissertation.

Gras, Pedro. 2013. Entre la gramática y el discuro: Valores conectivos de *que* inicial átono en español. In Daniel Jacob & Katja Ploog (eds.), *Autour de Que. El Entomo de Que*, 89–112. Frankfurt: Peter Lang.

Gras, Pedro. 2016. Revisiting the functional typology of insubordination: que-initial sentences in Spanish. In Nicholas Evans & Honoré Watanabe (eds.), *Insubordination*, 113–144. Amsterdam: John Benjamins.

Gras, Pedro & María Sol Sansiñena. 2015. An interactional account of discourse-connective *que*-constructions in Spanish. *Text & Talk* 35(4). 505–529.

Gras, Pedro & María Sol Sansiñena. 2017. Exclamatives in the functional typology of insubordination: evidence from complement insubordinate constructions in Spanish. *Journal of Pragmatics*. 115. 21–36.

Günthner, Susanne. 1999. Entwickelt sich der Konzessivkonnektor *obwohl* zum Diskursmaker? Grammatikalisierungstendenzen im gesprochenen Deutsch. *Linguistische Berichte* 180: 409–444.

Haiman, John. 1994. Ritualization and the development of language. In W. Pagliuca, (ed.), *Perspectives on Grammaticalization*, 3–28. Amsterdam: John Benjamins.

Heine, Bernd, Kaltenböck, Gunther & Kuteva Tania. 2016. On insubordination and cooptation. In Nicholas Evans & Honoré Watanabe (eds.), *Insubordination*, 39–64. Amsterdam: John Benjamins.

Heine, Bernd, Gunther Kaltenböck, Tania Kuteva & Haiping Long. 2017. Cooptation as a discourse strategy. *Journal of Linguistics* 55(4). 813–855.

Hilpert, Martin. 2015. Kollaborative Insubordination in gesprochenem Englisch: Konstruktion oder Umgang mit Konstruktionen? In Alexander Ziem & Alexander Lasch (eds.), *Konstruktionsgrammatik IV. Konstruktionen als soziale Konventionen und kognitive Routinen*, 25–40. Tübingen: Stauffenburg.

Huddleston, Rodney & Geoffrey K. Pullum. 2002. *The Cambridge grammar of the English language*. Cambridge: Cambridge University Press.

Kaiser, Sebastian. 2014. *Interpretation selbständiger Sätze im Diskurs. Syntax und Intonation in Interaktion*. Frankfurt, a.M.: Peter Lang.

Kaltenböck, Gunther. 2016. On the grammatical status of insubordinate *if*-clauses. In Gunther Kaltenböck, Evelien Keizer & Arne Lohmann (eds.), *Outside the clause: form and function of extra-clausal constituents*, 341–377. Amsterdam: John Benjamins.

Kaltenböck, Gunther, Bernd Heine & Tania Kuteva. 2011. On thetical grammar. *Studies in Language* 35(4). 848–93.

Lakoff, Robin. 1968. *Abstract syntax and Latin complementation*. Cambridge: The MIT Press.

Langacker, Ronald W. 2000. A dynamic usage-based model. In Michael Barlow & Suzanne Kemmer (eds.), *Usage-Based Models of Language*, 1–63. Stanford: CSLI Publications.

Laury, Ritva. 2012. Syntactically non-integrated Finnish *Jos* 'If'-conditional clauses as directives. *Discourse Processes* 49(3–4). 213–242.

Laury, Ritva, Camilla Lindholm & Jan Lindström. 2013. Syntactically non-integrated conditional clauses in spoken Finnish and Swedish. In Eva Havu & Irma Hyvärinen (eds.), *Comparing and contrasting syntactic structures. From dependency to quasi-subordination*, 231–270. Helsinki: Société Néophilologique 86.

Lindström, Jan, Camilla Lindholm & Ritva Laury. 2016. The interactional emergence of conditional clauses as directives: Constructions, trajectories and sequences of action. *Language Sciences* 58. 8–21.

Lombardi Vallauri, Edoardo. 2003. "Pragmaticizzazione" dell'incompletezza sintattica nell'italiano parlato: Le ipotetiche sospese. In Leoni F. Albano, F. Cutugno, M. Pettorino & R. Savy (eds.), *Il parlato italiano*. Napoli: Atti del Convegno Nazionale (Napoli, 13–15 febbraio 2003), D'Auria Editore, (Cd Rom).

Lombardi Vallauri, Edoardo. 2004. Grammaticalization of syntactic incompleteness: Free conditionals in Italian and other languages. *SKY Journal of Linguistics* 17. 189–215.

Lombardi Vallauri, Edoardo. 2010. Free conditionals. *Linguisticæ Investigationes* 33(1). 50–85.

Lombardi Vallauri, Edoardo. 2016. Insubordinated conditionals in spoken and non-spoken Italian. In Nicholas Evans & Honore Watanabe (eds.), *Insubordination*, 145–169. Amsterdam: John Benjamins.

Malčukov, Andrej L. 2013. Verbalization and insubordination in Siberian languages. In Martine Robbeets & Hubert Cuyckens (eds.), *Shared Grammaticalization: With special focus on the Transeurasian languages*, 177–208. Amsterdam: John Benjamins.

Mato-Míguez, Beatriz. 2014a. Are isolated *if*-clauses independent clauses? Evidence from spoken British and American English. In Paula Rodríguez-Puente, Teresa Fanego, Evelyn Gandón-Chapela, Sara Riveiro-Outeiral & Mª Luisa Roca-Varela (eds.), *Current research in Applied Linguistics: Issues on language and cognition*, 48–71. Newcastle upon Tyne: Cambridge Scholars Publishing.

Mato-Míguez, Beatriz. 2014b. *If you would like to lead*: on the grammatical status of directive isolated *if*-clauses in spoken British English. In Alejandro Alcaraz-Sintes & Salvador Valera-Hernández (eds.), *Diachrony and synchrony in English corpus linguistics*, 259–283. Bern: Peter Lang.

Mato-Míguez, Beatriz. 2014c. Looking into the relation between imperatives and isolated *if*-clauses: Evidence from spoken British and American English. In Esther Álvarez López, Emilia María Durán Almarza & Alicia Menéndez Tarrazo (eds.), *Building interdisciplinary knowledge. Approaches to English and American Studies in Spain*, 365–373. Oviedo: AEDEAN & KRK Ediciones.

Mato-Míguez, Beatriz. 2016. The expression of directive meaning: A corpus-based study on the variation between imperatives, conditionals and insubordinate *if*-clauses in spoken British English. In María José López-Couso, Belén Méndez-Naya, Paloma Núñez-Pertejo & Ignacio M. Palacios-Martínez (eds.), *Corpus linguistics on the move: Exploring and understanding English through* corpora, 291–312. Amsterdam & New York: Brill/Rodopi.

Mithun, Marianne. 2008. The extension of dependency beyond the sentence. *Language* 84 (1), 69–119.

Montolío Durán, Estrella. 1999. Las construcciones condicionales. In Ignacio Bosque & Violeta Demonte (eds.), *Gramática descriptiva de la lengua española III*, 3643–3738. Madrid: Espasa Calpe.

Moretti, Giovanni & Giorgio Orvieto. 1979. *Grammatica italiana, vol. 2: Il verbo*. Perugia: Benucci.

Narrog, Heiko. 2016. Insubordination in Japanese diachronically. In Nicholas Evans & Honoré Watanabe (eds.), *Insubordination*, 247–282. Amsterdam/Philadelphia: John Benjamins.

Ohori, Toshio. 1996. Remarks on suspended clauses: A contribution to Japanese phraseology. In Masayoshi Shibatani & Sandra A. Thompson (eds.), *Essays in Semantics and Pragmatics*, 201–218. Amsterdam: John Benjamins.

Ohori, Toshio. 2000. Framing effect in Japanese non-final clauses: Toward an optimal grammar-pragmatics interface. *Berkeley Linguistic Society* 23. 471–480.

Patard, Adeline. 2014. Réflexions sur l'origine de l'insubordination. Le cas de trois insubordonnées hypothétiques du français. *Langages* 196. 109–130.

Quirk, Randolph, Greenbaum, Sidney, Leech, Geoffrey and Svartvik, Jan. 1985. *A Comprehensive Grammar of the English Language*. London: Longman.

Robbeets, Martine. 2016. Insubordination and the establishment of genealogical relationship across Eurasia. In Nicholas Evans & Honoré Watanabe (eds.), *Insubordination*, 209–246. Amsterdam: John Benjamins.

Rodríguez Ramalle, Teresa M. 2008a. Estudio sintáctico y discursivo de algunas estructuras enunciativas y citativas del español. *Revista Española De Lingüística Aplicada* 21. 269–288.

Rodríguez Ramalle, Teresa M. 2008b. Marcas enunciativas y evidenciales en el discurso periodístico. In Inés Olza, Manuel Casado Velarde & Ramón González Ruiz (eds.), *Actas del XXXVII simposio de la sociedad española de lingüística (SEL)*, 735–744. Pamplona: Servicio de Publicaciones de la Universidad de Navarra.

Sansiñena, María Sol. 2017. Eliciting evidence of functional differences: The imperative vs. free-standing *que*-clauses in Spanish. In Daniël Van Olmen & Simone Heinold (eds.), *Imperatives and Directive Strategies*, 265–290. Amsterdam: John Benjamins.

Sansiñena, María Sol. 2015. The multiple functional load of *que*. An interactional approach to insubordinate complement clauses in Spanish. Leuven: University of Leuven dissertation.

Sansiñena, María Sol, Hendrik De Smet & Bert Cornillie. 2015a. Between subordinate and insubordinate. Paths toward complementizer-initial main clauses. *Journal of Pragmatics* 77. 3–19.

Sansiñena, María Sol, Hendrik De Smet & Bert Cornillie. 2015b. Displaced directives. Subjunctive free-standing *que*-clauses vs. imperatives in Spanish. *Folia Linguistica* 49(1). 257–285.

Schröder, Daniela. 2016. *That it should have come to this!* The challenging phenomenon of insubordination. In Fernanda Pratas, Sandra Pereira & Clara Pinto (eds.), *Coordination and subordination: form and meaning – selected papers from CSI Lisbon 2014*, 245–268. Cambridge: Cambridge Scholars.

Schwenter, Scott. 1996. The pragmatics of independent *si*-clauses in Spanish. *Hispanic Linguistics* 8. 316–51.

Schwenter, Scott. 1999. Sobre la sintaxis de una construcción coloquial: Oraciones independientes con *si*. *Annuari de Filologia* XXI(9). 87–100.

Schwenter Scott A. 2016. Independent *si*-clauses in Spanish: Functions and Consquences for insubordination. In Nicholas Evans & Honoré Watanabe (eds.), *Insubordination*, 89–112. Amsterdam: John Benjamins.

Stirling, Lesley. 1998. Isolated *if*-clauses in Australian English. In Peter Collins & David Lee (eds.), *The clause in English: In honour of Rodney Huddleston*, 273–294. Amsterdam: John Benjamins.

Traugott, Elizabeth Closs. 2017. 'Insubordination' in the light of the Uniformitarian Principle. *English Language and Linguistics* 21 (2). 289–310.

Traugott, Elizabeth Closs & Graeme Trousdale. 2013. *Constructionalization and constructional changes*. Oxford: Oxford University Press.

Van linden, An & Freek Van de Velde. 2014. (Semi-)autonomous subordination in Dutch: Structures and semantic-pragmatic values. *Journal of Pragmatics* 60. 226–250.

Verstraete, Jean-Christophe. 2007. *Rethinking the coordinate-subordinate dichotomy. Interpersonal grammar and the analysis of adverbial clauses in English*. Berlin: De Gruyter Mouton.

Verstraete, Jean-Christophe, Sarah D'Hertefelt & An Van linden. 2012. A typology of complement insubordination in Dutch. *Studies in Language* 36. 123–153.

Vries, Mark de. 2007. Invisible constituents? Parentheses as B-merged adverbial phrases. In Nicole Dehé & Yordanka Kavalova (eds.), *Theticals*, 203–234. Amsterdam: John Benjamins.

Vries, Mark de. n.d. The syntax of nonsubordination: Parenthesis, appositions and grafts. https://www.nwo.nl/onderzoek-en-resultaten/onderzoeksprojecten/i/20/1820.html (9/9/2017)

Weuster, Barbara. 1983. Nicht-eingebettete Nebensätze mit Verb-Endstellung. In Klaus Olszok & Edith Weuster (eds.), *Zur Wortstellungsproblematik im Deutschen*, 7–87. Tübingen: Niemeyer.

Yap, Foona Ha, Karen Grunow-Hårsta & Janick Wrona. 2011. Introduction: Nominalization strategies in Asian languages. In Foona Ha Yap, Karen Grunow-Hårsta & Janick Wrona (eds.), *Nominalization in Asian languages: Diachronic and typological perspectives*, vol. 1, 1–58. Amsterdam: John Benjamins.

Marianne Mithun

1 Sources and mechanisms

Abstract: As more descriptions have emerged of formally dependent clauses used as independent sentences, it has become clear that such constructions show rich variety not only in their functions, but also in their diachronic sources and pathways of development. A next step is to examine relationships among the two: the degree to which their origins and the processes they undergo shape their ultimate functions. Here it is shown that their sources may not be deterministic, but the mechanisms by which they develop can strongly affect the outcome. Insubordinate constructions are compared in two unrelated languages, Mohawk and Navajo. Both constructions have emerged from adverbial clauses, but via different mechanisms: matrix erosion in the first, and extension in the second. They now have nothing in common beyond the formal definition.

1 Introduction

Over the past decade, instances of what was previously a barely noticed phenomenon have been identified in a growing number of languages and described in ever finer detail, often with attention to usage documented in corpora of unscripted, interactive speech. It is now clear that 'the conventionalized main clause use of what, on prima facie grounds, appear to be formally subordinate clauses' (Evans 2007: 367) is widespread. But it is also clear there is considerable variation in the function, form, and scope of constructions defined in these terms. Evidence is emerging, furthermore, that they can develop from a variety of origins via a variety of mechanisms, raising intriguing questions about relationships between sources and processes of development on the one hand, and the nature of the outcome on the other. Here it is shown that a single source construction can serve as a point of departure for the development of entirely different insubordination constructions. The differences are shaped primarily by the processes by which they develop. Two genealogically and areally unrelated languages, Mohawk (Iroquoian) and Navajo (Athabaskan), both contain formally dependent clauses used as independent sentences. Both have sources in adverbial clauses. But they developed via different mechanisms, matrix erosion and extension, and, as a result, now differ completely in function and scope.

Marianne Mithun, University of California, Santa Barbara

https://doi.org/10.1515/9783110638288-002

2 Diversity of function, scope, form, and development

A wide variety of functions served by insubordination constructions has been documented, and the list continues to grow. Evans first discussed conventionalized interpretations involving interpersonal coercion (commands, permissives, abilitatives, threats), modal framing (quotation, perception, belief, inference, emotion), and particular local discourse contexts (negation, contrast, reiteration). Verstraete, D'Hertefelt, and Van linden (2012) describe seven functions of Dutch autonomous *dat* constructions in three domains: i) deontic (speakers' hopes or desires), ii) evaluative, and iii) discourse (expansion on previous comment by the speaker or another). Their first would correspond to Evans's modal framing, while their second and third would correspond to his discourse/elaborative functions. Lombardi Vallauri (2016) shows how *se* conditionals in Italian serve as offers/ requests, generic questions, reassurance, inhibition of action, and challenge/ protest. Floyd (2016) describes constructions in Cha'palaa of Ecuador that signal counter-assertion. Narrog (2016: 278) finds that insubordination constructions documented through the history of Japanese "crystallize around two preferred functions: (i) the subjective expression of the speaker's/writer's emotions, and (ii) the indirect expression of hearer-related speech acts". Importantly, Gras (2016), examining Spanish *que*, and Verstraete & D'Hertefelt (2016), describing Dutch, German, English, Swedish, and Danish constructions point to two recurring macro-functions of insubordination arising from their sources in dependent clauses: context dependency and non-declarative sentence modality.

Insubordinate constructions do vary in their scope: (i) the sentence, (ii), adjacent sentence pairs, or (iii) larger stretches of discourse. The dependency relations originally discussed by Evans are confined to the sentence (including an omitted matrix). But many others involve pairs of sentences or turns. Sansiñena, De Smet, and Cornillie (2015) discuss dyadically-dependent clauses in Spanish, French, German and English complementizer-initial answers in question-answer pairs. The answers can be construed as dependent on the matrix of the previous turn, so the scope of the construction extends over two sentences. The discourse connective insubordination discussed in Gras (2011, 2012), and Gras & Sansiñena (2015) similarly links adjacent sentences. Dwyer (2016) shows how insubordination constructions in modern Turko-Mongolic languages originate as co-constructed utterances in discourse. The Cha'palaa construction described by Floyd (2016) contradicts a statement or implicature of a previous conversational turn. D'Hertefelt and Verstraete (2014) distinguish two types of Swedish and Danish *at(t)* constructions: expressives, whose scope is confined to the sentence like those described by Evans, and elaboratives, in which speakers elaborate on a previous statement, either of their own or that of a previous speaker. Still other formally similar constructions show even larger scope. Mithun (2008, 2016a) describes constructions in several languages outside of Europe consisting of prosodically independent sentences which convey various aspects of discourse organization. Cristofaro (2016) discusses clausal disengagement in Italian, whereby speakers use insubordinate constructions to introduce a new discourse topic related to background knowledge shared by the hearer.

Formally, the insubordinate constructions first described by Evans contain, by definition, no trace of a matrix clause (2007: 366). Van linden and Van de Velde (2014) add another formal possibility, semi-insubordinate constructions. Fully autonomous insubordinate Dutch *dat* clauses lack an explicit matrix clause, while semi-insubordinate constructions contain an initial element, but one that is not a full clause.

Insubordinate constructions can emerge from a variety of sources, via a variety of mechanisms. Evans (2007) focuses on the simple ellipsis of a matrix clause. Heine, Kaltenböck, and Kuteva (2016: 39) describe a process they term *cooptation*: "Insubordinate clauses are [. . .] information units that are coopted from a construction type [matrix clause-subordinate clause] where the matrix clause is implied but not formally expressed]". Van linden and Van de Velde (2014), building on work by Croft (2000), cite *hypoanalysis*, whereby speakers come to reinterpret the interpersonal meaning of certain Dutch *dat* constructions as an inherent property of the subordinating conjunction rather than the complex sentence as a whole. The reinterpretation can then facilitate omission of the matrix. This proposal would shift the place of ellipsis from the first step in the developmental pathway outlined in Evans to a later position. D'Hertefelt and Verstraet (2014) cite *dependency shift* whereby a formally dependent clause comes to be dependent pragmatically on a previous turn. Mithun (2008, 2016a) characterizes the process involved in the development of constructions in Barbareño Chumash, Central Alaskan Yup'ik Eskimo, and Navajo as *extension of dependency* from the domain of syntax to that of discourse. Cristofaro (2016: 418) concludes that "individual insubordination patterns are compatible with several possible sources and developmental mechanisms, and it is possible that different instances of these patterns are produced in different ways, both cross-linguistically and within individual languages". She suggests that an obvious next step is to investigate correspondences between sources and mechanisms of development of structures on the one hand, and their functions on the other.

Here constructions that meet Evans's original basic formal definition of insubordination are compared in two unrelated languages, Mohawk and Navajo. Both languages show "the conventionalized main clause use of what, on prima facie grounds, appear to be formally subordinate clauses". But their functions are completely different: they share no semantic or pragmatic core, and they differ in scope. Both have emerged from adverbial clause constructions, but via different mechanisms, mechanisms which have shaped their modern functions.

3 Mohawk

The first construction comes from Mohawk, a language of the Iroquoian family indigenous to northeastern North America. It is based on the particle *tsi*, translatable variously as 'at/in/to/as/how/that'. There is no ancient documentation of the language that would permit us to trace its development philologically, but the arrays of constructions in which the particle occurs permit us to reconstruct likely pathways of development according to what we know about recurring tendencies of language change cross-linguistically. (All material cited here was drawn from unscripted, interactive speech.)

3.1 Simple adverbials

The Mohawk particle *tsi* is used to set off constituents that specify places, times, and manners. In (1) and (2) it forms locative expressions.

(1)   Mohawk place: Kaia'titáhkhe' Jacobs, speaker p.c.
      Wà:kehre' **tsi iakenheiontaientáhkhwa'** *ieiè:teron'.*
      I.thought **at** one.lays.the.dead.with.it   there.she.dwells
      'I thought maybe she was **at the hospital**.'

(2)   Mohawk place: Josie Day, speaker p.c.
      Thó **tsi tetiotóhsate'** *niahà:ke'* *wa'tkahséntho'.*
      there **at** it.elbow.extends there.I went I.cried
      'I went **to the corner** [of the porch] and cried.'

In (3) and (4) it forms temporal expressions.

(3)   Mohawk time: Watshennine Sawyer, speaker p.c.
      Tsi niióhseres *eniakón:ni'*
      at so.it.winter.is.long she.will.make
      '**In the winter** she would make

ne   wà:io
the it.is.fruit.in.liquid
jam.'

(4)   Mohawk time: Charlotte Bush, speaker p.c.
*Thonnéhtha'   ken **tsi** **niwakénhnhes?***
they.come.by Q   **at** so.it.is.summer.long
'Do they come **during the summer**?'

3.2 Adverbial clauses

Mohawk verbs can function as clauses in themselves, but the particle also sets
off locations and times designated by larger clauses, as in (5) and (6).

(5)   Mohawk locative clause: Josephine Horne, speaker p.c.
Thó   ki'   iá:ken'   iahonwaia'ténhawe'.
there in.fact   they.say   they.bodily.took.him.there
'They say they just took him up there

tsi   thonónhsote'   *ne ro'níha.*
to   there it him house stands   the he.is.father.to.him
to his father's place.'

(6)   Mohawk temporal clause: Minnie Hill, speaker
Tsi   tonsahnohtarhóhseron,
at   they.two.were.cleaning.around.again
'As they were cleaning up,

wahèn:ron',   raksà:'a,
he.said   boy
the boy said,

"Ó:ia'   na'thí:io."
other   so.it.is
'It is very unusual.'

Mohawk, like other Iroquoian languages, is what might be characterized as a fully
head-marking language. Grammatical relations are indicated only within the predicate, by pronominal prefixes, like *-honwa-* 3PL>3SG 'they>him' and *-hn-* 2DU.AGT
'they two' in the examples above. In all of the examples seen so far, the *tsi*

constructions designate places or times, but they do not themselves specify the relations of the place or time to the predication. The difference is subtle: most often terms designating places or times locate the situation in space or time. But the same kinds of constructions can serve as core arguments.

3.3 Complement constructions

The same particle *tsi* sets off manner clauses that can serve as complements.

(7) Mohawk complement clause: Billy Two Rivers, speaker p.c.
    Teiotierónnion' **tsi**   **nitewatenno:ten.**
    it.is.strange   **how**   so.our.words.are.a.kind.of
    '**How our words are** is strange' = 'Our language is strange.'

Manner complements are often formed with the particle *tsi* followed by the verb *ní:ioht* based on the verb root *-ht* 'be so'. This verb is often shortened to *ní:*, resulting in a routinized phrase *tsi ni: tsi* 'how', as in (8).

(8) Mohawk manner clause: Charlotte Bush, speaker p.c.
    Iáh ki' tetkaié:ri'   **tsi**   **ní:**   **tsi**   **rótston.**
    not just not.is.it.correct   **how**   so.it.is   **how**   he.is.dressed
    'It wasn't correct **the way he was dressed**.'

(9) Mohawk manner clause: Josie Day, speaker p.c.
    Iáh tewakaterièn:tare' oh *ní:*   **tsi**   **iewá:ko'.**
    not not.do.I.know   Q   how   **how**   I.arrived.there
    'I don't know **how I got there**.'

As in many languages, among them English and Russian, manner clauses can serve as complements of matrix verbs of perception (Kalinina and Sumbatova 2007). A Mohawk group crossing the U.S./Canada border was asked for identification. They responded to the immigration officer's request with the answer in (10).

(10) Mohawk perception matrix: Watshennine Sawyer, speaker p.c.
    Ió:ken   **tsi**   **onkwehón:we na'kwaia'tò:ten.'**
    it.is.visible   **how**   real.people   so.we.are.bodily.such.a.kind.of
    'You can see **how/that we're Natives**.'

The prosody of such Mohawk complement constructions often reflects information structure more closely than does the syntactic structure. The point of the response in (10) was that they were Native, so they should have free passage across the border. The syntactic construction consists of an initial matrix clause 'it is visible', followed by a complement clause 'that we are Native'. (Although constituent order is otherwise generally pragmatically determined, complement clauses routinely follow the matrix.) In pragmatically unmarked situations, a prosodic sentence typically begins with a high pitch on the first stressed syllable, then shows a steady reduction in pitch on each successive stressed syllable. In this instance, however, the pitch on the complement was as high as the matrix, a fact that makes it all the more prominent because of the expectation of declination. The pitch trace can be seen in Figure 1.

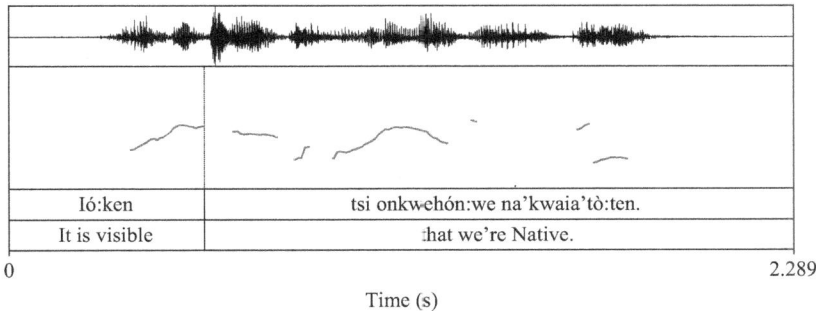

Ió:ken	tsi onkwehón:we na'kwaia'tò:ten.
It is visible	that we're Native.

0   2.289

Time (s)

Figure 1: Mohawk complement prosody and information structure.

Such patterns have been observed for other languages as well, among them English and Dutch (Verhagen 2005).

The *tsi* construction is also used with evaluative matrix verbs, as in (11).

(11) Mohawk evaluative matrix: Sisi Provevost, speaker p.c.
    Wakatshenón:ni   *kí:ken*
    I.am.happy   this
    'I was glad

    tsi, ...   ***enhaweientéhta'ne'***   *wahi'*
    that   he.will.come.to.know.how   TAG
    that he would learn this you know.'

And significantly, the same *tsi* construction occurs with degree complements, as in (12), (13), and (14).

(12) Mohawk degree complement: Billy Two Rivers, speaker p.c.
['When we're writing']

tewattó:kahs ***tsi*** ***kanontsistí:io's,*** *wáhe'.*
we.notice **how** it.is.good.heads.variously TAG
'we realize **how smart we are**, don't we.'

(13) Mohawk degree complement: Sisi Provevost, speaker p.c.
Ahsatkáhtho' ***tsi*** ***nihohehtí:io*** ***nòn:wa.***
you.should.see **how** so.he.is.garden.good now
'You should see **how nice his garden is now**.'

(14) Mohawk degree complement: Minnie Hill, speaker
Nakwáh tehotihenréhtha' ***tsi*** ***nihotkanón:ni wahotíniake'.***
so.much they shout **how** so.he.is.rich they.married.
'They were really bragging **how rich the guy she married was**.'

3.4 Semi-insubordination

As noted earlier, Van linden and Van de Velde (2014) introduced the term *semi-insubordination* to refer to autonomous constructions which contain an initial element that is not a full matrix clause. Mohawk contains constructions which resemble *tsi* complement constructions except that in place of an initial matrix clause, there is just a particle. An example with the particle *tó:ske* 'certainly' is in (15).

(15) Mohawk semi-insubordination: Ima Johnson, speaker
Ó:nen tó:ske ne onkwehón:we
'Then for sure the Native guy

tó:ske ***tsi*** ***rotshenón:ni.***
really **how** he.is.happy
was really happy.'

What is now the particle *tó:ske* 'really, certainly' is apparently an eroded form of a verb like *kat*ó*:kenske'* 'it is certain'. It now serves primarily as an intensifier, but the erstwhile complementizer *tsi* remains.

(16) Mohawk semi-insubordination
Ó *tó:ske* ***tsi*** ***ioiánere' thí:ken.***
oh really **how** it.is.good that
'Oh **it was so nice**.'

Another particle *kwahí:ken* 'very' serves a similar function, again in construction with a *tsi* complement. Examples are in (17) and (18).

(17) Mohawk semi-insubordination: Watshennine Sawyer, speaker p.c.
    Kwahí:ken **tsi**   **ionkwarihwiiohstòn:ne'.**
    very   **how** our.matter.had.been.good
    'We were **VERY religious**.'

(18) Mohawk semi-insubordination: Kanerahtenhawi Nicholas, speaker p.c.
    Kwahí:ken **tsi**   *niionkwashennón:ni*
    very   **how** we.are.happy
    'We are **very happy**

    tsi   *wa'onthón:tate'* …
    that   she.is.willing
    that she's willing … '

The origin of this particle *kwahí:ken* can still be discerned. It consists of the particle *kwáh* 'quite' plus the verb *í:ken* 'it is' (*i-ka-i* PROTHETIC-NEUTER-be).

This construction has been generalized so that any exclamative particle can occupy the place of *tó:ske* 'really' and *kwahí:ken* 'very'. The results are exclamative constructions, as in (19), (20), and (21).

(19) Mohawk exclamative: Watshennine Sawyer, speaker p.c.
    Há:ke **tsi**   *onhterá:ko'*
    gee   **how**   it.took.it.off
    'Gee, **what a load that took off**

    tsi   *kanonhtónnion*   *á:ke* …
    how   I.am.thinking   gee
    my mind … '

(20) Mohawk exclamative: Watshennine Sawyer, speaker p.c.
    Há:ke she's **tsi** *niion'wé:sen*   *nó:nen enhontóhetste'.*
    ah   then **how** so.it.was.pleasant when   they will pass
    'Ah **what a relief it was** when they had passed through.'

(21) Mohawk exclamative: Joe Deer, speaker
    Ó: **tsi**   *niiohsnó:re'* *tsi*   *wahaweientéhta'ne'.*
    oh **how** so.it.is.fast   how he.became.good.at.it
    'Oh **how quickly he learned it**.'

In general, exclamatives still contain an initial expressive element and the particle *tsi*. Occasionally the expressive is omitted, and on very rare occasions, even the particle *tsi*. (Further discussion is in Mithun 2016b.)

Exclamatives in some languages have been described as presupposing a quality and asserting that it holds to an unusually high degree. Presupposition may have been characteristic of the Mohawk constructions at some point, but this is no longer necessarily the case. The speaker of (21), for example, had said that a certain man learned to play the guitar, but there was no previous indication that he had learned quickly. This is of course not unlike their English counterparts (*How nice it is here!*) and the Dutch expressive independent complement constructions cited by D'Hertefelt and Verstraet. The exclamatives simply serve as expressives.

The marker *tsi* thus originated in constructions indicating place, time, and manner. The *tsi* construction was extended to marking clauses functioning as adverbials, to marking degree complements, to semi-insubordination constructions indicating intensity, and finally to semi-insubordinate exclamations. The fact that the scope of the construction is completely contained within the sentence makes sense in terms of its source: a single complex sentence. The mechanisms involved in its development, grammaticalization of an erstwhile matrix clause, then reanalysis of the construction requiring simply some kind of initial expressive marker, and the incipient shift of the expressive force from this initial element to the construction as a whole, also all took place within the context of the single sentence.

4 Navajo

Navajo, genealogically and geographically unrelated to Mohawk, is a language of the Athabaskan-Eyak-Tlingit family indigenous to the North American Southwest. It, too, contains a construction that could be described as "the conventionalized main clause use of what, on prima facie grounds, appear to be formally subordinate clauses" (Evans 2007: 367). It developed from a marker of adverbs, the dialectal and phonologically-conditioned enclitic = *go/=ho/=o/=ǫ*. Material cited here is drawn from unscripted conversation in the Navajo Conversational Corpus (Mithun 2015, funded by NSF Award 0853598). Special thanks go to Jalon Begay, Melvatha Chee, Miltina Chee, Warlance Chee, and Irene Silentman for their help with transcription and translation.

4.1 Simple adverbs

The enclitic derives adverbs. Some designate times, as in (22) and (23).

(22) Navajo time: nav007:00:00:58
 K'ad doo ádajit'į̓į̓' da níio,
 now not one.does not he.said
 '"Now people don't do that", he said,

 abíní=ó.
 morning=ADV
 in the morning.'

(23) Navajo time: nav007:00:33:34
 *Doo **náás=ó** hódoonííł da nisin.*
 not forward=ADV it.will.happen not I.think
 'I don't think it will happen **in the future.'**

The same enclitic derives manner adverbs, as in (24) and (25).

(24) Navajo manner: nav007:00:39:28
 *Áá **hazhóó'ó=go** bíhijiinííł nahalį̓o.*
 there careful=ADV one.adds.them.to.it it.seems.like
 'It seems like one adds them to it **slowly.'**

(25) Navajo manner: nav005:00:15:18
 *Tłééd̄ą̓ą̓' **nizhóní=go** da'iidą̓ą̓'.*
 last.night good=ADV we.ate
 'We really ate **well** last night.'

4.2 Adverbial clauses

The same enclitic *=go/=ho/=o/=ǫ* has been extended to form temporal adverbial clauses, as in (26) and (27).

(26) Navajo temporal adverbial clause: nav.007.00:00:16
 *Ałk'idą̓ą̓', **ádaniilts'iisí=go***
 long.ago we.all.were.young=ADV
 'Long ago, when all of us were young,

(my father would tell us all to wake up)

t'ah   **da'iilwosh=ó**   *ábíní=go.*
still   we.were.asleep=ADV morning=ADV
while we were still asleep early in the morning.'

(27) Navajo temporal adverbial clause: nav005.00:47:57
    Ch'íniijéi'=ó   *shį́į*   *chidí*   *nihátáadoogis.*
    we.walk.out=ADV probably vehicle they.will.wash.it.for.us
    'When we're done, we can get the vehicle washed.'

As in many languages, the construction used for 'when' clauses is also used for conditionals, clauses which provide background conditions for the main clause, as in (28) and (29).

(28) Navajo conditional clause: nav005:00:36:23
    T'áá sáhí **shił dahádíilyeed=o** *shį́į*   *t'óó yoo'ádíishaał.*
    alone   I.drive.off=ADV   probably I.will.just.get.lost
    'If I drive around by myself I'll probably get lost.'

(29) Navajo conditional clause: nav007:00:40:20
    Áá   *áko*
    INTNS   SO
    'It's OK,

    doo **ła'** **shikéé'**   **woosįį=hó**
    not   one   behind.me you.two.will.stand=ADV
    if you won't stand behind me

    shííghahjí *soozį̀.*
    beside.me you.two.stand
    then stand next to me.'

The simultaneity can indicate manner, as in (30) and (31).

(30) Navajo simultaneity: nav005:00:15:24
    Shizhéé' **naalǫ́=ǫ**   *nésh'į́.*
    my.saliva drip.off=ADV I.look.at.it
    'I was just looking at it **drooling**.'

(31) Navajo manner clause: nav005:00:15:40
    Áko **t'aá dzá=o** *kodi   adił   yáshti'*.
    so   aimless=**ADV** over.here self.with I.talk.to
    'I'm just talking to myself **for the fun of it**.'

As in many languages, speakers can echo parts of sentences across turns.

(32) Navajo manner across speakers: nav007:00:52:08
    A: **Tsxį́į́ł=go** *yee   yádaałti'   ya'*?
       fast=**ADV** with.it they.all.speak TAG
       'They speak it **quickly** right?'

    B: *Áá*   **tsxį́į́ł=o**
       very   fast=**ADV**
       'Pretty **quickly**.'

Such conversational structures have been described as sources for insubordinate constructions in a number of languages, but this does not appear to be a major factor in the development of the formally dependent autonomous sentence in Navajo. In Navajo insubordinate constructions, there is usually no possible matrix in the preceding context.

The basic uses of the Navajo enclitic *=go/=ho/=o/=ǫ* described so far are much like those of the Mohawk particle *tsi*, marking basic adverbs and adverbial clauses. But their paths of development from this point were quite different and have led to different results.

4.3 Distribution of information

It was noted in Section 1.2 that in Mohawk, as in many languages, the prosody of complement constructions can mirror their information structure more directly than their syntactic structure. The same is true of Navajo, though in part because it has distinctive tone, and in part because of general prosodic patterns in the language, this can be less obvious in pitch traces. Still, an example can be seen in Figure 2 with the sentence 'They said we'll walk around later'. The pitch of 'we'll walk around later', the most important information, is higher than that of the following 'they said'.

But Navajo sentences like this show something more interesting. Certain syntactic constructions mirror information structure more directly than their translation counterparts in many other languages. Verbs of saying and thinking are not only prosodically less salient than the message or the thought (the most

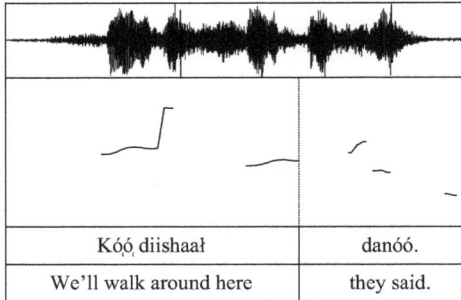

Kǫ́ǫ́ diishaał	danóó.
We'll walk around here	they said.

Figure 2: Navajo verb of saying.

important information), they are often grammatically subordinate to them as well. The verb 'they said' in the sentence shown in Figure 2 and analyzed in (33) is grammatically dependent, marked with the adverbial enclitic =o. 'They said they'd go there to explore' is literally 'I'll walk around here they saying'.

(33) Navajo subordinate verb of saying: nav005:00:18:36
  *Kǫ́ǫ́ diishaał **danó=ó.***
  here.about I.will.walk they said=**ADV**
  '**They said** they'd go there to explore.'

The same structure can be seen in (34) 'We were told to herd sheep'. The message 'you all herd' is syntactically the main clause, while 'we were told' is grammatically dependent, marked with the adverbial enclitic =o.

(34) Navajo subordinate verb of saying: nav007:00:11:15
  *Nida'nołkaad **nihi'danó=ó.***
  you.all.herd we.were.told=**ADV**
  '**We were told** to herd sheep.'

Verbs of thinking generally show the same pattern, where the content of the thought is more important than the fact of thinking.

(35) Navajo subordinate verb of thinking: nav005:00:19:11
  *Naasht'ézhígii át'é **nisǫ=ǫ.***
  Zuni it.is I think=**ADV**
  '**I think** it's a Zuni word.'

The pitch trace in Figure 3 shows that the verb 'I think' was pronounced with lower pitch than 'It's Zuni'. The lower pitch is in keeping with general patterns

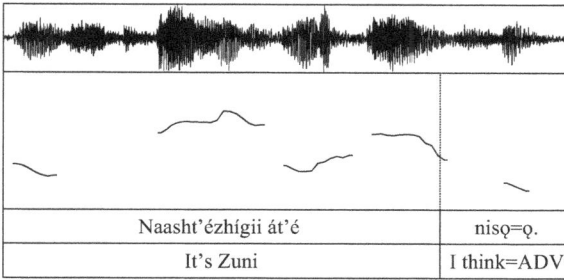

Naasht'ézhígii át'é	nisǫ=ǫ.
It's Zuni	I think=ADV

Figure 3: Navajo verb of thinking.

of declination through the course of an intonation unit, but it appears to be lower than it would be the case in a simple clause.

A similar pattern can be seen in (36) and (37) with the subordinate verb 'I think'. Their lower pitch can be seen in Figures 4 and 5.

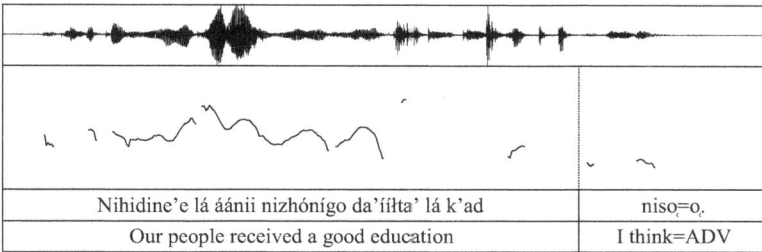

Nihidine'e lá áánii nizhónígo da'íiłta' lá k'ad	nisǫ=ǫ.
Our people received a good education	I think=ADV

Figure 4: Navajo verb of thinking.

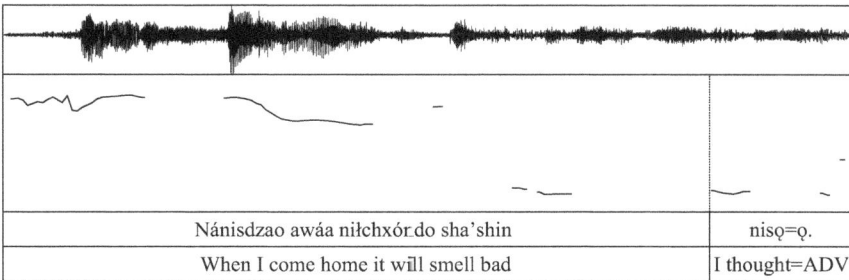

Nánisdzao awáa niłchxór do sha'shin	nisǫ=ǫ.
When I come home it will smell bad	I thought=ADV

Figure 5: Navajo verb of thinking.

(36) Navajo subordinate verb of thinking: nav001:00:17:10

Nihidine'é	*lá*	*áánii*	*nizhónígo*	*da'iiłta'*		*lá*	*k'ad*
our.people	EMPH	real	well	we.went.to.school		EMPH	now

nisǫ=ǫ.
I.think=ADV
'I was thinking our people received a good education.'

(37) Navajo subordinate verb of thinking

N'anisdzao	*awáa*	*niłchxóndo*	*sha'shin*	**nisǫ=ǫ.**
when.I.come.back	very	smell	possibly	I.thought=ADV

'**I thought to myself**, when I come home it will smell very bad.'

Constructions involving verbs of saying and thinking frequently take this form. Other verbs which would usually serve as matrix clauses in other languages but do not express the most important information of the sentence also appear subordinated in Navajo. The verb 'look like/seem' is subordinated in (38) and (39).

(38) Navajo subordinate 'seem': nav007:00:28:12

Éi	*nihá*	*áta'*	*dahalne'*	**nahałi=ǫ.**
that	for.us	between	they.tell	it.looks.like=ADV

'**It seemed like** they were interpreting for us.'

A pitch trace of this sentence is in Figure 6.

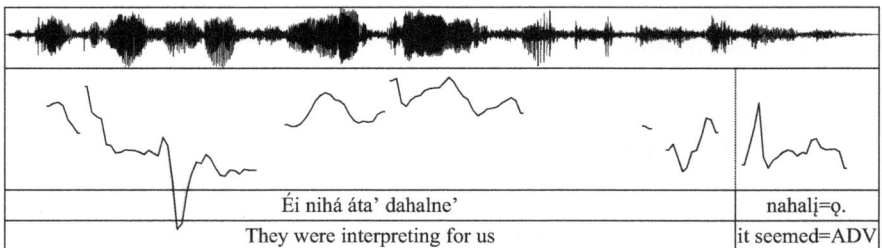

Éi nihá áta' dahalne'	nahałi=ǫ.
They were interpreting for us	it seemed=ADV

Figure 6: Navajo verb 'seem'.

(39) Navajo subordinate verb 'seem': nav.007:00:27:49

Łahóó	*ádaadin*	**nahałi=ǫ.**
parts	they.are.gone	it.looks.like=ADV

'**It seemed like** there were parts missing.'

The use of grammatical subordination to convey information structure can be seen with other verbs as well. The main information in (40) 'I was taught that back in 1500 the Europeans hadn't yet set sail for America' was that the Europeans had not yet set sail. The verb 'I was taught' was subordinate.

(40) Navajo subordinate verb 'I was taught': nav005:00:19:55
Nashi'di'neeztą́ą́=go *éi yahi*
I.was.taught=**ADV**   specifically
'I was taught that

1500   *yę́ę́dą́ą́'*
               then.in.the.past
back in 1500

k'ad   doo   bilagáana bił   dei'eeł   kojo.
now   NEG   Anglos   with.it they.float on.this.side
the Europeans hadn't yet set sail for America.'

4.4 Extension into discourse

The sensitivity of the grammar to information status has been extended a major step further in Navajo. The enclitic *=go/=ho/=o/=ǫ* that served a lexical function deriving adverbs within clauses, and was then extended to a syntactic function marking dependency of clauses within sentences, was extended further to mark the pragmatic dependency of independent sentences in discourse. It now occurs pervasively in prosodically independent sentences conveying comments that are subordinate to the main event line of a narrative or the main topic of a discussion: background information, parenthetical asides, explanations, and evaluative statements. These marked sentences are not dependent on a specific matrix clause, either spoken or unspoken, in the previous context of the same turn or that of another. Their context is the discourse situation. (In all of the examples cited here, the entire conversation was in Navajo, but free translations without the original Navajo are provided to supply context. For the Navajo, separate intonation units are shown on separate lines, and punctuation reflects prosody, with commas for medial phrases and periods for terminal intonation contours.)

Examples (41) and (42) show their use in explanations. Some men were discussing an area at the base of a mountain.

(41) Navajo explanation: nav002:00:04:15
'There's a lot of this thing called sumac berry.
They say there used to be a lot there in the ditch.'

Á'adę́ę́'	*shį́į́*	*tó,*
from.there	maybe	water

'Maybe water,

tó	*ch'ína'na=hó.*
water	it.crawls.outward=ADV

would run out from there.'

The final sentence carried the adverbializing enclitic *=ho*, because rather than adding to the description of the area, it was offered as a possible explanation for the profusion of the sumac. Prosodically, however, it constituted a complete sentence in itself, beginning with a full pitch reset, ending with a final terminal fall, and surrounded by pauses as can be seen in Figure 7.

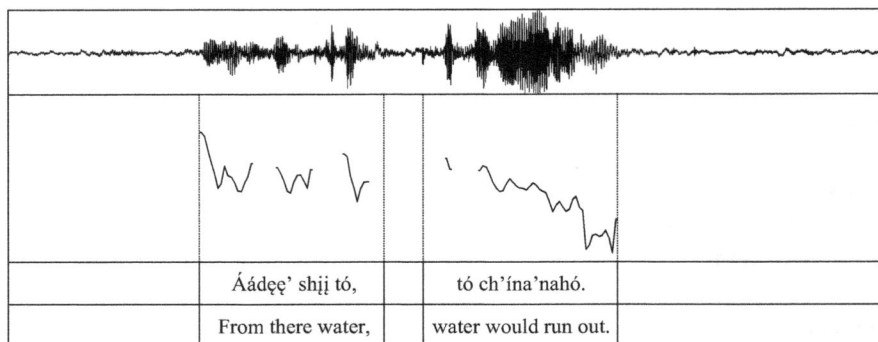

	Áádę̧ę' shį̧į tó,		tó ch'ína'nahó.	
	From there water,		water would run out.	

Figure 7: Navajo explanation.

At another point the men were discussing the status of the Navajo language, and where on the reservation children were speaking it. When one observed that children from Window Rock did not speak, another offered an explanation in a separate sentence marked by the adverbial enclitic.

(42) Navajo explanation: nav002:00:17:00

A:
Tséghahoodzánídoo	*nidaakaiígii*	*doo*	*Dinék'ehjíí*
from.Window.Rock	they.walk.around.NMLZ	NEG	in.Navajo

yádaałti'	*da*
they.speak	NEG

'It's always said that those from Window Rock don't speak Navajo.'

ha'níí	*łeh.*
it.is.said	usually

B: *Ąą'ą.*
'Uhuh.'

Aoo'í.
'Yes.'

Yaa   yádánizin=ó.
about.it   they are shy=ADV
'They're ashamed of it.'

This explanation occurred not only in a separate prosodic sentence, but also across turns. As can be seen in Figure 8, it, too, began with a pitch reset and ended with a terminal fall, followed by a pause.

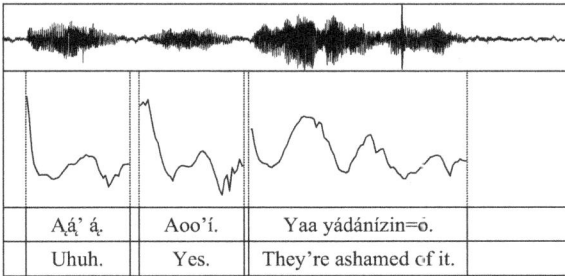

Ąą' ą.	Aoo'í.	Yaa yádánízin=ȯ.	
Uhuh.	Yes.	They're ashamed of it.	

Figure 8: Navajo explanation.

When this speaker then resumed his discussion, it was with another pitch reset, as can be seen in Figure 9.

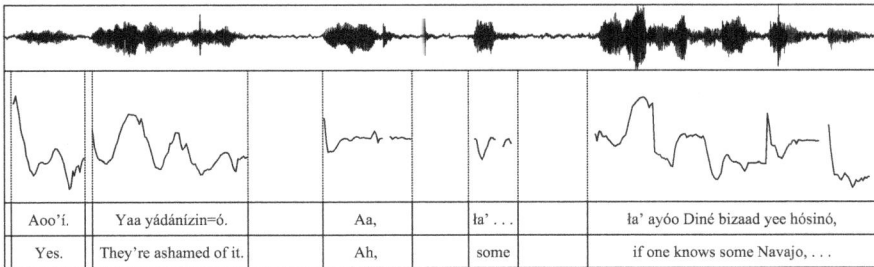

Aoo'í.	Yaa yádánízin=ó.	Aa,	ła' . . .	ła' ayóo Diné bizaad yee hósinó,
Yes.	They're ashamed of it.	Ah,	some	if one knows some Navajo, . . .

Figure 9: Navajo pitch reset.

The discourse context to which such sentences are pragmatically subordinate can be extensive. After recounting a series of events, the speaker in (43) added some incidental information, off the event line: 'My son was driving us around at the time'. It was in a separate prosodic sentence marked with the adverbial subordinator.

(43) Navajo asides: nav006:00:01:48

A: 'I first tried to take it [your blanket] over there . . . I told him to call to Two Grey Hills for me. But then my son said they weren't there. They told us they probably wouldn't be there until the next day. So then we went to this other place but it was closed. Again they weren't there. At that one place in Shiprock they call the Trading Place, right there. Remember that place I told you about where she was buying warp.'

B: 'Yes, over at that place, right? Oh yes, I remember that one place we drove by on the way out. It was closed.'

A: 'Because of that I also took it to that place again, but they weren't there. I was told the buyer was not available. They told me the buyer would be in the store the next day. That happened and so we left.'

Shiyáázh	*nihił*	*na'iłbąąs=o*	*éi.*
my.son	us	he.drove=ADV	that.

'My son was driving us around that time.'

B: *Aoo'o.*
'Yes'.

Speaker A then returned to her narrative, but after recounting a few more events, she added an explanation for why she could go to only one place: 'I had to take care of my mom, so that limited what I could do'. Her explanation was in a separate prosodic sentence marked with the adverbial subordinator. After this aside, she returned to her narrative.

(43′) A: 'We left from there and headed over there. We got to that one place.'

B: 'Yes.'

A: 'Ah. Where was it. We were only supposed to go that place.
That was where we were supposed to take your blanket.'

Shimá	*baa nishtł'a=go.*
my.mother	she.hampered me=ADV

'I had to take care of my mom, so that limited what I could do.'

'So we went to the auction.'

As can be seen in Figure 10, this =gɔ-marked sentence began with a full pitch reset and ended with a terminal fall. It was an independent sentence prosodically.

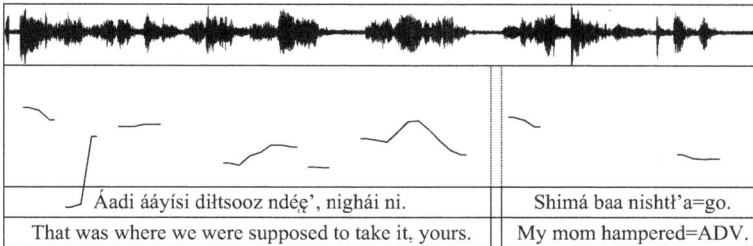

Áadi ááyísi diłtsooz ndę́ę́', nighái ni.	Shimá baa nishtł'a=go.
That was where we were supposed to take it, yours.	My mom hampered=ADV.

Figure 10: Navajo pitch reset and terminal fall.

Offline comments may offer explanations or simply supply additional information. They are not differentiated formally. The sentence in (44) below could be interpreted as an explanation or simply supplementary information. A woman told her friends that at a certain point, she had realized that her children did not know Navajo. She decided to bring them back to the reservation to live in a hogan with her grandmother. Both she (A) and another participant in the conversation (B) supplied some asides in independent sentences with formal subordinate marking (with overlap marked by brackets). Their asides provided information from their modern vantage point; information that was off the event-line of the narrative.

(44) Navajo aside: nav007:00:30:10
    A: 'I lived with my children there for maybe six months.
        So that water, we all hauled water.
        And things like wood, things like chopping wood.
        Still that is what they remember the most now.'

Áádą́ą́'	*um*	*áadi,*
there.past		there.at

    'Back then um, back then,'

    B: | *Áadi* | *da'diltłi'ígíí* | *ádin=o,* |
|---|---|---|
| there.at | they.are.lit.NMLZ | there.is.none=ADV |

        'There were no lights,
        [*electricity*.]'

A: [*da'diltłi'íi*] *ádaadin=o* *ą́ą́'ą́.*
there.are.lit there.were.none=ADV yes
'there were no lights.'

'When we lived with my grandmother was the only time we were all happy.'

A group was reminiscing about school experiences. Speaker A stepped back from her narrative to note that when they were young, children were in school the whole year, rarely going home.

(45) Navajo aside: nav007:00:27:24
   A: 'So I remember that when I went to school, and a White woman held up a drawing of a sheep. I remember she kept just saying "sheep". So all of us were Navajo. We Navajos were just looking at it, while she just kept saying "sheep". We were told not to speak Navajo. Only English.'

Níléí *um,*
That um

bini'ántą́ą́tsohdoo *ndi* *shį́į́* *át'é* *níléí,* ...
from.September but maybe it.is that
maybe starting from September

níléí *T'ą́ą́chil,*
over.there April
to April,

T'ą́ą́tsohji̧,
up.to.May
up to May

áá *áa* *da'íiníilta'=o.*
over.there over.there we.were.going.to.school=ADV
we were all going to school over there.'

   B: *Mm.*

Some Navajo language teachers were discussing what they do in their classes. One went through her daily routine, but left this topic briefly to comment on her grandmother's experiences with the language. The diversion was expressed as an independent prosodic sentence with the adverbial enclitic =*o*.

(46) Navajo aside: nav007:00:47:07
    'This is what I tell them when they attend my class.
    "This, like the way you all walked in, consider it your home.
    We are all here only to learn this language, our language.
    It's true that back then we were being chased around.
    We were told that our language would disappear.
    So I will make that my duty here.
    I'll teach you all my grandmother's language."'

    Éí   **tihooz'nii'=o.**
    that   she suffered=ADV
    'She suffered.'

The subordinating enclitic is used pervasively by Navajo speakers to add dimension to discourse, marking information which is off the event line of narrative or peripheral to the topic at hand. As with many discourse devices, speakers have choices in how they choose to shape their message, and not all speakers will make the same choices.

5 Theoretical implications

The emerging recognition of the diverse functions served by insubordinate constructions on the one hand, and their varied diachronic origins and pathways of development on the other, raise intriguing questions about relationships between the two. Here two constructions have been compared that emerged from similar points of departure in adverbial clause constructions, but differ completely in their modern functions. The Mohawk *tsi* construction and the Navajo *=go* construction share only Evans's original defining formal feature: both are formally dependent clauses used as independent sentences. They share no semantic or pragmatic characteristics, and they differ in scope. Their modern profiles were not determined at the outset by their sources, but are products of the pathways by which they developed.

    The Mohawk *tsi* construction is much like the kinds of insubordination first described in Evans 2007. It functions as an exclamative, serving to express intensive evaluation. This function has been described for similar constructions in many languages. It was cited by Evans for English *that* clauses and German *daß* clauses (2007: 403), by Kalinina and Sumbatova for the Nakh Daghestanian languages Bagwalal and Dargwa (2007: 184), for Dutch by Verstraete, D'Hertefelt, and Van linden (2012), and for Japanese by Narrog (2016: 278), among others.

The scope of the Mohawk construction is confined to a single sentence, like its source. It emerged from a single complex sentence construction, though not by instantaneous omission of an identifiable matrix. The particle *tsi* began as a place/time/manner nominalizer, which was extended to mark clauses denoting places, times, and manners. Because grammatical relations are specified in Mohawk on the predicate rather than dependents, these clauses contain no indication of their grammatical role. Because of their semantics, however, they most often serve an adverbial function. As in a number of other languages, they also came to serve as complements of certain matrix verbs. From there the routinization and erosion typical of grammaticalization turned some of those matrix verbs into simple particles. At a certain point, speakers apparently generalized the construction so that any exclamatory particles could occur in the initial particle position. The result is what is termed by Van linden and Van de Velde *semi-autonomous insubordinate* or *semi-subordinate* constructions. On rare occasions the initial particles are now beginning to be omitted from Mohawk *tsi* exclamatives, suggesting that this could be a stage along a pathway toward a full-fledged, autonomous insubordination construction. This could be viewed as an instance of what is termed *hypoanalysis* by Croft (2000) and Van linden and Van de Velde (2014), whereby the exclamative function was transferred from the original full complex sentence to the *tsi*-marked subordinate clause, or even the subordinating marker *tsi*, in turn facilitating the omission of the matrix. It could also be interpreted as an example of what Heine, Kaltenböck, and Kuteva (2016: 39) have termed *cooptation*, where the matrix clause is implied but not formally expressed.

The Navajo =*go* construction has an entirely different function from the Mohawk *tsi* construction: it serves as a discourse structuring device, permitting speakers to mark information that is incidental to the main thrust of the discourse. Its scope is different: it goes well beyond the sentence to the larger discourse, anywhere from a preceding remark to a lengthy narrative or discussion, often extending across turns from different speakers. The major process in its development was extension: The backgrounding function of the adverbial subordinator =*go* was generalized from marking the syntactic subordination of adverbial clauses within the sentence to marking the pragmatic subordination of sentences within discourse. Constructions with similar functions and histories can be seen in Central Alaskan Yup'ik and Barbareño Chumash (Mithun 2008, 2016a).

Though the Mohawk *tsi* construction and Navajo =*go* construction both emerged from adverbial clauses, different mechanisms produced quite different outcomes. The functions and scope of these modern constructions are the product of their subsequent histories, but, as seen here, such histories can be complex.

References

Cristofaro, Sonia. 2016. Routes to insubordination. In Nicholas Evans & Honoré Watanabe (eds.), *Insubordination*, 393–422. Amsterdam: John Benjamins.

Croft, William. 2000. *Explaining language change: An evolutionary approach*. Harlow: Longman.

D'Hertefelt, Sarah & Jean-Christophe Verstraete. 2014. Independent complement constructions in Swedish and Danish: Insubordination or dependency shift? *Journal of Pragmatics* 60. 89–102.

Dwyer, Arienne M. 2016. Ordinary insubordination as transient discourse. In Nicholas Evans & Honoré Watanabe (eds.), *Insubordination*, 183–208. Amsterdam: John Benjamins.

Evans, Nicholas. 2007. Insubordination and its uses. In Irina Nikolaeva (ed.), *Finiteness. Theoretical and empirical foundations*, 366–431. Oxford: Oxford University Press.

Floyd, Simeon 2016. Insubordination in interaction: The Cha'palaa counter-assertive. In Nicholas Evans & Honoré Watanabe (eds.), *Insubordination*, 341–366. Amsterdam: John Benjamins.

Gras, Pedro. 2011. *Gramática de construcciones en interacción*. Barcelona: University of Barcelona dissertation.

Gras, Pedro 2012. Entre la gramática y el discurso: Valores conectivos de *que* inicial átono en español. In Daniel Jacob & Katja Ploog (eds.), *Autour de Que. El Entomo de Que*, 89–112. Frankfurt: Peter Lang.

Gras, Pedro. 2016. Revisiting the functional typology of insubordination: Que-initial sentences in Spanish. In Nicholas Evans & Honore Watanabe (eds.), *Insubordination*, 113–144. Amsterdam: John Benjamins.

Gras, Pedro & María Sol Sansiñena. 2015. An interactional account of discourse-connective que-constructions in Spanish. *Text & Talk* 35 (4). 505–529.

Heine, Bernd, Gunther Kaltenbock, & Tania Kuteva. 2016. On insubordination and cooptation. In Nicholas Evans & Honoré Watanabe (eds.), *Insubordination*, 39–64. Amsterdam: John Benjamins

Kalinina, Elena & Nina Sumbatova. 2007. Clause structure and verbal forms in Nakh-Daghestanian languages. In Irina Nikolaeva (ed.), *Finiteness. Theoretical and empirical foundations*, 183–249. Oxford: Oxford University Press.

Lombardi Vallauri, Edoardo. 2016. Insubordinated conditionals in spoken and non-spoken Italian. In Nicholas Evans & Honoré Watanabe (eds.), *Insubordination*, 145–169. Amsterdam: John Benjamins.

Mithun, Marianne. 2008. The extension of dependency beyond the sentence. *Language* 84 (1). 264–280.

Mithun, Marianne. 2015. Navajo Conversational Corpus. Funded by the National Science Foundation, Award 0853598.

Mithun, Marianne. 2016a. Shifting finiteness in nominalization: From definitization to refinitization. In Claudine Chamoreau (ed.), *Finiteness and nominalization*, 299–324. Amsterdam: John Benjamins.

Mithun, Marianne. 2016b. Insubordinate exclamations. In Nicholas Evans & Honoré Watanabe (eds.), *Insubordination*, 369–393. Amsterdam: John Benjamins.

Narrog, Heiko 2016. Insubordination in Japanese diachronically. In Nicholas Evans & Honoré Watanabe (eds.), *Insubordination*, 247–282. Amsterdam: John Benjamins.

Sansiñena, María Sol, Hendrik De Smet & Bert Cornillie. 2015. Between subordinate and insubordinate. Paths towards complementizer-initial main clauses. *Journal of Pragmatics* 77. 3–19.

Van linden, An & Freek Van de Velde. 2014. (Semi-)autonomous subordination in Dutch: Structures and semantic-pragmatic values. *Journal of Pragmatics* 60. 226–250.

Verhagen, Arie. 2005. *Constructions of intersubjectivity: Discourse, syntax, and cognition.* Oxford: Oxford University Press.

Verstraete, Jean-Christophe, Sarah D'Hertefelt & An Van linden. 2012. A typology of complement insubordination in Dutch. *Studies in Language* 36. 123–153.

Verstraete, Jean-Christophe & Sarah D'Hertefelt 2016. Running in the family: Patterns of complement insubordination in Germanic. In Nicholas Evans & Honoré Watanabe (eds.), *Insubordination*, 65–88. Amsterdam: John Benjamins.

Jan Lindström, Ritva Laury and Camilla Lindholm

2 Insubordination and the contextually sensitive emergence of *if*-requests in Swedish and Finnish institutional talk-in-interaction

Abstract: This chapter reports a study of Swedish and Finnish insubordinate *om* and *jos* 'if' clauses from a synchronic perspective as the clauses emerge in interactional sequences of action. Insubordinate conditional clauses have the potential to function as complete directives without any main clauses: the recipients are able to treat them as such, responding to the directive as soon as the insubordinate clause is produced. The authors show that the emergence of insubordinate conditionals is anchored in projectable, often routinized interactional trajectories, in which the verbal action is enhanced with multimodal communication. Routinization and contextual cues play a particularly prominent role in the kind of data that are analyzed here: service encounters and medical consultations. Insubordinate conditional requests emerge in interaction in response to verbal and non-verbal actions done (and not done) by the recipients of the requests, and are thus a product of the interaction of participants in conversation.

1 Introduction

Conditional clauses are normally embedded as an adverbial constituent in a superordinate clause, which together build a conditional clause combination. When produced in initial position, the conditional clause then projects a superordinate clause to follow (see, e.g., Auer 2005); for example, *If you heat ice → it melts*. However, it is also known that in many languages, clause types ordinarily considered subordinate can, in some contexts, appear without superordinate clauses (e.g. Ford 1993; Clancy, Akatsuka, and Strauss 1997; Sansiñena, De Smet, and Cornillie 2015; Verstraete and D'Hertefelt 2016). Evans (2007) has introduced the concept *insubordination* to refer to the diachronic development towards syntactically independent uses of subordinate structures, or, in a synchronic view, to "the independent use of constructions exhibiting

Jan Lindström, Ritva Laury, Camilla Lindholm, University of Helsinki

https://doi.org/10.1515/9783110638288-003

characteristics of subordinate clauses" (Evans and Watanabe 2016: 2). According to Evans (2007), it is crosslinguistically common that conditional clauses are used without any superordinate clauses to make requests and offers and to express wishes – these are uses which he terms "if requests", "if wishes" and "if offers" (2007: 372). The objective of this study is to examine the contextual factors, including the speakers' embodied behavior, that contribute to the dialogic emergence and successful deployment of such 'if' requests in Swedish and Finnish talk-in-interaction. By 'if' requests we mean utterances like (1) and (2), which come from service encounters conducted respectively in Swedish and in Finnish[1]:

(1) *Om   jag   får   underskrift där   tack.*
     if   I   get- PRS signature   there thanks
     'If I can have (your) signature there, please.'

(2) *Sit   jos saisin   vielä teiän   ton   puhelinnumeron*
     then   if   get-COND-1SG   still 2PL-GEN   DEM-ACC   phone-number-ACC
     'Then if I could still get your phone number.'

In spoken interaction, such syntactically free-standing conditional clauses mostly communicate different kinds of directive actions, but these uses have been largely ignored in reference grammars. More attention has been paid to Swedish conventionalized conditional main clauses that express unaddressed potential or irrealis wishes (*Om hon bara kommer dit i tid!* 'If she only comes there in time'; *Om du var här* 'If you (only) were here') or counterfactual wishes (*Om jag bara hade varit där!* 'If I only had been there').[2] Finnish also has such uses, cf. *Jos se vaan tulee ajoissa* 'If s/he only comes in time'; *Oi jospa oisin saanut olla mukana* 'If only I had been able to be there'.

In what follows, we will first give an overview of some basic structural variations on Swedish and Finnish conditional clause combinations, leaving aside unaddressed desiderative or expressive uses that have been dealt with in many

---

1 We use the somewhat vernacular term "'if' request" in this study because of its functional transparency and practicality. In an earlier study (Lindström, Lindholm, and Laury 2016), which the present one builds on, we have called these structures *insubordinated conditionals used as directives* (ICDs). Other terms that have been used, possibly covering a wider spectrum of phenomena than that discussed here, include "suspended" or "free conditionals" (see Lombardi Vallauri 2016).

2 For a fuller account on different functional categories of insubordinate conditional and complement clauses in Germanic languages (including Swedish), see D'Hertefelt (2015) and Verstraete and D'Hertefelt (2016).

traditional descriptions. This background section is followed by a data presentation and an analysis that accounts for the interactional use and emergence of 'if' requests from a contextually sensitive point of view. The analysis is attuned to routinized trajectories of actions and embodied, nonverbal resources that accompany the realization of this type of directive action especially in certain kinds of institutional interaction. This study is thus a continuation to our prior work (Lindström, Lindholm, and Laury 2016), which concentrated on the sequential and structural emergence of insubordinate conditionals in both mundane and institutional interaction.

Interactional approaches to insubordination are still fairly uncommon, but we note the "dyadically dependent" analysis of insubordinate complement clauses that has been put forward by Sansiñena, De Smet, and Cornillie (2015), and specifically that of Spanish *que*-constructions in Gras and Sansiñena (2015); see also Floyd (2016) on "counter-assertions" in Cha'palaa. Similarly, Lombardi Vallauri's (2016) studies of conditionals in spoken Italian are of interest here. It should be noted that our analysis is concerned with a possibly initial component of a conditional clause combination which, from a canonical point of view, seems to lack a completion in the form of a superordinate consequent clause. This leaves out post-positioned conditional clauses which also may appear in a syntactically loose form, for example, as elaborative additions or re-completing increments to a prior statement (see Sansiñena, De Smet, and Cornillie 2015).

We want to stress that our analysis is strictly synchronic, based on an online-syntactical view of utterances and constructions emerging in talk-in-interaction here and now (see Auer 2005). For diachronic perspectives, we refer to the study by Beijering and Norde in this volume. We analyze Swedish and Finnish data in tandem in order to demonstrate general, and possibly even universal tendencies in the use of insubordinate conditional structures. In fact, there are more commonalities than differences in the usage, even though Swedish and Finnish are two structurally quite different languages: Finnish has, for example, a richer verb morphology, including dedicated person and conditional forms, while Swedish relies heavily on strict word-order patterns in marking grammatical relations.

2 Some variations of conditional clause-combining in Swedish and Finnish

Conditional clauses are initially marked with the subordinator *om* in Swedish and *jos* in Finnish, both corresponding to *if* in English. In the canonical view, the conditional clause is an adverbial clause which does not alone express an action (and thus, cannot stand alone); instead, it is combined with a superordinate (or matrix) clause which signifies the actual type of action, e.g. a question or a directive (Teleman, Hellberg, and Andersson 1999: 475), or expresses the condition under which the consequence in the main clause can be realized (Hakulinen et al. 2004: §1114). Swedish conditional clauses display typical features of subordinate clauses (with a fixed SVO structure and the placement of sentence adverbs, including the negator, before the finite verb), allowing the use of the modal auxiliary *skulle* 'would' only to convey a remote possibility in the conditional[3] (Teleman, Hellberg, and Andersson 1999: 646). In Finnish, conditional *jos* clauses are considered subordinate adverbial clauses integrated into their main clause, but they do not differ from main clauses in terms of word order or other syntactic features. Finnish has a morphological conditional, which can freely occur in *jos* clauses as well (see, e.g., the example in (2) above). However, insubordinate conditional clauses are not uncommon in spoken Finnish and Swedish (e.g. Kauppinen 1998; Laury 2012; Laury, Lindholm, and Lindström 2013; D'Hertefelt 2015); in such uses, they also retain the basic internal syntactic features of a typical conditional clause.

In Swedish, a standard conditional clause combination consists of a dependent clause expressing a condition (protasis) and a main clause expressing the consequence (apodosis). The main clause has inversion, which is a structural implication of the embedding of the first clause as an adverbial constituent in the latter clause (i.e. the clause combination displays the V2 order XVS in which the conditional clause is X). The examples in this section are taken from our data on institutional encounters (see *Data and method* below).

(3) *Om du vill,   kan   du köpa   ett program.*[4]
     if   you want.PRS can.PRS you buy-INF a   program
     'If you want, you can buy a program.'

The embedded syntactic relation is often clarified with a resuming *så* 'so' which is inserted between the adverbial clause and the main clause. Although this *så*

---

3 This constraint parallels with that for English *if*-clauses in which the auxiliary *should* can be used to convey a tentative meaning: *If you should wish to do so, please make your complaint as soon as possible* (see Quirk et al. 1985: 1093).
4 The clauses can, of course, come in a reversed order, e.g. *Du kan köpa ett program, om du vill* 'You can buy a program, if you want'. These combinations are not very common in our data (see also Auer 2000 on spoken German, Ford 1993 on spoken English), and the conditional clause in them usually has a softening function, for example, 'if you like', 'if you want', 'if it is possible'.

has evolved into a syntactic "dummy" it still projects the semantic relation of a consequence in the latter clause.

(4) *Om du   betalar för   dig   bara,*
    if you pay-PRS for   you.CBJ only
    så fixar vi   det sen.
    PRT fix-PRS we   that then
    'If you pay for yourself only, we (will) fix it then.'

When the conditional clause is followed by a question, the syntactic relation between the clauses is looser in that the initial clause is not embedded in the interrogative as a constituent. However, the two clauses can be bound together with an anaphoric adverb (*då* 'then') in a way that resembles a left dislocation (of the conditional clause):

(5) *Om   jag nu   måste   ta   penicillin,*
    if   I   now   must.PRS take.INF penicillin
    ska   jag be   å   få   då   Vibra?
    shall.PRS I ask.INF to   get.INF then   Vibra
    'If I must take penicillin, shall I ask for Vibra then?'

In Finnish, conditional clauses also most commonly occur in initial position (see Laury 2012: 215; Hakulinen et al. 2004: 1068), but unlike in Swedish, the word order in postposed main clauses can be direct. Since Finnish word order is, for the most part, "free", that is, pragmatically and not grammatically controlled (Vilkuna 1989), functions such as subordination are not marked by the order of constituents. In the next clause combination, concerning taking two medications at the same time, the main clause is marked as a consequent with *niin* 'so/then' similarly to the use of *så* in Swedish.

(6) *jos   molempia   ottaa   sen   kolme   kertaa*
    if   both-PL-PRT take-3SG   DEM-ACC three   time-PRT
    *päivässä **niin**   se   on,   rupee   oleen*
    day-INE   so   DEM   be-3SG begin-3SG be-INF
    aika   iso   annos   sitte   jo
    quite   large   dose   then   already
    'If (one) takes both (of them) three times a day, then it is, starts to be quite a large dose then'

Note that in the consequent clause, initiated with *niin* 'then/so', the word order is direct (SVX): the subject *se* 'it' precedes the verb *on* 'is'[5], which is then repaired to *rupee oleen* 'begins to be'. The adverb *sitte* 'then' in the consequent clause refers anaphorically to the matter expressed in the *jos* clause, similar to the use of *då* in the Swedish example (5) above.[6]

Viewed in a straightforward manner, insubordinate 'if' requests appear to be variations of these fuller conditional clause combinations in that the latter superordinate clause (the apodosis) is left unexpressed. However, we need to achieve a better understanding of the interactional and contextual factors that produce insubordinate conditional clauses as full-fledged interactional moves. In an earlier study (Lindström, Lindholm, and Laury 2016), we have discussed the sequential emergence of insubordinate and more canonical conditional constructions showing that the process is often stepwise and dependent on local interactional contingencies, not least the conduct of the co-participant (by complying or not with a request). In the present analysis we will sharpen this picture by taking into account multimodal aspects of communication.

3 Data and method

When collecting cases of insubordinate conditional clauses we have consulted several hours of recordings and transcripts of them in the Finnish and Swedish conversation archives at the University of Helsinki, including face-to-face and telephone conversations and ranging from everyday to institutional settings (see Laury, Lindholm, and Lindström 2013; Lindström, Lindholm, and Laury 2016). This larger data collection contains 185 instances of insubordinate conditional clauses, 121 in Swedish, 64 in Finnish. Specifically for the present study, we have used four sub-corpora of video-recorded institutional conversations, which give a good opportunity for a multimodal analysis.

For Swedish, we have studied a corpus of medical consultations and a corpus of box office encounters at a theatre. The former consists of 14 consultations and extends to 7 hours (Melander Marttala 1995), yielding 23 instances of 'if' requests; the latter consists of 83 brief encounters which amount to 3 hours

---

5 The subject *se* 'it' could be interpreted as representing the amount of medication resulting from taking both medications three times a day, which is then evaluated in predicate nominal as being a large dose.

6 As in Swedish (see note 4), Finnish conditional clauses can also come after the main clause, e.g. *Tähän voi maksaakin, jos haluatte* 'It's possible to pay here too, if you like'.

in total (Norrby et al. 2015) and contains six instances. In the majority of the cases it is the institutional party (physician or seller) who produces the request, but there are some instances in the service encounters in which the customer also uses an insubordinate conditional as a request.

The Finnish corpus consists of customer visits to a pharmacy and consultations with a small animal veterinarian. In the pharmacy data, there are altogether 58 customer visits. In these data, insubordinate conditionals are relatively rare; there are only four of them in 5 hours and 32 minutes of videotape. They also have a fairly routine context of use, as all but one involve requests for a telephone number. Insubordinate conditionals are slightly more common in the veterinary data consisting of 17 videotaped visits with a total duration of 3.5 hours and containing 7 'if' requests. All involve requests the veterinarian addresses to the pet owners, similar to the pharmacy data where all the insubordinate conditionals are requests made by the pharmacist to the customer. Thus, while the total duration of the Finnish data is comparable to the Swedish data, the number of insubordinate conditionals is smaller, only one third of what was found in the Swedish data (11 to 29).

The analytic methods are rooted in the traditions of Conversation Analysis and Interactional Linguistics (see Couper-Kuhlen and Selting 2001) augmented by a multimodal interaction analysis (see Mondada 2016). We thus pay special attention to the sequential, turn-by-turn emergence of speaker contributions and their grammatical shaping in conversational interaction as it is unfolding in real time. Moreover, the analysis keeps track of the coordination of verbal, embodied and other contextual resources utilized in communication.

4 Contextual and embodied resources in the emergence of 'if' requests

In an earlier study based on our larger data collection with more than a hundred instances (Laury, Lindholm, and Lindström 2013), we concluded that Swedish and Finnish insubordinate conditional clauses function most commonly as directives, i.e. to communicate actions which are designed to get someone to do something (see Ervin-Tripp 1976). These directives included the subcategories of suggestions, requests and proposals.[7] We have also noticed

---

7 In a *suggestion*, the agent as well as the beneficiary is Other, in a *request*, the agent is Other and the beneficiary is Self, in a *proposal*, both Self and Other are agents and beneficiaries (for this categorization of directive actions, see Couper-Kuhlen 2014).

that it is crucial for the dialogic emergence of 'if' requests that their use and interpretation is anchored in projectable interactional trajectories, in which the verbal action is enhanced with multimodal communication. This comes across in a prominent way in our sub-corpora of institutional interactions, which display routinized series of actions. The following extract, taken from a box office encounter, in which the customer is requesting a ticket from a staff member seated at a desk, illustrates both the use of a full conditional *om* clause combined with a consequent clause (l. 02–04) and a free-standing 'if' request (l. 09); in this extract and the following ones, the conditional clauses functioning as 'if' requests are highlighted in bold.

(7) Signature (055) (S=staff, C=customer)

```
01 S: nu  vill     den int göra   någo.    (0.5)
      now want-PRS it  NEG do-INF anything
      'now it isn't co-operating at all'

02    h om ja drar    de   här  via min  så
      if   I  draw-PRS this here via mine so
      'if I draw it here through mine'

03    (.) ((C gives her card to S))

04    funkar  de säkert  [#bättre#] (s-)
      work-PRS it surely  good-COMP
      'it probably works better'

05 C:                    [jå      ]
                          'yes'

06    (2.8) ((S draws C:s card through card terminal))

07 S: #jes#   så      ↑där. ((S gives card back to C))
      PRT     like    this
      'yes, here we go'

08    (5.0) ((S tears invoice out from card terminal))

09 S: mt     s:å om ja få(r)    underskrift #dä:r# *↑tack.
             So  if I  get-PRS signature    there   thanks
             'if I can get your signature here, please'
                                         *((C looks down
      at the invoice S has placed on the desk and reaches for a pen))
10    (2.1)
```

```
11 C: blev        de  ↑ändå  femtifyra?,
      become.PST  it  still  fifty-four
```
'oh, it ended up being fifty-four anyway?'

The extract is initiated by a comment from the staff member on the slow functioning of the customer's card terminal; the Swedish verb *vill* ('want') is used to describe the functional problems, ascribing the card terminal intentionality (i.e. a will of its own). This comment is followed by the staff member's proposal to deal with the customer's card in her own terminal. The proposal carries the form of a complex sentence expressing both the condition ('if I draw it through mine') and the consequent ('it probably works better'). The customer hands over her credit card and the staff member draws it through the card terminal. After handing over the card to the customer and tearing an invoice out from the terminal, the staff member makes a request to the customer to sign. In contrast to her previous directive move, this one (l. 08) has the form of a free-standing 'if' request. The verbal action is formed as a syntactically, prosodically and pragmatically complete "package". The turn-final *tack* ('please') does not project a continuation, rather, it re-completes the turn. The 'if' request is accompanied by the non-verbal action of handing over the invoice to the customer, who examines the invoice and takes a pen in her hand, thus signaling that she is about to comply and sign (see Figure 1); however, before signing, the customer asks for a clarification of the sum to be paid (l. 11).

Figure 1: The staff member hands over an invoice to the customer (facing the camera) simultaneously producing an 'if' request; the customer reaches for a pen to sign after the completion of the request; line 09–10 in extract (7).

The insubordinate conditional is produced in a routine transactional slot and it is combined with a physical action that enhances its interpretation, i.e. handing over a transactionally relevant artefact. The consecutive trajectory is hereby so strongly projected that it need not be said: compliance enables the completion of the purchase. Moreover, the customer's visible readiness to comply, conveyed by embodied action, makes a further elaboration of the request unnecessary.

The next extract, taken from a corpus of Swedish medical consultations, provides another illustration of a conditional *om* clause treated as a full-fledged request.

(8) Relax (LOP 1:9) (D=doctor, P=patient)

```
01 D: mm. kan du  ta       å   göra   så  här?,
      PRT can you take.INF and do-INF so  here
      'Mm. Can you do like this?'

02    (2.0) ((D lifts his hands behind his neck;
      P repeats the movement))

03 D: bra. (0.5) å   så  tibaka.
      good        and so  back
      'Good. And then back again.'

04    (3.0) ((D takes P's arms to a downward
      position))

05 D: .hh   så< (.) om du  *slappnar av  °där  så°.
            so      if you relax-PRS PRT there so
      'So (.) if you relax there'

                    *((D twists P's left arm))

06    (4.0)

07 D: mm. (0.5) jaha du  har      inte ont  i   nacken
      PRT       PRT  you have-PRS NEG  ache in  neck-DEF
      'Mm. Right, your neck isn't sore'
```

In the context of a physical examination, the doctor asks the patient to lift his hands up behind his neck (l. 01). The doctor first demonstrates the movement himself, and the patient complies with the request by repeating the doctor's movement (Figure 2a). The doctor assesses the patient's action (l. 03), and then continues by giving a verbal and an embodied instruction for further action; he first says 'and then back again', takes hold of the patient's arms and brings

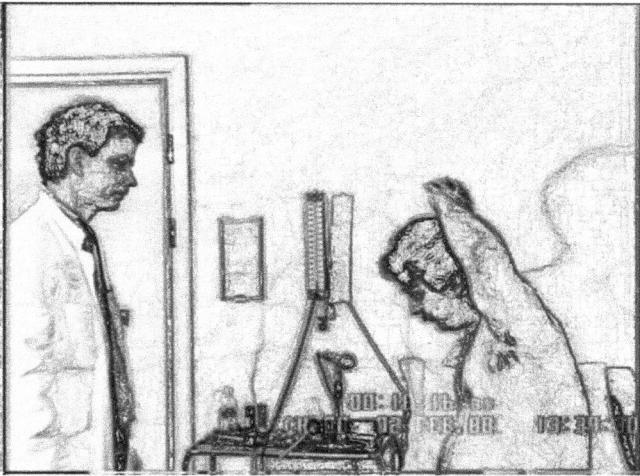

Figure 2a: The patient lifts his hands up behind his neck; line 02 in extract (8).

them back to the starting position in front of the body. The instruction to relax is expressed in a conditional clause (l. 05) and initiates a new sub-phase in the physical examination; the doctor puts his hands on the patient's left arm and makes a twisting movement. Note that the *om* request includes a final *så* ('so'). As mentioned earlier, *så* is often used to clarify the relation between the conditional clause and the main clause in standard conditional clause combinations. In this case, and recurrently in the doctor-patient data, *så* marks the request/ compliance interface: the production of *så* matches the completion of the arm movement to a relaxed down position (Figure 2b). In other words, rather than projecting a consequent to follow, *så* marks completed action, which is one of its many functions as an adverb (see Ottesjö and Lindström 2005). The doctor then goes on to performing the physical action (inspecting the arms) without any consecutive verbal expression referring to this action (l. 06). Such a verbal specification is made redundant by the fact that the doctor, through holding his hands on the patient's arm, can feel that the patient has complied by muscular relaxation.

In extracts (7) and (8) the 'if' requests were successful and complied with by the requestees. The next extract, taken from the corpus of box-office encounters, shows an instance where the request does not function in its own right. The staff member asks for the customer's telephone number. The customer, who is unfamiliar with the institution's practice of using the phone number to confirm the booking/purchase, reacts with confusion. Instead of providing the

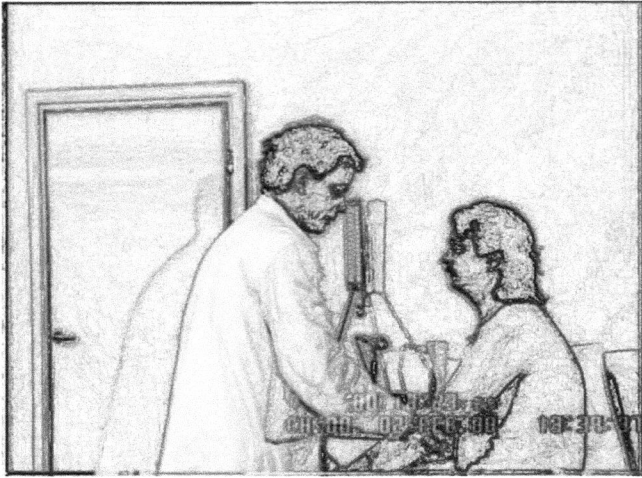

Figure 2b: The doctor holds the patient's arm when producing an 'if' request to relax, line 05 in extract (8).

asked-for number, the customer initiates a repair, signaling difficulty in hearing and understanding the previous move (l. 03). Thus, the staff member is asked to repeat and/or clarify the request expressed in line 01.

(9) Telephone number (088) (S=staff, C=customer)

```
01 S:  om ja får     ert     telefonnummer    ännu så.
       if I  get-prs your.v telephone-number yet  PRT
       'If I can have your phone number then'

02     (1.8) ((C looks confused, turns head closer to S))

03 C:  ett (ett va   sa)     ett telefonnum[mer]?,
       a   a   what say-PST a   telephone-number
       'A, (a what did you say), a phone number'

04 S:                                        [jå ]
                                             PRT
                                             'yes'

05     ja måst    få     in den som en bokning
       I  must.PRS get.INF in it  as  a  booking
       'I must register it as a booking'
```

```
06      före   ja kan sälja    den.
        before I   can sell-INF it
        'before I'm able to sell it'

07 C:   jaha. (0.4) eh (.) nu  de e   alltså-
        PRT              PRT   now it is PRT
        'okay, eh well, then it's a-

08      svensk   mobil  eh  telefonnummer    då.
        Swedish  mobile PRT telephone-number then
        'Swedish mobile eh phone number then'

09 S:   då    sätter  ja plus [förtisex] på den.
        then  put-PRS  I  plus forty-six  on it
        'then I'll put plus forty-six on the number'

10 C:                  [eh      ]      fyra sex (…)
                       PRT             four six
                       'eh four six …'
```

The customer's request for clarification is followed by an account by the staff member (l. 05–06). The account has the character of an (unexpressed) consequent indicating the reason for the 'if' request, e.g. 'If I can have your phone number (I can register a booking and sell the ticket)'. Note that the conditional clause in line 01 ends with a final *så* 'so', which, albeit not prosodically continuation-projecting, implies some sort of consecutive course of events by marking the request/compliance interface (see also extract (8) above). After the staff member has produced the account, the customer initiates the requested action of providing her phone number and the transactional business moves on.[8]

Extract (9) then provided an illustration of a case in which the 'if' request was not successful, as the other party did not have the necessary contextual knowledge of a routine transactional trajectory.[9] Generally, it is not evident what is left unpronounced in 'if' requests without a follow-up consequent but

---

8 We do not reproduce the customers' actual phone numbers in extracts (9) and (10) but only the beginning of the number series consisting of the country/operator prefix to indicate that the recipient complies with the request by producing a series of numbers.

9 Arguably, the unsuccessful outcome of the 'if' request in (9) does not depend on the insubordinate conditional format as such but on the lack of contextual cues. Our point is that the extract lucidly illustrates what kind of content may be left unexpressed in conditional directives, namely, the beneficial consequences of the requested action (e.g. 'If you do x, I can do y').

the implication is that it has to do with an outcome that is beneficial for the requester or possibly also for the requestee. In (9) the subsequent account makes this inferable relation explicit and is necessary for the action to continue, since it is called for by a repair initiative. However, in our data, extract (9) constituted an exception: insubordinate conditional requests are normally treated as sufficient to perform requested actions.

Our next example comes from our Finnish corpus of drugstore visits, and like the previous Swedish excerpt, involves a request for a phone number. As is common at Finnish pharmacies, the customer is sitting at the counter across from the pharmacist who has a computer screen in front of her. In all the cases with the Finnish *jos* requests in our pharmacy data, the medication the customer has a prescription for is not available; as a result, the pharmacist asks the customer for a phone number so the customer can be called when the medication arrives from the wholesaler. Here, it has been established already that the medication will be delivered at the pharmacy the next day.

(10) Apteekki 69W (P=pharmacist, C=customer)

```
01 P: joo.    maksatteko    nyt     vai:    noutaessa=
      PRT     pay-2PL-Q     now     or      fetch-INF-INE
      'ok. will you pay now or when you pick up?'

02 C: =huomenna    sitte    joo
      tomorrow     then     PRT
      'tomorrow then, yeah'

03    onks         se       mihi      aikaa
      be-Q-CLT     DEM      wh-ILL    time-ILL
      'what time will it be?'

04 P: .hhh noo ne  tavarat   tulee      meille yleensä
           PRT DEM thing-PL  come-3SG   1PL-ALL usually
      'well the goods are delivered usually'

05    ihan      siin       aamusta?       hh. et    sit
      quite     DEM-ESS    morning-ELA        COMP  then
      'first thing in the morning, so then'

06    sit    jos   on        kiire    niin  me  käyään tuolla
      then   if    be.3SG    hurry    so    1PL go-PASS DEM.LOC-ADE
      'if it is urgent we go over there'
```

```
07    penkoon   ne   läpi     mut yleensä me   ollaan ehitty
      dig-INF    3PL  through  but usually 1PL  be-PASS have.time
      'and dig through but usually we will have had time'
```

```
08    saada     niinku  ne     kaikki  [niinku purettua
      get-INF   PRT     DEM.PL all      PRT    unpack-PPL-PAR
      'to get them all like unpacked like'
```

```
09    niin iltapäivällä
      so   afternoon-ADE
      'by the afternoon'
```

```
10 C:                                        [(...)
```

```
11 C: okei
      PRT
      'ok'
```

```
12 P: .hh  me   ollaan        *kymmenest    neljään
           1PL  be-PRES.PASS  ten-ELA       four-ILL
      'we are (open) from ten to four'

                          *((Pharmacist moves to the left of the
                          computer and opens a drawer))
```

```
13 C: joo
      PRT
      'yeah'
```

```
14 P: tota
      PRT
      'um'
```

```
15 C: voiks     nää     maksaa   .hhhh
      can-Q-CLT DEM.PL  pay-INF
      'can I pay for these?'
```

```
16 P: anteeks
      apology-TRA
      'pardon'
```

```
17 C: voik-   voiks      nää      maksaa   sulle     tähä    [vai
      can-    can-Q-CLT  DEM.PL   pay-INF  2SG-ALL   DEM-ILL  or
      'can- can (I) pay for these here to you or?'
```

```
18  P:                                              [ne    voi
                                                    DEM.PL can
                                                    'you can'

19      maksaa    mulle    *mut    jos    mä  vielä  saisin
        pay-INF   1SG-ILL  but     if     1SG still  get-COND-1SG
        'pay me for them but if I could still get'

20      teiän     puhelinnumeron
        2PL-GEN   phone-number-ACC
        'your phone number'

                              *((Pharmacist gets pen ready and bends
                                over a piece of paper))

21  C:  joo nolla viis nolla ((…)) .
        PRT zero  five zero
        'yeah, zero five zero ...'

22  P:  joo
        PRT
        'yeah'
```

Having been established just prior that the prescribed medication would not be available until the next day, the customer asks about the time he could pick up his prescription (l. 03). Once this has been worked out, the pharmacist moves over to her left in search of what turns out to be a piece of paper (l. 12), which she puts down on the desk. While doing this, she misses the customer's question about paying for his other purchases (l.13–14), and there is a repair sequence (l. 15–16). Immediately after answering the customer's question (l. 17), the pharmacist makes her 'if' request. It is remarkably similar to the 'if' request in the Swedish example in (9). Besides being formatted as 'if' requests, both requests are done with the V-form, i.e. second person plural address pronoun (*ert* and *teiän,* respectively), and both contain an item, the Swedish *ännu* and the Finnish *vielä,* roughly equivalent to the English 'still, yet', indexing that the phone number is the next item due which needs to be established before the transaction is complete. Here, the phone number request is projected by embodied actions, the pharmacist's going over to the drawer to get the piece of paper for writing down the number (l. 12), as well as her bending over the paper and getting a pen ready to write (l. 19–20). The latter embodied action is timed so it begins exactly when the *jos* request is initiated. Unlike the Swedish request, this 'if' request is unproblematic, and the customer complies with the projected action, giving the phone number without delay. No verbal consequent is produced, and the transaction is brought to a close.

This is not the case with the 'if' requests the veterinarian makes to the owners of the pets examined in our other set of Finnish data. As noted by Somiska (2010), in each case, there is a consequent. However, the pet owner, to whom the 'if' request is addressed, complies with the request before the consequent is issued, both by doing the action requested and also, in most cases, with a verbal item doing compliance. Consider the following excerpt, in which the veterinarian is examining a turtle.

(11) SG 436 Konna (V=veterinarian, O=owner)
```
01 V: #mä laitan# painon     tohon  ylös
      1SG put-1SG weight-ACC DEM-ILL up
      'I will put down the weight over there'

02    ennen    ku    mä   ↑unohdan    ↑sen?,
      before   PRT   1SG  forget-1SG  DEM-ACC
      'before I forget it'

      (0.5) ((Vet places turtle on table, facing the owner))

03 V: vähäj   jos otat    *vasta[an    ettei    lähe,
      a.little if take-2SG against     COMP-NEG  leave
      'if you would hold it a little so (it) won't start (getting)'

                          *((Owner places hands on turtle))

04 O:                      [joo
                           PRT
                           'ok'
      (1.0)

05 V: pöyält   alas  =>kyl ne<  monestit tohon  pöydän
      table-ABL down  PRT  DEM.PL often    DEM-ILL table-GEN
      'down from the table, they do often at the table's'

06    reunalle kun   ne  menee ni [sit  ne    sillai,
      edge-ALL  when DEM.PL go-3SG so then    DEM.PL DEM-MANN
      'edge when they go, so then they (seem to think) like'

07 O:                               [#mmm#

08 V: (0.8)    ((Vet mimics a turtle))

09 O: £mheh heh heh he .hhh£
```

```
10 V: mä  oon  aika  korkeella £en    meekkään£.
      1SG be-1SG fairly high-ADE  NEG-1SG go-CLT
```
'I'm pretty high up, I guess I won't go after all'

At this point in the visit, the veterinarian has just weighed the turtle, has lifted it off the scales and is examining its nose, the trouble spot, holding the turtle close to her face. She then announces that she will write down the turtle's weight (l. 01–02). The owner is standing on the opposite side of the examining table from the vet. The vet turns the turtle around, places it on the examining table, holding it with two hands so that it is facing its owner, and issues the *jos* request. Before the veterinarian's hands are off the turtle, and before the word *vastaan* is said, the owner reaches out her hands and grabs the turtle as the veterinarian releases it, (Figure 3), and then produces a verbal compliance, *joo* 'yeah' (line 04), showing again that the insubordinate conditional functions independently as a request.

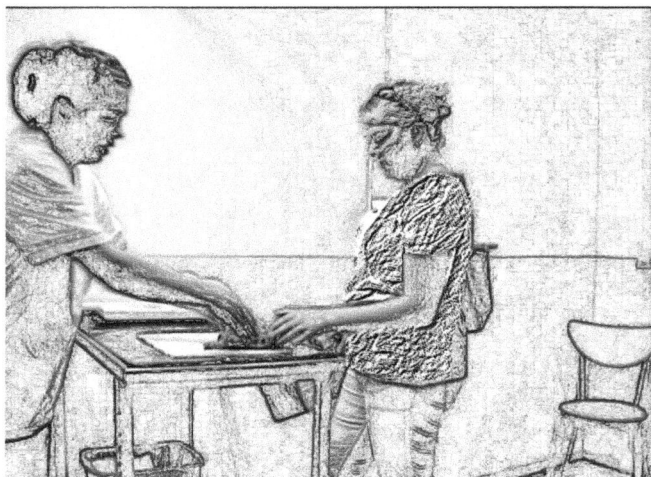

Figure 3: The veterinarian places the turtle on the table when producing an 'if' request to the customer to hold the turtle; the customer places her hand on the turtle; line 3 in extract (11).

In this excerpt, the consequent is in the form of a negative consecutive *ettei* 'so+NEG' clause, which follows the *jos* request immediately. However, the owner's compliance, both verbal and embodied, comes before the *ettei* clause begins. It is also true that the veterinarian's request is projected by her embodied action of placing the turtle on the table facing the owner, so that she can comfortably reach her pet; also, the imminent action of taking her hands off the turtle calls for an action from the owner, to take care of the turtle. Thus we can see that the 'if' request is projected by an embodied preface and complied with by another embodied action before the consequent is produced. Note also that the request is mitigated immediately after the consequent; latched with the consequent clause *ettei lähe pöyält alas* 'so it won't get off the table', the vet explains that when the turtle gets to the edge of the table, it is able to see how high up it is, and changes its mind – thus holding the turtle might not be necessary after all. This subsequent hedging probably does politeness work in the institutional context in which directives to the customer may be dispreferred.

5 Conclusions

In this article, we have discussed the use of insubordinate conditional *jos* and *om* 'if' clauses as directives in Finnish and Swedish conversation. We showed that such conditional clauses are responded to by the recipients of the directives in ways which show that they do not wait for a main clause to be produced – readiness to comply may be signaled either verbally or through embodied action. This indicates that such 'if' requests are conventionalized as directives and function as such without projecting a consequent (an apodosis) to emerge; in most of our instances, the issuer of an 'if' request does not show any orientation (for example, prosodically) to continue past the conditional move. These facts would suggest that the Finnish and Swedish usage has reached the final stage 4, i.e. full conventionalization and reanalysis as a main clause, in Evans' (2007) model of the evolutionary trajectory towards insubordination.

On the other hand, the emergence of insubordinate *om* and *jos* 'if' directives is contextually sensitive to a high degree, enhanced by situational and embodied resources in communication. Although the verbal consequent is left unsaid, a consecutive trajectory of action is strongly projected in the service encounter and medical interaction data we have analyzed. Thus, the 'if' requests are produced together with embodied actions which facilitate action ascription, for instance, by handling a transactionally relevant artefact (such as an invoice to sign, a paper and a pen to make notes with). Similarly, familiarity with the routine trajectory of actions, for example, knowledge of what kind of information is relevant to be produced where and when, helps identify the target of the directive move. We could even say that the whole array of these contextual resources – consisting of talk (the 'if' request proper), embodied action (bodily orientation), situational affordances (artefacts projecting a measure) and transactional "scripts" for the order of actions – render the production of a consequent clause to an 'if' request redundant. Rather, the consequent is something that is produced when it becomes apparent that the contextual cues do not work for a successful identification of the directive action (see extract (9) above and Lindström, Lindholm and Laury 2016 for further examples). In this sense, the "free-standing" nature of 'if' requests is strongly relativized as they in practice do not occur independently from other (i.e. nonverbal) communicative resources which may communicate the "consequent", i.e. the relevance of the asked-for action for the subsequent trajectory of actions. These features then would place the evolutionary status of Finnish and Swedish 'if' requests closer to stage 3 in Evans' (2007) model for the process of insubordination, i.e. "conventionalized ellipsis" which involves some restriction of pragmatic interpretation (cf. Lombardi Vallauri 2016 on Italian).

However, we find that there are reasons to take a critical stance to Evans' (2007) stepwise evolutionary model, which builds on the concept of ellipsis before the stage of conventionalization. We can see in our data that the 'if' requests are clearly understood as directives, and complied with, even when the main clause is subsequently produced and no ellipsis, in effect, has taken place, e.g. in extract (11) above. Furthermore, the ellipsis explanation may not be adequate if one takes into account ontogenesis: Kauppinen (1998) shows that insubordinate *jos* 'if' requests emerge in Finnish child language acquisition prior to the embedded use of 'if' clauses; thus, it does not seem logical that any main clause is ellipted, since the child has not acquired the clause combination yet. Against this background it is not quite clear that the emergence of insubordinate 'if' requests of the type we have studied here can be fitted into the Evans model.

Generally, by involving conditionality, 'if' requests suspend the consequences that the nominated action would have, i.e. they are not verbalized. Such directives are less direct in that they thus leave room for interpretation for the recipient as to the desirability of the proposed action. This kind of conditional indirectness can be seen as an orientation towards the dispreferred nature of many directive actions and may be useful, for example, in service encounters. There is also a noticeable element of mutual sense-making in the deployment of 'if' requests in that they emerge on-line, as collaborative actions of the participant issuing the directive and their addressees, and in response to the actions performed by both participants. Such co-activity, which involves recognition of upcoming interactional trajectories, builds on intersubjectivity, i.e. a sufficient level of shared understanding between the interlocutors.

Acknowledgments: The research reported in this study was conducted in the *Finnish Centre of Excellence in Research on Intersubjectivity in Interaction*, based at the University of Helsinki (intersubjectivity.fi). The data from Swedish box-office encounters were collected for the research program *Interaction and Variation in Pluricentric Languages* (IVIP), funded by Riksbankens Jubileumsfond (Grant M12-0137:1). The data on Swedish medical consultations was collected and processed by Ulla Melander Marttala for her doctoral thesis, and the Finnish data were videotaped and transcribed by Päivi Hakamäki (the pharmacy data) and by Outi Somiska (the veterinary data) for their MA theses; we thank all of them for their generosity in sharing their data with us. We have slightly modified their transcripts. We also want to thank the editors of this volume and two anonymous reviewers for their very useful comments on an earlier version of this chapter.

References

Auer, Peter. 2005. Projection in interaction and projection in grammar. *Text* 25 (1). 7–36.

Clancy, Patricia M., Noriko Akatsuka & Susan Strauss. 1997. Deontic modality and conditionality in discourse. A cross-linguistic study of adult speech to young children. In Akio Kamio (ed.), *Directions in functional linguistics*, 19–57. Amsterdam: Benjamins.

Couper-Kuhlen, Elizabeth. 2014. What does grammar tell us about action? *Pragmatics* 24 (3). 623–647.

Couper-Kuhlen, Elizabeth & Margret Selting. 2001. Introducing interactional linguistics. In Margret Selting & Elizabeth Couper-Kuhlen (eds.), *Studies in interactional linguistics*, 1–22. Amsterdam: Benjamins.

D'Hertefelt, Sarah. 2015. *Insubordination in Germanic: A typology of complement and conditional constructions*. Leuven: University of Leuven dissertation. https://lirias.kuleuven.be/handle/123456789/509450.

Ervin-Tripp, Susan. 1976. Is Sybil there? The structure of some American English directives. *Language in Society* 5 (1). 25–66.

Evans, Nicholas. 2007. Insubordination and its uses. In Irina Nikolaeva (ed.), *Finiteness: theoretical and empirical foundations*, 366–431. New York: Oxford University Press.

Evans, Nicholas & Honoré Watanabe. 2016. The dynamics of insubordination. In Nicholas Evans & Honoré Watanabe (eds.), *Insubordination*, 1–37. Amsterdam: John Benjamins.

Floyd, Simeon. 2016. Insubordination in interaction. The Cha'palaa counter-assertive. In Nicholas Evans & Honoré Watanabe (eds.), *Insubordination*, 341–365. Amsterdam: Benjamins.

Ford, Cecilia E. 1993. *Grammar in interaction. Adverbial clauses in American English conversation*. Cambridge: Cambridge University Press.

Gras, Pedro & Maria Sol Sansiñena. 2015. An interactional account of *que*-constructions in Spanish. *Text & Talk* 35 (4). 505–529.

Hakulinen, Auli, Maria Vilkuna, Riitta Korhonen, Vesa Koivisto, Tarja-Riitta Heinonen & Irja Alho. 2004. *Iso suomen kielioppi* [The comprehensive grammar of Finnish.] Helsinki: Suomalaisen Kirjallisuuden Seura.

Kauppinen, Anneli. 1998. *Puhekuviot, tilanteen ja rakenteen liitto: tutkimus kielen omaksumisesta ja suomen konditionaalista.* [Speech patterns, a union of context and structure: a study of language acquisition and the Finnish conditional.] Helsinki: Suomalaisen Kirjallisuuden Seura.

Laury, Ritva. 2012. Syntactically non-integrated *jos* 'if' conditionals as directives. *Discourse Processes* 49 (3–4). 213–242.

Laury, Ritva, Camilla Lindholm & Jan Lindström. 2013. Syntactically non-integrated conditional clauses in spoken Finnish and Swedish. In Eva Havu & Irma Hyvärinen (eds.), *Comparing and contrasting syntactic structures. From dependency to quasi-subordination*, 231–270. Helsinki: Société Néophilologique.

Lindström, Jan, Camilla Lindholm & Ritva Laury. 2016. The interactional emergence of conditional clauses as directives: constructions, trajectories and sequences of action. *Language Sciences* 58. 8–21.

Lombardi Vallauri, Edoardo. 2016. Insubordinated conditionals in spoken and non-spoken Italian. In Nicholas Evans & Honoré Watanabe (eds.), *Insubordination*, 145–169. Amsterdam: Benjamins.

Melander Marttala, Ulla. 1995. *Innehåll och perspektiv i samtal mellan läkare och patient: en språklig och samtalsanalytisk undersökning.* [Content and perspective in doctor-patient conversations: a linguistic and conversation analytic investigation.]. Uppsala: Uppsala University dissertation.

Mondada, Lorenza. 2016. Challenges of multimodality: language and the body in social interaction. *Journal of Sociolinguistics* 20 (3). 336–366.

Norrby, Catrin, Camilla Wide, Jenny Nilsson & Jan Lindström. 2015. Address and interpersonal relationships in Finland-Swedish and Sweden-Swedish service encounters. In Catrin Norrby & Camilla Wide (eds.), *Address practice as social action. European perspectives*, 75–96. Houndsmills, Basigstoke Hampshire: Palgrave Macmillan.

Ochs, Elinor, Emanuel A. Schegloff & Sandra A. Thompson (eds.). 1996. *Interaction and grammar*. Cambridge: Cambridge University Press.

Ottesjö, Cajsa & Jan Lindström. 2005. Så som diskursmarkör ['So' as a discourse marker]. *Språk och stil* 15. 85–127.

Quirk Randolph, Sidney Greenbaum, Geoffrey Leech & Jan Svartvik. 1985. *A comprehensive grammar of the English language*. London: Longman.

Sansiñena, Maria Sol, Hendrik De Smet & Bert Cornillie. 2015. Between subordinate and insubordinate. Paths toward complementizer-initial main clauses. *Journal of Pragmatics* 77. 3–19.

Somiska, Outi. 2010. *Eläinlääkärin pehmeät direktiivit.* [The veterinarian's soft directives.]. Helsinki: University of Helsinki, Department of Finnish MA thesis.

Teleman, Ulf, Staffan Hellberg & Erik Andersson. 1999. *Svenska Akademins grammatik.* [The Swedish Academy grammar.] Volume 4. Stockholm: Svenska Akademien.

Verstraete, Jean-Christophe & Sarah D'Hertefelt. 2016. Running in the family. Patterns of complement insubordination in Germanic. In Nicholas Evans & Honoré Watanabe (eds.), *Insubordination*, 65–87. Amsterdam: Benjamins.

Vilkuna, Maria. 1989. *Free word order in Finnish: its syntax and discourse functions*. Helsinki: SKS.

Appendix

Transcription symbols (cf. Ochs, Schegloff, and Thompson 1996: 461–465)

.	falling intonation
,	level intonation
;	slightly falling intonation
?,	slightly rising intonation
?	rising intonation
↑	rise in pitch
<u>en</u>	emphasis indicated by underlining
:	lengthening of a sound
[	utterances starting simultaneously
]	point where overlapping talk stops
(.)	micropause, less than 0.2 seconds
(0.5)	silences timed in tenths of a second
> <	talk inside is at a faster pace than the surrounding talk
< >	talk inside is at a slower pace than the surrounding talk
en<	glottal stop
en-	cut off
=	"latching", i.e. no silence between two adjacent utterances
#en#	creaky voice
£en£	smile voice
°en°	talk inside is more quiet than the surrounding talk
(en)	uncertain transcription
( )	inaudible words
hh	audible exhalation (the more h's, the more aspiration)
.hh	audible inhalation (length as above)
*	point of coordinated verbal and non-verbal action
((reaches for a pen))	specification of the type of non-verbal action
((. . .))	omitted verbal material

Glossing abbreviations

ABL	ablative
ACC	accusative
ADE	adessive
ALL	allative
CLT	clitic
COMP	complementizer
COND	conditional
COP	copula
CMP	comparative
DEF	definite
DEM	demonstrative

DET	determiner
ELA	elative
ESS	essive
FN	first name
GEN	genitive
GNR	generic 3rd person pronoun (cf. 'one')
ILL	illative
IMP	imperative
INE	inessive
INF	infinitive
1INF	1st infinitive
LN	last name
NEG	negation
PAR	partitive
PASS	passive
PL	plural (1PL reads 'first person plural')
PRS	present tense[10]
PRT	particle
PST	past tense
PTC	participle
REFL	reflexive (pronoun)
SG	singular (1SG reads 'first person singular')
TRA	translative
Q	question clitic
V	second person politeness form
VOC	vocative
WH	wh-question word

---

10 Present tense and nominative case are default for Finnish glossing and are not marked.

Karin Beijering and Muriel Norde

3 Adverbial semi-insubordination constructions in Swedish: Synchrony and diachrony

Abstract: The term 'adverbial semi-insubordination' refers to constructions with subordinate word order that differ from regular clause combining constructions. In a Swedish sentence such as *kanske att han inte kommer* 'maybe that he not comes', the presence of the subordinator *att* as well as the position of the sentence adverb *inte* 'not' suggests that we are dealing with a subordinate clause, yet this clause is not preceded by a full matrix, but by an epistemic adverb alone. The construction is found in several European languages and has been puzzling syntacticians for decades. Attempts to account for adverbial semi-insubordination are generally tied to a specific syntactic framework, with the unsurprising result that there is little consensus on the syntactic status of either the epistemic adverb or the *att*-clause. In this paper, we argue that the phenomenon can only be fully understood from a diachronic perspective. Focusing on Swedish, we will first present corpus data of adverbial semi-insubordination in Modern Swedish. Subsequently, we will zoom in on the historical development of the most frequent epistemic adverb in this construction, *kanske* 'maybe', which derives from the VP *kan ske* 'can happen'.

1 Introduction

In this paper, we will outline the synchronic properties as well as the historical development of a Swedish construction in which an epistemic sentence adverb like *kanske* 'maybe' or *möjligen* 'possibly' is followed by a subordinate clause introduced by the general subordinator *att* 'that'.[1] These constructions bear the formal hallmarks of subordinate clauses – the presence of the conjunction *att* and subordinate word order. The latter is shown by the position of the sentence adverbials (*inte* 'not' in (1a) and *inte alltid* 'not always' in (1b)), which precedes

---

[1] Semi-insubordination constructions may also be introduced by the conjunction *om* 'if', as in *Sannerligen om jag har glömt den än.* 'Indeed if I have forgotten it yet.'(Stroh-Wollin 2008: 58), but this construction type will not be discussed in this paper.

Karin Beijering, University of Oslo
Muriel Norde, Humboldt University of Berlin

https://doi.org/10.1515/9783110638288-004

the finite verb. Note that they follow the finite verb in the corresponding declarative main clauses (1a') and (1b').[2]

(1) a. *Kanske att   killen   inte är interesserad.*   [GP04][3]
       Maybe   that the guy   not is interested.
       'Maybe the guy is not interested.'

   a'. *Killen   är inte interesserad.*
       The guy   is not interested.
       'The guy is not interested'

   b. *Möjligen att   det inte alltid   finns   några direkta*   [GP04]
       Possibly that it not always are found some direct
       mål.
       targets
       'Possibly, there are not always direct targets'

   b'. *Det   finns   inte alltid   några direkta mål.*
       There are found not always   some direct   targets.
       'There are not always direct targets.'

Following Van linden and Van de Velde (2014: 231–5), we will term these constructions 'adverbial semi-insubordination'. As we will show in this section, the constructions in (1a-b) display a number of unusual properties. First, the subordinate *att*-clauses are not preceded by a full matrix clause; instead they are introduced by a sentence adverb which seems to function at matrix clause level (cf. Van linden and Van de Velde 2014: 231). Alternatively, one could argue that the sentence adverb co-occurs with a complementizer and plays a main predication role (cf. Ramat and Ricca 1998: 212).

The initial adverb in semi-insubordination constructions typically expresses modal, evaluative or attitudinal meanings (Ramat and Ricca 1998; Aelbrecht 2006; Van linden and Van de Velde 2014), but members from other word classes may introduce a semi-insubordinate *att*-construction as well. These include (the neuter singular form of) adjectives (e.g. *klart* 'obvious') or nouns (e.g. *tur* 'luck') as in the examples in (2). Note also that adjectives and nouns in this position may be further modified (e.g. *vilken tur* 'what luck' in (2b)).

---

2 As Swedish is a Verb Second language, the finite verb always comes in second place in declarative main clauses; adverbs occur after the finite verb.

3 The abbreviation 'GP04' refers to the subcorpus Göteborgs Posten 2004. See Section 3.2 for more details about the corpora we used for this study.

(2) a. **Klart** **att** det är stor skillnad mellan dom.   [GP04]
 Obvious that there is big difference between them
 'Obviously, there is a big difference between them.'

 b. **Vilken tur** att hon tackcde ja till erbjudandet.   [GP04]
 What luck that she thanked yes to the offer
 'It is very fortunate that she accepted the offer.'

Apart from the modal and evaluative initial elements in (1) and (2), there is a wide variety of rhetorical items that may occur in initial position.[4] These are used to express the speaker's reasoning towards the *att*-clause in relation to prior discourse (e.g. *plus* 'plus' in (3a)). Furthermore, semi-insubordinate *att*-constructions may feature various types of interjections, including social formula (e.g. *tack* 'thanks' in (3b)) and curses (e.g. *fan* 'damn it (lit. devil)').

(3) a. det gör fruktansvärt ont, **plus att** det blöder en massa [GP12]
 it does terribly pain, plus that it bleeds a lot
 'it's terribly painful, plus it bleeds a lot'

 b. **Tack** **att** ni format mig till den jag är!   [GP06]
 Thanks that you made me to whom I am
 'Thanks that you made me who I am!'

 c. **fan** **att** jag inte blev advokat   [GP04]
 damn that I not became lawyer
 'Damn it, I should have become a lawyer'

As noted above, we will focus on semi-insubordination constructions involving epistemic sentence adverbs. These are of particular interest because they cannot be explained in terms of partial ellipsis of the matrix, as has been suggested for nominal and adjectival initial constituents (Aelbrecht 2006; Julien 2009). This becomes clear from the contrastive examples in (4): in (4a), a full matrix clause *det är klart att* 'it is obvious that' replaces the single adjective *klart* 'obvious' in the semi-insubordinate construction in (2a). However, it is not possible to paraphrase an epistemic semi-insubordinate construction in the same way, compare the ungrammaticality of (4b).

---

4 See Beijering (2016) on different types of initial constituents in Norwegian semi-insubordinate *at*-constructions

(4) a. *Det är klart   att   det   är stor skillnad   mellan   dom.*
It   is   obvious   that   there   is   big   difference   between   them.
'Obviously, there is a big difference between them.'

b. **Det är kanske att   killen   inte är intresserad.*
It   is   maybe   that   the guy   not   is   interested.

In the remainder of this paper, we will outline the structural and functional properties of adverbial semi-insubordination constructions in Swedish. We aim to show that purely synchronic accounts cannot satisfactorily explain all current syntactic properties of these constructions and therefore need to be complemented by diachronic data.

This chapter is organized as follows: Section 2 sets out the theoretical preliminaries to the present study. Section 3 presents a synchronic case study of contemporary adverbial semi-insubordination constructions in Swedish. Section 4 reports on a diachronic study of semi-insubordination constructions introduced by epistemic sentence adverbs. Section 5 provides an overall analysis and discussion of interrelated synchronic and diachronic issues regarding semi-insubordination constructions. Finally, Section 6 contains a concluding summary.

2 Preliminaries

2.1 Definitions and delimitation

The notion of semi-insubordination needs to be clearly delineated from both subordination and insubordination. *Subordination* involves a hierarchical dependency whereby a subordinate clause is both dependent on, and embedded in, a full matrix clause, as in (5).

(5) *Det förvånar mig **att du hann med tåget!***
It   surprises   me   that   you   reached   the train!
'I'm surprised that you caught the train!'

Insubordination is a cover term for "the conventionalized main clause use of what, on prima facie grounds, appear to be formally subordinate clauses" (Evans 2007: 367). This concerns the independent use of formally dependent clauses, for instance autonomous *att*-clauses like (6).

(6) *Att du hann med tåget!*[5]
That you reached   the train!
'[I'm surprised] that you caught the train!'

Insubordination has both a synchronic and diachronic link to subordination. From a synchronic perspective it is "the independent use of constructions exhibiting prima facie characteristics of subordinate clauses" (e.g. subordinate word order, conjunctions and complementizers). Diachronically it concerns "the recruitment of main clause structures from subordinate structures" (Evans and Watanabe 2016: 2).

Semi-insubordination, finally, involves "constructions [which] consist of a subordinate [that]-clause that is preceded by just a [sic.] one element which seems to function at matrix clause level. Crucially, this element conveys the attitudinal (including epistemic) assessment of the propositional content expressed in the [that]-clause" (Van linden and Van de Velde 2014: 231).

(7) *Så bra att du hann med tåget!*
How good that you reached   the train!
'Luckily you managed to catch the train!'

Semi-insubordination is related to insubordination in that both constructions represent a linguistic mismatch between form and function (i.e. subordinate marking in combination with main clause use). They differ from one another in that insubordinate or autonomous *att*-clauses (in (6)) lack an overt matrix element, whereas in case of semi-insubordination (in (7)) the *att*-clause is introduced by a single matrix element only.

2.2 Previous accounts of semi-insubordination and hypotheses on its origin

The peculiar syntactic status of semi-insubordination constructions has puzzled linguists for decades. Using different labels,[6] some authors have described the prototypical semantic and structural properties of semi-insubordinate clauses, but the discursive functions and properties are generally left underinvestigated.

---

5 Example (6) is from D'Hertefelt & Verstraete (2014: 91), who in turn quote Delsing (2010: 17). Examples (5) and (7) are adapted from example (6).
6 Semi-insubordination constructions are also known as 'Adverb + complementizer construction' (Ramat & Ricca 1998), 'X +that-clauses' (Aelbrecht 2006), 'minimal matrices' (Julien 2009).

What all extant accounts of semi-insubordination have in common is that they take their point of departure in a sentence-level representation and analysis of this construction type.

Previous accounts represent different variants of a complex clause analysis: i) complex clause without Subject-Predicate construction (Bos 1963), ii) Adverb + complementizer construction (Ramat and Ricca 1998), iii) dependent clause which is subordinated to an implicit neustic 'I say so' component (Nørgård-Sørensen 2001), iv) complex clause with partial matrix clause ellipsis (Aelbrecht 2006), v) clause subordinated to a one-word matrix clause (Julien 2009), vi) subordinate clause preceded by a single matrix constituent (Van linden and Van de Velde 2014), and vii) independent complement clause with main clause traces (D'Hertefelt 2015).

The above studies are primarily synchronic in nature, but three developmental scenarios for the rise of semi-insubordination constructions can be derived from the literature: (i) (partial) ellipsis of the matrix clause (Aelbrecht 2006; Evans 2007; Julien 2009; Van linden and Van de Velde 2014), (ii) condensation of higher predicates into (formulaic) stance markers (Ramat and Ricca 1998; Norde et al. 2014; D'Hertefelt 2015, and (iii) extension of dependency markers beyond the sentence level (Mithun 2008), in parallel with discourse connectives (cf. Nørgård-Sørensen 2001; Lindström and Londen 2008).

Of particular interest for the present study is Evans' (2007; 2009: 4; Evans and Watanabe 2016) 'historical trajectory of the formation of insubordinated clauses' in Figure 1. His diachronic account of insubordination comprises four stages. The first stage, subordination, includes full constructions with an overt main clause. At the second stage, the overt main clause is elided, but any grammatically compatible main clause can be 'reconstructed' by the hearer. The reconstruction of syntactically permitted main clauses becomes restricted by convention at the third stage. At the fourth stage, the construction acquired a specific meaning of its own, and it may not be possible to restore any elided material (Evans 2007: 370–5).

Subordination	Ellipsis	Conventionalized ellipsis	Reanalysis as main clause structure
A	B	C	D
Biclausal construction, with subordinate clause	Ellipsis of main clause, any contextually appropriate material can be recovered	Restriction on interpretation of ellipsed material	Conventionalized main clause use of formerly subordinate clause

Figure 1: A diachronic model of insubordination (Evans and Watanabe 2016: 3).

Evans does not discuss semi-insubordination constructions in relation to his diachronic model of insubordination. On the basis of Figure 1 he explicitly excludes "instances where complement-taking predicates embedded in main clauses reduce to formulaic particles, parenthetical phrases etc." (Evans 2007: 385) from insubordination phenomena. In these cases of 'clause union' a main and subordinate clause are condensed while retaining semantic elements of both, whereas in cases of insubordination only material from the subordinate clause is overtly expressed.

However, since semi-insubordination is assumed to be related to insubordination, and semi-insubordinate constructions are considered to contain a 'defective' or 'minimal' matrix clause, one could think of semi-insubordination as an intermediate stage on the way to insubordination. That is, "the ellipsis of the original main clause need not be instantaneous, but [...] the pathway from complex constructions towards insubordination could also go via gradual erosion of the original main clause" (D'Hertefelt 2015: 178).

Another problem with Evans's ellipsis account, as noted in Traugott (2017: 293), is that, in contemporary English at least, the prosodic patterns of elliptical clauses and semi-insubordination clauses differ. Furthermore, her diachronic study of semi-insubordination constructions (which she calls "monoclauses introduced by a subordinator") often occur as partial responses to questions and assertions, they are "simply chunks usable in negotiated interaction" (Traugott 2017: 293).

2.3 Challenges to diachronic models of change

Semi-insubordination constructions are not only difficult to account for within traditional syntactic analysis, they have also been claimed to be problematic for unidirectionality tendencies in the domain of clause combining and grammaticalization. Clause combining in general is a contentious issue in grammaticalization studies. Standard definitions of grammaticalization are generally morpheme-based and focus predominantly on the change from lexis to grammar for individual grams (rather than syntactic constructions), resulting in stronger syntactic integration and internal dependencies.[7]

---

7 However, it is now generally accepted that grammaticalization may also involve expansion at different linguistic levels (cf. Traugott & Trousdale 2013: 100–107 on 'grammaticalization as reduction and increased dependency' and 'grammaticalization as expansion').

However, changes in clausal structure may instantiate cases of grammatic-alization if one defines it broadly "so as to encompass the motivations for and development of grammatical structures in general, then processes of clause combining clearly fall squarely within its domain" (Hopper and Traugott 2003: 176). On this broad view of grammaticalization, "the changes giving rise to [pat-terns of (semi-)autonomous subordination] go against the directionality ob-served for a number of grammaticalization processes within the domain of clause-combining, in which it is main clause construal in paratactic organiza-tion that gives rise to subordination patterns rather than the other way around" (Van linden and Van de Velde 2014: 247).

Thus, the emergence of (semi-)insubordinate constructions is assumed to violate "the cline of clause combing" in (8) which schematically represents the rise of complex sentences through coordination or subordination (Hopper and Traugott 2003: 178).

(8) parataxis > hypotaxis > subordination
    -dependent +dependent +dependent
    -embedded -embedded +embedded

The three clustering points on the cline represent different degrees of depen-dency. Parataxis (or relative independence), in (9a), applies to the juxtaposition of two (or more) nuclei, which are related to one another by inference only. Hypotaxis (or interdependency), in (9b), concerns a nucleus and one (or more) clauses which cannot stand by themselves and which are typically not entirely integrated within any constituents of the nucleus. Subordination (or complete dependency), in (9c), involves a margin which is wholly included within a constituent of the nucleus.

(9) a. *Fort Sumter has been fired on. My regiment leaves at dawn.*

    b. *Before leaving Krishnapur, the Collector took a strange decision.*

    c. *That the Titanic sank was unexpected.*
    [examples by from Hopper and Traugott (2003: 179, 183–184)]

The 'problem' with (semi-)insubordination constructions is that (formally) sub-ordinate clauses gain in autonomy when they acquire conventionalized main clause use. Because of this, (semi-)insubordination constructions could be con-sidered instances of degrammaticalization at the level of clause-combining (Van linden and Van de Velde 2014: 248). In order to conceptualize this, Norde's (2009: 120) morpheme-based definition of degrammaticalization in (10) which operates at the content level ('degrammation'), content-syntactic level ('deinflectionalization') and at the morphosyntactic level ('debonding'), would have to be extended so as to include changes at the sentence level.[8]

(10) Degrammaticalization is a composite change whereby a gram in a specific context gains in autonomy or substance on more than one linguistic level (semantics, morphology, syntax, or phonology).

The cline of clause combining predicts that the overall tendency in clause combining is towards increased syntactic integration and dependency. Hence, legitimate counterexamples would have to proceed along the lines of (11), ultimately leading to clause separation.

(11) subordination > hypotaxis   > parataxis
      +dependent   +dependent   -dependent
      +embedded   -embedded   -embedded

In order to assess the implications of adverbial semi-insubordination constructions for unidirectionality issues, we will outline the history and current usage of these constructions.

3 Synchronic study: Epistemic adverbs in semi-insubordination constructions

3.1 Introduction

Our first case study, based on synchronic corpora, focuses on *kanske* and other epistemic adverbs in contemporary semi-insubordination constructions in Swedish. On the basis of Van linden and Van de Velde's (2014) characterization of semi-insubordination, we will describe the prototypical grammatical and functional properties of adverbial semi-insubordinate *att*-constructions. In our analysis, special attention will be paid to the larger discursive context and actual usage of adverbial semi-insubordination constructions. These functional

---

8 Van linden & Van de Velde (2014: 248) point to this possible analysis, but note that "it may be questioned whether it is desirable at all to range the constructions studied here with instances of degrammaticalization, and we'd rather refrain from taking a position in this matter."

aspects of semi-insubordination have not been discussed in great detail in previous studies. The implications of these findings for theoretical assumptions about the structural status and the rise of semi-insubordination constructions will be discussed in Section 3.4.

3.2 Sources and method

The data for the synchronic study of epistemic adverbs in semi-insubordinate *att*-constructions were extracted from the subcorpora *Göteborgs-Posten* (GP) at *Språkbanken* (Borin, Forsberg and Roxendal 2012). These subcorpora cover the years 2004–2013 and comprise 192.27 million tokens.[9] They were queried for specific strings consisting of an epistemic adverb followed by the subordinator *att*. The following epistemic sentence adverbs were examined: *antagligen, förmodligen, kanhända, kanske, måhända, möjligen, möjligtvis, sannolikt, troligen, troligtvis* all meaning 'maybe', 'possibly', 'probably' or 'presumably'.

3.3 Results

Adverbial semi-insubordinate *att*-constructions as such appear to be an infrequent phenomenon in the GP corpora. Semi-insubordination constructions headed by *kanske* are most frequent, followed by *möjligen* and *möjligtvis*. There are only a few attestations of other epistemic sentence adverbs in this construction, as shown in Table 1. The final column in Table 1 relates the number of occurrences of a specific adverb in semi-subordination constructions to the token frequency of this adverb in the corpus as a whole. The figures in Table 1 show that adverbial semi-insubordinate *att*-constructions involving these epistemic adverbs are a rare phenomenon. The only adverb that features more than a handful of tokens is *kanske* 'maybe', but in view of the fact that this is the adverb with the highest token frequency generally (note that there are adverbs that occur with higher relative frequency), not even *kanske* is particularly common in this construction.

Semi-insubordinate *att*-clauses introduced by epistemic sentence adverbs typically have assertion intonation (cf. Bos 1963; Julien 2009) and take the form of a declarative clause. They are also possible as interrogative clauses, but these

---

9 <https://spraakbanken.gu.se/korp/#?stats_reduce=word&cqp=%5B%5D&corpus=gp2004, gp2005,gp2006,gp2007,gp2008,gp2009,gp2010,gp2011,gp2012,gp2013>

Table 1: Overview of initial epistemic sentence adverbs in semi-insubordinate att-constructions.

Adverb	Number of Adverb in semi-insubordination construction in GP 2004–2013	Total occurrences of Adverb in GP 2004–2013	$\log_2$ of ratio
kanske	133	84922	−9.31857
möjligen	20	6023	−8.23434
möjligtvis	14	955	−6.092
antagligen	4	4021	−9.97334
sannolikt	3	9016	−11.5533
troligen	3	8609	−11.4867
måhända	3	563	−7.55203
förmodligen	2	8713	−12.089
kanhända	1	85	−6.40939
troligtvis	1	2420	−11.2408

are only found with *kanske* (10 tokens) and *måhända* (1 token). Most previous studies discussed and analyzed the semantic and grammatical properties of isolated (and sometimes reconstructed) examples of semi-insubordination, without considering the larger context in which these constructions occur. However, as Traugott (2017) correctly notes, semi-insubordination cannot be fully understood if the interactional context is not taken into account. It turns out that the adverbial semi-insubordination constructions in our sample are syntactically independent, but they are always bound to a preceding proposition in discourse. In other words, they represent continuations of, or additional comments to, a previous stretch of discourse. This may be an epistemic assessment of the content of the att-clause in relation to prior statements as in (12).

(12) - *Än så länge kan man inte se att rekryteringen avtar.*
     *Det är ju en evighetsprocess! **Möjligen att** vi kan se ett resultat om fem år.*
     '-Thus far one cannot see that the recruitment is decreasing.
     It is a never-ending-story! Possibly (that) we can see a result in five years.'
     [GP 2006]

In this example, *kanske* can be paraphrased as '(I deem) it possible that we see a result in five years'. The *kanske att*-constructions denotes a future possibility by which the speaker mitigates his/her prediction about the results of a new policy to prevent recruitment by criminal gangs.

Epistemic adverbs in interrogative semi-insubordinate *att*-constructions fulfill a hedging function. In example (13) *måhända* functions as a question particle in a polite (indirect) request to the addressee to provide the recipe of 'halim bademjon'.

(13) *Har sökt som en dåre efter receptet men inte lyckats.*
 ***Måhända att** du kan lyckas bättre? Tack på förhand, Karina.*
 '[I] have searched like a fool for the recipe but did not succeed.
 Perhaps (that) you can do better? Thanks in advance, Karina.'
 [GP 2008]

Epistemic semi-insubordinate *att*-clauses are often used to provide a tentative answer to a question, especially when introduced by elements meaning 'presumably': *förmodligen, sannolikt, troligen* and *troligtvis* (as in 14).

(14) *Men vad krävs för att man ska bli riktigt gammal?* ***Troligtvis att** man inte gravt* [sic] *missköter sin kropp.*
 'But what is required to become really old? Presumably [it is required] that you do not seriously abuse your body'
 [GP 2013]

Finally, semi-insubordinate *att*-clauses may also function as a tentative explanation or justification of a previous statement, as in example (15).

(15) *Han besväras av något i halsen, men fortsätter.* ***Kanske att** höstens fukt påverkar hans stämband?*
 'He is bothered by something in his throat, but continues. Perhaps (that) the autumn moisture is affecting his vocal chords?'
 [GP 2006]

As is evident from the examples in (12)-(15), the preceding discourse context may contain a variety of clause types, declarative, interrogative and exclamative. As such, adverbial semi-insubordination constructions appear in different types of adjacency pairs. The examples furthermore show that epistemic semi-insubordinate *att*-constructions fulfill a variety of discourse functions (requests, explanations, justifications, responses, etc.; cf. Van linden and Beijering 2016 for a functional taxonomy of Dutch *misschien dat*-constructions). Initial epistemic sentence adverbs function primarily as hedges or question particles conveying tentativeness and politeness rather than expressing the speaker's evaluation of the likelihood or truth of the content of the *att*-clause. The examples in (12)-(15) also show that the semi-insubordinate *att*-constructions function as evaluative continuations or additional comments to a prior statement, which reflects a pragmatic, sequential, dependency with respect to the foregoing context.

3.4 Discussion

When taking a closer look at the corpus examples, we note that they do not fully comply with Van linden and Van de Velde's (2014: 231) characterization of semi-insubordination (cf. Section 2.1). Though *kanske* and related sentence adverbs qualify as single matrix constituents in the sense that they convey an epistemic assessment of the propositional content expressed in the *att*-clause, they do not seem to function at matrix clause level.

Neither the 'single matrix element', nor the *att*-clause can be used independently (both within original context, or as context-free independent statements). The parts are mutually dependent on one another in order to form a meaningful unit (cf. ('12) and ('15)).

('12) [*Det är ju en evighetsprocess!*]
　　*Möjligen att vi kan se ett resultat om fem år.
　　*Möjligen att vi kan se ett resultat om fem år.
　　*Möjligen att vi kan se ett resultat om fem år.

('15) [*Han besväras av något i halsen, men fortsätter.*]
　　*Kanske att höstens fukt påverkar hans stämband?
　　*Kanske att höstens fukt påverkar hans stämband?
　　? Kanske att höstens fukt påverkar hans stämband?

An interesting and useful concept in this respect is the distinction between 'predication subordination' and 'discourse subordination' (Lindström and Londen 2008: 146). Predication subordination is typical of syntactically dependent clauses (e.g. *Jag tror att han kommer* 'I think that he comes'). Discourse subordination takes into account the sequential/incremental dependencies typical of narrative discourse and conversational language. It accounts for constructions that are pragmatically, but not syntactically, dependent on a 'discoursal antecedent.' On this view, the conjunction 'that' does not have a subordinating role at the sentence level, but a 'sequential back-linking' function at the discourse level i.e. "[to] point back to a preceding discourse source and respond to this and expand from this" (Lindström and Londen 2008: 145).[10]

The corpus data point to a sequential/incremental dependency at the discourse level, rather than to a hierarchical/grammatical dependency between initial element and complement clause at the sentence level. The constructions in (12–15) extend beyond the sentence level in that they represent various types of continuations and additional comments to prior statements. Accordingly, a sentence-based characterization assuming a grammatical/hierarchical dependency between the 'single matrix constituent' and the *att*-clause cannot account for these constructions. Therefore semi-insubordination constructions are better analyzed as discourse units.

4 Diachronic study: The history of *kanske* 'maybe' and related epistemic adverbs

4.1 Introduction

It is generally assumed that *kanske* is a univerbation of the verb phrase *kan ske* 'can happen', which formed part of a full main clause *det kan ske att X* 'it can happen that X'. This origin in a VP would explain the clausal properties of the present-day adverb (cf. Lundin 1997; Andréasson 2002; Beijering 2010). In this diachronic case study, we test the hypothesis, put forward by Wessén (1968), that the development from *det kan ske att* went through five successive stages, including loss of the expletive pronoun *det* 'it' and of the subordinator *att*. These stages should be seen as gradual transitions, as the developmental stages overlap and their instantiations may therefore occur simultaneously.

At stage I the verb phrase *kan ske* forms part of a full matrix clause in which the formal subject *det* 'it' is more or less obligatory. At stage II the formal subject *(det)* is no longer part of the verb phrase, but the complementizer *att* 'that' cannot be omitted. Omission of the complementizer *att* is possible at stage III. At stage IV, inversion of the subject and finite verb is possible, which results in standard declarative V2 clauses. Once V2 word order is possible, at stage V, the verb phrase is reanalyzed as a sentence adverb and *kanske* may now also occur clause-internally.

---

10 See Lehti-Eklund (2002), Verstraete et al. (2012), Weinert (2012), Anward (2014) and Wide (2014) for more studies on the discourse function of 'that' and 'that'-clauses.

The five stages in the development of *kanske*, according to Wessén (1968: 15), are exemplified with present-day Swedish equivalents of the phrase '*Maybe that he comes already today*' in (16). The synonymous univerbated adverbs *kan hända* > *kanhända* 'can happen'; *må hända* > *måhända* 'may happen'; *tör hända* > *törhända* 'may happen' went through a similar development.

(16) I.   *(Det) kan   ske*   *att   hcn*   *kommer redan   idag.*
          '(It)   can   happen   that   he   comes   already today.'

     II. *Kanske / kan ske*   *att   hcn*   *kommer redan   idag.*
          'Maybe / may be   that   he   comes   already today.'

     III. *Kanske*   *hcn*   *kommer redan   idag.*
          'Maybe   he   comes   already today.'

     IV. *Kanske*   *kommer han*   *redan   idag.*
          'Maybe   comes   he   already today.'

     V.   *Han*   *kommer kanske*   *redan   idag.*
          'He   comes   maybe   already today.'

In present-day Swedish, *kanske* occurs in canonical positions for sentence adverbs (adverbial *kanske* in V2 clauses; cf. stage IV and V), and in positions where it is followed by subordinate word order (subordinating *kanske* in non-V2 clauses; cf. stage II and III). Combinations of a modal auxiliary and a main verb with a referential subject (as in stage I), are still found as well. Adverbial semi-insubordinate *att*-clauses as we find them today may thus reflect an earlier stage in *kanske*'s development (i.e. stage II).

4.2 Sources and method

The diachronic study of *kanske* is based on Norde, Rawoens and Beijering (2014). This study traces the development of the verbal predicate *kan ske* 'can happen' and competing constructions, such as *kan hända* 'can happen' and *må ske* 'may happen', from Old Swedish to Modern Times. The historical corpus data were collected from *Fornsvenska textbanken*[11] (1375–1525s; cf. Delsing 2002), *Litteraturbanken*[12] (1700–1800s) and *Språkbanken*[13] (1900–2000s). Since *kanske*

---

11 <http://project2.sol.lu.se/fornsvenska/>
12 <http://litteraturbanken.se>
13 <https://spraakbanken.gu.se/>

and related adverbs have their origin in a verb phrase, the query consisted of all possible spelling variants of the univerbated adverbs (*måhända, kanhända* 'perhaps' and *törhända* 'perchance'), the modal forms (*kan, må, tör* 'can/may') and the main verbs (*ske* and *hända* 'happen'). Texts from non-annotated corpora were examined by means of the concordance tool in *WordSmith Tools* (Scott 2004).

4.3 Results

Queries of the historical corpora that formed the basis for Norde et al.'s study yielded 108 epistemic verb phrases (see Table 2) and 160 epistemic sentence adverbs.

Table 2: Epistemic verb phrases.

MAIN VERB	AUXILIARY	Late Old Swedish (ca. 1375–1525)	Early Modern Swedish (ca. 1526–1732)
hända	*kan*	2	46
	må	2	1
	tör	–	15
	lär	–	–
ske	*kan*	5	34
	må	2	–
	tör	–	1
	lär	–	–
total		**11**	**97**

Despite the relatively low frequencies of the verb phrases and corresponding adverbs, it is possible to trace a number of morphosyntactic and semantic changes in the development of *kanske*. The change from Stage I to Stage II, i.e. the loss of the formal subject pronoun, is illustrated in examples (17a) and (17b). In (17a), the subject pronoun (often spelled *thz* in Old Swedish) is present, whereas it is absent in (17b). These examples also show that the matrix clause did not (yet) have a fixed word order, as evidenced by the inversion of subject and finite verb in (17a), or the insertion of an adverb between the modal auxiliary and the main verb (17b-c). Furthermore, the auxiliary was not only found in the present tense, but in the past tense as well, as in (17c).

(17) a. *Nu* **kan thz ske** *at thu sigher wæl swa.*
Now can it happen that you say well so
'Now it may happen that you do say so.'
[ST I, ca. 1460]

b. **Kan wäl ske,** *at någen kan wara komin i stade.*
Can well happen that someone can be come in stead
'It could well be the case, that someone else came instead.'
[Horn, ca. 1657]

c. **kunde väl skee,** *att the och vij måtte bliffva goda*
Could well happen that they and we would become good
venner.
friends
'It could happen that we become good friends.'
[Gyll, ca. 1640]

Instances of the verb phrase *kan ske* accompanied by a formal subject are decreasing towards the Early Modern Swedish period. On the basis of Wessen's (1968) hypothesis about the history of *kanske*, this is what one would expect. However, in light of the rise of obligatory (expletive) subjects from the 16th century onwards, omission of *det* is a remarkable tendency (cf. Falk 1987, 1992, 1993; Platzack 1985). The fact that these epistemic verb phrases develop towards subjectless adverbial clauses shows that these constructions can no longer be regarded as standard matrix clauses (on the assumption that a matrix should at least contain a subject and a tensed verb).

The transition to Wessén's stage III, i.e. loss of the complementizer *att*, is also attested in our historical corpus data. Overall, subordinate clauses without a complementizer are supposed to be a rare phenomenon during the Old Swedish period (ca. 1225–1525; Wessén 1965: 275–277). In the following Early Modern Swedish period, epistemic verb phrases and adverbs occur with (18a) and without *att* (18b):

(18) a. *Det* **kan wäl hända** *at den stora dumma skaran beröfwar*
It may well happen that the big stupid crowd robs
honom.
him
'It may well be that the big stupid crowd robs him.'
[Argus, 1700s]

b. ***Kan   hända*** *det   torde   ock   ha   sin   nytta.*
  Could happen it   would also have its usefullness
  'Perhaps it would be useful in some way.'
  [Argus, 1700s]

Table 3 shows the frequencies of epistemic verb phrases with and without expletive subject *det* and complementizer *att*. Note that epistemic verb phrases
may occur without a subject but with a complementizer, but not the other way
around (as predicted by stage I-III in Wessén's developmental trajectory for
kanske). However, Wessén's claim that the loss of the subject pronoun and the
subordinator went hand in hand with the univerbation of the epistemic verb
phrase is not borne out by the data – for instance, in (18b) above, both the subject pronoun and subordinator are missing, yet there is not univerbation.

Table 3: Formal subject det and complementizer att in epistemic verb phrases.

MAIN VERB	MODAL FORM	Late Old Swedish (ca. 1375–1525)				Early Modern Swedish (ca. 1526–1732)			
		+ DET + ATT	+ DET – ATT	– DET + ATT	– DET – ATT	+ DET + ATT	+ DET – ATT	– DET +ATT	– DET – ATT
hända	*kan*	1	–	1	–	7	–	14	6
	må	2	–	–	–	1	–	–	–
	tör	–	–	–	–	–	–	4	6
ske	*kan*	1	–	4	–	–	–	5	7
	må	1	–	–	–	–	–	–	–
	tör	–	–	–	–	–	–	1	–
total		5	0	5	0	8	0	24	19

Apart from problems with the chronology of the changes, Wessen's (1968)
study fails to acknowledge the occurrence of epistemic verb phrases in other
syntactic positions. They do not only occur sentence-initially, but also as parenthetical insertions, especially in texts from the Early Modern Swedish period (as in (19a-c); note also the use of the preterite in the last example).

(19) a. *Det fån I   se **kan skie**   om några åhr, sade han.*
   That get you.PL see can happen in some years said he
   'Perhaps you get to see it in a couple of years, he said.'
   [Argus, 1732–4]

b. *Deras offer   får   man, **kan ske**,   ej   taga något skäl*
   Their sacrifice should one, can happen, not take some reason
   utaf, (...)
   of
   'Their sacrifice cannot be used as an argument (...)'
   [hogstrom-lm, 1747]

c. *så hade the   och icke heller ähn nu   sett   någin fiende*
   so had they also not either still now seen some enemy
   *för   sig,   **kunde skie**   icke heller finge see.*
   before themselves could happen not either got   see
   'Still they had not yet seen an enemy in front of them, perhaps they
   would not get to see one either.'
   [Brahe, ca. 1585]

We will return to the significance of these parenthetical constructions in the
next section.

4.4 Discussion

In their account of adverbial semi-insubordination constructions, Ramat and Ricca
(1998) distinguish between univerbated adverbs (e.g. *kanske* 'maybe') and derived
ones (e.g. *probablement* 'probably'). For constructions with initial derived adverbs
they argue that these structures are possible because of 'the extension of the predicative construction "it is + ADJ + that ..." to adverbial constructions, probably via
those adverbs which are formally identical to adjectival forms [...]: 'it is + ADJ/
ADV + that ...' → 'ADV that ..."" (Ramat and Ricca 1998: 214). This developmental
trajectory is particularly plausible in languages without a clear formal distinction
between adverbs and adjectives (such as Russian or Dutch).

   Another scenario applies to univerbated adverbs. Their occurrence in semi-
insubordination constructions can be diachronically accounted for by their origin in a higher predicate. Structurally there are two subtypes of univerbated
adverbs: forms with and without an agglutinated complementizer (e.g. Serbian /
Croatian *možda* 'perhaps' < 'can that' contains an agglutinated complementizer
(= *da*); Norwegian *kanskje* 'perhaps' < 'it may/can happen' does not contain
a complementizer, but may co-occur with a complementizer).[14] According to

---

14 See also Ramat & Ricca's (1998: 231) structural typology of non-derivational sentence
adverbs.

Ramat and Ricca, clausal univerbations that retain the complementizer have to derive from main predicates, whereas those without a complementizer may originate in both main and parenthetical clauses (1998: 233).

Following Ramat and Ricca's account, the presence of *kanske*, *kanhända* and *måhända* in Modern Swedish adverbial semi-insubordinate *att*-constructions (see Section 3) can be diachronically explained by their origin in a predicate. Obviously however, this is not true for the epistemic adverbs that do not originate in a predicate, such as *möjligen* 'possibly' or *förmodligen* 'presumably'. Since Swedish uses clear morphological marking to distinguish between adverbs and adjectives, an explanation in terms of extension of a predicative adjectival construction for adverbs with identical adjectival forms is not likely either (cf. Ramat and Ricca 1998). The occurrence of non-univerbated epistemic sentence adverbs could therefore be a case of analogical extension on the basis of *kanske*, modelled after its possibility meaning.

The history of *kanske*, as outlined in our diachronic case study, shows the importance of taking into account diachronic facts in synchronic analyses. Evans (2007) already pointed out a 'crucial formal difference' between insubordination and semi-insubordination constructions (cf. Section 2.2), which means that these are actually two different construction types. If semi-insubordination were an intermediate stage on the historical trajectory of insubordinated clauses (cf. Figure 1), one would expect to find instances of independent *att*-clauses (like in (6)) for which an epistemic matrix can be reconstructed. The data show that the *att*-clauses following *kanske* are not insubordinate clauses, because they do not constitute syntactically and pragmatically independent units which are consistently used with subordinate marking (cf. Section 3).

To sum up, the data support the idea that the original clausal properties of the predicate *(det) kan ske (att)* persist in current epistemic semi-insubordinate *att*-constructions. A diachronic account in terms of reduction of epistemic verb phrases is therefore the most likely developmental scenario for *kanske att*-clauses (cf. Wessén 1968; Ramat and Ricca 1998; Norde et al. 2014).

5 A counter-example to unidirectionality?

All previous accounts of semi-insubordination assume an origin in a full-blown matrix, which (abruptly) disappeared or (gradually) condensed into a single matrix element. As a consequence, the semi-autonomous status of formally subordinate 'that'-clauses makes them eligible counter-examples to the cline of clause-combining, in which it is main clause construal in paratactic organization that gives rise to subordination patterns rather than the other way around (cf. the 'clines of clause combining' in (8) and (11)).

For insubordination constructions, Evans (2007, 2009) has claimed that these form a counter-example to unidirectionality tendencies in grammaticalization processes whereby subordinate clauses develop from material in main clauses. That is, "[i]nsubordination proceeds in the opposite direction (i.e. subordinate clauses recruited to provide material for new main-clause types)" (2009: 2).

If the development of adverbial semi-insubordination constructions were indeed a case of degrammaticalization, that would be remarkable because degrammaticalization is very rare cross-linguistically (Norde 2009: 122), but adverbial semi-insubordination is not (Traugott 2017: 294). In the remainder of this section however, we will argue that the adverbial semi-insubordinate constructions discussed in this paper are *not* examples of degrammaticalization.

First of all, the reverse of clause combining should be a gradual process of 'clause separation', by which a subordinate (+embedded) construction, via an intermediate hypotactic (-embedded) status, ends up as a paratactic construction (i.e. two main clauses). The corpus data do not support such a development.

The rise of adverbial semi-insubordination constructions rather represents a case of advanced grammaticalization in that it involves (further) reduction of a complex sentence construction. The original epistemic matrices in a complex clause condense into formulaic stance markers, parenthetical phrases, etc., which is comparable to the emergence of "evidential parentheticals" (Hopper and Traugott 2003: 207–209). This would involve "integration of structure via a shift from multiclause to single clause structure" (Hopper and Traugott 2003: 207). The former margin (= subordinate clause) has been reanalyzed as a single nucleus, "and the former nucleus (= a full-blown matrix, e.g. *I think*) has been demoted to something that looks like a sentence adverb (comparable with *evidently, apparently*, etc.)" (Hopper and Traugott 2003: 209).

This scenario is in accordance with our diachronic data and recent functional analyses of 'main' and 'subordinate' clauses in complement-taking predicate (CTP) constructions. Thompson (2002) analyzes the 'main clause' parts in these constructions as "epistemic/evidential/evaluative formulaic fragments expressing speaker stance toward the content of a clause" (Thompson 2002: 125). In a similar vein, Verhagen (2005) considers the 'matrix elements' to be 'grammaticalized expressions for intersubjective coordination', whereas he regards the 'complement clauses' as 'main carrier of discourse continuity.' In addition to the functional reanalysis, there has been an extension of dependencies beyond the sentence level (cf. Mithun 2008; Lindström and Londen 2008). The *att*-clause is not embedded in a single matrix constituent ('predication subordination'), but the entire semi-insubordination construction is sequentially/incrementally and pragmatically dependent on a stretch of prior context ('discourse subordination'). A parallel can be drawn with Lindström and Londen's (2008) analysis of the complex connectives (*så att* 'so (that)', *men att* 'but (that)', and *för att* 'for (that)') in Swedish. For constructions introduced by these complex connectives they observe that the first item specifies the semantic relation/function (causal, adversative and consecutive) and *att* denotes sequential back-linking. This insight can also be extended to semi-insubordinate *att*-constructions: the initial element specifies either a speaker oriented assessment (evaluative semi-insubordination) or the speaker's reasoning (discursive semi-insubordination), and *att* serves to point back to prior context (cf. examples (12)-(15)).

Traugott (2017) rejects the analysis of adverbial semi-insubordination as degrammaticalization for a different reason – she argues they these are not the result of ellipsis, but constructions typical of dialogue (whereby they are dependent on a matrix in a preceding utterance).

6 Concluding summary

Like most prior studies of semi-insubordination, the present study had its point of departure in a sentence-level representation and analysis of these constructions. Initially, we adopted the characterization of semi-insubordination by Van linden and Van de Velde (2014: 231) as our working definition. Indeed, from a sentence-level perspective, semi-insubordination constructions like (1–3) undoubtedly go against well-known patterns of clause combining and subordination. However, a number of problematic issues pop up with respect to the terminology and analysis of actual corpus data in terms of the working definition.

We addressed the difficulties posed by semi-insubordination constructions for traditional syntactic analysis and unidirectionality issues in the domain of clause combining and grammaticalization. We reviewed previous accounts of and hypotheses on the rise of semi-insubordinate constructions against our own empirical study. Our data support a developmental path in terms of (further) reduction of complex sentence constructions, accompanied by a functional shift of the 'minimal matrix' and subordinate clause, as well as an extension of dependencies at the discourse level.

We have argued that although adverbial semi-insubordination constructions are syntactically independent, they are always bound to a preceding proposition in discourse. Moreover, the epistemic sentence adverb often has special pragmatics too, in the sense that it fulfills various hedging functions. The discursive properties of adverbial semi-insubordinate constructions cannot be accounted for within previous sentence-based accounts of its structural status (e.g. Aelbrecht 2006; Julien 2009), as these analyses assume a hierarchical/grammatical dependency between the 'minimal matrix clause' and the 'that'-clause.

As shown by the examples in Section 3, adverbial semi-insubordinate constructions extend beyond the sentence boundary and operate at the discourse level. The data point to a discursive use of *att* in adverbial semi-insubordination constructions. In Swedish (like English), 'that' is in general an optional element in complement constructions. However, *att* tends to be non-omissible from the semi-insubordinate *att*-constructions in Section 3.4. Moreover, the Swedish *att*-clauses are not always overtly marked as syntactically 'subordinate clauses'. In absence of a negation marker or sentence adverb in between the subject and finite verb, subordinate word order in the *att*-clause does not become syntactically manifest.

Since adverbial semi-insubordination constructions function as additional comments or continuations to previous (complete) statements and questions, they always occur discourse-internally. This reflects a sequential/incremental dependency at the discourse level, rather than a hierarchical/grammatical dependency at the sentence level. Because of their responsive relation to prior statements, the adverbial semi-insubordination constructions in this paper are best analyzed as dependent discourse units (e.g. as part of an adjacency pair, or turn continuation).

Although the term *semi-insubordination* suggests otherwise, it appears to be fundamentally different from *insubordination* (i.e. "the conventionalized main clause use of what, on prima facie grounds, appear to be formally subordinate clauses" (Evans 2007: 367)). Insubordination involves 'abrupt' ellipsis of the main clause in a complex construction whereby only material from the 'original' subordinate clause is retained in the resultant insubordinate construction (Evans 2007: 386). Therefore semi-insubordination is explicitly excluded from insubordination phenomena because it represents instances of clause union or fusion (e.g. reductions of predicates into formulaic phrases), and therefore contains material from both clauses (Evans 2007: 386). Another observation is that the 'subordinate clause' in semi-insubordinate constructions is often not an *insubordinate* one. That is, the 'subordinate' *att*-clause on its own cannot be used autonomously (cf. the adapted examples in ('12) and ('15) in Section 3.4).

All of this does not mean that *subordination* is irrelevant in the context of semi-insubordination: these constructions do have a diachronic origin in a complex clause. More specifically, there has been a structural and functional reanalysis of a complex clause from the sentence to the discourse level similar to 'instances where complement-taking predicates embedded in main clauses reduce to formulaic particles, parenthetical phrases etc.' (Evans 2007: 385). This involves "integration of structure via a shift from multiclause to single clause structure" (Hopper and Traugott 2003: 207), "whereby the former margin (= subordinate clause) has been reanalyzed as a single nucleus, 'and the former nucleus (= a full-blown matrix, e.g. *I think*) has been demoted to something that looks like a sentence adverb (comparable with *evidently, apparently*, etc.)" (Hopper and Traugott 2003: 209).

Moreover, we have shown that purely synchronic analyses cannot account for the peculiar properties of adverbial semi-insubordination constructions. For example, the predominance and puzzling syntactic properties of semi-insubordination constructions headed by the epistemic sentence adverb *kanske* 'maybe' is explained with reference to its diachronic development. This epistemic sentence adverb originated via univerbation of a higher predicate (i.e. *(det) kan ske (att)* '(it) may happen' > *kanske* 'maybe'). On this assumption, present-day *kanske att*-constructions have retained the predication properties of the original verb phrase *(it) may happen/be (that)*.

The overall findings regarding the grammatical status and discourse use of semi-insubordination constructions in Swedish square with conclusions and insights from other recent studies on 'insubordination artefacts' (Struckmeier and Kaiser (this volume)), 'illusory insubordination and semi-insubordination' (Wiemer (this volume)) and 'apparent insubordination' as discourse patterns (Debaisieux et al. (this volume); Traugott 2017).

Acknowledgements: We wish to thank the participants of the workshop on (Semi-)independent subordinate constructions, the reviewers and Gunther Kaltenböck for useful suggestions and constructive comments on this paper. Beijering's work on this chapter was partly supported by a postdoctoral fellowship (grant number 12L7715N, awarded by the Research Foundation-Flanders (FWO)) at the University of Antwerp (2014-2017).

Sources

Språkbanken (Korp)
Göteborgsposten corpora [GP 2003–2014]
<https://spraakbanken.gu.se/swe/resurser>

Appendix. Historical texts (Norde, Rawoens and Beijering 2014)

Abbreviation	Text	(Approximate) year	Number of words
Late Old Swedish [ca. 1375–1525]			
Bir	*Birgittas uppenbarelser I*	1380s	106 740
HML	*Helga manna leverne*; Codex Oxenstierna	1385	30 025
KM	*Karl Magnus Saga*	end of the 1300s	10 930
SVM	*Sju vise mästare*	end of the 1300s	16 240
Bild	*Codex Bildstenianus*	first half of the 1400s	88 520
Barl	*Barlaam och Josaphat*	1440s	27 029
KrL	*Kristoffers Landslag*	1442	56 500
ProsKrön	*Prosakrönikan*	1450s	4 730
Va	*Namnlös och Valentin*	1450s	15 215
ST	*Själens tröst I*	1460	132 060
Läke	*Läkebok no. 1*	latter half of the 1400s	109 279
Did	*Didrikssagan*	end of the 1400s	48 855
Luc	*Lucidarius*	1487	28 187
StimAm	*Stimulus Amoris*	1498–1502	26 600
SK	*Själens Kloster*	early 1500s	25 485
PMB	*Peder Månssons Bondakonst*	1510	41 517
Early Modern Swedish [ca. 1526–1732]			
NT 1526	*Markusevangeliet i Nya Testcmented*	1526	14 187
Troj	*Historia Trojana*	1529	44 380
Petri	*Olaus Petris krönika*	1530	108 000
Swart	*Peder Swarts krönika*	1560	51 940
Brahe	*Per Brahes krönika*	1585	26 380
AV	*Anna Vasas brev*	1591–1612	8 060
Gyll	*Carl Carlsson Gyllenhielms anteckningar*	1640	53 010
Horn	*Agneta Horn: Beskrifningh öfwer min wandringestidh*	1657	40 460
Hiärne	*Urban Hiärne: Stratonice*	1665	11 030
Columbus	*Samuel Columbus: Måål-roo eller Roo-måål*	1675	20 260
Spegel	*Haqvin Spegel: dagbok*	1680	32 720
Stål	*Jon Stålhammar: brev*	1700–1708	44 780

(continued)

Abbreviation	Text	(Approximate) year	Number of words
Runius	Johan Runius: Prosastycken på svenska	1710	30 200
Argus	Olof von Dalin: Then Swänska Argus	1732–1734	213 160
Gyllenborg	Carl Gyllenborg: Swenska Sprätthöken	1740	28 478
Högstr-lm	Per Högström: Beskrifning öfwer Sweriges Lapmarker	1747	17 990
Qvirs	Mag. Joh. Qvirsfeld: Himmelska örtegårds-sällskap Litteraturbanken	1758	6 783
VN1	Vitterhetsnöjen 1	1769	17 137
VN2	Vitterhetsnöjen 2	1770	14 320
VN3	Vitterhetsnöjen 3	1772	20 011
VN4	Vitterhetsnöjen 4	1781	18 937
EnbomFf	P.U Enbom: Fabriks-flickan	1796	14 961
EnbomMS	P.U. Enbom: Medborgeligt skalde-försök	1793	8 291
LenngrenNO	A.M. Lenngren: Några ord til min k. Dotter, i fall jag hade någon	1794	3 488
LenngrenTC	A.M. Lenngren: Thé-Conseilen	1777	2 098
VF1	Våra Försök 1	1753	15 049
VF2	Våra försök 2	1754	34 554
VF3	Våra försök 3	1756	31 699

References

Aelbrecht, Lobke. 2006. IP-ellipsis in Dutch dialects. In Jeroen van de Weijer & Bettelou Los (eds.), Linguistics in the Netherlands 2006, 1–14. Amsterdam: Benjamins.

Andréasson, Maia. 2002. Kanske- en vilde i satsschemat [Meddelanden från Institutionen för svenska språket 41]. Göteborg: Institutionen för Svenska Språket.

Anward, Jan. 2014.'att'. Språk och stil 13. 65–85.

Beijering, Karin. 2010. The grammaticalization of Mainland Scandinavian MAYBE. In Edit Bugge & Lidun Hareide (eds.), Seven mountains Seven Voices, 1–21. Bergen: University of Bergen. https://bells.uib.no/index.php/bells/issue/view/20

Beijering, Karin. 2016. Semi-insubordinate at-constructions in Norwegian: Formal, semantic and functional properties. Norsk Lingvistisk Tidsskrift 34 (2). 161–182.

Borin, Lars, Markus Forsberg & Johan Roxendal. 2012. Korp – the corpus infrastructure of Språkbanken. In Calzolari, Nicoletta, Khalid Choukri, Thierry Declerck, Mehmet Uğur Doğan, Bente Maegaard, Joseph Mariani, Jan Odijk, Stelios Piperidis (eds.), Proceedings of the Eighth International Conference on Language Resources and Evaluation LREC'12, 474–478. Istanbul: ELRA.

Bos, Gijsbertha F. 1963. Een verwaarloosd zinstype. In De Groot A.W. & H. Schultink (eds.), *Studies op het gebied van het hedendaagse Nederlands*, 174–194. Den Haag: Mouton.

Delsing, Lars-Olof. 2002. Fornsvenska textbanken. In Svante Lagman, Stig Ohlsson Örjan & Viivika Voodla (eds.), *Svenska språkets historia i Östersjöområdet*, 149–156. Tartu: Tartu University Press.

Delsing, Lars-Olof. 2010. Exclamatives in Scandinavian. *Studia Linguistica* 64 (1). 16–36.

D'Hertefelt, Sarah. 2015. *Insubordination in Germanic: A typology of complement and conditional constructions*. Leuven: University of Leuven dissertation. https://lirias.ku leuven.be/bitstream/123456789/509450/1/DHertefelt_Insubordination+in+Germanic.pdf

D'Hertefelt, Sarah & Jean-Christophe Verstraete. 2014. Independent complement constructions in Swedish and Danish: Insubordination or dependency shift? *Journal of Pragmatics* 60. 89–102.

Evans, Nicholas. 2007. Insubordination and its uses. In Irina Nikolaeva (ed.), *Finiteness. Theoretical and empirical foundations*, 366–432. Oxford: Oxford University Press.

Evans, Nicholas. 2009. Insubordination and the grammaticalisation of interactive presuppositions. Paper presented at the Conference on Methodologies in determining Morphosyntactic Change, Museum of Ethnography Osaka, March 2009. http://www.r.min paku.ac.jp/ritsuko/english/symposium/pdf/symposium_0903/Evans_handout.pdf

Evans, Nicholas & Honoré Watanabe (eds.). 2016. *Insubordination*. Amsterdam: Benjamins.

Falk, Cecilia. 1987. Subjectless clauses in Swedish. *Working Papers in Scandinavian Syntax* 32. 1–26.

Falk, Cecilia. 1992. Pro-drop in Early Modern Swedish. *Folia Linguistica Historica* XIII. 115–132

Falk, Cecilia. 1993. Non-referential subjects and agreement in the history of Swedish. [Special issue on Null Subjects in Diachrony]. *Lingua* 89. 143–180.

Hopper, Paul J. & Elizabeth Closs Traugott. 2003 [1993]. *Grammaticalization*. Cambridge: Cambridge University Press.

Julien, Marit. 2009. Plus(s) at(t) i skandinaviska – en minimal matris. *Språk och Stil* 19. 124–141.

Lehti-Eklund, Hanna. 2002. Om *att* som diskursmarkör. *Språk och stil* 11. 81–118.

Lindström, Jan & Anne-Marie Londen. 2008. Constructing reasoning: The connectives *för att* (causal), *så att* (consecutive) and *men att* (adversative) in Swedish conversations. In Jaakko Leino (ed.), *Constructional Reorganization*, 105–152. Amsterdam: Benjamins.

Lundin, Katarina. 1997. *Från verbkombination till adverb*. Lund: University of Lund Bachelor thesis.

Mithun, Marianne. 2008. The extension of dependency beyond the sentence. *Language* 84 (1). 69–119.

Norde, Muriel. 2009. *Degrammaticalization*. Oxford: Oxford University Press.

Norde, Muriel, Gudrun Rawoens & Karin Beijering. 2014. *Från matrissats till satsadverb? En diakron studie av adverbet kanske*. https://www.academia.edu/20378714/Från_matris sats_till_satsadverb_En_diakron_studie_av_adverbet_kanske

Nørgård-Sørensen, Jens. 2001. Plus at – en ny konjunktion i dansk. *Danske studier* 96. 65–84.

Platzack, Christer. 1985. Syntaktiska förändringar i svenskan under 1600-talet. In Sture Allén, Lars-Gunnar Andersson, Jonas Löfström, Kerstin Nordenstam & Bo Ralph (eds.), *Svenskans beskrivning* 15, 205–221. Göteborg: Göteborgs universitet.

Ramat, Paolo & Davide Ricca. 1998. Sentence adverbs in the languages of Europe. In Johan van der Auwera & Baoill Dónall P. Ó. (eds.), *Adverbial constructions in the languages of Europe*, 187–273. Berlin/New York: De Gruyter.

Scott, Mike. 2004. *WordSmith Tools version 4*. Oxford: Oxford University Press.

Stroh-Wollin, Ulla. 2008. 'Det känner fan inte någon Oscar Segerqvist!' Om bl.a. popularitet och formellt fundament i svenskan. *Språk och stil* 18. 38–66.

Thompson, Sandra A. 2002. "Object complements" and conversation: Towards a realistic account. *Studies in language* 26 (1). 125–163.

Traugott, Elizabeth Closs. 2017. 'Insubordination' in the light of the Uniformitarian Principle. *English Language and Linguistics* 21 (2). 289–310.

Traugott, Elizabeth Closs & Graeme Trousdale. 2013. *Constructionalization and constructional changes*. Oxford: Oxford University Press.

Van linden, An & Freek Van de Velde. 2014. (Semi-)autonomous subordination in Dutch: Structures and semantic-pragmatic values. *Journal of Pragmatics* 60. 226–250.

Van linden, An & Karin Beijering. 2016. *Misschien (dat): Semi-insubordinate constructions versus canonical adverbial uses*. Paper presented at the Linguists' Day 2016 of the Linguistic Society of Belgium, Université catholique de Louvain, 13 May 2016.

Verhagen, Arie. 2005. *Constructions of intersubjectivity: Discourse, syntax, and cognition*. Oxford: Oxford University Press.

Verstraete, Jean-Christophe, Sarah D'Hertefelt & An Van linden. 2012. A typology of complement insubordination in Dutch. *Studies in Language* 36 (1). 123–153.

Weinert, Regina. 2012. Complement clauses in spoken German and English: Syntax, deixis and discourse-pragmatics. *Folia Linguistica* 46 (1). 233–265.

Wessén, Elias. 1965. *Svensk språkhistoria. I Ljudlära och ordböjningslära*. Stockholm: Almqvist & Wiksell.

Wessén, Elias. 1968. Ett fornsvenskt vardagsord Fsv. maxan – da. måske – sv. kanske. *Nysvenska Studier* 47. 5–16.

Wide, Camilla. 2014. Constructions as resources in interaction: Syntactically unintegrated att 'that'-clauses in spoken Swedish. In Boogaart, Ronny, Timothy Colleman & Gijsbert Rutten (eds.), *Extending the scope of Construction Grammar*, 353–380. Berlin: De Gruyter.

Björn Wiemer

4 On illusory insubordination and semi-insubordination in Slavic: Independent infinitives, clause-initial particles and predicatives put to the test

Abstract: Recently, claims have been made on the diachronic rise of insubordinated and semi-insubordinated clauses on a broader cross-linguistic basis. For instance, independent infinitival clauses have been treated since Evans (2007) as paradigm examples of insubordination, and Dutch complement clauses depending on predicative units of nominal origin and without verbal morphology have been analysed as prominent instances of semi-insubordination (Van linden and Van de Velde 2014). This article shows that structures in Slavic languages which are, on the face of it, similar to the aforementioned structures cannot be regarded as insubordination or semi-insubordination, since in diachronic terms their development is a different one. To this effect, the article contains in-depth studies on the use and status of three different structures: (i) independent clauses with infinitival predicates in the history of several Slavic languages, (ii) largely equivalent *da*-headed finite clauses in Balkan Slavic, and (iii) with regard to purported semi-insubordination, so-called predicatives with clausal complements, mainly in Russian and West Slavic. All these structures are shown to qualify as diachronically primary in the history of this language group, in the sense that they were not derived from more complex structures; if changes occurred, these can be characterized as analogical expansion, syntactic reanalysis and categorial differentiation.

Based on these descriptive findings, the available facts allow us to make a principled case for the necessity of a case-by-case investigation of clause structures that look similar in contemporary languages but may turn out to result from radically different diachronic processes. In fact, these processes may rest on fundamentally different preconditions and may take opposing directions (in terms of increase vs. decrease of material, or in terms of morphosyntactic complexity). Alleged cases of (semi-)insubordination can thus turn out to be artefacts of anachronistic approaches toward syntactic structures if these structures are assessed merely on a synchronic basis. In addition, semi-insubordination may be an areally restricted phenomenon inasmuch as the preconditions for

Björn Wiemer, Mainz University

https://doi.org/10.1515/9783110638288-005

changes to patterns that are salient in specific languages (e.g., an almost obligatory use of finite verbs, including copulae) are not necessarily available elsewhere.

1 Introduction:
Definitions and formulation of the problem

In various Slavic languages, we encounter clause types which could be argued to represent instances of insubordination or semi-insubordination, at least if one looks at their contemporary make-up. Evans introduced the concept of insubordination referring to "the conventionalized main clause use of what, on prima facie grounds, appear to be formally subordinate clauses" (Evans 2007: 367). The main processes leading to this stage are ellipsis of the original main clause and the reanalysis of the remaining part as a clause that bears all hallmarks (intonation, illocution, etc.) of independent sentences; simultaneously, insubordinate clauses often acquire meanings that are untypical of the dependent clauses from which they derive, and no 'feeling of ellipsis' remains. Prominent examples have been utterances starting with a unit that, on a synchronic account, counts as a complementizer, conjunction and/or relativizer (e.g., *As if he would know me!*)[1] and infinitives used with a directive illocution (e.g., Russ. *Dver' ne **zakryva-t'***[IPFV]-INF 'Don't **close** the door!'). In other cases infinitives as independent clausal nuclei have been shown to be convenient means in reactive dyadic turns, such as echo-questions with a specific illocutive load (e.g., Germ. *Ich und ihm glauben?!* 'Me and believe him?!', i.e. 'Why/How should I believe him?', or 'How can you expect me to believe him?'; see also ex. (12) below). Although the latter ones can hardly be explained as results of insubordination (at least in Evans's diachronic sense), they make salient a specific feature which has been connected to what "formally subordinate clauses" means, namely: the conventionalized use of <u>morphologically</u> non-finite forms – i.e. those which do not show the maximum range of tense-mood and agreement marking admitted in the respective language – as predicates of independent sentences (cf. Dwyer 2016: 188).[2]

---

1 Cf., for instance, Gras (2016) on Peninsular Spanish, Verstraete et al. (2012), Verstraete and D'Hertefelt (2016) on Germanic, Brinton (2014) on English *as if*.
2 Finiteness is a complex of very different parameters on the morphological, syntactic, semantic and pragmatic level which do not necessarily correlate (cf. Nikolaeva 2013 for a recent comprehensive treatment). All three cases from Slavic which I am going to discuss show mismatches between these levels insofar as on at least one of these levels some feature is not canonical for finite clauses. All of them, however, have independent illocution.

Semi-insubordination, in turn, has even more recently been applied as an umbrella notion capturing different phenomena which, for one reason or other, have been considered as located "halfway" between subordination and insubordination. These are constructions which contain material from an assumedly deleted main clause. Such phenomena were excluded from insubordination by Evans (2007: 384). A structure that has figured prominently as illustrating semi-insubordination is sentences with a clausal complement that depends on a predicative unit with nominal origin and without verbal morphology, as in the following Dutch example (cited after Van linden and Van de Velde 2014: 231):

(1) ***chance***   *dat*   *mijne* *radio* *hier*   *nog* *opstaat*
     good.luck COMP my   radio   here   PTC   be.on.PRS
     '**Luckily** my radio is still on (here).', or more literally:
     '(It is) **good luck** that my radio is still on here.'

The complement introduced by *dat* 'that' appears as an argument of the noun *chance* 'good luck' which here functions as the predicative nucleus of a matrix clause, but there is no NP serving as subject of this predicate. On the background of structures with some canonical coding of arguments and finite morphology on some verb it has been assumed that the single matrix constituent *chance* cannot by itself constitute a full main clause, and that the *dat*-clause depends on an elliptical trunc of a main clause. This assumption bears the diachronic implication that a structure like *chance dat P* (NP – COMP – V_{FIN}) continues some other, more elaborate structure in which nominal predicates like *chance* were furnished with a "full" entourage of arguments and accompanied by some finite verb (e.g., a copula). In Slavic languages we encounter sentence patterns that correspond to the structure in (1). Compare, for instance, examples from Polish (2), Macedonian (3) and Croatian (4):

(2) ***Szkoda***, *że*   *nie* *przyjdzi-esz.*
     pity   COMP NEG come[PFV]-FUT.2SG
     'It's a **pity** that you won't come.'

(3) ***Sramota*** *što* *ja*   *bruka-at*   *pesna-ta*
     shame   COMP she.ACC disgrace[IPFV]-PRS.3PL song[F].SG-DEF.ART.SG.F
     na *Vojo.*
     on PN
     'It's a **shame** that Vojo's song is being disgraced.'
     (https://www.facebook.com/filip.t.petrovski/.../1636339743266558)

(4) **Šteta** *što   Marija nije   doš-l-a.*
    shame COMP PN.NOM NEG.AUX.3SG come[PFV]-PRF-SG.F
    'It's a **pity** that Marija hasn't come.'

In fact, from a structural-synchronic viewpoint, the Dutch pattern and the Polish, Macedonian, or Croatian pattern are identical, i.e. any standard analysis of constituency and dependency relations would lead to the same result. Despite – or maybe, because – of this, the question arises whether the chronology of changes, in particular the relation to clausal complementation, is the same for all cases. More specifically, do finite clausal complements of predicative nouns in Slavic result from semi-insubordination – as has been assumed for Dutch (see above), but also for Swedish, French and Spanish (Van linden and Van de Velde 2014: 247)?

Actually, if we dig more deeply into the genesis of independent infinitives (§2.1) and their functional equivalents in South Slavic which are headed with the connective *da* (§2.2), we discover that, most probably, these patterns diachronically preceded the subordination constructions (i.e. complex sentences) with which they have become associated in structural descriptions of the respective contemporary languages. The case of adjectives and nouns functioning as predicates with clausal complements (as in (2)-(4)) is different; their rise should be analysed as the result of analogical expansion, both in a semantic and a syntactic sense, of simple clause patterns based on nominal predicates without agreement controllers (§2.3). However, as with the first two cases, no process of syntactic reduction has occurred. I will, therefore, argue that in Slavic none of these patterns can be regarded as an instantiation of (semi-)insubordination – at least not if we take insubordination as the endpoint of some diachronic process and as it was initially defined by Evans (2007). In fact, if we claimed that the phenomena from Slavic addressed below illustrate (semi-)insubordination, we would turn upside down the diachronic relation between subordination and looser patterns of clause linkage.

The article is structured as follows. In Section 2, I will sketch each of the debatable patterns in Slavic from the point of view of their structural properties in contemporary descriptions and then each time look at their respective diachronic development. Section 3 compares the structure discussed in §2.3 with a seemingly identical pattern in modern Dutch and shows that these patterns are results of radically different diachronic processes. The methodological conclusions to be drawn from a joint assessment of the factual material and the theoretical underpinnings are formulated in the concluding section 4.

2 The phenomena: Synchronic account and diachronic background

The description of facts from Slavic will focus on Russian, Polish and Old Church Slavonic. However, as far as available language-specific accounts allow, I will check the picture for other Slavic languages as well. A comment on the terminology concerning periods of Slavic languages seems appropriate here. Common Slavic (approx. 300–700 AD) is considered to have been a relatively homogeneous dialect continuum that existed prior to the first written attestations of Slavic. Old Church Slavonic (OCS) is the first documented variety of Slavic; in a sense, it was created on a kind of koiné of South Slavic spoken in the 9th century AD in the Aegean region. At that time the Slavic dialect continuum can be assumed to have been still sufficiently homogeneous to supply intercomprehensibility. The oldest documents used in the literature referred to below are from the late 10th century. The oldest East Slavic documents are from the 11th century, and 'early East Slavic' will mean the period up to the end of the 14th century. Since then we may speak of Old Russian[3] and Old Ukrainian. Old Polish and Czech refer to the period from the 14th to, more or less, the 16th century. Note that, although OCS still reflected the structure of Common Slavic to a large extent, it was no direct predecessor of the East or West Slavic varieties. Its influence on literary forms of East Slavic (and ultimately on standard Russian) has been tremendous, although the impact is largely restricted to certain morphonological processes, verb forms and derivation. In the domain of clause combining it is less considerable, at least as concerns the time after the 14th century.

Sections §§2.1–2 are based on Wiemer (2017; 2018), so the reader is referred to these articles for more details. The reason why facts and arguments from these extensive studies are taken up in this article is the desire to show what all the phenomena from Slavic languages discussed here have, to some extent, in common (see §2.4).

2.1 Independent infinitives

Main clauses with infinitival predicates are widespread in modern Russian, but less so in other Slavic languages. All types of independent infinitives (IndInfs) have a very simple structure, the absolutely predominant one is shown in [1]:

---

3 The label 'Old Russian' (Russ. *drevnerusskij*) is often (rather misleadingly) used as a cover term for ancient East Slavic (until the end of the 14th century) in its entirety.

the infinitive usually combines with a dative NP which denotes the most agent-like argument of the verb and, thus, a potential agent. In addition, an inflected copular verb can be used to indicate tense and mood. The dative NP can be "left out" in particular subtypes of this construction or if the referent is obvious from the situation, e.g. because it refers to the speaker by default (see (5)).[4]

[1] potAg$_{DAT}$ – (ESSE –) INF.

The status of the ESSE-verb will be clarified below (see especially §2.3.3).

IndInfs that correspond to this structure imply a modal meaning, more precisely the meaning of circumstantial (a.k.a. dynamic) or deontic (im)possibility. This can be demonstrated with sentences having a certain exclamative load used to rhetorically deny a possibility (5) and with sentences in which the negated IndInf conveys prohibition or unnecessariness (6):

(5) *I   kak   tut   by-l-o   **uderža-t'-sja**   ot   slez!*
  and how here be-PST-N refrain[PFV]-INF-RM from tear-(GEN.PL)
  'And how one/I could **withhold** tears!' (F. A. Abramov: "Prjasliny". Moskva, 1974)

(6)[5] *Emu   **ne sdava-t'**   ėt-ot   ėkzamen.*
  he.DAT NEG pass[IPFV]-INF DEM-ACC.SG.M exam[M]-(ACC)
  '**He doesn't have to / cannot pass** the exam.'

(i)   *Zapretili ved'.* 'For they have forbidden it.'   → prohibition
(ii) *On uže sdal ego v prošlom godu.* 'He already   → unnecessariness
   passed it last year.'

The same non-epistemic modal meanings can be expressed more explicitly with modal auxiliaries or auxiliary-like constructions, which take infinitives in their scope, regardless of whether they induce clauses without nominatival subjects (see (7) and (6a)) or with a nominatival subject (see example (6b)):

---

4 In the general past (marked with {l}) the verb form indicates lack of agreement, since it invariably takes the neuter-singular ending (*by-l-**o***). In Russian, the copula is obligatorily omitted in the indicative present, but in constructions with the IndInf it lacks in the indicative present in other Slavic languages as well (also at previous stages).

5 The negated infinitive is of ipfv. aspect. Denial of circumstantial possibility is correlated with pfv. verbs. Thus, the specific modal domain is regulated by aspect, but the entire clausal construction is associated with non-epistemic modality. The same distribution of aspect choice (with/without negation) applies for infinitives in the scope of modal auxiliaries (as in ex. 7).

(7) *Ne*   *by-l-o*   *sil*   /
     NEG   be-PST-N   power-(GEN.PL)
     nel'zja   *by-l-o*   *uderža-t'-sja*   *ot*   *slez.*
     AUX.NEG.POSS   be-PST-N   refrain[PFV]-INF-RM   from   tear-(GEN.PL)
     'One couldn't withhold tears.' (more lit.: *there was no strength / possibility of withholding tears.*)

(6) a. *Emu*   *nel'zja*   *by-l-o*   *sdava-t'*   *ėkzamen.*
       he.DAT   AUX.NEG.POSS   be-PST-N   pass[IPFV]-INF   exam-(ACC)
                                    non-finite auxiliary complex
       'He didn't have to pass the exam.'

     b. *On*   *ne*   *može-t*   *sdava-t'*   *ėkzamen.*
       he.NOM   NEG   can-PRS.3SG   pass[IPFV]-INF   exam-(ACC)
                                    finite auxiliary complex
       'He cannot [= is not allowed to] pass the exam.'

At face value, sentences (5) and (6) could count as illustrations of insubordination. However, this is not justified from a diachronic point of view: the clause pattern with the IndInf definitely preceded patterns with more explicit expressions of modal meanings (such as modal auxiliaries; see §2.3.3). IndInfs were attested since the oldest documented times of East Slavic (11th century). See an example from the 13th century:

(8) *a*   *dvorjan-omъ*   *tvo-imъ,*   *knjaž-e,*   **xodi-ti**
     and   nobleman-DAT.PL   your-DAT.PL   duke-VOC.SG   walk[IPFV]-INF
     po   *pošlin-e.*
     according.to   tradition-DAT.SG
     'and your noblemen, Duke, should **behave** as it used to be.' (Dogovornaja gramota Novgorodskaja 1264 g.)

IndInfs even made up the absolute majority of clauses without a nominatival subject ('impersonal sentences'), and about two thirds of IndInfs occurred in main clauses, i.e. not in clausal arguments or adjuncts (Borkovskij 1968: 159). This structure was therefore well-established already by that time.

     For modern Russian examples like (5) – (6) the structure in [1] can be taken as diachronic point of departure, since there is no reason to assume that it was not inherited from Common Slavic, i.e. from the time before internal dialectal differentiation began to increase. This holds true even if we admit the possibility that the clause pattern in [1] evolved from the reanalysis of a yet earlier pattern which explains the modal semantics of this structure and the prove-nance of the dative-marked potential agent. The non-epistemic modal mean-ing of pattern [1] can be explained as resulting from the goal/purpose semantics of the infinitive which it inherited from its predecessor, the dative of the verbal noun (*nomen actionis*), and which into our days has remained quite prominent in East Slavic (as well as in Baltic; cf. Ambrazas 1995). There seems to be a diachronic connection between the pattern in [1] and nominal sentences like the following one[6]:

(9) *takov-a*   *pravd-a*   *uzja-ti*   *rusin-u.*
     such-NOM.SG.F right[F]-NOM.SG take[PFV]-INF Russian[M]-DAT.SG
     'These are the rights a Russian must (should, can?) enjoy.'

From a semantic viewpoint, the structure in (9) provides a locus for ambiguity: in one interpretation, the nominatival NP *takova pravda* looks like a possessee of the dative-NP *rusinu* (see [2a]), but it can also be interpreted as the undergoer (i.e. more patient-like argument) of the infinitive (see [2b]). In either case (*takova pravda uzjati* ≈ 'such rights are to take' and *takova pravda rusinu* ≈ 'such rights are for/belong to a Russian') we are dealing with an inherently modal utterance, with possibility or necessity determined only by context. In the latter interpretation, the infinitive constitutes the predicate of the clause [2b], in the former it should be taken as a goal-adjunct of *pravda* 'right' [2a]. Now, regardless of whether (9) can be understood as representing predicative possession,[7] the relation between the infinitive and the nominatival NP as a predicate-argument relation (with the nominatival NP expressing the under-goer) and the dative-NP as a potential agent must have resulted from reanaly-sis. [2a-b] pictures reanalysis in, as it were, two variants: the dependency relations on the left side assume that no BE-verb need be postulated (or that it functioned only as a tense-mood marker), the illustration on the right side im-plies an existential BE-verb as the highest node (or head) of the clause. However, an explanation in terms of reanalysis does not depend on whether one wants to assume an existential BE-verb (often realized as zero) or not:

Subsequently, this reanalysis became manifest in a case marking shift which made the newly interpreted argument relation of the nominatival NP

---

6 (9) is from early East Slavic and was originally cited in Potebnja ([1874] 1958: 406). Večerka (1996: 93–94) gave analogous examples for OCS.

7 The diachronic relation to the MIHI EST-type (known, e.g., from Latin) is far from certain (cf. Holvoet 2003 for a critical assessment).

(as undergoer) to the verb (infinitive) visible by morphological encoding: NOM → ACC (*rusinu uzjati takovu*.ACC *pravdu*.ACC).[8]

Some researchers have assumed that the construction in [1] and its purported source construction in [2a] contained an existential BE-verb (*byti*) which could, for the earliest stages, be considered as the syntactic head of the clause, with the infinitive as its dependent; this is what the right half of Figure 1 would suggest. As we saw above, this assumption is unnecessary. Moreover, it does not sound likely in view of many facts reported for ancient Indo-European languages: existential verbs very early must have turned into copulas which functioned as mere markers of tense-mood and agreement categories (person, number); cf. Disterheft (1980: 40–49), but see also §2.3.3. But even if we shared this assumption, the infinitive acquired the status of the highest clausal node with the disappearance of the BE-verb. And in case there was no such existential verb, and *byti* just a copular tense-mood marker, the infinitive was the clausal head from the start, i.e. already in the earliest attested times. Whatever syntactic theory one abides by, it is crucial to understand that nothing in the whole process can qualify as insubordination. The reanalysis occurred in the confines of a simple sentence. The details of the relation between an earlier stage (largely prior to written documentation) in [2a] and a subsequent stage in [1] and [2b] may have partially remained obscure; however, as said above, we may safely assume that [1] was the starting point for IndInfs in the individual Slavic languages.

In other Slavic languages (beyond East Slavic and specifically Russian), IndInfs have been attested with the aforementioned modal meanings as well. See, for instance, example (10) from a 14th-century translation from Middle High German into Czech; here, the IndInf occurs despite the fact that the MHG original contained modal or volitional verbs. Czech could have calqued these constructions, but, obviously, it employed an inherited construction:

(10)   *t-omu*   *nám*   *jest*   *kněžstv-a*   ***pomáha-ti***
       DEM-DAT.SG.M   1PL.DAT   be.PRS.3SG   duchy[N]-GEN.SG   help[IPFV]-INF
       'We have to **help** him (to get) the duchy.' (Dal 98; L)

---

8 This shift happened except in those parts of the East Slavic territory, in which the Nominative Object established itself more firmly, i.e. the region of Pskov-Novgorod and north to it (cf. Mendoza 2008 for a recent comprehensive account). The NOM>ACC-shift can also be observed with fossilized infinitives of perception verbs which have entered into the fuzzy class of predicatives (e.g., Pol. *widać* 'see', *słychać* 'hear' + ACC; see §2.3). With their Czech equivalents argument marking varies (NOM or ACC), but the diachronic relation between the case choices remains obscure (Holvoet 2003: 470). However, in whatever direction the construction becomes reanalyzed is of no concern for insubordination, since all changes have occurred in the confines of simple sentences.

$$
\begin{array}{ll}
[2a] & \textit{takova pravda} \bullet\!\!-\!\!\!-\!\!\!-\!\!\bullet \textit{rusinu}, \quad \text{OR:} \textit{takova pravda} \qquad \textit{rusinu} \\
& \qquad\qquad \downarrow \qquad\qquad\qquad\qquad\qquad\quad \downarrow \\
& \qquad\quad \textit{uzjati} \qquad\qquad\qquad\qquad\qquad \textit{uzjati}
\end{array}
$$

Figure 1: Reanalysis from adnominal-adjunctival to predicative infinitive.

MHG originals: (rhymed) *wir **suln** in zcum horczogtum entpurn* (Jir. 11) 'We **should** support him for/to get the duchy.'; (prose) *dem **wolle** wir das lant eingeben* (Jir. 278) 'We **have to/should** pass over the land'.

In more recent West Slavic the IndInf has become much more restricted.[9] Regardless of where it has "survived", its functions are associated to states of affairs that are presented as irreal (e.g., hypothetical or counterfactual). The same functional characteristics can be ascribed to *da*-clauses with morphologically finite predicates in South Slavic; this clause type has ousted infinitives as heads of both main and subordinate clauses particularly in Balkan Slavic (see §2.2).

Apart from the predominant pattern of IndInfs just discussed there exists the so-called 'narrative infinitive', which can occur only in continuation of a preceding stretch of discourse and which normally implies an ingressive meaning. In comparison to other IndInf-types it is very infrequent. See a Russian example from Puškin's cited after Nikolaeva (2007: 153), where this phenomenon is analyzed at length:

(11) *Korol'*   *rasskaza-l*   *anekdot.*
      king[M]-(NOM.SG)   tell[PFV]-PST-(3SG.M)   joke[M]-(ACC.SG)
      Carevn-a   ***xoxota-t'.***
      princess[F]-NOM.SG   laugh[IPFV]-INF
      'The king told a joke. **The princess started laughing.**'

---

9 In modern Polish, for instance, the IndInf is largely limited to deontic functions with the speaker or the addressee as the implied potential agent (mostly in questions) and to generalized prohibitions (with negation, e.g. *Nie dotykać przewodów!* 'Don't touch the wires!', at railway stations).

In contrast to the modal IndInfs with a dative-marked NP of a potential agent, narrative infinitives combine with a nominatival NP. The same syntactic pattern (NP$_{NOM}$ – INF) is found in utterances like (12) from contemporary Russian; they typically carry a pragmatic load of indignation and are used in echo-replicas, while the narrative infinitive does not convey any specific pragmatic meaning.

(12) *Ja   i   obmanyva-t'   svo-ego   drug-a?!*
     1SG.NOM and deceive[IPFV]-INF POSS.REFL-ACC.SG.M friend[M]-ACC.SG
     'I and deceive my friend?!'

In both cases the infinitive combines with a nominatival subject, and one can argue that both need to be embedded into some linguistic context.[10] In contrast, the properly modal IndInfs with the dative-marked potential agent can be uttered in isolation. These considerations, together with the different syntactic structure, lead us to believe that the narrative infinitive and the 'infinitive of indignation' are of a different origin than the predominant pattern of IndInfs. However, I am unaware of any earlier structure from which the contemporary NP$_{NOM}$ – INF-constructions might have derived via main clause ellipsis or via reanalysis; there are no indications that they have ever been embedded.

2.2 Complementizer vs. clause-initial particle

South Slavic shows a cline of infinitive loss: in Bulgarian and Macedonian, the infinitive has been lost almost entirely as a morphological form of the verb, while the further one moves from there to the north-west, the better the old functions of the infinitive and the form itself are preserved. The štokavian dialect continuum (basically Serbian-Croatian) is transitional between Slovene in the north-west corner and Bulgarian and Macedonian in the south-east; the infinitive exists as a form, but seems to be avoided more and more, the further one moves to the south-east. The syntactic functions of the infinitive have largely been taken over by a construction that consists of verb forms inflected for tense and agreement categories (person, number) preceded by the proclitic *da*. Inasmuch as these inflectional characteristics can be regarded as core symptoms of morphological finiteness, we may say that *da* always attaches to

---

10 For other features of either construction and some diachronic background cf. Wiemer (2017: §3.1, §4.1).

a finite verb (V_{FIN}). This yields a primitive template which is the basis of all constructions relevant for the following discussion:

[3] *da* + V_{FIN} .

The syntactic status of this proclitic and of the constructions it introduces has been (and still is) an object of controversies. Although it cannot be denied that *da* plays a central role in clausal complementation, it fulfils many other functions as a connective on various levels of morphosyntax. In modern Macedonian and Bulgarian it functions as (i) a complementizer (although a peculiar one; see below), (ii) a conjunction (see ex. (14)), (iii) a connective in auxiliary and phasal verb complexes which links the lexical verb (V_{FIN}) to an auxiliary or phasal verb (see ex. (15)), and (iv) a clause-initial particle in independent clauses (see (16) – (18)). Modern Balkan Slavic *da* is a strict verbal proclitic, it can be separated from the verb in the complement only by another proclitic; as a consequence, it does not always occupy the first position in the complement clause, but separates the complement predicate from its subject argument (see ex. 13). Compare the following examples from contemporary Macedonian[11]:

Functions of *da* in Balkan Slavic (here for Macedonian)
(i)   clausal complementation, e.g. in object control:

(13)   *Nareduva-m   Marija da   dojd-e   vednaš.*
       order[IPFV]-PRS.1SG PN   COMP come[PFV]-PRS.3SG immediately
       'I demand that Marija come immediately.'

(ii)   adverbial subordination, e.g. conditionals:

(14)   *Da   ima-m   pari,   ḱe si   kupa-m   kola.*
       CONJ have[IPFV]-PRS.1SG money FUT REFL.DAT buy[PFV]-PRS.1SG car.PL
       'If/When I have money, I will buy myself a car.'

(iii) connective in auxiliary/phrasal verb complexes, e.g. modal auxiliaries:

(15)   *Mora-at   da   doaǵa-at.*
       must-PRS.3PL CON come[IPFV]-PRS.3PL
       'They must come.'

---

11 These examples are cited from Wiemer (2014; 2017), with more references of standard descriptions therein. Miševska Tomić (2006: ch. 6) provides a comprehensive overview of the contemporary distribution of *da*-clauses in Balkan Slavic. Specifically on Macedonian cf. Kramer (1986) and Miševska Tomić (2012: ch. 12).

(iv)   initial particle in independent clauses, e.g.

(16)   *Da   gi   prečeka-te!*   quasi-imperative, hortative
       CON them.ACC wait[PFV]-PRS.2PL
       'You should wait to welcome them!'

(17)   *Da   go   bj-ax   nameri-l-a*
       CON he.ACC AUX-IMPF.1SG find[FFV]-PRF-SG.F
       tuk!   optative (counterfactual)
       here
       'If only I would have found him here!'

(18)   *Da   se   zakolja-m?*   rhetorical question
       CON RM   stab_to_death[PFV]-PRS.1SG
       'Shall I stab myself to death?'

(19)   *Da   ima-š   pari,*
       CON   have[IPFV]-PRS.2SG   money
       a   da   žive-eš   kato
       and   CON   live[IPFV]-PRS.2SG   like
       bednjak!
       poor_man   in coordinated clauses
       'To have money and to live as a poor man!'

As different as these constructions (and *da*'s functions) are from a syntactic point of view, *da* always functions to mark some sort of irreality, or suspension of assertiveness.[12] This includes epistemic or emotional distancing as in the rhetorical question (with "illocutionary negative polarity") in (18) and the expression of indignation as in (19).[13] Indignation is typically associated with reactions to other people's behaviour, in particular to their speech acts. We, thus, find *da*-clauses also in a certain kind of echo questions. (18) is of this kind, but compare also a Bulgarian example in (20), which is an equivalent of the Russian sentence in (12):

---

12 The situation differs in South Slavic north-west of Balkan Slavic: in Serbian and further to the north-west *da* has become the neutral complementizer. However, if it introduces independent clauses, it suspends assertiveness.

13 Indignation shares with admirative utterances the feature that the speaker cannot but admit that a certain state of affairs holds, but they would not have expected it. On the different concepts of 'distance' cf. Sonnenhauser and Meermann (2015).

(20) Bulgarian *Az   da   pluva-m?!*
              1SG.NOM CON spit[IPFV]-PRS.1SG
              'Me and spit?!'

This condensed survey shows that IndInfs and independent *da*-clauses (i.e. the structure *da*+V_{FIN}) show a large overlap of functions, both in terms of some cognitive-semantic load (suspension of assertiveness) and in discourse-conditioned, but sufficiently stable pragmatic associations.[14] In fact, the primitive template in [3] carries the same semantic load as do IndInfs in Russian (and earlier stages of Slavic languages). However, note as well that neither IndInfs nor independent *da*-clauses are restricted to (or particularly typical of) utterances that are embedded in dyadic pairs of face-to-face communication (these are at stake only in echo-replicae signalling indignation).

The natural question that now arises is: how does the pattern *da*+V_{FIN} in independent clauses (listed above under (iv)) relate diachronically to the same pattern employed in unanimously subordinated clauses (listed under (i-ii)) and complex predicates (see (iii))? The answer, though less straightforward than it was regarding IndInfs, points to the same direction: *da*'s occurrence in syntactically independent clauses diachronically preceded its employment as a subordinator (conjunction, complementizer, connective in complex predicates). Here I will give only a survey of the most important findings concerning *da*'s functional development in South Slavic; a more elaborate discussion with extensive references can be found in Wiemer (2017: §4.3; 2018: §§3.1–3).

The most accepted view on the etymology of *da* is that it descended from the ablative form of an IE demonstrative (**dōd*.ABL) probably meaning something like 'from then onwards' (cf. Grković-Major 2004, among others). An alternative, less accepted etymology was suggested by Gołąb (1984: 171). According to him, *da* descended from the imperative singular **dadjь!* of the Proto-Slavic verb **dati* 'give'. This etymology would neatly explain why *da*, irrespective of its syntactic status, occurred first with an optative or hortative[15] function. However, Gołąb (1984: 179) claimed that the verbal origin of *da* applied only to its use as a particle ("mood marker"), while the homonymous complementizer (his "conjunction") derived from the demonstrative pronoun. We are left with this somewhat strange (and certainly unverifiable) claim. Regardless of whether this etymology is correct or not, by Old Church Slavonic times *da* already

---

14 Actually, the only clause-type not attested for Russian IndInf is conditionals. Moreover, the correspondence with *da*-clauses pertains into the narrative infinitive. Cf. Wiemer (2017: §3.3) for the discussion of an equivalent use of *da*-clauses in Bulgarian.
15 Consider the generally well-attested path from 'give' to 'let' (e.g. in analytical causatives).

appeared as a ubiquitous particle at the beginning of clauses, and its function was associated with unrealized states of affairs (see below). In East and West Slavic *da* by and large has faded away. In Russian it has survived as an affirmative marker ('yes'), as an adversative conjunction (also on NP-level, e.g. *staryj da malyj* 'old and/but small'), or as a sort of switch-reference marker on clause level, sometimes with a hortative function (e.g. Russ. *Da pomogi ty emu nakonec!* 'Will you help him, at last!'), which shows up also in rather lexicalized phrases like *Da zdravstvuet X!* 'May X live/be healthy!'. Note that in all these usage types (except in NP-coordination) *da* occurs at the beginning of non-embedded clauses.

In Old Church Slavonic, *da* was used as a 'particle' in different clause types, but all of them shared one feature: they all referred to irreal (or unrealized) situations, and the finite verb occurred predominantly in the present indicative. *Da* appeared (i) in non-embedded clauses with directive function (ex. (21)), (ii) after predicates of volition, command or with apprehensive semantics (ex. (22)), or (iii) in final or, more rarely, consecutive clauses (ex. (23)):

(21) *ne trъplju uže žaždi.*

da	***po-črъp-i***	*ubo*	*vod-y*	*se-a.*
CON	PFX-scoop-PRS.3SG	PTC	water[F]-GEN.SG	DEM-GEN.SG.F

'I don't stand the thirst any longer. **Scoop**, then, a bit of this water.'
(Vita Cyrilli 12, MMFH II, 94; Večerka 1996: 77)

(22)

tetъk-a	*bo-itъ*	*sę*
aunt[F]-NOM.SG	be.afraid-PRS.3SG	RM

da	***ne***	*otъrъve-n-a*	*bǫd-etъ.*
CON	NEG	reject-PP-NOM.SG.F	be-FUT.3SG

'The aunt is afraid **lest** she will be repudiated.'
(Suprašalski sbornik 133, 11–12; Večerka 2002: 401)

(23)

těmže	*tъšt-ǫ*	*sę*	***da***	*abije*	*vъ-stan-ǫ.*
thus	hurry-PRS.1SG	RM	CON	soon	PFX-stand.up-PRS.1SG

'I therefore hurry up to stand up soon.' (lit. . . . **that** *I soon stand up*)
(Suprašalski sbornik 141. 6–7; Večerka 2002: 325)

From (ii), it could easily evolve into a complementizer, in (iii) it was easy to become a conjunction. Gołąb (1954: 70–71), following Vondrák (1908: 517), assumed that *da* first existed as a particle before it took part in the formation of tighter syntax (i.e. subordination). The examination of the extensive data in Večerka (1993; 1996) leads us to the same conclusion. Ammann and Van der

Auwera (2004: 304–306) argued against this view and claimed that main clauses headed by *da* are a comparatively late development. Their position would amount to an argument in favour of insubordination via ellipsis (i.e. in accordance with Evans 2007). However, they did not take into consideration some facts and methodological aspects which I am going to discuss now.

Although the diachronic primacy of the particle use and, thus, the primacy of non-subordinated *da*-clauses cannot be proved unrefutably on the basis of the earliest written documents in Slavic, most considerations speak in favour of this assumption. The crucial methodological problem is that we cannot assume to be dealing with complementation (or, more broadly, subordination) just because, in some stretch of discourse, we see a clause that begins with *da* and immediately follows a clause with a predicate which has the semantic potential of a complement-taking predicate (CTP). Here I give only two examples. In (24), *da* introduces a clause with a final or consecutive sense (the verb is in the supine); but this does not entail that this *da*-clause depended structurally on the preceding clause, because it can be read as inserted direct speech with an optative or a hortative meaning. The same applies even after verbs denoting manipulative verbal behaviour where the *da*-clause contains a verb in the indicative present; this is illustrated in (25):

(24)　*i*　　*posl-a*　　　　　°*csrъ*　　　*po filosof-a*　　　*brat-a*
　　　and　send[PFV]-AOR.3SG　tsar-(NOM)　for philosopher-ACC　brother-ACC
　　　jego.　*vъ*　　　*kozar-y.*
　　　his　　to　　　khazar-ACC.PL
　　　da　　*poja-tъ*　　　*i*　　　　*sъ*　*soboju*　*na*　*pomoštъ.*
　　　CONJ(?)　take[PFV]-SUP　him.ACC　　with　self.INS　on　help-(ACC)
　　　'and the tsar sent for his brother, the philosopher. to the khazars. **in order** to take him with him as support.'
　　　(Vita Methodii 4; Večerka 1996: 30)

(25)　*star'c-i.*　　　　　*nausti-šę*　　　　　*narod-y.*
　　　venerable_men-NOM　incite[PFV]-AOR.3PL　folk-ACC.PL
　　　da　　　　　*ispros-ętъ*　　　　*varaav-ǫ.*
　　　COMP(?)　　　ask[PFV]-PRS.3PL　　PN-ACC
　　　'The venerable men. incited the folks. **that** they (may) ask for Barrabas.'
　　　(Matthew 17, 20; Večerka 2002: 395)

The notorious problem of distinguishing indirect from direct speech in ancient texts, among others in Old Church Slavonic, is well-known to specialists (cf. Daiber 2009 for a recent critical account). A strong criterion to decide in favour of direct speech, and against subordination, would be a clear sign of independent illocutive force in the *da*-clause. Unfortunately, this can be demonstrated only rarely (obviously because clauses with first- or second-person subjects are infrequent in the relevant text corpora), and I am unaware of any such example with a *da*-clause in Old Church Slavonic. Anyway, analyzing the *da*-clause in (24) as a clausal adjunct to the preceding clause, or the *da*-clause in (25) as a complement of the predicate *naustišę* 'they incited, encouraged', would mean to project an understanding of modern (written) syntax onto the OCS text. The *da*-clauses clearly catch up with the preceding context in terms of discourse coherence, but we cannot prove that they depended on the immediately preceding clauses in structural terms. One cannot really disprove it, either. We may therefore ask who is to be charged with the burden of proof: the adherents of complementation and adverbial subordination, or those who support the opposite view, or those who remain agnostic in this respect?

To take sides for any position, some more circumstances have to be considered. Let us start with comparative evidence. *Da*'s function as an optative-hortative marker was very prominent in Old Church Slavonic. Optatives and hortatives do not need the support of preceding linguistic context and can be uttered "out of the blue". Markers of analytical optatives or hortatives in other languages (closer to our time) arose from fossilized (often also truncated) verb forms in independent sentences; compare Russ. *Pust' / puskaj* (< *pustit'/puskat'* 'let, release'), Pol. *niech* (< Old Polish *niechać* 'let'), Latvian *lai* (< **laid* = imperative of *laist* 'let' in older Latvian). All of these reinterpreted forms occur with the present indicative (as did *da* in the overwhelming majority of OCS examples and as it still does in modern South Slavic languages), but only some of these markers have turned into subordinators. This happened to Ltv. *lai*. The source construction from which *lai* developed into a complementizer (with a specific modal load) were directive speech acts (ex. (26)) which could then be reported, so that *lai* ended up after suitable CTPs in indirect speech or after desiderative CTPs (ex. (27)); cf. Holvoet (2016: 237, 253, 260), Holvoet and Konickaja (2011: 5–10). This, however, was the endpoint of a development leading from looser to tighter syntax. Thus, sentences of the type (26) illustrate the initial point of the developmental path, while sentences of the type in (27) are the product of a much more recent development.[16]

---

16 Examples cited from Holvoet and Konickaja (2011: 4) and Holvoet (2016: 229).

(26) Latvian **Lai** *Jān-is nāk mums līdzi!*
            HORT PN-NOM come.PRS(3) 1PL.DAT together
            '**Let** John come with us!'

(27) Latvian *Es grib-u,*
            1SG.NOM want-PRS.1SG
            lai tu atbrauc paciemo-tie-s.
            COMP 2SG.NOM come.PRS(2SG) visit-INF-REFL
            'I want you to come on a visit.'
            (lit. . .., or: . . . COMP.IRR *you come*)

We can observe preceding stages of this developmental path in modern Polish and Russian. Thus, for instance, Pol. *niech* cannot be interpreted as an 'irreality complementizer' even if it occurs in an appropriate context after a potential CTP. Compare the ungrammatical sentence in (28) for Polish, which would be almost an item-by-item translation of the Latvian sentence (27):

(28) Polish **Chc-ę, niech nas odwiedzi /*
            want[IPFV]-PRS.1SG HORT 1PL.ACC visit[PFV].PRS-(3SG)
        odwiedzi-sz
        visit[PFV].PRS-2SG
        intended 'I want him / you to visit us.'
        literally 'I want let (he) visits us / (you) visit us.'

Although one can construct contexts in which *niech* refers to the clause immediately preceding it and containing a verb generally used as a CTP, *niech* would not be interpreted as a complementizer. Consequently, the status of the *niech*-clause as a complement to the predicate in the preceding clause can be doubted as well:

(29) Polish *Wsta-ł i powiedzia-ł:*
            rise[PFV]-PST-(3SG.M) and say[PFV]-PST-(3SG.M)
            niech nas odwiedzi.
            HORT us.ACC visit[PFV].PRS-(3SG)
            'He rose and said: let him visit us.'

The conventional means of linking a clausal argument to a CTP in Polish are the complementizers *że* 'that' and *żeby* 'that, in order to' (with variants), which are in opposition to each other as markers of 'real(ized)' (*że*) vs. 'unreal(ized)' (*żeby*) situations. Notabene, one can make a case that these contemporary complementizers themselves derive from particles used in loosely juxtaposed clauses; the argument here, again, very much hinges on the diachronic time-frame and reference point (see below).

Regardless of this, if the diachronic path from a marker of directive speech acts and unrealized situations toward a complementizer (as reconstructed by Holvoet) has been attested elsewhere, why should it not apply to South Slavic *da*? Admittedly, the etymology of *da* probably differs from Ltv. *lai*, Pol. *niech* and Russ. *pust'*, but these morphemes share with Balkan Slavic *da* (and Pol. *żeby*) a core function as markers of unrealized situations and, on all accounts, this function has been diachronically stable. This common function, however, says nothing about the syntactic status of these markers or about the syntactically independent or dependent status of clauses which they head. To decide on the latter, one needs independent criteria that allow subordination in structural terms to be diagnosed in a noncircular way.

This brings us to a second consideration which is based on linguistic common sense and on basic hypotheses of evolutionary linguistics. Before a larger, more complex construction falls apart (or a part of it is elided) this larger construction must have existed in the first place. That is, before a subordinated clause can become independent from its matrix clause (and the latter be "lost"), there must have been a complex sentence composed of both these items. One cannot disintegrate a complex unit which has not previously become integrated. The notion of subordination implies that two (or more) simpler, but distinct clauses started demonstrating an asymmetrical structural relation; the ultimate symptom of this asymmetry is that the purported subordinate clause does not carry its own illocutionary force. Thus, if *da* started serving as a subordinator it must have first appeared as a clause-initial particle.

It sounds implausible that complex sentences (composed of at least two simpler units) were the first to appear in diachrony (cf., for instance, Givón 2009). However, to assess this, one has to agree on a diachronic point of departure from which onwards one looks at historical (i.e. written) data, or up to which one wants to reconstruct a stage prior to written documents. The choice of this reference point influences one's analysis and evaluation of diachronic processes, as it focuses our attention on a particular "window" in diachrony, i.e. a certain time interval in a language's history. Thus, if we want to claim that main clauses headed by *da* have resulted from insubordination via ellipsis we draw our attention to processes taking place between stage (b) and (c) in [4]. But how do we know that stage (b) was not the result of a change that led from an even earlier stage (a) at which *da* happened to consistently appear at the beginning of independent clauses?[17]

[4] a. [clause 1] + [clause 2 (= *da*-clause)] juxtaposition (*da* as a particle)
    b. > [clause 1 *da*-[clause 2]] clausal integration (*da* as a subordinator)
    c. > ~~[clause 1]~~ [*da*-clause] insubordination by ellipsis and reanalysis

The problem is that we cannot "see" a change from (a) to (b) on the basis of written documents. But, apart from the common sense reasoning on complexity just presented, it does not seem very plausible to assume that the salient function of *da* in directive speech acts which we observe for the earliest attested stages of Slavic and which occurred in non-embedded clauses, is a manifestation of the disintegration of complex sentences, i.e. resulted from a change (b) > (c). Ammann and Van der Auwera (2004) seem to assume exactly this, and this assumption implies that optative and hortative functions were diachronically secondary to *da*'s function as a complementizer and conjunction. Comparative evidence on functionally equivalent units and on clause linkage with other particles in Old Church Slavonic (see above) makes this reasoning unlikely.

That said, let us now look at slightly later periods in South Slavic. According to Grković-Major (2004: 198), in Old Serbian (12th-15th centuries) *da* had to be analyzed as a paratactic or adjunctive connective, usually with an optative or hortative function. See one of her examples from 13th century writings ("Stare srpske povelje i pisma"):

(30) *Ta vi   ni   ste   rek-l-i   da*
     CON 2PL.NOM 1PL.DAT be.PRS.2PL say[PFV]-PRF-PL CON
     se stane-mo.
     RM meet[PFV].PRS-1PL
     'Well, you told us. Let's meet!'

The second part (*da se stanemo* 'Let's meet!') could still be interpreted as direct speech, loosely attached to the preceding verb form *ste rekli* 'you(PL) said'. The hortative potential of *da* was compatible with one of the possible readings of the speech act verb, namely: that it was used as a directive (and not in order to

---

17 Of course, the same applies to morphological complexity. For instance, complex word forms (e.g., stem/root+suffix) are the result of gradual coalescence of formerly free (i.e. juxtaposed) morphemes.

introduce a report on an accomplished fact). Initially, this semantic compatibility was established on mere discourse-based grounds, without tighter syntax. Subsequently, these loose ties were strengthened via reanalysis. This step is schematized in Figure 2 with the corresponding clause pair in modern Serbian (which in principle still allows for both syntactic interpretations):

(30a)   *Ta vi ste nam rekli* | *da se sastanemo.*   (juxtaposed clauses; hortative)
(30b) > *Ta vi ste nam rekli   da se sastanemo.*   (CTP + complement clause; indirect speech)
        'Well, you told us to meet / that we should meet.'

    clause-initial particle   >   complementizer

Figure 2: Reanalysis: juxtaposition > complementation.

The clause *da se sastanemo* 'Let us meet' in (30a) carries its own illocutionary force, whereas in (30b) this clause no longer has an independent illocution. Correspondingly, the status of *da* changes to that of a complementizer; this is tantamount to saying that the formerly juxtaposed *da*-clause has been reinterpreted as an argument of the predicate in the preceding clause.

There is more to be said about the evolution of *da* in South Slavic,[18] but all further steps in this evolution just support the assumption that *da* became more and more strengthened in its role as a subordinator, that its association with the finite verb as a proclitic increased and that it gradually narrowed its structural scope. This becomes particularly evident in *da*'s role as a connective in auxiliary complexes, which corresponds to a rather late developmental step (not earlier than during the 16th century). For the issue of insubordination these processes are tangential. Most relevant for this issue is the fact that the reanalysis pictured in Figure 2 was possible only under favourable (and certainly frequent) discourse conditions: clause-initial *da* occurred immediately after clauses with predicates whose semantics made them suitable as CTPs (first of all, verbs denoting speech act or cognitive attitudes; see ex. (25)). Other suitable contexts were those with final semantics (as in ex. (24)).

In conclusion to this subsection let me emphasize the following. Since *da*+V_{FIN} in Balkan Slavic has supplanted the infinitive in practically all its functions, it is interesting to note that diachronic relations to source constructions are strikingly similar for both. For this reason, the issue that can be taken against an analysis in terms of insubordination is practically the same for *da*-clauses as it is for IndInfs.

---

18 Cf. Wiemer (2017: §4.3.2; 2018: §3.3) for comprehensive summaries.

Let us now turn to a different case which superficially resembles semi-insubordination (see §1). Remarkably, it is also connected to the role of infinitives, at least during the incipient stages.

2.3 Expressing cognitive or emotive stance with predicatives

This subsection is devoted to a specific class of predicative expressions which has been widely discussed in Slavist literature, but which seems to be rather unknown beyond these circles. I will thus give first an outline of the phenomenon in modern Slavic languages (§2.3.1), prior to dwelling on the diachronic background (§2.3.2). Particular attention is paid to the role of the BE-verb (byti) in §2.3.3, before I will resume (§2.3.4.).

2.3.1 Predicatives as a fuzzy class in modern Slavic languages

Consider the following examples:

(31) Russian **Spasibo,** čto xot' tut skaza-l-i pravd-u.
thanks COMP at_least here say[PFV]-PST-PL truth-ACC
'**Thanks** that you said the truth at least here.'
(NKRJa; Ju. O. Dombrovskij: *Fakul'tet nenužnyx veščej*, č. 5. 1978)

(32) Polish *za komunizmu dolar drogi był,*
szkoda że obali-l-i...
pity COMP turn_down[PFV]-PST-PL.VIR
przestanie się opłacać jeżdżenie do Ameryki...
'During communism the dollar was expensive. It's a **pity** that they turned it [i.e. communism] down. It will not anymore be paying to go to America...'
(NKJP; E. Redliński: *Szczuroczycy*. 1997)

(33) Macedonian **Sreḱa** što ostan-a živ.
luck COMP remain[PFV]-AOR.3SG alive-(SG.M)
'It's **luck** that he remained alive.'
(internet: puls24.mk, 09/04/2016)

All three examples contain a predicative noun, or a noun-like unit carrying an expressive illocution, with a clausal argument introduced by a THAT-complementizer

(Russ. *čto*, Pol. *że*, Mac. *što*). This noun therefore qualifies as a complement-taking predicate (CTP), although it is not accompanied by any markers of morphosyntactic finiteness (tense, mood, person-number). At face value, sentences like (31) – (33) resemble the Dutch example (1) quoted at the beginning. The question arises whether their diachronic genesis is the same, in particular whether sentences like (31) – (33) can be regarded as manifestations of semi-insubordination.

In order to answer this question (see §3.1), the sentence pattern illustrated by (31) – (33) has to be assessed from a diachronic perspective and against other non-verbal predicates that are capable of taking clausal arguments. Clausal arguments divide into finite and infinitival ones. We should then realize that the discussion of semi-insubordination has been concerned only with sentences in which the clausal complement of the non-verbal predicate (CTP) is finite and linked to that predicate by a complementizer; concomitantly, the CTP itself (or better: the matrix clause for which it represents the nucleus) is void of morphosyntactic features of finiteness. Therefore, if we want to answer the question about the rise of the sentence pattern reflected in (31) – (33), we have to establish the diachronic relation between clausal and non-clausal arguments and, as for clausal arguments, between finite and infinitival complements of non-verbal CTPs; we furthermore have to inquire whether there has been any reduction of morphosyntactic finiteness with the CTP (i.e. in the matrix clause) and, if yes, what significance such process might have had for the rise of predicatives. This last issue will be tackled in §2.3.3. The subsequent sketch of the contemporary stage of predicatives in Slavic languages focuses on Russian and West Slavic, because their comparison provides a good basis to flesh out those structural and distributional facts which have allowed certain non-verbal lexical items to acquire salience as a specific, though fuzzy class. As we will see, predicatives with finite clausal complements form only a small minority within this class (§2.3.1.3), and all available data lead to the conclusion that they were latecomers (§2.3.2). For a better understanding of the synchronic significance of predicatives with finite clausal complements I continue by spelling out the main properties and etymological subclasses of predicatives (§2.3.1.1) and by showing how morphological differentiation can favour the discrimination of predicatives from related categories (§2.3.1.2).

2.3.1.1 Properties and subclasses of predicatives

It is crucial to realize that non-verbal CTPs with finite clausal complements are knowledge-related, i.e. either they specify some epistemic or evidential notion, or they evaluate some presupposed fact. This implies that their clausal complements convey propositions.[19] For instance, in (31) – (33) the complement codes a proposition. Moreover, in these sentences the proposition of the complement is presupposed as being true, i.e. its truth value would not be affected if the predicative noun were negated. Consequently, this noun can be qualified as a factive predicate (in the sense defined by Kiparsky and Kiparsky 1970). In other cases, however, negation of a predicative noun influences the truth value of the propositional complement clause; compare, for instance, a fragment from a Polish internet forum (punctuation of original not adapted):

(34) *Ja mam kundelka i co? i uw[a]żam że jest to najmądrzejszy pies na świecie.*

Nie	**prawda**	*że*	*z*	*rasow-ymi ps-ami*
NEG	truth	COMP	with	pure-bred_dog-INS.PL
trzeba	*obchodzi-ć*	*się*	*w*	*sposób specjaln-y.*
AUX.NEC	treat[IPFV]-INF	RM	in	manner_special-ACC.SG

'I have a tike, so what? And I think that this is the smartest dog in the world. It's **not true** that pure-bred dogs have to be treated in a special way.'
(NKJP; http://www.forumowisko.pl/lofiversion/index.php/t48416-0.html, 25/10/2007)

All predicative nouns illustrated so far bear some relation to knowledge, either knowledge is presupposed (with factive predicates) or it is somehow modified (as in ex. (34)). However, among nouns used as predicative nuclei of clauses with clausal complements, knowledge-related predicatives form only a smaller group. In turn, nouns as predicative nuclei that are able to take clausal arguments constitute only a tiny subclass of lexemes that have become known as 'predicatives' (Russ. *predikativy*) among Slavists. This notion serves as an umbrella term for predicative units of diverse morphological, mostly non-verbal, origin whose core function is defined syntactically:

[P1] Predicatives supply the nucleus of a sentence, either a simple or a complex one. They function as main predicates[20] in clauses without agreement controllers (i.e. without a nominatival subject).[21]

---

19 For a detailed treatment and explanation cf. Boye (2012).

20 Cf. Isačenko (1965: 36).

21 This excludes adjectives in the nominal declension (a.k.a. 'short forms'; see fn. 26) which distinguish gender and number, so that they act as agreement targets on clause level. In East and West Slavic they are practically restricted to forms of the nominative in predicative use. For our purpose they are of no importance and can therefore be ignored, although they have been included in many accounts of predicatives.

This syntactic property can be accepted as the only feature that unites all lexemes which have been related to this "category" (see however fn. 21). Another, though more debatable property is a semantic one:

[P2] Predicatives refer to transient states.[22]

Transient states may be either physiological (Pol. *Zimno mi* 'I'm cold') or emotional (Russ. *Nam strašno ot tvoix slov* 'We are frightened by your words'), they may concern weather (Russ. *Na ulice stalo syro* 'It became damp outside', Czech *oblačno* 'cloudy', *ošklivo* 'nasty') or other environmental phenomena (Russ. *Vokrug temno* 'It's dark around', Pol. *Na sali zrobiło się duszno* 'In the room it became sultry').[23] Emotional states can imply deontic judgments like Pol. *Jak ci nie wstyd!* 'How dare you!' or **Wstyd** *mu było, bo postąpił nieuczciwie* 'He was ashamed [lit. (it) was **shame** to him] because he didn't behave honestly', while other judgments about temporary states can easily be associated with circumstantial modality, as, e.g., in Russ. *Emu bylo* **legko** *tak postupit'* 'It was **easy** for him to behave that way' (vs. non-modal *Emu bylo* **legko** *na duše* 'He felt peace of mind', lit. 'To him (it) was **easy** on the soul'). Predicatives with these two modal, but non-epistemic meanings (or implicatures) typically take infinitival complements; I will return to this issue below.

Two other properties to be considered for predicatives are the following ones:

[P3] Predicatives can combine with the copula, but not with modal auxiliaries. The copula serves to mark clausal categories (tense, mood), but it tends to be left out or even must be left out (see §2.3.3).

[P4] Predicatives can occur with infinitives (as do auxiliaries), but they do not form complex predicates with them. Instead, the infinitive functions as an argument of the predicative.[24] (The same applies to *da*-clauses as equivalents of infinitives.) This property is a consequence of [P1].

---

22 Because of this property the lexemes discussed here have also been called 'category of state' (Russ. *kategorija sostojanija*). This term is unfortunate, first of all because the notion of state has often been treated too loosely.

23 The experiencer of this state is generally coded with the dative. The same concerns the judging subject of knowledge-related predicatives; however, many of these predicatives do not allow this subject to be expressed at all (e.g., Pol. *widać* in ex. (42)).

24 Compare with Germ. *Es ist Zeit/schlecht...* *(zu)+INF 'It's time/bad *(to)+INF' (→ predicatives) vs. *Man kann/darf/muß...* (*zu)+INF 'One can/must (*to)+INF' (→ modal auxiliaries).

Other properties may possibly be listed, but these would add only to a sort of checklist: many units allotted to this category do not fulfil all conditions, and none of the conditions is by itself sufficient to delimit predicatives from other classes of predicates. For decades, the range of predicatives as a class and the properties which delimit them from major syntactic categories or from adverbials have been issues of considerable debate in Slavic and particularly in Russian linguistics. The main bone of contention was the question of whether predicatives form a distinct syntactic category (minor part of speech), and further issues have been raised by their internal subclassification.[25]

While we are here interested primarily in the question how predicatives started to appear with clausal arguments, one may in fact argue whether predicatives are really a category in their own right, inasmuch as they are parasitic on other categories (major parts of speech, adverbs, PP-adverbials). The etymological link to their mostly non-verbal sources usually remains transparent, and many grammarians have treated them as homonyms of sentential or manner adverbs, adjectives in the neuter gender, or nouns. The main subclasses of predicatives show the following provenance:

1. The neuter singular of the (former) nominal declension (a.k.a. 'short forms') of adjectives and *n/t*-participles (marked with {o}).[26] See, for instance, Russ. *dosadno* 'annoying', *očevidno* 'obvious', *ploxo* 'bad', *ponjatno* 'understandable', *zamečatel'no* 'remarkable', Pol. *chłodno* 'cold', *duszno* 'sultry', *przykro* 'unpleasant', *smutno* 'sad', Czech *lehko* 'easy', *teplo* 'warm', *vlhko* 'dampy'. (See further in §2.3.1.2.)

2. The nominative singular of nouns. Compare, for instance, Russ. *grex* 'sin', *len'* 'laziness', *oxota* 'willingness, wish', *pora* '(suitable) time', *žal'* 'pity', Pol. *szkoda* 'pity', *wstyd* 'shame', *żal* 'pity', Czech *hanba* 'shame', Mac. *grev* 'sin', *maka* 'torture', *sramota* 'shame', *strav* 'fear', Croat. *šteta* 'damage, harm', *žao* 'pity'.

3. Fossilized forms of verbs, e.g. Pol. *widać* 'see', *słychać* 'hear', *czuć* 'feel', *stać* 'stand'. These are infinitives which are the only remnants of their

---

25 An early overview was given by Isačenko (1955). For more recent critical surveys (with further references) cf. Bonč-Osmolovskaja (2009: 157–160) concerning Russian, and Lehmann (2001) including also Polish.

26 Originally, Slavic adjectives inflected liked nouns, but already during the Common Slavic period pronouns of the Indo-European **j*-stem encliticized to adjective stems before they agglutinated and finally fused with them. The result was a new declension by which the adjective inflection became consistently distinct from the inflection of nouns (Townsend and Janda 2003: 138–142; Wiemer 2011: 741–742). I will correspondingly distinguish between pronominal and nominal forms (and declensions).

former paradigm (*widać, słychać*) or which have become isolated from their paradigms in the specific meaning they have as predicatives (*czuć* 'smell', *stać* 'afford').[27]
4. Lexicalized prepositional phrases or univerbations, for instance Russ. *spasibo* 'thank you' (< *spasi Bog* 'may God save (you)'), *navesele* 'exhilarated' (< *na vesel-e*), *nagotove* 'ready' (< *na gotov-e*), *zamužem* 'married (about women)' (< *za muž-em* 'behind the man/husband').

Therefore, the whole debatable category is like a sink which assembles units of different origin. Nonetheless, it cannot be denied that their syntactic behaviour differs from the behaviour of predicative adjectives, of ordinary verbs or nouns. This behaviour was captured in the syntactic property [P1] given above, which can be considered as the core property of predicatives. Central units of this fuzzy class are exclusively used in predicative function (and thus have lost other properties typical of nouns, adjectives, or adverbs).[28] By ending up in this "sink", lexemes lose some of the properties which are characteristic of the respective part of speech from which they derive (and with which they usually remain 'homophonous'). For instance, in (35a) Russ. *pora* '(it is) time (to do X)' (< *por-a*[F].NOM.SG 'suitable time') serves as the predicative nucleus of a simple sentence, and it does not trigger agreement with the past tense copula (*byl-o*.N), whereas in (35b) *pora* occurs as the subject-NP and triggers gender-number agreement on the past tense form of the predicate *nastala* 'began, commenced'. As a noun, *pora* continues to inflect (e.g., after prepositions as in *v letn-juju por-u*.ACC.SG.F 'in summer time'):

(35) a. *Pora*   *by-l-o*   *exa-t'*.   → predicative
         time.INDECL   be-PST-N   go/ride[IPFV]-INF
         'It was (high) time to go.'

       b. *Nasta-l-a*   *letn-jaja por-a*   → noun
          commence[PFV]-PST-SG.F   summer_time-NOM.SG.F
          'The summer time began.'

Compare also the following Polish example in which a predicative of adjectival origin (*przykro* 'unpleasant') is coordinated with a predicative that derives from a masculine noun (*wstyd* 'shame'):

---

27 For details and further references cf. Grzegorczykowa (1990) and Wiemer (2009). For Czech equivalents cf. MČ/III (1987: 214–215).
28 This suggestion was put forward (somewhat indirectly) already by Isačenko (1955: 64).

(36) *By-ł-o   jej   najzwyczajniej* **przykro**   *i*   **wstyd.**
be-PST-N her.DAT plainly   unpleasant and shame
'She plainly felt **unpleasant** and **ashamed.**'
lit. 'For her (it) was plainly **unpleasant** and **shame.**'
(NKJP; Z. Górniak: *Siostra i byk.* Warszawa, 2009)

Loss of agreement features is not consistent. For instance, Vinogradov (1986: 345)
listed examples with the Russian nouns *pora* '(suitable) time' and *len'* 'idleness
(> feel idle, lazy)'. Both are feminine, but they occur as predicates with and
without agreement on the copula: *len' byl-o.*SG.N / *byl-a.*SG.F *zanimat'sja* '(we, I,
you, they) were too lazy to deal with sth.'.

2.3.1.2 Degrees of morphological differentiation
Among all predicatives, those derived from adjectival stems (and inflected participles) constitute the subclass with the highest type (and probably also token)
frequency. This certainly holds true for all Slavic languages. See examples from
representatives of East, West, and South Slavic, each of them with a clausal argument conveying a proposition:

(37) Russian *I   mne   by-l-o   **dosadn-o   i***
             and   1SG.DAT be-PST-N annoying-N and
             ***strann-o,** čto*
             strange-N COMP
             ona   ne   ponima-et
             she.NOM   NEG   understand[IPFV]-PRS.3SG
             togo, čto ponimaju ja (...).
             'And for me it was **annoying** and **strange** that she didn't un-
             derstand what I understood.'
             (NKRJa; M.P. Arcybašev: *Žena.* 1905)

(38) Polish **Jasn-e,** *że   moż-esz   nas   odwiedzi-ć.*
             clear-N COMP can-PRS.2SG 1PL.ACC visit[PFV]-INF
             'Of course, you can visit us.'
             (lit. '**Clear** that you can visit us.')

(39) Macedonian **Arn-o** *što   molče-še.*
                  good-N COMP keep.silent[IPFV]-IMPF.2SG
                  'It's **good** that you were keeping silent.'
                  (by courtesy of E. Bužarovska)

However, Slavic languages differ with regard to whether and how consistently predicatives derived from adjective stems can be distinguished from cognate adverbs morphologically (i.e. on the basis of their endings), and to which extent both can be distinguished from the neuter singular nominative form of cognate adjectives. Adverbs derived from adjective stems go back to the neuter singular of the nominal adjective inflection in {o} (see fn. 26), or they take the suffix {'e} (with a palatalized stem-final consonant). This inflection occurs also with participles marked with the *n/t*-suffix, which is why in the following I will treat them on a par with adjectives (see ex. 40a) and (40b)). As allomorphs of adverb endings, {o} and {'e} are unevenly distributed over Slavic. Languages differ as to whether they show a morphological distinction between the short neuter form of adjectives and adverbs, and as to whether, in turn, adverbs differ morphologically from predicatives. Standard Russian does not make such a distinction. Compare, for instance, the differences in syntactic status of the form *zabavno* (< *zabavn-* 'funny') in (40a) – (40c), in which the zero copula (see fn. 29) is not indicated:

(40) a. *Pis'm-o*   *napisa-n-o*   / *zabavn-o.*
　　　 letter[N]-NOM.SG   write[PFV-PP-NOM.SG.N   funny-NOM.SG.N
　　　　　　　　　　　　　　　　　　　　　　　　　　　 predicative participle /
　　　　　　　　　　　　　　　　　　　　　　　　　　　 adjective (neuter)
　　　 'The letter has been [lit. *is*] written / is funny.'[29]

　　 b. *Pis'm-o*   *napisa-n-o*   *zabavn-o.*   manner adverb
　　　 letter[N]-NOM.SG write[PFV]-PF-NOM.SG.N funny-**ADV**
　　　 'The letter is written in a funny way [lit. *funnily*].'

　　 c. *Zabavn-o,*   *čto*   *ty*   *mne*   *napisa-l*
　　　 funny-**PRED**   COMP   2SG.NOM   1SG.DAT   write[PFV]-PST-(SG.M)
　　　 pis'mo.   predicative
　　　 letter[N]-ACC.SG
　　　 (*Ja by ne ožidal.*)
　　　 'It is funny that you have written me a letter. (I did not expect it.)'

The situation is different in West Slavic, where a predicative can often (though not consistently) be distinguished morphologically from the adverb and the neuter form of predicative adjectives (which continue the pronominal declension). In Polish, for instance, the nominal adjectival declension has decayed (except for

---

29 In Russian, copular and auxiliary *byt'* 'be' is omitted obligatorily in the present indicative (see §2.3.3).

a few remnants), but many predicatives keep the former neuter singular ending of the nominal declension in {o} (ex. (41a)), which differs from the most widespread ending of adverbs in {'e} (ex. (41b)) and from the neuter ending of the adjective in {e} (without palatalization of the stem-final consonant; ex. (41c)):

(41) a. *Mił-**o***   *mi*   *by-ł-o*   *Pan-a*   *pozna-ć.*
           nice-PRED   1SG.DAT   be-PST-N   Sir-ACC.SG   acquaint.with[PFV]-INF
                                                                               predicative
                                                                               (= clausal nucleus)
           'It was **nice** to make your acquaintance.'

      b. *Mił-**e***   *się*   *z*   *Pan-em*   *pogawędzi-ł-o.*   manner adverb
           nice-ADV   RM   with   Sir-INS.SG   chat[PFV]-PST-N
           'It was nice to have had a chat with you.', more lit.: '**Nicely** one chatted with you.'

      c. *Spotkani-**e***   *z*   *Pan-em*   *by-ł-o*   *bardzo* *mił-**e**.*
           encounter[N]-NOM. SG   with   Sir-INS.SG   be-PST-N   very   nice-NOM.SG.N
                                                                               predicative adjective
           'The meeting with you was very **nice**.'

From the diachronic point of view, predicatives ending in {o} just retain an ancient stage, which existed prior to the rise of the pronominal adjective declension (where West Slavic forms in {e} come from); see fn. 26. Most of the adjectival stems which, at the earliest stages, prepared the ground for the category of predicatives had the ending {o} (see §2.3.2). At that time this was still to be interpreted as the neuter gender (of the nominal declension) used as the default if the clause lacked an agreement controller. Simltaneously, {o} and {'e} were employed as markers of adverbs; but in standard Russian {'e} ceased to be productive and {o} is the predominant suffix of adverbs derived from adjectival stems. As a consequence, adverbs and predicatives based on adjectival stems cannot be distinguished. In West Slavic the situation is rather reversed: {o} and {'e} must have existed in parallel for a long time without a clear functional distribution before {o} became marginalized and "specialized" as a marker of predicatives. This morphological differentiation which is most pronounced in West Slavic has contributed to the consolidation of predicatives; in standard Russian the salience of predicatives could have increased only on the basis of behavior properties, both with predicatives derived from adjectives and with those derived from nouns (see §2.3.3).

These findings supply the background against which Slavic predicatives deriving from nouns and capable of taking finite clausal complements are to be evaluated.

2.3.1.3 Predicatives with clausal arguments

Although we still lack systematic empirical findings, we can safely assume that predicatives which derived from nouns and which can take clausal complements with finite morphology and that are introduced by a complementizer are in a clear minority.[30] This is confirmed by my cursory searches in electronic corpora. In any case, such complements are possible only with knowledge-related predicatives, i.e. they either have to carry some epistemic-evidential value or add some emotional or moral evaluation of a proposition that is taken for granted.[31] For the latter case see the factive predicatives in (31) – (33), (37) and (39); an epistemic predicative was exemplified in (34), (42) illustrates an evidential predicative:

(42) Polish **Widać** *że* *jest* *w ciąż-y.*
　　　　　　 evident COMP be-PRS.3SG in pregnancy-LOC
　　　　　　 'It is **obvious** that she is pregnant.'

Predicatives with clausal arguments that do not code propositions, but states of affairs (SoAs)[32] typically occur with the infinitive, a complementizer marking irreality (Russ. *čtoby*, ex. 43) or with equivalent *da*-constructions in Balkan Slavic (see §2.2). They often, but not always, convey a deontic or circumstantial meaning, and this can become manifest in the choice of a marked complementizer, as in the following examples:

---

30 As for modern Russian, the findings by Bonč-Osmolovskaja (2009) indicate that the type-frequency of clausal complements of predicatives is equally low regardless of whether the clause is headed by an infinitive (14%) or whether it has a finite verb and is introduced by a complementizer (15%). The highest type frequency is with predicatives for which no 'stimulus' is explicitly expressed (49%). On the level of token frequency, finite clausal arguments are in a clear minority; this complementation pattern dominates only for three predicatives: *jasno* 'clear', *izvestno* 'known', *ponjatno* 'understandable'. However, Bonč-Osmolovskaja's figures take into account only predicatives that occur together with dative experiencers (as, e.g., in ex. (36)), and her investigation was restricted to publicistic sources and the belles-lettres.
31 Note that the inverse is not true: not all factive predicates require a finite complement. See, for instance, the Polish example in (41a): the infinitival complement refers to a presupposed fact; it can however be rephrased with a finite complement (***Miło** (mi) było, że Pana poznałem* lit. 'It was **nice** (for me) that I got to know you.').
32 In contrast to propositions, states of affairs do not implement reference to the denoted situation and therefore do not underlie truth conditions. For a systematic treatment of the difference cf. Boye (2012).

(43) Russian **Nužn-o,**   *čtoby*   *golos*   *biznes-a*
necessary-N   COMP   voice[M]-NOM.SG   business-GEN
zvuča-l
sound[IPFV]-PST-(SG.M)
gromče, čem on zvučal ran'še.
'It's **necessary** that the voice of business sounds louder than it
sounded before.'
(NKRJa; D. Viktorov: *Stena* // "Biznes-žurnal", 10/23/2003)

(44) Macedonian **Arn-o**   *e*   *da*   *molč-iš.*
good-N   be.PRS.3SG   COMP   keep.silent[IPFV]-PRS.2SG
(compare with ex. 39)
'It were **good** if [lit. *that*] you kept silent.'

Note, finally, that predicatives either do not allow a copula to be added in the
present indicative at all (Russian, more or less also Polish), or the present-
indicative copula tends to be avoided or is facultative (e.g., Macedonian, Czech).
Lack (or even prohibition) of the copula is, apart from lack of an agreement controller (i.e. nominatival subject), an important feature of predicatives which has
to be traced back diachronically. I will return to this point in §2.3.3.

By now, we have already seen that many independent processes were involved in the emergence and consolidation of predicatives. Some more factors
will be dwelt upon in the remainder of this section. Heterogeneous factors have
converged, although their particular weight differs among Slavic languages:
roughly, in West Slavic morphological differentiation has proved more important
than in (standard) Russian, where, in turn, syntactic distribution is a more prominent factor. In any case, however, the share of predicatives derived from nouns
appears to be rather inconsiderable, judged in terms of type and token frequency.

2.3.2 The diachronic source of predicatives

Let us, then, turn to diachrony: how can the rise of predicative nouns and adjectives with clausal arguments in Slavic be explained? It seems obvious that
this process can be understood only on the broader backdrop of the development of sentence patterns in which no agreement controller (i.e. a subject-NP
in the nominative) was available. This point can be approached in terms of
Keenan (1976): to which extent has a differentiation in behaviour properties of
non-verbal clausal nuclei been indicated by their coding properties (i.e. morphological endings)?

A critical note concerning the data is in order. What follows is a sketch not only for reasons of space, but also for the reason that the corpora and previous studies on diachronic syntax in Slavic languages so far have very little to offer for a systematic investigation of the issue at stake here. Even comprehensive and detailed treatments of the rise and changes of clause patterns and clause combining in various Slavic languages give scarce, if any, valuable information about the development of clausal complements of non-verbal parts of speech. One does find elaborate discussions on infinitival constructions (and of their da+V_{fin}-equivalents in South Slavic), on nominal predicates and on simple clauses which lack agreement between nominatival subject-NPs and predicates,[33] but to date there is no connection between complementation and non-verbal predicates that are potential CTPs. As concerns electronic corpora, only some of them are annotated for older stages of Slavic languages, but even if annotations exist they are not very suitable to be exploited for the sort of syntactic quests relevant to our purpose. In addition, practically all predicatives are notoriously homonymous with forms of other parts of speech (as their sources). Thus, the amount of work that should be performed with corpora in order to pinpoint relevant constructions in complementation would have surpassed my capacities for the current contribution. Regardless of this, a thorough perusal of extant literature on the diachronic syntax of Slavic languages has allowed to confront the "Slavic case" of predicatives with clausal complements with the "Dutch case" of semi-insubordination referred to in the beginning (see ex. 1). A systematic reconstruction of the rise of clausal complements of predicatives has to be postponed to a later occasion.

To tell the most relevant conclusion in advance, knowledge-related predicatives with finite clausal complements and a complementizer are most probably the last ones that became established after a long process of analogical extension from clause patterns known since Common Slavic. Let us now order the facts.

2.3.2.1 Old Church Slavonic

In OCS, among non-verbal predicates we find quite a few that were already able to take clausal complements, but these were headed by infinitives.[34] According to Večerka (1993/II: 129; 1996/III: 105–107), such complements could be found

---

33 E.g., early East Slavic $grěx\breve{\delta}$.NOM.SG.M $slad\breve{b}k$-o.N 'Sin is sweet' (cf. Sabenina 1983: 59–60 or Wiemer 2012).
34 In many traditional accounts on old stages of Slavic languages these infinitives were analysed as (non-canonical) subjects of nominal predicates; cf., for instance, Borkovskij (ed.) (1983) on early East Slavic.

with comparative forms of adverbs (e.g., *uńeje* and *dobrěje* '(is) better') and with the following units[35]:

(45) *dobro, blago* 'good', *lěpo, dostoino, podoba / na podobǫ, godъ / godě* 'befits, suitable', *ljubo* 'suited', *tęžъko* 'difficult', *lъgъko / legъko, udobъ* 'easy', *moštъno, (ne)vъzmožъno, (ne) lъdze / lъzě* '(not) possible', *lětъ, lětъjǫ* 'allowed', *trěbě, potrěba, potrěbъno, nǫžda, nevolja / nevolě* 'necessary, compulsory'.

Most of these forms were marked with the neuter ending of the nominal declension (which at that time was still productive); in this declension the neuter SG-NOM forms were often homonymous with the corresponding adverbs. They could be used without a copula (ex. (46) – (47), (50)), but it seems that more often than not a copula occurred (ex. (48) – (49), (51)). Instead of an infinitive, a *da*-clause could be employed as a complement (see ex. (48)); this fact illustrates that the "replacement" of the infinitive (discussed in §2.2) developed from an already existing, though minor pattern:

(46) **legъk-o**   bo   oč-ima   tvo-ima   °vlk-o
     easy-N   because eyes-INS.PL your-INS.PL   lord-VOC.SG
     umrъtvi-ti   i   *oživi-ti.*
     put.to.death[PFV]-INF and reanimate[PFV]-INF
     'because it is **easy**, Lord, with your eyes to put to death and to reanimate'
     (Euchologium Sinaiticum 78b 22–23)

(47) **ne lъzě**   sъpas-ti   sę inako
     NEG can.INDECL   salvage[PFV]-INF   RM other.way
     'One **cannot** salvage oneself in another way.'
     (Suprašalski sbornik 370. 16–17).

(48) **nevъzmožъn-o**   estъ   da   ne   prid-ǫtъ
     impossible-N   be.PRS.3SG   COMP NEG come[PFV]-PRS.3PL
     sъblazn-i.
     temptation-NOM.PL

---

35 The infinitives *(ne) viděti* '(not) see', *(ne) slyšati* '(not) hear' are also relevant. Obviously, already in OCS times they had started to isolate from their paradigms and functioned as independent predicates of "impersonal" sentences denoting circumstantial (im)possibility, e.g.: *glasa že jemu ne běaše* **slyšati** 'He couldn't **hear** the voice', lit. 'For him (it) was not (to) hear the voice' (Suprašalski sbornik 116. 26; cited after Večerka 1996/III: 106). I have, however, not found any examples with a clausal argument.

'It is **impossible** that no temptation will come.'
(Luke 17, 1)

(49) **dobrěe** emu   bi   by-l-o
     better   him.DAT SUBJ be-PST-N
     ašte   ne   bi   rodi-l-ъ   sę   °čk-ъ.
     if   NEG   SUBJ be.born[PFV]-PRF-SG.M REFL man[M]-NOM.SG
     'It would have been **better** for him if man had never been born.'
     (Matthew 14, 21)

These predicatives showed affinity to circumstantial or deontic modality (e.g.,
'it is easy (for X) to do V' evokes the implicature 'X can do V'). By contrast,
knowledge-related predicatives appear to have been very rare. Večerka (1996/
III: 117) notes that they existed, and that they even had clausal arguments introduced by *jako* 'that', but then he mentions only the adjective-based *(j)av-ě* 'is
obvious, evident' (< *(j)av-* 'obvious') and the participial derivatives *vědo-m-o*
and *věs-t-o* '(is) known' (< *věd-ě-ti* 'know'), e.g.

(50) **jav-ě**   bo   jako   ot   ijudov-a   kolěn-a
     obvious-ADV because COMP from Jewish-GEN.SG.N provenance[N]-GEN
     vъsьj-a
     all-GEN.SG.N
     °g-ъ naš-ъ. °is.
     lord_our_Jesus[M]-NOM.SG
     'because it is **obvious** that our Lord Jesus is from the Tribe of Judah.'
     (Epistle to the Hebrews 7, 14)

(51) **vědom-o** bo   jestь   jako sam-ъ   stvor-i
     known-N because be.PRS.3SG COMP self-NOM.SG.M create[PFV]-AOR.3SG
     °mtrъ.
     mother-ACC
     'for it is **known** that he himself created the mother'
     (Besedy na evangelie papy Grigorija Velikogo 25, 162aβ 17 sq)

I did not find any knowledge-related nouns which might have been qualified as
predicatives.

2.3.2.2 The relation between predicatives and modal auxiliaries

Predicatives can also be found in other languages, both in ancient and modern
ones (compare Germ. **Schade**, daß P '(It is a) **pity** that P'). Lexical equivalents of

the units mentioned under (45) and neuter forms of adjectives were used as predicatives in ancient Greek; some of them occurred also in Latin. For instance, Latin *opus* shifted from its use as a noun in the meaning 'work' to a deontic predicative ('necessary') and could then lack agreement with the copula and a modifier (e.g., *multa* mihi **opus** *sunt* 'I have much to do'); Isačenko (1955: 53–54). Since in Slavic many of the early "candidates" for the predicative category were associated to non-epistemic modality, one wonders how they came to be distinguished from modal auxiliaries.

Some of the units listed for Old Church Slavonic under (45) were developing into modal auxiliaries, which at that period were still a nascent category, and no modal auxiliary with a stable epistemic function yet existed (Hansen 2001: 275–279). From a syntactic point of view, Slavic modals can be delimited from predicatives in that modals combine only with an infinitive to form complex predicates with a shared argument structure (in particular, a coreferential subject which remains implicit with the infinitive), while predicatives have their own arguments. As for the expression of arguments, predicatives are much more flexible: they can combine with different morphosyntactic formats of complements, and argument structures may differ (so that there also is no coreference requirement for any argument). Modals are more like operators on other predicates, while predicatives have independent syntactic status as predicates (hence their name). However, predicatives and modal auxiliaries can have common source expressions, like those in (45) – (49), all of which are associated with deontic or circumstantial modality, but not with epistemic meanings.

In fact, to tell apart a circumstantial possibility modal from a predicative proves impossible with infinitival complements as in (46) – (47). What distinguishes a predicative with infinitival complement from a full-fledged modal, say, in modern Russian? Compare:

(52) *S*   *toboj*   **trudn-o**   *soglasi-t'-sja*   → predicative
      with 2SG.INS difficult-N agree[PFV]-INF-RM
      'It **is hard / difficult** to agree with you.'

(53) *S*   *toboj*   **nel'zja**   *soglasi-t'-sja.*   → full-fledged modal auxiliary
      with 2SG.INS AUX.NEG.POSS agree[PFV]-INF-RM
      'One **cannot** agree with you.'

(54) *S*   *toboj*   **nevozmožn-o** *soglasi-t'-sja.* → peripheral modal auxiliary
      with 2SG.INS impossible-N agree[PFV]-INF-RM
      'It **is impossible** to agree with you.'

All three sentences can be uttered to refer approximately to the same situation and to the speaker's personal attitude toward the action at stake (to agree or not with the interlocutor). But only *nel'zja* in (53) counts as a modal auxiliary because, apart from circumstantial impossibility, it can also mark deontic impossibility (i.e. prohibition); that is, it is polyfunctional within the core domain of modality (defined via the opposition of necessity and possibility).[36] By contrast, *nevozmožno* in (54) is semantically restricted to circumstantial impossibility; for this reason it is at best a peripheral modal, although in other respects, first of all syntactically, it behaves like *nel'zja*. *Trudno* in (52), in turn, does not count as a modal because a modal meaning can only be inferred ('it is difficult to V' implies 'one cannot V'), and this inference can be drawn only for circumstantial impossibility. That is, neither does *trudno* conventionally code a modal meaning, nor is it polyfunctional.

This brief comparison shows that modal auxiliaries and predicatives may have overlapping distributional properties in their syntactic behaviour, but differ in their range of functional distinctions (modals are more flexible within modality) and complement types (many predicatives are more flexible). If we look back, again, at the relative diachronic starting point reflected in Old Church Slavonic, we see that a distinction between modal auxiliaries and predicatives proved impossible if complementation was restricted to infinitives. Inversely, one can conclude that modal auxiliaries and predicatives originated in partially identical source expressions and became differentiated from each other via more clear-cut syntactic distribution. In other words: representatives of these two classes started complying to different syntactic templates (viz. whether argument structure was shared with a verb or not); concomitantly, the semantic requirements for predicatives have in general been much looser than for auxiliaries, which, in contrast, were more flexible within the domain of modality proper. Since representatives of either category comply with the respective central properties to different degrees, it it not surprising to find cases of overlap. For instance, Russ. *nužno* marks necessity, but belongs only to the inner periphery of modal auxiliaries, since it also behaves like a deontic predicative (see ex. (43)).

2.3.2.3 Development from early East Slavic into Russian
Dictionary entries and comprehensive studies on diachronic syntax indicate that the situation for early East Slavic very much resembled Old Church Slavonic.

---

36 For this definition cf. Van der Auwera and Plungian (1998). I am using the criteria on modals developed by Hansen (2001; 2004). In the European-wide survey by Hansen and De Haan (2009: 515), the requirement that modals combine with infinitives was dropped and the polyfunctionality criterion became the most important one for units to be considered as full-fledged modals.

Borkovskij (1968: 182) reports that predicatives with an emotional-evaluative meaning were not much rarer than modal predicatives (some of them might have been characterized as nascent modal auxiliaries). By contrast, neuter *n/t*-participles as predicative nuclei became more frequent only after the 14th century (Borkovskij 1968: 170–171). They became particularly frequent, at least on token level, for speech act verbs, and this yielded object control constructions with infinitival complements (e.g., *velěno ěxati* '(it has been) ordered to go').

These observations allow for the cautious indirect conclusion that initially the lion's share of predicatives must have been derived from adjectival stems: the amount of predicatives deriving from nouns was very limited, while the role of neuter forms of *n/t*-participles as predicatives increased considerably only after the 14th century. We may assume that both adjectives and participles as nuclei of clauses without canonical subjects (i.e. without agreement controllers) created a pattern to which the comparatively few nouns able to take clausal complements could contribute by analogy. Very likely the inventory of such nouns fluctuated. For early East Slavic (11–14th c.) we find *běda* 'trouble, misfortune', *blago* 'weal, good', *ne dosug* 'no spare time' (> *nedosug* in modern Russian), *sram/sorom* 'shame',[37] *strax* 'fear', *utešenie* 'consolation', *zloba* 'malice', *žal'* 'pity' (Borkovskij 1968: 189–190, 1983: 60–62; SDJa 1990/III: 233). Many of these have not been mentioned for subsequent periods or reappeared only considerably later. For instance, by the 17th century only *grex* 'sin', *sram* 'shame', *styd* 'shame', *nevolja* 'lack of freedom', and *vremja* (*veremja*) 'time' were attested, then *pora* '(suitable) time', *(ne)oxota* '(lack of) willingness', *len'* 'laziness', *beda* 'misfortune', *strax* 'fear', and *užas* 'horror, awe' (re-)entered the scene. A more considerable increase of predicatives deriving from nouns seems to have taken place in the 19th century (Švedova 1964: 322–324). At that time *pravda* 'truth' was well attested as a predicative, too, although it was considered to have been used in this function already earlier (Pospelov 1964: 78–79).

Diachronic dictionaries consulted for these key words do not register usage with finite clausal arguments; similarly, in the relevant literature one only exceptionally comes across such usage. For instance, in his eloquent discussion of predicatives Vinogradov (1986: 330–347) casually mentions but one such instance with the now obsolete *nevidal'* ≈ 'something hitherto unseen' (1986: 345)[38]:

---

37 *Sorom* is the East Slavic correspondence to South Slavic (i.e. OCS) *sram*. No difference in meaning is known, and only *sram* has survived into modern Russian. Other units from this list that testify to OCS influence are *blago, strax,* i *utešenie*.

38 Dal' ([1881] 1956/II: 505) registered it only as a parenthetical.

(55) **Nevidal'**,   čto   on   pridvorn-yj   sovetnik.
unseen.thing COMP he.NOM at.court-NOM.SG.M counselor[M]-(NOM.SG)
'It is an **incredible thing** that he is court councillor.'
(Gogol': Ženit'ba. 19th c.)

Likewise, Borkovskij (1983: 62) quotes in passing examples with complementi-
zer-like iže (or ježe) from early East Slavic (11–14th c.), but this connective[39]
was followed by an infinitival complement conveying deontic or related modal
meanings; for instance:

(56) ne   bo   malo **blago** jestъ   iže   nudi-ti
NEG because little weal be.PRS.3SG COMP force[IPFV]-INF
rabota-ti   °st-yimъ
work[IPFV]-INF saints-DAT
'because there it is no little **good** for the saints to force to work'
(Sreznevskij 1955–56/I: column 90)

Many predicatives took infinitival complements with generalized (omnitempo-
ral) meaning, e.g.

(57) **Straxъ** vide-ti   gnev-u   Bož-ogo.
fear   see[IPFV]-INF anger-GEN of.God-GEN
'It is **terrifying** to see God's anger.'
(Barkulabovskaja letopis', l. 165, 16–17th century; cit. from Borkovskij
1983: 61)

Finite clausal arguments appear to have been missing, or were extremely rare,
also with predicatives derived from adjective stems.

Browsing through standard treatments of diachronic syntax in other Slavic
languages yields the same picture, and, as far as I am aware, no specialized investigations exist.

We can summarize our observations by specifying the following directions
of development of sentences with non-verbal predicative nuclei with lacking
agreement controllers (nominatival subjects):

---

39 They go back to IE. *j-pronouns used as relativizers. Such instances (also for translational
equivalents of ex. 56) were commented on by Večerka (1996/III: 106–107) for Old Church
Slavonic. He noted that they were rare and might have been influenced by Greek literary
traditions.

1) syntactic form of the complement: infinitive > finite verb (+ complementizer)
2) function of the complement: SoA > proposition
3) PoS origin of the predicatives: no clear preference/direction discernible, but most
                                        probably development started with adjectival stems

Figure 3: Chronological relation for predicatives and their arguments.

Of course, the development in the form of the complement is closely connected to its functional development: as we have seen, predicatives and modal
auxiliaries had common source expressions, but epistemic or other knowledge-
related meanings became established as the latest ones; only these meanings
entail propositional complements which, in turn, seem to be the precondition
for finite complements to arise.

2.3.3 On the role of *byti* 'be'

One wonders whether the presence or absence of the BE-verb (OCS *byti*) could
have played a role in the expansion of predicatives, in particular as concerns their
use with finite clausal complements. The answer to this question is twofold; we
can approach it from a diachronic-empirical and from a more theoretical point of
view. From the empirical point of view, *byti* 'be' in the present indicative retreated
after the 14th century in East Slavic. This process seems to have affected particularly predicatives of adjectival origin (Borkovskij 1983: 66). The process, however,
must have started much earlier; *byti* happened to be "omitted" with nominal predicates already in Old Church Slavonic (see §2.3.1.1). This process increased during
early East Slavic, i.e. already by the 14th century, and generally it has advanced
further than in the rest of Slavic. It also affected BE as an auxiliary clitic used in
originally compound tenses (perfect with the *l*-participle > general past), BE as an
auxiliary in the (resultative) passive as well as existential BE. Although the fate of
existential BE has remained investigated poorly, the general retreat of BE with nominal predicates is well-known, and it contributes to inner-Slavic (south)west-
(north)east clines.[40] In accordance with this cline, contemporary standard Russian
presents the most advanced stage with respect to all usage types of *byti*: in the
present indicative it has an almost obligatory zero copula and auxiliary (e.g., in
the resultative passive); this copula form occurs only in some pragmatically highly
restricted contexts, which are not at stake here. As concerns existential BE, in the

---

40 For a recent overview concerning BE as an auxiliary cf. Meermann and Sonnenhauser
(2016), on BE in East Slavic cf. Kopotev (2015).

present indicative only the former (and now paradigmatically isolated) 3.SG-form *est'* has survived, which is used only with narrow scope (i.e. if the existence of the referent is asserted emphatically). Before this general retreat of BE, *byti* had already turned into a copula serving as a tense-mood and agreement marker. This must have happened already during Common Slavic, since this stage can be observed in the earliest Slavic written attestations,[41] as did continuations of **es-/*bhū-* in many other Indo-European branches (Isačenko 1955: 49, 55).

From a theoretical point of view, one may ask why the propensity, or avoidance, of using a BE-verb should at all be relevant for the rise and status of predicatives. As predicative nuclei the latter constitute the highest node in dependency structure, although they are uninflected for clause-level categories. Copular BE marks only agreement and tense-mood, i.e. those clause-level categories which have been regarded as symptoms of morphological finiteness. Copular BE is nothing but an operator, it is not a constituent. Expletive (a.k.a. dummy) subjects have been unknown in Slavic (except for some of its westernmost exponents); if the copula occurs in the PRS.IND.3SG-form in clauses without agreement controllers, its role is reduced to mark default tense and default mood with non-verbal predicates.

Admittedly, if a BE-verb is used in combination with a nominal predicate that lacks a canonical subject as an agreement controller, it might also be considered an existential verb, however I am ignorant of convincing argumentation in favour of such a treatment.[42] Existential verbs are usually regarded as one-place predicates with an NP as their argument; compare (58) with (59) from modern Russian and both with (60), which reproduces a part of (56) from early East Slavic:

(58) *Vokrug by-l-**a***   / ∅*est'*/ *bud-et*   *tišin-a.*
      around be-PST-**SG.F** / zero /   be-FUT.3SG silence[F]-NOM.SG
      'Around there **was** / is / will be silence.'

(vs.) *Vokrug by-l-**i***   / ∅*est'* / *bud-ut*   *derev'j-a*)
      around be-PST-**PL**   / ZERO /   be-FUT.3PL tree[N]-NOM.PL
      'Around there were / are / will be silence.'

(59) *Vokrug by-l-**o***   / ∅*est'* / *bud-et*   *tixo.*
      around be-PST-**SG.N** / ZERO /   be-FUT.3SG quiet[N?]
      'Around it **was** / is / will be quiet.'

---

41 As for East Slavic cf. Borkovskij (1949: 117–120; 1968: 153), with reference to Istrina (1923: 48, 54).

42 It is usually conceded that the difference between existential and copular use of BE becomes blurred, in particular with predicatives (cf., for instance, MČ/III 1987: 212). The main reason is that predicatives do not have referential subjects as agreement controllers.

(60) ... *blag-o*   *jest'*   *iže* ...
     weal/good[N?]-(NOM.SG ?) be.PRS.3SG COMP
     '... weal/good is that ...'

In (58) the noun *tišina* 'silence' occurs in the nominative and triggers number-gender agreement (in past tense) on BE; here, BE can be treated as an existential verb without objections. (59), in contrast, contains a cognate adjective stem with a neuter ending (*tix-o* 'quiet'), and BE can hardly be treated as an existential verb, since *tixo* does not serve as its argument. It is not even clear whether the neuter form of BE should be regarded as a sign of agreement with *tixo*; rather, it is *tixo* which functions as the predicate, without any NP that might control agreement on itself. Finally, in (60), one cannot really decide whether *blago* is to be treated as a noun (meaning 'weal') in an argument function to *jest'* (i.e. an existential verb) or rather as the clausal nucleus (meaning '(it's) good') in relation to which *jest'* is just an operator. It is thus plausible to assume that with nouns (or adjectives in the neuter) that started functioning as clausal nuclei, the status of the BE-verb (copular or existential?) could be disambiguated only when lack of agreement became obvious (see examples in §2.3.1.1): in clauses in which nouns function as predicates and there is no agreement controller, these nouns themselves lose behaviour properties of nouns, and the BE-verb, in turn, no longer behaves like a head of such a noun and, thus, does not show number-gender agreement with that noun. As a consequence, it cannot any longer be analysed as an existential verb. The general retreat of BE in the indicative present does not change this analysis: if there is no BE-verb, one cannot "see" anything, and if BE occurs in the past (where gender is distinguished) it takes the neuter ending.

Now, as mentioned above, the extent to which the BE-verb in the present indicative has retreated differs among Slavic languages. In all respects Russian shows the strongest propensity toward such avoidance. Ukrainian and Belarusian, then Polish seem to come next; Polish uses the present-indicative form of BE in the (resultative) passive, but not with predicatives deriving from adjectives ending in {o} (see §2.3.1.2) and not with most of the predicatives deriving from nouns. In the rest of Slavic the BE-verb is quite well (though not consistently) represented in these contexts.

The natural conclusion to be drawn from the reported facts and principled theoretical considerations is that the decrease and loss of *byti* in the present indicative cannot be regarded as an immediate cause of the rise of predicatives. Avoidance and loss of the BE-verb (in all its functions: existential, auxiliar, copular) and the rise of predicatives are parallel, but independent processes in Slavic. This conclusion is partially supported by Zatovkaňuk (1958: 203), who pointed out that predicatives appeared to have developed to an equal degree in Old Czech and early East Slavic, although Czech at that time showed a much weaker tendency to avoid *byti* (and this has continued into the present time). In a similar vein, Isačenko (1955: 59) observed that, in early East Slavic, the copula was lacking most consistently in clauses with adjectival forms which ended in {o} or {ě} (> {'e} or {'a}) and whose meaning was evaluative (e.g., *ljubo* 'pleasant', *lěpo* 'suitable', *divno* 'strange', *ugodno* 'convenient', *tjažko* 'difficult', *zlo* 'bad', *dostoino* 'honorable', *čjudno* 'wonderful'), and with words of "nouny" provenance and a modal meaning (e.g., *(ne)lъzě, nevolja* < NEG + *volj-a* 'freedom.NOM', *nadobě* < *na* 'on' + *dob-ě* '(suitable) time.LOC'). These practically coincide with the lists given by Večerka for Old Church Slavonic (see §2.3.2.1).

Nonetheless, even if no direct causal relationship between avoidance (or lack) of BE and the emergence of predicatives can be established, predicatives are associated with the lack of present-indicative BE with respect to their coding and behaviour properties: if predicatives contrast with other syntactic classes – namely, with predicative neuter adjectives, adverbs, or "full" nouns – it is predicatives which lack the present-indicative copula, while the contrasting word classes allow or even require it. Modern Russian does not allow BE at all. Polish does not allow it with predicatives of adjectival origin marked with {o} (e.g., **Jest mi miło poznać Pana* 'It is a pleasure for me to get to know you'), with fossilized infinitives (e.g., **Jest słychać kroki* 'One can hear steps'; **Jest widać, że P* 'One can see that P') and with most predicatives originating from nouns (e.g., **Jest szkoda, że P* 'It's a pity that P'),[43] but it allows for the copula with predicative neuter adjectives (e.g., *(Jest) całkiem możliwe, że P* 'It's very possible that P'). Here, copular BE can be used, but need not; which of the two realizations is older, requires a thorough investigation (and the establishment of a diachronic starting point: Common Slavic or the earliest attestations of Polish?). Whatever diachronic direction may turn out to be the correct one, it would not tell us much about semi-insubordination. It could, however, contribute to an explanation of how other diachronic processes helped the emergent category of predicatives to consolidate itself.

I refrain from more details on other Slavic languages in this regard, because they do not substantially add to the point made here: nouns have become involved in the fuzzy category of predicatives; a knowledge-related subclass of this category (fueled from noun, adjective, or verb stems) is capable of taking

---

43 Note that these are the same predicatives deriving from nouns and infinitives which do not show agreement with the copula in the past tense (*Szkoda był-o, że P* 'It was a pity that P'; *Widać był-o, że P* 'It was evident that P').

finite clausal complements, but also tends to occur without a BE-verb in their own clause (i.e. in the matrix clause). This make them appear similar to semi-subordinated structures as those postulated for Dutch and some other languages.

2.3.4 Resumptive remarks

We may, therefore, argue that predicatives become more salient when they are not accompanied by a copula. Possibly, a decrease in the use of the BE-verb has indirectly supported their formation and, as it were, made them more easily discernible, inasmuch as predicatives tend to differ in their distribution with copular BE from word classes from which predicatives are recruited. Together with lack of agreement controllers and the semantics of transient states these are hallmarks of this peculiar class of non-verbal predicates.

From the available descriptions and corpus data we can infer that predicatives with propositional complements, in particular nouns, were latecomers to this class and have remained small in number. This is tantamount to saying that clausal complements with morphologically finite predicates appeared at a very late stage in the history of predicatives. Furthermore, it follows that a structure like

[5] $\text{noun}_{\text{PRED}} - [\text{COMP} + V_{\text{FIN}}]$

without a subject-NP (in the nominative) is nothing but an analogical extension of a simple sentence pattern that was already well developed at the time when Slavic entered the scene of written documentation: nonverbal predicate + $\text{NP}_{\text{OBLIQUE}}$ / INF, with the argument and/or a copular BE often remaining facultative. Nothing was "cut away" from any previous more complex structure; the opposite happened: a simple clause pattern was extended by finite clausal complements to semantically suitable non-verbal expressions used as predicates. Moreover, expletive subjects have never been present, so that the nonverbal predicate just represents the diachronically original and persistent nucleus of the whole construction in [5].

2.4 What do the three phenomena have in common?

The tight analogy between IndInfs and equivalent *da*-clauses is obvious. In Balkan Slavic (and to a large extent in the rest of South Slavic as well) – where infinitives were lost as a morphological category –, they are related diachronically in that *da*-clauses took the place of infinitives in all their occurrences as heads of clausal arguments or adjuncts, but also as heads of independent sentences. They are also related to IndInfs in the sense that in both cases main clause uses are most probably older, diachronically speaking, and not the result of insubordination. In neither case can diachronic primacy ultimately been proven on the basis of historical (i.e. written) evidence (nor can it be disproved), but all arguments resting on comparative evidence, internal reconstruction and linguistic common sense converge in that clauses with infinitival heads or, respectively, clauses headed by *da* were first used as non-embedded clauses. One may argue that, since these clauses consistently betray a certain modal or illocutionary load (both in the modern languages and at earlier stages), at least some variants of usage typically depend on preceding discourse. However, this sort of (original) pragmatic dependence is not the issue of insubordination as a diachronic process in the sense of Evans's four-stage model.

As concerns predicatives, they are structural opposites of IndInfs and *da*-clauses in that infinitival clauses (in North Slavic) and *da*-clauses (in South Slavic) can express arguments of certain predicatives, and in that predicatives are predominantly of non-verbal origin. Predicatives are also, in a sense, diachronic antipodes of IndInfs and *da*-clauses: predicatives are rather endpoints of a longer process, not the starting point, in particular when we have in mind predicatives with finite clausal complements. However, as I tried to show, an essential part in the formation of predicatives (as a class of predicating expressions with peculiar behaviour and coding properties) was played by infinitival complements of adjectival and participial stems and a gradual discrimination from another nascent category, namely modal auxiliaries. Part of this discrimination amounts to the fact that predicatives take their own arguments, and the parallel with infinitival and *da*-clauses consists in the fact that complex clauses appeared at more advanced, not during incipient stages. Actually, for predicatives, the appearance of finite clausal complements with a complementizer is the result of an analogical extension that presupposes this discrimination.

Let us now compare the rise of predicatives with finite clausal complements to semi-insubordination which has been described for superficially identical structures in Dutch.

3 Comparison with semi-insubordination in Dutch

Van linden and Van de Velde (2014) analyzed contemporary (Flemish) Dutch utterances which they regarded as manifestations of semi-insubordination. They distinguished two types. I will discuss only the first one, because for the second we do not find any equivalents with an identical structure in

Slavic languages. In the sentence type which is of relevance here "a single matrix constituent is followed by a *dat*-clause which functions as its propositional complement" (Van linden and Van de Velde 2014: 227).[44] Consider first the following pair of examples (glossing here and in the following adapted):

(61) a. *Dat   hij   dat   nog   mocht   meemaken!*
       COMP   3GS.M this PTC   could   experience.INF
       'I never thought he would live to experience this!'
       (lit. 'That he was able to experience this, after all!')

    b. *Het   is prachtig dat   hij   dat nog mocht   meemaken!*
       3SG.N is great   COMP 3GS.M this PTC could   experience.INF
       'It is great that he was able to experience this!'

Dat is the neutral (or default) complementizer of Dutch. In (61a) the whole sentence starts with this complementizer, and it looks like a good illustration of insubordination in the sense of Evans (2007), i.e. based on the ellipsis of a matrix clause on which the *dat*-clause originally seems to have depended. (61b) would then represent the pattern from which (61a) might have developed: a complex sentence consisting of a matrix predicate (CTP) with a clausal complement; it is this clausal complement that is "left" in (61a).[45] Now, consider that modern Dutch allows also for sentences like (61c):

(61) c. *Prachtig dat   hij dat   nog mocht   meemaken!*
       great   COMP he that   PTC could   experience
       '(It is) great that he was able to experience this.'
       (by courtesy of A. Van linden)

We are tempted to assume that the *dat*-clause is an instance of semi-insubordination, since the structure in (61c) is somehow intermediate between (61b) and (61a); more material is "left" from the assumed predecessor construction

---

44 Another way to characterize this utterance type is to say that "a subordinate *dat*-clause (. . .) is preceded by just one element which seems to function at matrix clause level" (Van linden and Van de Velde 2014: 231).

45 Instead of a predicative adjective (*is prachtig* 'is great') the purported ellided main clause might have contained a finite verbal predicate, for instance:

(61d) *Dat   ik   dat   nog mocht   meemaken, had ik   nooit   gedacht!*
      COMP 1SG this PRT   could   experience had 1SG never   thought!
      'I had never thought that I would be able to experience this!'

(61b) than it is in (61a). (61c) may be considered intermediate in terms of diachronic development as well. This development might look as follows:

[6] clausal complementation (subordination) (61b)
     > semi-insubordination   (61c)
     > insubordination   (61a).

Notabene, such diachronic ordering is reasonable, but has not yet been confirmed on an empirical basis (A. Van linden, p.c.).

Note furthermore that Dutch shows the same variety of non-verbal lexemes
able to function as independent CTPs (in constructions like (61c)) as are attested in Slavic (see §2.3). We observe adverb-like lexicalizations of verb forms
(62), predicative adjectives (62–63), and nouns (64 and ex.1 in §1). The only crucial difference in comparison to Slavic languages is that predicative adjectives
and adverbs lack inflectional suffixes[46]:

(62) ***Misschien / Goed*** *da*   *Kris* *kom-t!*
     perhaps / good   COMP PN   come-PRS.3SG
     '**Maybe** / **Good** [i.e. *it's a good thing*] that/ Maybe Kris is coming!'

(63) <xphile> *LordLeto:hoe kunde in pine naar de laatste mail gaan van ne*
              folder ? [. . .]
     <xphile> *andersom sorteren ?:)*
     <xphile> *aha*
     <xphile> *cool*
     <xphile> **stom**   *da'k*   *daar* *nie* *aangedacht* *heb*
              stupid   COMP.1SG   there   NEG   thought.of   have
     'X: LordLeto, how can you go to the last e-mail in a folder in Pine?, by
     sorting the other way round? X: Oh yeah, cool! It is so **stupid** that
     I haven't thought of this myself *wink*.'
     (CONDIV, IRC, Leuv 3)

(64) *Een* **opluchting** *dat* *ik*   *weer wedstrijden kan spelen*
     a   relief   COMP 1SG   again games   can play.INF
     'It is a **relief** that I can play games again.'

---

46 The same applies to German, which in most respects shows the same phenomena as does
modern Dutch (at least superficially so). Examples (62) – (64) are cited from Van linden and
Van de Velde (2014: 227, 231).

Van linden and Van de Velde argue that, in modern Dutch, this structural model always conveys interpersonal meaning, as they mark a mirative or otherwise evaluative comment by the speaker on some fact, or wish, stated in the complement. This function has become an inherent feature of the construction itself, while it was only an accidental, contextually conditioned function to its predecessors in Middle Dutch. Compare two examples (cited from Van linden and Van de Velde 2014: 242); (65) has a factive CTP and complement, (66) expresses a desire:

(65) *Dat wij van rouwen niet ontzinnen Dat es wonder*
COMP 1PL of grief NEG lose.mind DEM is wonder
'That we don't lose our minds in grief, that is a wonder'

(66) *Dat ghi dit zwijcht: dats mijn begheren.*
COMP 2SG DEM be.silent that.is my wish
'That you be silent about this, that is my wish'

Van linden and Van de Velde therefore suggest to treat such cases as instantiations of hypoanalysis, a term adopted from Croft (2000) and referring to "a form-function reanalysis such that a contextual semantic/functional property is reinterpreted as an inherent property of a syntactic unit" (Van linden and Van de Velde 2014: 241). Crucial is the fact that independent (61a)-type sentences carry the same emotional and illocutionary load as (61b)-type and (61c)-type sentences do, in which the unit conveying this load is embedded under a CTP. In (61b)- and (61c)-type sentences this load harmonizes with the meaning of the predicative unit, but in (61c) this predicative unit does not have morphosyntactic marks of finiteness.

If we judge these utterance types on their face value and assume their diachronic relation as indicated in [1], an analysis in terms of ellipsis (as in Evans 2007) and an interpretation as hypoanalysis (after Croft 2000) need not be mutually exclusive, but can combine to emphasize different aspects of the same diachronic process. This is considered by Van linden and Van de Velde, but they advocate a hypoanalysis account because also other patterns of (semi-)insubordination discussed by them share identical illocutionary (and interpersonal) functions; an account in terms of ellipsis would not do justice to the fact that the purported source construction had a wider range of functions in Middle Dutch (2014: 244–245). Their argument, thus, amounts to the following: in the modern language we find complements of predicative expressions which are deprived of verbal morphology. Semi-insubordination is assumed because earlier stages are attested in which (presumably) such structures were used only as subordinate clauses. The main clause contained an evaluative non-verbal predicate with a finite copula; the former "stayed" in its place, while the copula disappeared. Moreover, only those sentences have served as a diachronic starting point into semi-insubordinated patterns which were fraught with specific interpersonal meaning. This meaning was conventionalized from invited inferences (following Traugott and König 1991 and others).

Now, in a comparison with Slavic predicatives discussed in §2.3 two issues should be clarified. First, have the syntactic changes which have been favourable for predicatives with finite clausal arguments in Slavic been the same as the processes which have produced the superficially identical structure in contemporary Dutch? Second, what is the role of interpersonal meanings in sentences with predicatives as CTPs? As for the last question, predicatives with finite clausal arguments typically convey the same interpersonal meanings as do those which have been highlighted for the modern Dutch construction (see §2.3.1). These meanings, however, arise because semantically suitable predicatives appeared via analogy with a previously established pattern. Interpersonal functions are just a side effect and, in this respect, tangential to Slavic predicatives. As such, predicatives do not have special attitudinal or interactional functions, like such ones which are regarded as typical of (semi-)insubordination.

This brings us to the first question. Evidently, the diachronic processes which have to be assumed in the "Dutch case" and in the "Slavic case" differ. First, in Slavic, predicatives with clausal complements containing a finite verbal predicate and "linked" to the predicative by a complementizer occurred relatively late. The subclass of predicatives which are able to have clausal arguments with a propositional status is rather restricted since it requires the predicative to be lexically (i.e. inherently) related to knowledge about facts (which are either presupposed or provide the operandum of modification by that predicative). Second, the most plausible explanation for the appearance of predicatives with finite clausal arguments is expansion by analogy from a simple clause pattern in which the complement of the predicative was either an NP or a PP (Pol. *Widać rzekę* 'The river can be seen / is visible'), an infinitive (Russ. *Stranno tak dumat'* 'It is strange to think this way'), or absent (as with metereological predicatives like Russ. *Stalo svetlo* 'It became light').

Thus, instead of hypoanalysis we are dealing with analogical expansion. The model for this expansion rests on certain preconditions with quite deep roots in diachronic Slavic morphosyntax, which, for their most part, are not shared with Dutch and other Germanic languages. Germanic languages amply use adjectives as predicates with such finite clausal complements (e.g. Germ. *Es ist gut / bemerkenswert / traurig, daß P* 'It's good / remarkable / sad that P'). However, such sentences differ from their Slavic counterparts in three respects:

(i) in Germanic a BE-verb is used much more consistently than, for instance, in Russian, Polish or Macedonian; (ii) in Germanic, if BE is used and there is no agreement controller (canonical subject), the predicative adjective needs the accompaniment of an expletive subject (Engl. *it*, Germ. *es*, Dutch *het*); (iii) adjectives do not inflect for gender and number if they are used predicatively. Criteria (i-ii) hold true for predicative nouns, too. Thus, in these Germanic languages, adjectives or nouns, used as clause predicates, cannot show any particular coding or behaviour properties if there is no agreement controller, and they normally require an expletive subject. The construction type discussed by Van linden and Van de Velde as a case of semi-insubordination becomes salient on this background, as both a BE-verb and an expletive subject are missing. By contrast, the absence of an expletive subject is nothing extraordinary in Slavic languages, nor is the lack of a BE-verb in a language like Russian or, more generally, in the eastern half of Slavic.

A schematic presentation of the differences between the case of semi-insubordination made for Dutch sentences like (1) and (61c), on the one hand, and for Slavic predicatives with a clausal complement realized by a finite verb and a complementizer, on the other hand, is given in Figures 4a-b:

Stage 1: $[S_{EXPLETIVE} - COP - ADJ/NOUN]_{claus1} - [COMP - S - V_{FIN}]_{clause2}$
Stage 2: > $(COP -) ADJ/NOUN] - [COMP - S - V_{FIN}]$
Stage 3: > $COMP - S - V_{FIN}$

Figure 4a: Semi-insubordination > Insubordination (e.g. Dutch).

Apart from the direction of change between Stages 1 and 2, another difference possibly lies in the question whether in Slavic (Figure 4b) the structure [COMP – S – V_{FIN}] can be interpreted as some Stage 3 (= insubordination) after Stage 2 (= predicatives with finite clausal complements), in analogy to the Dutch case (see Figure 4a). Since this issue is not central to the argument against semi-insubordination in Slavic, let me only remark that syntactically independent sentences corresponding to the pattern [COMP – S – V_{FIN}] do occur in Slavic, but probably never with the default THAT-complementizer. Instead, a complementizer marking irreal (or unrealized) states of affairs would occur; see, for instance, Russ. *Čtoby ja v èto poveril!* ≈ 'As if I were to believe in this!' or the Macedonian examples (18–19). As we saw, predicatives with finite clausal complements (Stage 2 in Figure 4b) are, as a rule, factive; for such complement clauses Slavic languages use unmarked complementizers (Russ. *čto*, Pol. *że*, etc.)

Stage 1:   ADJ/NOUN – INF / NP$_{\text{OBLIQUE}}$

Stage 2:   > ADJ/NOUN – [COMP – S – V$_{\text{fin}}$]   (= propositional complement)

Figure 4b: Predicatives with clausal complements (Slavic).

or a special complementizer (like Macedonian or Serbian-Croatian *što*).[47] Simultaneously, apart from Balkan Slavic (see fn. 47), I am unaware of cases in which a syntactically independent structure [COMP – S – V$_{\text{FIN}}$], with a default complementizer, would carry a mirative function; for Dutch, however, this has been reported (Van linden and Van de Velde 2014: 244, see also example (61a)). In view of these facts it is rather doubtful that Stage 2 in Figure 4b could serve as a basis for main clauses that are headed by marked complementizers and denote unrealized states of affairs.

4 More general conclusions

Cristofaro's (2016) recent contribution to the field of insubordination started with the observation that, although the notion of insubordination has been used both from a synchronic perspective (i.e. to describe "a pattern whereby an independent clause is structurally similar to a subordinate one") and from a diachronic vantage point (namely, as a "process that assumedly gives rise to this pattern, one whereby a former subordinate clause comes to be used independently"), the diachronic perspective has so far "received comparatively less attention" (2016: 395). And she concluded, among other things, that "diachronic evidence should also be collected in order to distinguish between insubordination and superficially similar patterns that originate through different processes" (2016: 420). The study which has been presented here is meant as a contribution to this diachronic desideratum, and one of its principal aims has been to demonstrate that patterns that are superficially identical on the level of contemporary languages, may turn out as the results of radically different diachronic processes. In fact, these processes may have rested on fundamentally different preconditions and taken opposite directions (in terms of increase vs. decrease of material, or of morphosyntactic complexity). But these processes have converged, which has led to structures that are identical at face value. If these structures differ with respect to their discourse-pragmatic potential, this

---

47 Balkan Slavic also uses *da*, provided the complement is not only factive, but also marks a mirative illocution (see the Macedonian example 19).

discrepancy may be explained by their divergent histories. The last point concerns, in particular, the degree to which interpersonal meanings become associated with salient construction types.

In conclusion, let me thus compare the findings worked out above with more widely known cases discussed in connection with (semi-)insubordination.

IndInfs serve practically the same array of functions as those that have been figured out for insubordinate clauses beginning with a connective (complementizer, conjunction, relativizer), such as, for instance, Spanish *que* (Gras 2016: 115): directives (optatives, hortatives), evaluative modality, echo-sentences, etc. The same holds true for the structural equivalents of infinitive clauses in South, particularly in Balkan Slavic, i.e. for *da*-clauses. IndInfs in Russian fall into the same two macrogroups which were identified for Spanish insubordinated *que*-clauses by Gras (2011, 2016: 116, 125–135), namely: (i) modal and (ii) discourse connective ones. The former includes not only modal meanings in the narrow sense (circumstantial, deontic), but also related illocutionary functions; in general, they "deal with the speakers' attitude towards the proposition" (Gras 2016: 116). In Russian and other Slavic languages (if IndInfs still occur), modal IndInfs clearly predominate, and they usually allow or even require a dative-NP marking the potential agent. These IndInfs need not be reactive on preceding discourse.

Admittedly, discourse connective functions can be figured out for another construction, namely, Russian IndInfs with a nominatival subject-NP. These are comparatively infrequent, but depend on discourse, i.e. can never occur in isolation or as the first sentence in a chain of utterances. The so-called 'narrative infinitive' has consecutive value (in typically monological speech), the 'infinitive of indignation' is typical for echo-replicae (thus, of dialogues). Again, these non-modal functions are covered by Balkan Slavic *da*-clauses as well, but (in contrast to the two classes of IndInfs in Russian) they are not distinguishable from 'modal *da*-clauses' (in the wide sense) on structural grounds. One can argue that discourse connective IndInfs (and their *da*-clause equivalents) are characterized by pragmatic dependence on the preceding discourse (either narrative and monological or dyadic in face-to-face communication). It is, however, a safe guess that, on text level, discourse connective IndInfs constitute a clear minority in comparison to modal IndInfs.

More importantly, the modal and interactive uses of IndInfs in Russian both seem to reach back to a general pattern in the structural resources common in Slavic from times prior to written documentation: infinitives (like other morphologically non-finite forms) suspend assertiveness and are therefore prone to marking independent non-declarative speech acts. This includes all sorts of directives, but also modal utterances in the proper sense. This insight makes an analysis in terms of insubordination (understood as a diachronic process) inappropriate. Rather, we should say that verb forms without agreement, tense and mood marking (in languages which otherwise do apply such marking) are still associated with suspended assertiveness (which can be exploited for diverse discourse pragmatic purposes). These structures, then, need not be "derived" from any presumably earlier, morphosyntactically more complex structure. It is only the background of structures with a higher degree of overt complexity (namely, tense-mood and agreement marking) which provides a background of some default in which main clause phenomena with morphosyntactically non-finite predicates look like "deviations" or anyway become salient.

A similar reasoning was promoted by Mithun (2008: 107): "syntactically subordinate clause forms might come to be identified as less assertive than main clause forms. Speakers might then begin to select them in certain contexts for that implication. There need never have been a specific matrix clause that was omitted." The claim becomes even more radical if we need not postulate any "main clause ellipsis", because lowered assertiveness was associated with non-finite morphology even before it started being used in embedded clauses, and this is what the Slavic cases analyzed above demonstrate.

That being said, it should become obvious that the chronology of stages (or construction types) has to be established thoroughly, and a diachronic starting point has to be determined. Otherwise we will get into troubles saying what the "initial" stage was. For instance, the modal IndInf may well go back to an earlier pattern (at least superficially associated with predicative possession), but this pattern is irrelevant for that (however long) segment in the history of Slavic languages for which the rise and differentiation of IndInfs can sensibly be claimed and analyzed (see §2.1). The same applies to *da*-clauses (see §2.2).

In principle, an identical remark concerns predicatives with finite clausal complements. They are antipodes of IndInfs and *da*-clauses insofar as they carry exactly complementary evaluative meanings operating on propositions (epistemic, evidential, mirative), and I have identified them as endpoints of a diachronic development, not as initial stages. But the question of what exactly counts as initial stage needs to be settled. The rise of predicatives can be studied from the earliest written documentation, i.e. for roughly the last 1,000 years (although with many gaps). The Dutch construction qualified as an instance of semi-insubordination by Van linden and Van de Velde has been traced back to Middle Dutch (1150–1500). What would change in our assessment of (semi-)insubordination if we were able to look at preceding stages?

This diachronic caveat has a typological-comparative counterpart. Consider again Slavic predicatives. They are not as such associated with mirative (or other evaluative) meanings, and the extended structure with finite clausal complements becomes salient because a non-verbal predicate lacks a copula. From the typological point of view this may not be a particularly surprising situation.

For instance, as reported by Cristofaro (2016), nominalized verb forms can be used as independent predicates without a copula in Musqueam (Salish). This pattern does not induce any mirative effect (in contrast to, for instance, Chantyal, Tibeto-Burman; Cristofaro 2016: 411). Moreover, "most word types in the language can occur in predicative function without a copula [. . .]. It is then possible that, when used in predicative function, nominalized forms have always been self-standing clauses in their own right, and there never was any additional material in the first place" (Cristofaro 2016: 419). This comes very close to what we observed in the history of Slavic predicatives, while the Dutch case analyzed by Van linden and Van de Velde can be interpreted as an instance of semi-insubordination only because the propensity to having a copula and expletive subjects is an areal feature of some languages in western Europe.

I hope to have shown that superficially identical syntactic phenomena can differ radically in their genesis. Reliance only on a synchronic account of these phenomena can lead to an inadequate assessment in terms of (semi-)insubordination, in fact, alleged cases of insubordination can even turn out as artefacts of anachronistic approaches toward syntactic structure. In addition, semi-insubordination may be an areally restricted phenomenon inasmuch as the preconditions for changes to patterns (constructions) that are salient for specific languages are not given elsewhere. This said, I want to emphasize that my analysis focused on the <u>diachronic</u> relation between clause patterns and clause linkage (according to Evans's 2007 'five-stage-model'); the range of the functional potential of contemporary clause (or utterance) patterns that have become associated with (semi-)insubordination – especially for spoken discourse – have been of minor concern. I do not deny that these synchronic aspects of the respective phenomena deserve more systematic research, but at present we obviously also need to understand better how discourse-driven (semi-)insubordination and (semi-)insubordination from a diachronic perspective are to be related to each other. The same concerns hypoanalysis and probably other notions which have been brought into the discussion since the issue of insubordination has been raised.

Acknowledgments: For their consult as informed native speakers I am indebted to Eleni Bužarovska, Liljana Mitkovska (Macedonian), Karolína Skwarska, Bohumil Vykypěl (Czech), and Jasmina Grković-Major (Serbian). I am also obliged to Mikhail Kopotev for a couple of succinct remarks and bibliographical support, as well as to two anonymous reviewers. Furthermore, I appreciate Ulrike Stange's thorough proofreading and the painstaking formatting by Julia Schmidt. None of these persons shall however be blamed for any remaining shortcomings or mistakes, as the sole responsibility for this paper is mine.

Abbreviations

1	first person
2	second person
3	third person
ACC	accusative
ADV	adverb
AOR	aorist
ART	article
AUX	auxiliary
CON	connective (OCS and Balkan Slavic *da* with unclear status)
CONJ	conjunction
COMP	complementizer
DAT	dative
DEF	definite
DEM	demonstrative
F	feminine
FUT	future
GEN	genitive
HORT	hortative
IMPF	imperfect
INDECL	indeclinable
INF	infinitive
INS	instrimental
IPFV	imperfective
IRR	irreal situation
LOC	locative
M	masculine
N	neuter
NEG	negation
NOM	nominative
PFV	perfective
PFX	prefix
PL	plural
PN	proper name
POSS	possessive
PP	past passive participle
PRF	perfect
PRED	predicative
PRS	present
PST	past
PTC	particle
REFL	reflexive pronoun
RM	reflexive (light) marker
SG	singular
SUBJ	subjunctive

SUP	supine
VIR	virile
VOC	vocative

References

Ambrazas, Vytautas. 1995. Lietuvių kalbos bendraties konstrukcijų raida [The evolution of infinitive constructions in Lithuanian]. *Lietuvių kalbotyros klausimai* 33. 74–109.

Ammann, Andreas & Johan van der Auwera. 2004. Complementizer-headed main clauses for volitional moods in the languages of South-Eastern Europe: A Balkanism? In Olga Mišeska Tomić (ed.), *Balkan Syntax and Semantics*, 293–314. Amsterdam & Philadelphia: Benjamins.

Bonč-Osmolovskaja, Anastasija A. 2009. Dativnye sub"ektnye konstrukcii s predikativami na *-o/-e* [Constructions with predicatives in *-o/-e* and a dative subject]. In Ksenija L. Kiseleva, Vladimir A. Plungjan, Ekaterina V. Raxilina & Sergej G. Tatevosov (eds.), *Korpusnye issledovanija po russkoj grammatike: Sbornik statej*, 157–183. Moskva: Probel-2000.

Borkovskij, Viktor I. 1949. *Sintaksis drevnerusskix gramot* [The syntax of Old Russian official documents]. L'vov: Izdatel'stvo L'vovskogo gosudarstvennogo universiteta.

Borkovskij, Viktor I. 1968. *Sravnitel'no-istoričeskij sintaksis vostočnoslavjanskix jazykov: Tipy prostogo predloženija* [A comparative-diachronic syntax of East Slavic languages: Types of the simple sentence]. Moskva: Nauka.

Borkovskij, Viktor I. (ed.). 1983. *Struktura predloženija v istorii vostočnoslavjanskix jazykov* [The structure of the sentence in the history of East Slavic languages]. Moskva: Nauka.

Boye, Kasper. 2012. *Epistemic meaning: A crosslinguistic and functional-cognitive study*. Berlin & Boston: De Gruyter Mouton.

Brinton, Laurel J. 2014. The Extremes of Insubordination: Exclamatory *as if! Journal of English Linguistics* 42 (2). 93–113.

Cristofaro, Sonia. 2016. Routes to insubordination: A cross-linguistic perspective. In Nicholas Evans & Honoré Watanabe (eds.), *Dynamics of insubordination*, 395–424. Amsterdam & Philadelphia: Benjamins.

Croft, William. 2000. *Explaining Language Change: An Evolutionary Approach*. Harlow: Longman.

Daiber, Thomas. 2009. Direkte Rede im Russisch-Kirchenslavischen: Zum pragmatischen Wert des *jako recitativum*. In Juliane Besters-Dilger & Achim Rabus (eds.), *Text – Sprache – Grammatik. Slavisches Schrifttum der Vormoderne: Festschrift für Eckhard Weiher*, 363–386. München & Berlin: Sagner.

Dal', Vladimir. 1956 [1881]. *Tolkovyj slovar' živogo velikorusskogo jazyka*, t. II: I-O [Explanatory dictionary of the living Great Russian language, vol. II: I-O]. Moskva: Gosudarstvennoe izdatel'stvo inostrannyx i nacional'nyx slovarej.

Disterheft, Dorothy. 1980. *The syntactic development of the infinitive in Indo-European*. Columbus: Slavica Publishers.

Dwyer, Arienne M. 2016. Ordinary insubordination as transient discourse. In Nicholas Evans & Honoré Watanabe (eds.), *Dynamics of insubordination*, 183–208. Amsterdam & Philadelphia: Benjamins.

Evans, Nicholas. 2007. Insubordination and its uses. In Irina Nikolaeva (ed.), *Finiteness: Theoretical and Empirical Foundations*, 366–431. Oxford etc.: Oxford University Press.

Givón, Talmy. 2009. *The genesis of syntactic complexity: Diachrony, ontogeny, neuro-cognition, evolution*. Amsterdam & Philadelphia: Benjamins.

Gołąb, Zbigniew. 1954. Funkcja syntaktyczna partykuły *da* w językach południowo-słowiańskich (bulgarskim, macedońskim i serbo-chorwackim) [The syntactic function of the particle *da* in South Slavic languages (in Bulgarian, Macedonian and Serbocroatian)]. *Biuletyn Polskiego Towarzystwa Językoznawczego* XIII. 67–92.

Gołąb, Zbigniew. 1984: South Slavic *da* + Indicative in Conditional Clauses and its General Linguistic Implications. In Kot K. Shangriladze & Erica W. Townsend (eds.), *Papers for the V. Congress of Southeast European Studies: Belgrade, Sept. 1984*, 170–198. Columbus, Ohio: Slavica Publishers.

Gras, Pedro. 2011. *Gramática de Construcciones en interacción. Propuesta de un modelo y aplicación al análisis de estructuras independientes con marcas de subordinación en español*. Barcelona: Universitat de Barcelona.

Gras, Pedro. 2016. Revisiting the functional typology of insubordination. Insubordinate *que*-constructions in Spanish. In Nicholas Evans & Honoré Watanabe (eds.), *Dynamics of insubordination*, 113–143. Amsterdam & Philadelphia: Benjamins.

Grković-Major [Grković-Mejdžor], Jasmina. 2004. Razvoj xipotaktičkog *da* u starosrpskom jeziku [The development of hypotactic *da* in Old Serbian]. *Zbornik Matice Srpske za filologiju i lingvistiku* 47 (1–2). 185–203.

Grzegorczykowa, Renata. 1990. Geneza i współczesne funkcje konstrukcji z bezokolicznikami: *czuć, słychać, widać, znać, stać* [The development and contemporary functions of constructions with the infinitives *czuć, słychać, widać, znać, stać*]. *Poradnik językowy* 1990 (8). 564–571.

Hansen, Björn. 2001. *Das slavische Modalauxiliar: Semantik und Grammatikalisierung im Russischen, Polnischen, Serbischen/Kroatischen und Altkirchenslavischen*. München: Sagner.

Hansen, Björn. 2004. Modals and the boundaries of grammaticalization: The case of Russian, Polish and Serbian-Croatian. In Walter Bisang, Nikolaus P. Himmelmann & Björn Wiemer (eds.), *What makes Grammaticalization? A Look from its Fringes and its Components*, 245–270. Berlin & New York: Mouton de Gruyter.

Hansen, Björn & Ferdinand De Haan. 2009. Concluding chapter: modal constructions in the languages of Europe. In Björn Hansen & Ferdinand de Haan (eds.), *Modals in the Languages of Europe. A Reference Work*, 511–559. Berlin & New York: Mouton de Gruyter.

Holvoet, Axel. 2003. Modal constructions with 'be' and the infinitive in Slavonic and Baltic. *Zeitschrift für Slawistik* 48 (4). 465–480.

Holvoet, Axel. 2016. Semantic functions of complementizers in Baltic. In Kasper Boye & Petar Kehayov (eds.), *Complementizer Semantics in European Languages*, 225–263. Berlin & Boston: De Gruyter Mouton.

Holvoet, Axel & Jelena Konickaja. 2011. Interpretive deontics: A definition and a semantic map based mainly on Slavonic and Baltic data. *Acta Linguistica Hafniensia* 43 (1). 1–20.

Isačenko, Aleksandr V. 1955. O voznikovenii i razvitii "kategorii sostojanija" v slavjanskix jazykax [On the rise and development of the "category of state" in Slavic languages]. *Voprosy jazykoznanija* 1955 (6). 48–65.

Isačenko, Aleksandr V. 1965 *Grammatičeskij stroj russkogo jazyka v sopostavlenii s slovackim. Morfologija* I-II [The grammatical structure of Russian in comparison to Slovak. Morphology I-II], 2nd edn. Bratislava: Izdatel'stvo Slovackoj Akademii nauk.

Istrina, Evgenija S. 1923. *Sintaksičeskie javlenija Sinodal'nogo spiska 1-j Novgorodskoj letopisi* [Syntactic phenomena of the Synodal recension of the First Novgorodian Chronicle]. Petrograd.

Keenan, Edward. 1976. Towards a universal definition of 'subject'. In Charles N. Li (ed.), *Subject and Topic*, 303–333. New York etc.: Academic Press.

Kiparsky, Paul & Carol Kiparsky. 1970. Fact. In Danny D. Steinberg & Leon A. Jakobovits (eds.), *Semantics*, 345–369. Cambridge etc.: Cambridge University Press.

Kopotev, Mikhail. 2015. Reconstruction and idiomaticity: The origin of Russian verbless clauses reconsidered. *Folia Linguistica Historica* 36. 219–243.

Kramer, Christina Elizabeth. 1986. *Analytic modality in Macedonian*. München: Sagner.

Lehmann, Volkmar. 2001. Prädikative als unpersönlich gebrauchte Adjektive: Zur Grammatik von Adjektiven im Polnischen und Russischen. In Viktor S. Chrakovskij, Maciej Grochowski & Gerd Hentschel (eds.), *Studies on the Syntax and Semantics of Slavonic Languages*, 253–263. Oldenburg: BIS.

MČ/III. 1987. Daneš, František & Jan Petr (eds.), Mluvnice češtiny, t. 3: *Skladba* [Czech grammar, vol. 3: Syntax]. Praha: Academia.

Meermann, Anastasia & Barbara Sonnenhauser. 2016. Das Perfekt im Serbischen zwischen slavischer und balkanslavischer Entwicklung. In Alena Bazhutkina, & Barbara Sonnenhauser (eds.), *Linguistische Beiträge zur Slavistik. XXII. JungslavistInnen-Treffen in München, 12. bis 14. September 2013*, 83–110. München: Sagner.

Mendoza, Imke. 2008. Überlegungen zur Entstehung des Nominativobjekts im Altrussischen. In Peter Kosta & Daniel Weiss (eds.), *Slavistische Linguistik 2006/2007: Referate des XXXII. und des XXXIII. Konstanzer Slavistischen Arbeitstreffens*, 299–317. München: Sagner.

Mišeska Tomić, Olga. 2006. *Balkan sprachbund morpho-syntactic features*. Dordrecht: Springer.

Mišeska Tomić, Olga. 2012. *A Grammar of Macedonian*. Bloomington, Ind.: Slavica Publ.

Mithun, Marianne. 2008. The extension of dependency beyond the sentence. *Language* 84 (1). 69–119.

Nikolaeva, Irina. 2007. Constructional Economy and nonfinite independent clauses. In Irina Nikolaeva (ed.), *Finiteness: Theoretical and Empirical Foundations*, 138–180. Oxford etc.: Oxford University Press.

Nikolaeva, Irina. 2013. Unpacking finiteness. In Dunstan Brown, Marina Chumakina & Greville G. Corbett (eds.), *Canonical Morphology and Syntax*, 99–122. Oxford etc.: Oxford University Press.

Pospelov, Nikolaj S. 1964. Razvitie predloženij "odnočlennoj" struktury [The development of "one-component" sentences]. In Viktor V. Vinogradov & Nina Ju. Švedova (eds.), *Izmenenija v stroe složnopodčinennogo predloženija v russkom literaturnom jazyke XIX veka*, 20–82. Moskva: Nauka.

Potebnja, Aleksandr A. 1958 [1874]. *Iz zapisok po russkoj grammatike*, t. I-II [From the notes on Russian grammar, vol. I-II] (ed. by V. I. Borkovskij). Moskva: Izdatel'stvo Prosveščenie.

Sabenina, Anna M. 1983. Iz istorii dvukomponentnyx neglagol'nyx predloženij [From the history of non-verbal sentences with two components]. In Viktor I. Borkovskij (ed.), *Struktura predloženija v istorii vostočnoslavjanskix jazykov*, 9–101. Moskva: Nauka.

SDJa 1990: *Slovar' drevnerusskogo jazyka (XI-XIV vv.)*, t. III [Dictionary of Old Russian (XI-XIV centuries), vol. III]. Moskva: Russkij jazyk.

Sonnenhauser, Barbara & Anastasia Meermann (eds.). 2015. *Distance in language: Grounding a metaphor*. Cambridge: Cambridge Scholars Publishing.

Sreznevskij, Izmail I. 1955–56. *Materialy dlja slovarja drevnerusskogo jazyka*, t. I [Materials for a dictionary of Old Russian, vol. I]. Graz: Akad. Druck- und Verlags-Anstalt. [Reprint from St. Petersburg 1893.]

Švedova, Nina Ju. 1964. Izmenenija v sisteme prostogo predloženija [Changes in the system of the simple sentence]. In Viktor V. Vinogradov & Nina Ju. Švedova (eds.), *Izmenenija v sisteme prostogo i osložnennogo predloženija v russkom literaturnom jazyke XIX veka*, 20–369. Moskva: Nauka.

Townsend, Charles E. & Laura A. Janda. 2003. *Gemeinslavisch und Slavisch im Vergleich: Einführung in die Entwicklung von Phonologie und Flexion*. München: Sagner.

Traugott, Elisabeth Closs & Ekkehard König. 1991. The semantics-pragmatics of grammaticalization revisited. In Elisabeth Closs Traugott & Bernd Heine (eds.), *Approaches to grammaticalization*, vol. 1: *Focus on theoretical and methodological issues*, 189–218. Amsterdam & Philadelphia: Benjamins.

van der Auwera, Johan & Vladimir A. Plungian. 1998. Modality's semantic map. *Linguistic Typology* 1 (2). 79–124.

Van linden, An & Freek Van de Velde. 2014. (Semi-)autonomous subordination in Dutch: Structures and semantic-pragmatic values. *Journal of Pragmatics* 60. 226–250.

Večerka, Radoslav (1993): *Altkirchenslavische (altbulgarische) Syntax*, II: *Die innere Satzstruktur*. Freiburg: Weiher.

Večerka, Radoslav (1996): *Altkirchenslavische (altbulgarische) Syntax*, III: *Die Satztypen: der einfache Satz*. Freiburg: Weiher.

Večerka, Radoslav (2002): *Altkirchenslavische (altbulgarische) Syntax*, IV: *Die Satztypen: der zusammengesetzte Satz*. Freiburg: Weiher.

Verstraete, Jean-Christophe, Sarah D'Hertefelt & An Van linden. 2012. A typology of complement insubordination in Dutch. *Studies in Language* 36 (1). 123–153.

Verstraete, Jean-Christophe & Sarah D'Hertefelt. 2016. Running in the family. Patterns of complement insubordination in Germanic. In Nicholas Evans & Honoré Watanabe (eds.), *Dynamics of insubordination*, 65–87. Amsterdam & Philadelphia: Benjamins.

Vinogradov, Viktor V. 1986 [1947]. *Russkij jazyk: Grammatičeskoe učenie o slove* [Russian language: A grammatical treatment about the word], 3rd edn. Moskva: Vysšaja škola.

Vondrák, Václav. 1908. *Vergleichende slavische Grammatik*, vol. II: *Formenlehre und Syntax*. Göttingen: Vandenhoek & Ruprecht.

Wiemer, Björn. 2009. *Widać* und *słychać*: zum Schicksal zweier erstarrter Infinitive. In Tilman Berger, Markus Giger, Sibylle Kurt & Imke Mendoza (eds.), *Von grammatischen Kategorien und sprachlichen Weltbildern – Die Slavia von der Sprachgeschichte bis zur Politsprache: Festschrift für Daniel Weiss zum 60. Geburtstag*, 615–632. [Sonderausgabe]. *Wiener Slawistischer Almanach* 73. München & Wien & Berlin: Sagner.

Wiemer, Björn. 2011. *Grammaticalization in Slavic languages. In* Bernd Heine & Heiko Narrog (eds.), *Handbook of Grammaticalization*, 740–753. Oxford etc.: Oxford University Press.

Wiemer, Björn. 2012. Zum wechselnden Status nicht-kongruierender Prädikationstypen im nördlichen Slavischen und Litauischen. In Andrii Danylenko & Serhii Vakulenko (eds.), *Studien zur Sprache, Literatur und Kultur bei den Slaven: Gedenkschrift für George*

Y. Shevelov aus Anlass seines 100. Geburtstages und 10. Todestages, 31–57. München & Berlin: Sagner.

Wiemer, Björn. 2014. *Mora da* as a marker of modal meanings in Macedonian: on correlations between categorial restrictions and morphosyntactic behaviour. In Werner Abraham & Elisabeth Leiss (eds.), *Modes of Modality. Modality, Typology, and Universal Grammar*, 127–166. Amsterdam & Philadelphia: Benjamins.

Wiemer, Björn. 2017. Main clause infinitival predicates and their equivalents in Slavic Why they are not instances of insubordination. In Łukasz Jędrzejowski & Ulrike Demske (eds.), *Infinitives at the Syntax-Semantics Interface: A Diachronic Perspective*, 265–338. Berlin & Boston: De Gruyter.

Wiemer, Björn. 2018. On triangulation in the domain of clause linkage and propositional marking. In Jasmina Grković-Major, Björn Hansen & Barbara Sonnenhauser (eds.), *Diachronic Slavonic Syntax: The Interplay between Language Contact and Internal Factors*, 285–338. Berlin & Boston: De Gruyter Mouton.

Zatovkaňuk, Mikoláš. 1958. K vzniku a vývoji neosobních predikativ [On the rise and evolution of impersonal predicatives.] *Československá rusistika* 1958 (4). 201–215.

Corpora

NKJP: *Narodowy korpus języka polskiego*, http://nkjp.pl/
NKRJa: *Nacional'nyj korpus russkogo jazyka*, http://www.ruscorpora.ru/

Gunther Kaltenböck
5 Delimiting the class: A typology of English insubordination

Abstract: This chapter proposes a heuristic for delimiting the class of insubordination in English and for identifying different subtypes. It argues that a usage-based approach is best suited for capturing the defining feature of insubordination, viz. its form-function mismatch. This is because usage-based grammar assumes a close link between actual language use and its mental representation, i.e. language structure, with the latter emerging out of the former – often with a substantial time-lag. Accordingly, insubordination is analysed on two different levels: on the level of syntactic structure, which distinguishes between syntactic dependence and independence, and on the level of usage, which distinguishes between pragmatic dependence and independence. Syntactic independence is seen as primary and delimits insubordination from subordination. The secondary criterion of pragmatic (in)dependence allows for the distinction of two subcategories: stand-alone and elaborative insubordination. The proposed criterion of syntactic independence not only provides for a relatively clear-cut identification of insubordination, it also highlights the similarity of insubordination with a range of other, so-called extra-clausal structures (e.g. parenthetical uses of subordinate clauses). This larger category of syntactically independent constructions includes the special case of semi-insubordination, which is argued to fall outside the category of insubordination proper on the basis of its internal syntactic structure.

1 Introduction

Insubordination, "the conventionalized main clause use of what, on prima facie grounds, appear to be formally subordinate clauses" (Evans 2007: 367), has received increased interest in recent years, especially since the seminal publications

---

Notes: I'm deeply indebted to the two reviewers and Karin Beijering for their detailed and constructive feedback as well as to all the participants of the insubordination workshop at the SLE conference in Leiden 2015, whose contributions helped me get a better understanding of the many aspects surrounding (semi-)insubordinate clauses. Needless to say, any remaining shortcomings are all mine.

Gunther Kaltenböck, University of Graz

https://doi.org/10.1515/9783110638288-006

by Evans (2007) and Mithun (2008) on this topic. It has also been referred to by a range of other terms, such as "independent" subordinate clause (e.g. D'Hertefelt and Verstraete 2014), "isolated" (e.g. Stirling 1998; Mato-Míguez 2014), "autonomous" (Van linden and Van de Velde 2014), "free" (e.g. Lombardi Vallauri 2004, 2010), or "non-integrated" subordinate clause (e.g. Laury 2012; D'Hertefelt 2015: 155). I will stick here to the term insubordination, which has become the most widely used, although "independent subordinate clause" may be a descriptively more adequate label. As with the term itself, there is also considerable variation in its application. It has been used for a range of different structures, such as the ones in (1) to (4).

(1) *If you come over here.*

(2) *I'll top up my tea, **if you don't mind**.*

(3) A: *Is it obligatory to hand in a paper?*
    B: *If you want a grade.*

(4) *Funny that he should say that.*

Example (1) illustrates the stand-alone, and probably most typical, form of insubordination (e.g. Evans 2007). Example (2) represents a pragmatically dependent insubordinate clause (e.g. Mithun 2008; D'Hertefelt and Verstraete 2014), and example (3) what has been referred to as a dyadic instance of insubordination (e.g. Gras 2012, 2016; Sansiñena et al. 2015; Gras and Sansiñena 2015). Example (4), finally, illustrates what Van linden & Van de Velde (2014) call a semi-insubordinate construction (see Sections 3 and 5 for a discussion of each of these types).

There is thus little consensus on which constructions are to be subsumed under the concept of insubordination, with different studies applying the term in different ways (see also Mithun, this volume). This is not really surprising though. While formal marking as subordinate – as indicated in Evans' definition above – is relatively easy to identify, at least for English clauses, Evans' other criterion, that of "conventionalized main clause use", is open to some interpretation. In addition, as noted by D'Hertefelt (2015: 155), "[t]he issue of delimiting insubordination has received relatively little explicit attention in the literature so far". This is problematic, however, since clear category boundaries are essential prerequisites for corpus retrieval and establishing the functional potential and diachronic development of the class.

The present paper tries to close this gap by proposing a heuristic for delimiting the class of insubordination and for identifying different subtypes. It does so by adopting a usage-based approach, which seems best suited for capturing the defining feature of insubordination, viz. its form–function mismatch: a formally subordinate clause is used as if it were an independent clause. A usage-based perspective can account for this as it assumes a close link between actual language use and language structure, i.e. our mental categories, in the sense that the latter develops out of the former (e.g. Langacker 2000; Haiman 1994). The basic assumption is that language change starts at the level of language use and may over time, with sufficient frequency, crystallize into new syntactic structures. Syntactic structure therefore naturally lags behind changes on the usage level and may be considered more conservative in that firmly entrenched patterns are more resistant to change, particularly with respect to abandoning certain formal features such as a subordinator (e.g. Torres Cacoullos and Walker 2009). The mismatch between syntactic form and usage in the case of insubordination can thus be explained by a 'bottom-up' development from usage to structure and the time it takes for changes in usage to seep into linguistic structure.

In line with a usage-based approach, then, this paper assumes two levels of analysis, viz. syntactic structure and pragmatic use: on the level of syntactic structure it distinguishes between syntactic dependence/independence, on the level of usage it distinguishes between pragmatic dependence/independence. Syntactic independence is seen as primary in that it allows for a clear delimitation of the class from subordination. While all insubordinate clauses are syntactically independent, only some of them – the more central cases – are also pragmatically independent. The secondary criterion of pragmatic (in)dependence thus introduces an internal stratification of the category and the distinction of two types of insubordination: stand-alone insubordination and elaborative insubordination. Accordingly, only examples (1) and (2) above are cases of insubordination, the former stand-alone and the latter elaborative, but not examples (3) and (4) (which are analysed as subordination and semi-insubordination respectively, as discussed in Sections 3.3 and 5).

The paper is structured in the following way. Section 2 briefly reviews previous proposals for identifying insubordination. Section 3 then outlines a usage-based approach to the delimitation of insubordination with the two types, stand-alone and elaborative, discussed in 3.1 and 3.2 respectively. Section 3.3 contrasts these uses with cases of subordination proper. Section 4 sets insubordination in the context of syntactic independence more generally and argues for the inclusion of parenthetical subordinate clauses and various other categories previously identified in the literature. Section 5, finally, discusses semi-insubordination and argues that it is best excluded from the category of insubordination. Section 6 provides a brief conclusion.

2 Previous proposals for identifying insubordination

As noted in the introduction, explicit discussions of the delimitation of insubordination are conspicuously absent in the literature. Most studies adopt Evans' (2007: 367) definition, where "main clause use" is typically interpreted as 'occurring without an accompanying main clause' (e.g. Stirling 1998: 273; Lombardi Vallauri 2010: 51). There are two rare exception to this, which will be briefly reviewed in this section: Schwenter (2016) provides a catalogue of criteria for identifying insubordinate *si*-clauses in Spanish, and D'Hertefelt (2015) offers a detailed discussion of the external delimitation of insubordination in Germanic languages.

2.1 Schwenter (2016): Spanish *si*-clauses

Schwenter (2016) discusses useful criteria for the identification of insubordination but is limited in its scope to Spanish *si*-clauses. He proposes the following four tests for distinguishing insubordinate *si*-clauses from ordinary (elliptical) conditional clauses:

(i)   Different behaviour with negative polarity items: Independent *si*-clauses, but not conditional clauses, require *no* with a negative polarity item such as 'any doubt': e.g. *Si yo no tengo duda alguna* ['SI I don't have any doubt']

(ii) The inability of independent *si*-clauses to coordinate with another independent *si*-clause: e.g. A: *Julia no va a aprobar el examen* ['Julia won't pass the test'] B: *¡Si ha estudiado mucho y (*si) lo sabe todo!* ['SI she's studied a lot and she knows it all!']

(iii) The inability of independent *si*-clauses to embed under a verb of cognition or communication (e.g. 'to say'): e.g. A: *Vamos a comprar un coche Nuevo* ['Let's buy a new car'] B: # *¡Juan dice que si no tenemos dinero!* ['Juan says that SI we don't have money'] (# indicates infelicitous use).

(iv) The use of sentential adverbs (such as *obviamente* 'obviously'), which must be within the scope of *si* in an independent *si*-clause: e.g. *Si obviamente no vienen,* as opposed to #*Obviamente si...* ['SI obviously they won't come]

Of these four criteria only (ii) and (iii) apply to English. As for (ii), English, unlike Spanish, does allow coordination with another insubordinate *if*-clause, as attested by the following corpus example:

(5) [driving instructor] *Right we're going to do this one at a time **If you'd like to go to your machines** and Gareth **if you'd like to lead** <,,>*
(ICE-GB:s2a-054-017)[1]

However, coordination is a useful test for the syntactic independence of insubordinate *if*-clauses since they coordinate with other main clauses, as illustrated by the following example (cf. also Mato-Míguez 2014).

(6) [lecturer] *And uhm <,> pharmacology companies are very interested in uh pursuing this this line of research <,,> So **if we sort of settle down and** <,> **look at a tiny part of one of the pathways** and the particular enzyme that I I'm researching into is phospholypase C <,>*
(ICE-GB:s2a-034-110)

As for (iii), the inability to embed under a verb of cognition or communication is a good indication for the syntactic independence of an English *if*-clause too. The only potential caveat here is the possibility of a (non-subordinate) direct speech reading, as in (7), which would allow for an independent *if*-clause.

(7) *He said '**if you'd like to come next door**'.*

For the purpose of identifying insubordinate *if*-clauses in English, therefore, further criteria are required (see Kaltenböck 2016).

2.2 D'Hertefelt (2015, 2018): Insubordination in Germanic

In her study of insubordination in Germanic languages D'Hertefelt (2015: 155–176; see also 2018) argues that so-called elaborative complement constructions, as in (8), and post-modifying conditional clauses, as in (9), are not cases of insubordination but rather the result of an alternative grammatical mechanism, namely that of dependency shift (cf. also D'Hertefelt and Verstraete 2014: 93–99). This mechanism "describes cases in which conjunctions that typically mark subordinate dependency on the propositional level can also come to express dependencies on the discourse level, often going hand in hand with loss of clause-internal subordinate marking" (D'Hertefelt and Verstraete 2014: 97; cf. also e.g. Günthner 1996 for German *weil* 'because' and *obwohl* 'although').

---

1 ICE-GB refers to the British component of the International Corpus of English (Nelson et al. 2002).

(8) Swedish (D'Hertefelt and Verstraete 2014: 96)
    A: *jag vill att dom ska ha fasta regler (...)*
    B: *m'm*
    A: *riktlinjer (följer ju dom)*
    B: *m'm*
    A: *ja*   **att**   **man**   **e0**   **strukturerad**   *(...)*
        yes   COMP   one   be.PRS   structured
    'A: I want them to have fixed rules [lit. want that they...]
    B: mm
    A: directions (follow those)
    B: mm
    A: yes that one is structured'

(9) English (Dancygier and Sweetser 2005: 265)
    "So you will keep him?" Macon said.
    *"Oh, I guess," she said. **"If you're desperate."***

There are two reasons given for excluding the two construction types from the category of insubordination. First, they are always discourse dependent on the previous discourse and therefore "cannot be considered main clauses in their own right" (D'Hertefelt and Verstraete 2014: 96). Second, they may display ambiguous subordinate marking in some languages. For instance, they may have main clause word order or may take interrogative or imperative form.

Identifying these instances as a separate category captures the undeniable fact that there is a difference between them and clear cases of insubordination. However, excluding them from the category of insubordination altogether and postulating a different mechanism for their development seems somewhat premature based on the study of synchronic data alone. Given that there is still no generally accepted view on the diachronic development of insubordination (e.g. Evans' 2007 ellipsis hypothesis, Mithun's 2008 functional extension, Van linden and Van de Velde's 2014 hypoanalysis, Heine et al.'s 2016 cooptation; see also Mithun, this volume) it seems best not to pre-empt any possible developmental paths. Moreover, the fact that elaborative clauses may show syntactic features of main clauses (such as interrogative and imperative form) can be explained as insubordinate clauses reducing their form-function mismatch (see Section 1) and bringing their form in line with their "main clause use".[2] It therefore

---

2 It was argued by a reviewer that the assumption that elaborative insubordination may use main clause features to bring their form in line with their increasingly main clause use may be

seems advisable not to exclude pragmatically dependent subordinate clauses *a priori* from the category of insubordination.

3 A usage-based approach to delimiting insubordination

Having reviewed some previous criteria proposed for the delimitation of insubordination, this section suggests an alternative approach based on a usage-based model of language (e.g. Haiman 1994; Langacker 2000; Bybee 2010). From a usage-based perspective there is a close link between concrete language use and our mental linguistic categories (i.e. linguistic structure) in the sense that the latter is seen as arising from the former as a conventionalisation of recurrent patterns in language use. As Du Bois (1985: 359–360) puts it, "recurrent patterns in discourse tokens exert pressure on linguistic types". However, the usage–structure relationship is not just a one-way street. While structure is distilled out of usage, it is also true that linguistic structure – once in place – will, in turn, exert some influence on usage. Linguistic structure, although derived

---

at odds with their pragmatically secondary status, as it invites the inference that these elaborative insubordinations are – in formal terms – one step ahead of pragmatically independent (i.e. stand-alone) insubordinations. The argument put forward here is indeed that the boundary between primary and secondary use is a permeable one and a pragmatically dependent insubordination may be used as a pragmatically independent one. As illustrated by the following example, a *because*-clause, which in its insubordinate use is typically pragmatically dependent (cf. example (11)), may also be pragmatically independent, as signalled by interrogative word order.

(i)   A: *Mm That's a very good question*
(ii)   B: ***Because why can't you consult a psychiatrist and see wha I mean a friendly one and see what the correct response is*** (ICE-GB s1a-031-131)

However, we clearly cannot expect there to be a one-to-one correlation between pragmatic independence and the use of main clause features, as illustrated for instance by pragmatically independent *if*-clauses (e.g. example (23)). Different syntactic types show differing propensities for adopting main clause features. This seems easier for some adverbial clauses (e.g. *because, although*) than for others (e.g. *if*-clauses). *That*-complement clauses only allow it when the complementizer has been omitted. Moreover, there are also other formal features for signalling pragmatic independence, such as prosody (e.g. Kaltenböck 2016) or the use of putative *should* (*That I should live to see this!*) or the modal particle *only* (*If only you'd phoned!*) (see also Kaiser and Struckmeier, this volume).

from previous acts of usage, is thus a phenomenon in its own right and constrains subsequent acts of usage (e.g. Harder 2003; Boye and Harder 2007: 572).

There are thus two types of linguistic description of an utterance: it can be described on the usage-level as an actual communicative event, and on the level of syntactic structure as an instantiation of specific structural patterns (cf. Boye and Harder 2007: 572). In a usage-based model these two levels are seen as linked, allowing it to accommodate dynamic aspects of language such as language change. In this view, then, language change originates on the level of use, the more adaptive of the two, which is more responsive to the needs from the external 'environment' (DuBois 1985). The level of structure, on the other hand, is, by its very nature, more preservative and persistent. This is necessary to give the system sufficient stability to allow for communication. Ultimately, however, changes on the usage-level can be expected to impact also on the level of structure, albeit with some time lag.

For an adequate description of insubordination we therefore need to take into account both the level of usage and the level of structure and relate them to each other. On the level of usage we can distinguish between communicatively 'primary' vs. communicatively 'secondary' use. 'Primary' use means that the clause has its own illocutionary force (e.g. directive or exclamative) and can therefore stand alone. In other words, it is pragmatically independent from the surrounding co-text. 'Secondary' use, on the other hand, includes clauses which are pragmatically related to some previous or following co-text and therefore lack the ability to stand alone. On the level of syntactic structure, it is possible to distinguish between syntactically independent and syntactically dependent clauses. Syntactic dependence is equivalent to the clause being a constituent of a larger structure, while syntactic independence means that it is not.

As illustrated in Table 1, the two sets of criteria only partially overlap with syntactic dependence implying pragmatic dependence but pragmatic dependence extending into syntactically independent clauses. This allows for the identification of three different types of formally subordinate clauses: stand-alone insubordination, elaborative insubordination, and subordination proper.

Before looking at the three types in more detail, let me briefly discuss the two criteria on each level. Starting with the difference between syntactic dependence and independence, this is illustrated by the following examples:

(10) *Mary's late for work **because she got stuck in a traffic jam***.

(11) *Mary's late for work, **because I can't see her car in the car park***.

Table 1: Types of formally subordinate clauses in English[3].

Structure:	Syntactically independent no constituent of a larger structure		Syntactically independent constituent of a larger structure
Usage:	Pragmatically dependent 'primary' use	Pragmatically dependent 'secondary' use	
	Stand-alone Insubordination	**Elaborative Insubordination**	**Subordination**

As variously noted in the literature (e.g. Rutherford 1970; Kac 1972; Hooper and Thompson 1973; Lakoff 1974; Stenström 1998; Haegeman 2003; Verstraete 2007, 2008), the two adverbial clauses differ in that in (10) it is syntactically integrated and as such part of the constituent structure of the matrix clause, while in (11) it is a syntactically external disjunct and the first clause merely an "associated clause" (Haegeman 2003: 318) rather than a matrix clause. Semantically, the external status is reflected in the fact that the *because*-clause in (11) is outside the propositional content of the first clause and plays no role in determining the truth conditions of the utterance (Kac 1972). It is therefore "non-restrictive" (Rutherford 1970). Whereas in (10) the *because*-clause gives a reason for Mary's lateness, in (11) it provides a justification for the assertion made by the speaker in the first clause: It gives the reason why the speaker believes that Mary is late for work (e.g. Lakoff 1974: 330–331; Verstraete 2008: 198).

Various tests have been proposed for distinguishing syntactically external adverbial clauses from those that are syntactically integrated (e.g. Stenström 1998: 128–9; Espinal 1991; Verstraet 2008: e.g. chapter 7; see also Debaisieux and Deulofeux, this volume; von Wietersheim and Featherston, this volume). As illustrated by the examples below, unintegrated clauses cannot be the focus of an *it*-cleft, as in (12b), they cannot be the focus of a variant of the pseudo-cleft, as in (13b), or serve as a response to a *wh*-question, as in (14b).

(12) a. *It is **because she got stuck in a traffic jam** that Mary's late for work.*
    b. **It is **because I can't see her car in the car park** that Mary's late for work.*

(13) a. *The reason Mary's late for work is that **she got stuck in traffic**.*
    b. **The reason Mary's late for work is that **I can't see her car in the car park**.*

---

3 Formally subordinate clauses include those introduced by a subordinator or non-finite clauses, but not necessarily cases of zero-*that*, as their syntactic status cannot always be unambiguously identified.

(14) a. *Why is Mary late for work?* **Because she got stuck in traffic.**
    b. **Why is Mary late for work?* **Because I can't see her car in the car park.**

These tests also apply to non-finite clauses (Quirk et al. 1985: 629). Compare:

(15) a. *Mary drove all the way to Maine* **(only) to visit some friends.**
    b. *It was* **only to visit some friends** *that Mary drove all the way to Maine.*

(16) a. *Mary drove all the way to Maine* **(only) to find that her friends had moved to Florida.**
    b. **It was* **only to find that her friends had moved to Florida** *that Mary drove all the way to Maine.*

For complement clauses an *it*-cleft is not an option since it does not allow a *that*-clause as its focus. Instead, passivization may be used.[4] E.g.

(17) a. *I understood* **that it's not out on video** (ICE-GB:s1a-006-65)
    b. **That it's not out on video** *was understood by me.*

(18) a. *I'm inclined to favour your first suggestion,* **that we shelve the proposal until after the election** (Huddleston and Pullum 2002: 966)
    b. **That we shelve the proposal until after the election* *was inclined to favour your suggestion by me.*

As for the second set of criteria, on the usage level, the distinction between pragmatically dependent and independent clauses can be established by their ability to stand alone. This independence from preceding co-text is a result of their own illocutionary force, as illustrated by the directives and exclamatives in (19) to (21). And it is in that sense that they can be seen as having 'primary' usage function, as opposed to some ancillary, elaborative function with regard to some other utterance or discourse content.

(19) **If you'll just come next door** (ICE-GB:s1a-089-159)

(20) **To think that she could be so ruthless!** (Quirk et al. 1985: 841)

---

4 As noted quite rightly by a reviewer, the passive version in (17), although strictly speaking possible, would not really be used by native speakers. Note, however, that its acceptability can be improved by adding extra weight to the predicate: e.g. . . .*was clearly understood by me and everyone else in the room.*

(21) ***That it should have come to this!*** (Huddleston and Pullum 2002: 944)

Unlike syntactic (in)dependence, for which the above mentioned tests provide a useful heuristic, the difference between pragmatic dependency and pragmatic independency is less clear-cut. The gradient link between the two can be illustrated by the exclamative *if*-clause in (22).

(22) ***If ever I heard the like of that!*** (OED s.v. *if*, conj. and n. A.I.7)

Although exclamative clauses have their own illocutionary force and therefore can easily stand alone, they may also, as is implied in this example, be a reaction to some previous utterance and in that sense may not be completely pragmatically independent. However, it is clear that in this example the retrospective link is not a result of the complementizer but of the anaphoric pronoun *that*. In most cases the larger context of a specific example can be expected to clarify the question of pragmatic (in)dependence but potential cases of indeterminacy cannot be ruled out.

The following sections briefly discuss and illustrate the two types: stand-alone insubordination (3.1), pragmatically dependent insubordination (3.2). They will be contrasted with cases of subordination in Section 3.3.

3.1 Stand-alone insubordination

Stand-alone insubordinate clauses are pragmatically independent and as such by necessity also syntactically independent (see Table 1 above). They occur without an associated matrix clause and have their own illocutionary force, which is typically that of a directive, optative or exclamative (cf. Verstraete and D'Hertefelt's 2016 deontic and evaluative types).

In terms of their syntactic form they include 'adverbial' clauses,[5] as in (23), *that*-clauses ('complement clauses'), as in (24), and non-finite clauses, as in (25).

(23) ***If only Denis Betts could have picked that ball up and got it out to Offiah*** But he couldn't <,,> (ICE-GB:s2a-4-377)

(24) ***That I should live to see such ingratitude!*** (Quirk et al. 1985: 841)

---

5 I use the term 'adverbial' here in inverted commas as in their insubordinate (i.e. extra-clausal) uses they have lost their adverbial status.

(25) *She just looked fantastic.* **To think that she lost the same amount of weight as her uniform weighs**. (COCA2009:SPOK:NBCToday)[6]

The range of stand-alone insubordinate clauses in English is fairly restricted. *If*-clauses are clearly the most productive, which can be attributed to the fairly generic semantic relation they construe between two states or events: i.e. that of a simple concomitance without further specifying the relation between them (Lombardi Vallauri 2004: 214; see also Lindström et al., this volume). This makes conditional clauses much more versatile than other adverbial clauses, such as *since-* or *when*-clauses, which are semantically more constrained (e.g. time, cause-effect, purpose, concession) and therefore do not lend themselves so easily to being detached from preceding discourse.

Occasionally there are cases of stand-alone *if*-clauses which appear adjacent to an independent clause looking superficially similar to a matrix clause, as in (26). Here the second clause does however not syntactically govern the *if*-clause (cf. the syntactic tests of independence discussed above) and can be omitted without affecting the felicity of the *if*-clause, owing to the fact that the *if*-clause has its own illocutionary force of a directive.

(26) *Now **if you come round here** we have the Indian roll <,,> (ICE-GB:s2a-059-050)

3.2 Elaborative insubordination

The term 'elaborative' is borrowed from D'Hertefelt and Verstraete (2014: 92f; cf. also Verstraete and D'Hertefelt 2016), who use it in a more restrictive sense for a specific type of independent complement construction in Swedish and Danish. It is used here to refer to all those formally subordinate clauses which are syntactically independent, but pragmatically dependent in the sense that they relate to another utterance or discourse content on which they elaborate in some way by providing further information, a clarification, a comment, an explanation etc. This category covers essentially what Verstraete et al. (2012) and D'Hertefelt (2015) call the "discursive" type of insubordination and what Mithun (2008: 107) refers to as extension of dependency beyond the sentence: "They relate sentences to a larger discourse or pragmatic context [...] they are dependent but not necessarily subordinate".

---

6 COCA refers to the Corpus of Contemporary American English (Davies 2008).

As indicated in the quote above, elaborative insubordinations may relate not only to a specific verbal co-text but also to a pragmatic context (cf. also Gras and Sansiñena 2015: 526–527). The inclusion of contextual dependence may seem to introduce a potential problem for delimitation from stand-alone cases such as *If you'd like to go next door* (as discussed in 3.1), which could be argued to require also a specific pragmatic situation. Let us compare this example with the following two cases of pragmatically dependent insubordinate clauses.

(27)   *There are crisps in the cupboard **if you're hungry**.*

(28)   ***If you're hungry*** [said by a speaker pointing at a packet of crisps on the table]

The example in (27) illustrates a so-called Austin conditional or speech act conditional (e.g. Dancygier 1998: 103; also Haegeman 1984: 487). It is syntactically independent from the preceding clause but tied to it pragmatically. Similarly, the *if*-clause in (28) is pragmatically tied to a specific gesture: it is dependent on the act of pointing at the packet of crisps. Without this pragmatic link the *if*-clause would not be meaningful. This is different from a stand-alone *if*-clause such as *If you'd like to go next door* above, which can 'survive' alone as a meaningful unit even if stripped of its immediate situational context. Stand-alone insubordinations are thus more independent than elaborative insubordinations, although the possibility of occasional indeterminacy between them cannot be completely excluded (as illustrated by example (22) above).

All formal types of subordinate clauses can be used as pragmatically dependent insubordinate clauses. The examples below illustrate adverbial clauses (29), *that*-clauses (30), and non-finite clauses (31).

(29) a.   *There's one I was going to show you because it it made my hair stand on end <,> It 's a bit scary this <,> **if I can find it** <,,> No Can't find it*
(ICE-GB:s1a-037-236)

   b.   A: *But it's worth booking both at the same time so that cos it costs less I think*
      B: *I didn't know it was a huge <,> thing <,> **Because Karen and I have been to see most of his plays***
      (ICE-GB:s1a-025-256)

   c.   B: *Well I mean it would be nice to have a holiday but uh*
      A: *Yeah yeah yeah yes yeah I'm sure it would <,,> I think you ih Well I don't know I think I always feel I'd like to get away from the place for a bit*

B: *Yeah **Although I did have three weeks in sunny Shepherd's Bush of course*** (ICE-GB:s1-095-285)

(30) a. *But I agree very much with what Melvyn and John both said <,> **that the arts are vital to our lives a central part of what goes on in London*** (ICE-GB:s1b-022-77)

b. *I think most neurologists would would uhm say the same **that you that one can distinguish <,> hysteria from malingering*** (ICE-GB:s1b-070-39)

(31) a. ***To be sure**, Pamela is a better companion for a lady than a monkey or a harlequin.* (BNC:drama)[7]

b. ***Speaking generally**, one might pronounce these islands entirely destitute of wood.* (BNC:non-fiction)

c. ***Stated briefly**, these theories argued that employees would demonstrate high levels of effort and performance. . .* (BNC:commerce)

As can be seen from the examples, the clauses in bold are all syntactically separate from their linguistic environment (as evidenced e.g. by their inability to become the focus of an *it*-cleft, as discussed above), but pragmatically they depend on the presence of a particular utterance or discourse content. The linguistic co-text to which they relate typically precedes the insubordinate clause, which is reflected by some of the terms in the literature: e.g. "postposed free subordinate clauses" (Lombardi Vallauri 2004: 213), "post-modifying independent conditional clause" (D'Hertefelt 2015). However, they may also precede the co-text they relate to, as illustrated by the more formulaic examples in (31) and (32).

(32) a. ***If you like** that's a measure of <,> uh how much people are paid. . .* (ICE-GB:s2a-037-023)

b. *# **As you know**, the issue of climate change is polarizing.* (COCA2015:SPOK:NBC)

The syntactic independence of insubordinate clauses raises the question as to the exact status of the subordinator, particularly in pragmatically dependent cases, where some co-textual link persists. Since the 'subordinator' no longer introduces a truly subordinate clause it is best considered a discourse link or, in Huddleston and Pullum's (2002: 1354) terms, an "indicator", which indicates

---

7 BNC refers to the British National Corpus (Davies 2004).

the nature of the semantic link to the host construction (or anchor). It thus has mainly a discourse connective function, in that "it ties what follows it, typically an independent sentence, to previous discourse" (Mithun 2008: 108). For instance, *because* in example (29b) above expresses a discourse link between two utterances which is not necessarily causal (e.g. Kac 1972: 629; Stenström 1998: 130). It is even possible for an indicator to adopt a meaning which is substantially different from that of its original subordinator use. Compare, for instance, the temporal meaning of the subordinator *when* in (33) and the contrastive meaning in (34).

(33) **When she arrives** *she will be greeted by trumpets* <,> (ICE-GB:s2a-020-100)

(34) C: *It's easy to make* <,> *See I mean you shouldn't have seen all the preparation bits I should have like just whipped up this amazing meal and you'd have gone God Mark you must have spent hours slaving over the stove And I would have said yeah you know*
  D: *Mm Taco bar* <unclear-word> *Leicester Square*
  C: **When it really only took me fifteen minutes** <,>
  (ICE-GB:s1a-071-320)

Similar changes in meaning have been noted for other subordinator-indicator pairs, such as *while, as, since, so that* (Verstraete 2007: 193–196; Verstraete 2008; also Haegeman 2003: 329–30; Günthner 1996).

3.3 Subordination

Subordination proper is distinguished from insubordination by the fact that the subordinate clause is a constituent of a matrix clause (syntactically dependent) and consequently (by implication) also pragmatically dependent on it. As a syntactically integrated element the subordinate clause can, for instance, be the focus of an *it*-cleft and can be questioned (see above). This is true for complex sentences produced by a single speaker as well as for dyadic instances of subordinate clauses, where the subordinate clause is produced in a different turn from that of its matrix clause. As illustrated by the examples below, such dyadic uses of subordinate clauses may either complete the matrix clause produced by another speaker (examples (35) and (36)) or provide an answer to an open question (examples (37) and (38)). In both cases they are construed as dependents of a matrix clause in the previous turn.

(35) B: *Uh uh it's obligatory is it to have something in a company report*
C: **If you've got more than a hundred in the uh workforce** (ICE-GB:s1b-062-138)

(36) B: *I was sort sort of asking him again*
A: *Yes <,>* **Cos you want to get back together** <,> (ICE-GB:s1a-050-052)

(37) A: *How do you know that*
B: *Well* **Because I've been to the Soviet Union I suppose a good few times** (ICE-GB:s1a-014-071)

(38) A: *What were you trying to put across*
B: **That we had supports already in the wall** (ICE-GB:s1b-069-140)

Dyadic uses of subordinate clauses, as the ones above, result from the interaction of speech participants who are jointly constructing a complex sentence (cf. Lindström et al. 2016, and this volume). This is particularly obvious where the subordinate clause completes another speaker's independent clause, as in (35) and (36), and in doing so construes it as its matrix clause.[8] Note that in all these examples the subordinate clause can occur as the focus of a corresponding *it*-cleft: e.g. *It is (only) if you've got more than a hundred in the uh workforce that it's obligatory is it to have something in a company report*. However, not all instances of this type neatly separate the two clauses into two turns, as is illustrated by the following example, where the *that*-clause is already initiated in the first speaker's turn.

(39) B: *I don't think he really tries to hide the fact that he's like*
C: **that he steals her money** (BNC; Sansiñena 2015: 190)

In the question-answer sequences in (37) and (38) the subordinate clause is similarly construed as depending on the matrix verb in the question: e.g. *I know that because...*, *I was trying to put across that we...* (cf. Sansiñena et al. 2015: 4), as evidenced, for instance, by the *it*-cleft test (*It is because I've been to the Soviet Union a good few times that I know that*) and the passivisation test (*That we had supports already in the wall was put across*).

---

8 Bowie and Aarts (2016) refer to this type as "clausal extension", while for Ono and Couper-Kuhlen's (2007) such syntactically integrated extensions are "increments".

Dyadic uses of subordinate clauses such as in (37) and (38) have been discussed in some detail by Sansiñena (2015: 180–190) and Sansiñena et al. (2015), where they are shown to have functions which overlap to some extent with those of insubordinate clauses. In terms of the criterion of syntactic independence, as suggested here, they are however outside the category of insubordination.[9]

Excluding dyadically constructed complex sentences like the ones above from the category of insubordination does however not diminish their potential role in the emergence of insubordinate clauses. This has in fact been suggested by Lombardi Vallauri (2010: 74), who sees the origin of insubordinate Italian *if*-clauses in the omission of the main clause for performance reasons, such as dialogic interruptions. In a similar vein, Sansiñena et al. (2015: e.g. 6.17) argue that dyadically dependent complement clauses provide the intermediate stage in Evans' (2007) ellipsis account for the development of insubordination, even if not all the discourse functions of insubordinate clauses can be traced back to dyadically dependent clauses (cf. also Sansiñena 2015: 197; Hilpert 2015).

Dyadic subordinate clauses may of course qualify for inclusion in the category of insubordination, viz. the pragmatically dependent type. In that case they are not construable as projections of a matrix clause. The examples below illustrate this dyadic type of syntactically independent, yet pragmatically dependent subordinate clauses, as discussed in 3.2 above.

(40) A: *So people are ignoring what the students want the*
B: *Well yeah By and large I **If if you must put it like that*** (ICE-GB:s1a-068-292)

(41) A: *Yre you a are you generally a quick writer*
B: *Yes When I'm taking notes I have to be fairly quick*
A: *Mhm And d'you use a biro*
B: *Yes*
A: *D'you find that easier*
B: *Yes I think it is an option now*
A: ***Because one way of improving writing is to use a <,> a fountain pen*** *<,>*
(ICE-GB:s1a-059-271)

---

9 A similar position is taken by Evans (2007: 418) in his discussion of an example by Ford and Thompson (1986: 368).

(42) A: *And and if one was a psychiatrist and supposing she'd said that to*
a psychiatrist what would they say <,,>

B: *Mm That's a very good question*

A: **Because why can't you consult a psychiatrist and see wha I mean**
a friendly one and see what the correct response is
(ICE-GB:s1a-031-131)

(43) A: *And uh obviously if they do break as happened here injury may be sus-*
tained You'd have that in mind would you <,> *You'd be aware of that*
possibility

B: **That there could be a possibility that would happen** <,,>
(ICE-GB:s1b-067-54)

These examples of dyadic subordinate clauses can be distinguished from the syntactically integrated ones by the tests outlined above: e.g. *It is only if you must put it like that that people are ignoring what the students want; What are you aware of? *That possibility that there could be a possibility that would happen*. The link to the previous turn is simply a pragmatic one. In (41), for instance, *because* provides a discourse link with a preceding speech act: "I'm asking this because. . ." In example (42) the purely discourse connective function of *because* is further highlighted syntactically by interrogative word order, a typical main clause phenomenon (Green 1976).

To conclude, the distinction between syntactically independent and syntactically dependent subordinate clauses applies irrespective of whether they are produced within a single speaker turn or dyadically, that is, in a different turn from that of its potential matrix clause.

3.4 Granularity: A need for further distinction?

For the three-fold classification above (stand-alone insubordination vs. elaborative insubordination vs. subordination) I have suggested two different parameters, viz. syntactic (in)dependence and pragmatic (in)dependence, with the former being the primary criterion for distinguishing between subordination and insubordination. This raises the question whether there are any further parameters that need to be considered in making the typology more fine-grained.[10] Although this question cannot be answered in full within the scope of the present

---

10 I'm grateful to one of the reviewers for drawing my attention to this issue.

chapter, it seems there is indeed room for further fine-tuning, as it were, especially in view of the important work by Verstraete (e.g. 2007) on the interpersonal
dimension of clause combining. In the following I will briefly point out two areas
where additional parameters may allcw for further subsective gradience (Aarts
2007) of the category of elaborative insubordination.

One possible additional parameter is the expression of a modal value in the
'subordinate' clause, as suggested by Verstraete (2007). He distinguishes four different types of complex sentences, viz. coordination, modal subordination, free
subordination, and bound subordination, on the basis of three interpersonal parameters, viz. speech function, modal value, and scope, as illustrated in Table 2.

Table 2: Verstraete's (2007: e.g. 132) types of complex sentences with parameters and
relations between parameters.

Scope: integration into the speech act of main conjunct	[– Scope] ↑	[– Scope] ↑	[– Scope] ↑⟋→	[– Scope]
Modality: modal values expressed in the secondary conjunct	[+ Modality] ↑	[+ Modality] ↑⟋→	[– Modality]	
Speech Function: non-declarative clause types (mood) allowed	[+ Speech Function]	[– Speech Function]		
	Coordination	**Modal subordination**	**Free subordination**	**Bound subordination**

Verstraete's parameter of scope indicates whether the secondary clause falls
within the scope of the illocutionary force of the main clause and is therefore
part of its propositional content ([+ Scope]) or not ([– Scope]). It separates
'bound subordination' from all other types and thus marks the boundary between speaker-related uses (coordination, modal and free subordination) and
state-of-affairs-related uses (bound subordination) (Verstraete 2007: e.g. 232).
Although the notion of scope is essentially an interpersonal one, it can be
tested for by clefting and *wh*-questioning and is as such roughly equivalent to
my notion of syntactic (in)dependence, which in my account separates subordination from insubordination.

On the other hand, the parameter of pragmatic (in)dependence in my typology, i.e. whether the clause has its own illocutionary force, relates to both

Verstraete's parameters of modality (expression of a modal value in the 'subordinate' clause) and speech function (whether it allows for non-declarative clause types, viz. interrogative or imperative). As he argues, "speech function forms one of the two grammatical components of illocutionary force, together with modality" (Verstraete 2007: 106). His additional parameter of modality thus allows for a more fine-grained distinction of my category of elaborative insubordination into those that express a modal value (modal subordination) and those that don't (free subordination). His category of 'coordination' is comparable to my 'stand-alone insubordination', but somewhat more restrictive in allowing only for non-declarative mood.

A second area where further distinction may be necessary is between different syntactic types of elaborative insubordination. As discussed in 3.2, the category of elaborative insubordination comprises structures that are syntactically quite disparate, such as independent complement clauses as in (44) (cf. D'Hertefelt and Verstraete 2014) and adverbial clauses introduced by a subordinator, such as the *because*-clause in (45) (repeated from 11) (cf. e.g. Verstraete 2007: ch. 9).

(44) *The excuse he gave – **that the train had been late** – seemed to satisfy the boss* (Huddleston and Pullum 2002: 1358)

(45) *Mary's late for work, **because I can't see her car in the car park**.*

In their ordinary sentence grammar use as subordinate clauses, these two types are clearly different, with complement clauses being part of the argument structure of the main clause and adverbial clauses not. In their insubordinate uses, however, these two syntactic types have been lumped together in the category of elaborative insubordination. Although it can be assumed that the syntactic differences in their sentence grammar uses do not automatically carry over to their insubordinate uses (as stipulated by the cooptation hypothesis, e.g. Heine et al. 2017), there may still be important functional differences which need to be captured. In the examples above, for instance, the insubordinate clause in (44) elaborates on the textual element *excuse*, clarifying the exact nature of the excuse. In the words of D'Hertefelt and Verstraete (2014: 92–93) the insubordinate clause here is used to "elaborate on or clarify an aspect of [the] previous discourse to guarantee proper understanding between speaker and interlocutor". In (45), on the other hand, the insubordinate clause elaborates on the speech act itself, providing a justification for the speaker's assertion that Mary is late for work (cf. Verstraete 2007: 197–200). We could also say that the insubordination in (44) is more oriented towards text/discourse organisation, making sure that the speaker's utterance is fully understood, while in (45) it is oriented more towards the speaker-hearer relationship by providing support for the speaker's assessment of the situation (cf. Kaltenböck, Heine, and Kuteva's 2011 distinction of different components of the situation of discourse). The exact functional difference, however, still requires further investigation.

4 A broad church: Syntactic independence as a larger category

The proposed identification of insubordination in terms of syntactic independence has the advantage of bringing together under one heading linguistic categories that are clearly related but often treated separately in the literature.

The category of elaborative insubordination includes, first and foremost, 'adverbial clauses', which have been discussed in the literature under various guises, such as "extradiscursory clauses" (Kac 1972), "non-restrictive subordination" (Rutherford 1970), "epistemic conditional" (Sweetser 1984), "conversational *if*-clauses" (Dancygier 1998), "premise conditional" (Haegeman 2003) and "peripheral adverbial clause" (Haegeman 1984). All of them are identified as being syntactically external to the host clause and are characterised as semantically non-restrictive in that they do not modify some propositional content but instead relate to another utterance or the larger discourse on a pragmatic level.

In addition to adverbial clauses, non-finite adjunct clauses and complement clauses have been identified above as further categories of elaborative insubordinate clauses. Non-finite clauses typically have metatextual function, conveying the speaker's comment on the way they are speaking (cf. Quirk et al's 1985: 1072 style disjuncts), as illustrated in (31) above. *That*-complement clauses, on the other hand, elaborate on the content of a noun phrase and in that sense are, what Huddleston and Pullum (2002: 1358) call, "content-specifying" (cf. also Quirk et al's 1985: 1072 content disjuncts), as illustrated in (30) above.

One category that has not yet been discussed but is also included by virtue of its syntactic independence is that of non-restrictive relative clauses. Most accounts of non-restrictive relative clauses assume a non-syntactic link to their host/antecedent. For Fabb (1990), for instance, the relationship between a non-restrictive relative clause and its host holds only on the level of discourse structure. Similarly, Burton-Roberts (1999: 38–40) argues that the pronoun-antecedent relationship is only contextually interpretable and therefore does not invoke (syntactic) coindexing but (semantic-pragmatic) coreference. This pragmatic link is particularly obvious in dyadic uses such as the following.

(46) A: *Well Toni's put an order in <,>*
     B: **Which means it'll come next month** (ICE-GB:s1a-017-102)

(47) B: *You can justify anything through Yes*
     A: *Well yes That's right*
     B: *Yes <,,>*
     A: **Which reminds me** *apparently well I say apparently theology is a Greek well it's a Greek deriv derivative*
        (ICE-GB:s1a-053-264)

By the same token, the category of elaborative insubordination also needs to include the type of nominal relative clause illustrated in (48). While non-restrictive relative clauses are retrospective, this type is exclusively prospective (forward-looking) in its discourse orientation.

(48) **What's more surprising**, *he didn't inform his parents.* (Quirk et al. 1985: 1117)

A further grammatical category that is covered by the criterion of syntactic in-dependence is that of parenthetical clauses, that is clauses interpolated within a host clause as in (49) and (50).

(49) *The representations I had seen **if I remember rightly** were dated the sixth of of November* (ICE-GB:s1b-058-021)

(50) *Fiona **as you know** does set design* (ICE-GB:s1a-093-131)

Clauses such as these are sometimes subsumed under the heading of 'comment clauses' (e.g. Quirk et al. 1985: 1112–1118) and are often highly formulaic. As parentheticals they are, by definition, syntactically independent information units which are not governed by their host clauses (e.g. Kaltenböck 2007 for discussion) and thus qualify for inclusion under elaborative insubordination. This view is also supported by the fact that most of the parenthetical (i.e. inter-polated) clauses are positionally flexible and may equally occur in initial and final position. Note, however, that parenthetical use is not restricted to elabora-tive insubordination. Stand-alone insubordinate clauses may also be inserted into a host clause, as illustrated by example (51).

(51) *I invite you this evening* <,,> *to come* <,> *and basically to enjoy the slides* <,,> *but also* <,> ***if you have a taste for such things*** *to read between the lines* (ICE-GB:s2a-040-3)

The category of pragmatically dependent insubordination thus unites a range of constructions, which are typically discussed separately in a grammar: insubordinate adverbial clauses, insubordinate complement clauses, non-restrictive relative clauses, and parenthetical clauses. Subsuming all of them under one heading allows us to capture their functional and formal similarity as well as their difference from 'ordinary' elements of sentence grammar.

In addition, the criterion of syntactic independence enables us to see insubordinate clauses not as an isolated, somewhat unusual grammatical category, but as part of a larger family of constructions, that of extra-clausal constituents (Dik 1997), also referred to as supplements (Huddleston and Pullum 2002) or theticals (Kaltenböck et al. 2011, Heine et al. 2013). The category of theticals comprises a range of different linguistic units, such as parentheticals, formulae of social exchange, vocatives, imperatives, interjections, all of which share typical properties: They are (i) syntactically independent, (ii) typically set off prosodically from the rest of an utterance, (iii) semantically non-restrictive, (iv) tend to be positionally mobile, and (v) may be elliptical. Insubordinate clauses share these properties and therefore qualify as a further category of theticals (see Heine at al. 2016). Insubordinate clauses also share the typical discourse functions of theticals, which have been identified as relating to the immediate Situation of Discourse, more specifically the components of Speaker-Hearer Interaction, Speaker Attitude, and Text Organisation.

By including insubordination as a special category of theticals we can capture the fact that it is not a marginal phenomenon, representing an "irregular" or "minor" category (e.g. Quirk et al. 1985: 838ff; Stirling 1998: 289). Instead they can be seen as the result of a more general discourse strategy (viz. cooptation; e.g. Heine et al. 2017) and part of a larger grammatical domain, thetical grammar.[11]

---

11 It is clear that the inclusion of insubordination in the larger family of theticals does not preclude the necessity for further subcategorization. As noted by a reviewer, for instance, elaborative insubordinations are different from stand-alone insubordinations in that the latter, unlike the former, always lack an anchor utterance.

5 A special case: Semi-insubordination

The term semi-insubordination is used by Van linden and Van de Velde (2014) for subordinate *dat*-clauses in Dutch which are preceded by a single matrix constituent. These vestiges of a matrix clause can be adjectival, adverbial, or nominal and express interpersonal meaning in that they convey "the speaker's attitudinal assessment of the propositional content expressed by the *dat*-clause" (Van linden and Van de Velde 2014: 235). An example of an adjectival matrix head is given in (52).

(52) Dutch (Van linden and Van de Velde 2014: 231)
    Stom da'k   daar nie aangedacht heb
    stupid CONJ.I there not thought.of   have
    'It's so stupid that I haven't thought of this myself'

Semi-insubordination has also been investigated for Spanish by Sansiñena (2015: 143–172), who notes that the element preceding the *que*-clause expresses either the speaker's subjective evaluation or some epistemic or evidential value. For a discussion of adverbial semi-insubordination in Swedish see Beijering and Norde (this volume). In English, semi-insubordination has largely gone unnoticed.[12] This is somewhat surprising as it is far from infrequent in corpus data. Typical examples are given below.

(53) a. **Sorry** *that Larry's not here* (COCA:2010:SPOK:CNNMisc)
    b. *Well,* **funny** *you should ask, Florence.* (COCA:1999:SPOK:NBCToday)
    c. **Strange** *how the Lebanon should be covered with them* (BNC:KC9Sconv)
    d. **Glad** *to hear it!* (BNC:KSVSconv)
    e. **Lovely** *being here* (COCA2002SPOK:NBCToday)

(54) a. **Pity** *that she had not lived longer* (COCA1997:FIC:WomanHouse)
    b. **No way** *this is legit* (COCA2012:SPOK:ABCPrimetime)
    c. **Pleasure** *to have you here* (COCA2012:SPOK:CBSThisMorning)
    d. **A shame** *not being able to hear* (BNC:K8VW:fictprose)

As can be seen from the examples, the matrix element can take the form of an adjective or noun (occasionally with an indefinite article), as illustrated in (53)

---

12 Cf. however some brief observations by Bolinger (1977: 73), Kaltenböck (2003: 251–252) and D'Hertefelt (2015: 176–178) as well as a detailed study of one particular pattern of semi-insubordination by Gentens et al. (2016), viz. *No wonder that...*

and (54) respectively.[13] Syntactically, these matrix predicates can be reconstructed as *it*-extrapositions with an ellipted anticipatory *it* and copula *is* (e.g. *It is funny / a pity that...*) or as an exclamative clause (e.g. *How funny that you should ask!, What a pity that she had not lived longer!*).[14] Somewhat less frequently the matrix elements can also be reconstructed as first person copulative matrix clauses (e.g. *I am sorry / glad that...*) or, occasionally, as an existential *there* construction (e.g. *There's no way that...*). Semantically, the lexical items in matrix predicate position typically represent emotive predicates (Kiparsky and Kiparsky 1970), which include adjectives such as *amazing, crazy, funny, good, great, nice, odd, strange, lucky, glad, sorry, happy* and nouns such as *shame, pity, pleasure, joy*.

For the subordinate clause, too, there are different possibilities: (i) a *that*-clause (examples (53a) and (54a) above), (ii) a zero-*that* clause (53b and 54b), (iii) a *how*-adverbial clause (53c), (iv) a *to*-infinitival clause (53d) and (54c), (v) an -*ing* clause (53e) and (54d). The typical structure of semi-insubordination in English can therefore be sketched out as in Table 3.

Table 3: Typical structure of semi-insubordination in English.

Matrix element	Subordinate clause
Adjective, Noun	*That*-clause, zero *that*-clause, *how*-clause; *To*-infinitive, -*ing* clause

Functionally, the matrix element of semi-insubordination expresses a speaker comment on the proposition expressed in the subordinate clause. The matrix element, in other words, is prospective (forward-looking) in its discourse orientation with its scope being over the subordinate clause. This is important as it distinguishes semi-insubordination from superficially similar syntactic strings, as in the example in (55) below. Here the adjective *sorry* does not provide a comment on the proposition "you raised the issue about what we don't know". As noted by Sansiñena (2015: 153), it represents a separate discourse move from the following clause. Thus, it is not possible to insert a *that*-complementizer without changing the meaning of the utterance (cf. **I'm sorry that you raised the issue...*).

---

13 Exceptionally, the matrix element can also be a prepositional phrase (*about time*), an intransitive verb (*seems*) or a transitive (imperative) verb (*remember*), but not an adverb (unless one includes *Maybe that she misunderstood him*) (see Kaltenböck in prep.).

14 Note, however, that reconstruction as an exclamative is not possible for semi-insubordination with a *how*-clause; cf. **How funny how he managed to do it.*

(55) A: *OK*
    B: *Jane, sorry you raised the issue about what we don't know* (COCA:2005: SPOK)

With semi-insubordination, on the other hand, the matrix predicate has scope over the immediately following subordinate clause and as such is prospective. Depending on the syntactic and prosodic form of the subordinate clause and its information status it is possible to distinguish different functional types of semi-insubordination (Kaltenböck in prep.). What they all have in common, though, is the expression of a speaker's subjective (emotional) attitude towards the content of the subordinate clause. Unlike its typical structural alternative, *it*-extraposition (e.g. *It is funny that...*), a semi-insubordinate construction lacks the use of an impersonal anticipatory *it,* which has the function of "'objectifying' a modality" (Collins 1994: 19), presenting it as if it were some generally accepted view rather than the speaker's personal judgement. Biber et al. (1999: 977) refer to this as 'implicit attribution of stance to the speaker/writer'. Semi-insubordination, by comparison, with its lack of an explicit subject attributes the comment of the predicate more directly to the speaker and the hic et nunc of the situation of discourse. This deictic anchoring is something that semi-insubordination shares with its other structural alternative, exclamative clauses (e.g. *How funny that he should say that!*), which have been noted to have "indexical function of expressing speaker perspective" (Michaelis 2001: 1040). In that sense semi-insubordination can be seen as a subjectivising construction.

The intrinsic speaker perspective of semi-insubordination is frequently exploited in literary texts, where it shifts the perspective from author narration (third person) to the subjective perspective of a character (first person). This is illustrated in the following example, where semi-insubordination presents the utterance as the character's first person thoughts in contrast to the preceding third person narration.

(56) *He was quite cold. He opened the door; a dark hall.* **Funny; the place didn't smell like the McHoans' house did.** (BNC:G0AW:fictprose)

With a clearer picture of the syntactic and functional peculiarities of semi-insubordination we can now turn to the question whether it should be included under the general heading of insubordination. As has become obvious from the discussion above, the syntactic status of semi-insubordination constructions is far from clear (see also D'Hertefelt 2015: 176). In terms of their external syntax they are like stand-alone, independent clauses and conform to the criteria of pragmatic and syntactic independence suggested for insubordination in Section 3. In terms of their internal syntax, however, they are identifiable as a subordinate clause governed by a matrix element.

A further problem for classification as insubordination are cases such as in (57) to (59), where what is commented on is not a subordinate clause but a noun phrase with a relative clause.

(57) **Funny _the way_ territories persist.** (BNC:J13W:fictprose)

(58) **Strange _the tricks_ that life plays.** (BNC:BMRW:fictprose)

(59) **Odd, _the things_ people get worked up about.** (BNC:GWBW:fictprose)

These examples, however, need to be included in the class of semi-insubordination based on their functional and structural similarity with the more prototypical members of this category. Their inclusion in the category of semi-insubordination is also consistent with Huddleston's (1984: 452) discussion of the construction _It is_ [matrix predicate] [the+N+relative clause], where he argues for their status as extrapositions since the NP is semantically close to a subordinate interrogative clause, e.g. _how the territories persist._ As noted above, semi-insubordination can typically be reconstructed as an instance of _it_-extraposition.

In view of the presence of a matrix element and examples such as in (57) to (59) above, the position adopted here is to exclude cases of so-called semi-insubordination from the category of insubordination. This of course raises the question of how to account for them in a grammar of English. One option is to treat them as elliptical _it_-extraposition (e.g. _[It is] funny that he should say that_), but this would fall short of accounting for their subjectivising function, which is absent with _it_-extraposition.

A better solution is to treat them as a category of theticals, as discussed in Section 4 above. This accounts for their syntactic independence and semantic non-restrictiveness, which are defining features of theticals, as well as their subjectivising function and deictic centeredness in the here and now. As noted in Section 4, theticals are very much located in the immediate situation of discourse with the expression of speaker attitude being one of the typical manifestations of this pragmatic function. Including semi-insubordination in the family of thetical constructions thus has the advantage of capturing the similarity of semi-insubordination with insubordination proper while still acknowledging their difference as two separate construction types.

6 Conclusion

As pointed out in the introduction, the category of insubordination has received a number of interpretations and has been applied to a range of different constructions, such as the ones in examples (1) to (4). The present paper has made suggestions for a clearer delimitation of the class based on a usage-based approach, which involves two separate, yet linked, levels of analysis: language usage and syntactic structure. For each of the levels two criteria are identified (as discussed on Section 3): syntactic dependence vs. independence on the level of syntactic structure, and pragmatic dependence vs. independence on the usage level. The criterion of syntactic independence is proposed as primary, which allows for a clear distinction from the category of subordination. Pragmatic (in)dependence, as a secondary criterion, allows for the distinction of two subtypes of insubordination: stand-alone insubordination and elaborative insubordination.

There are a number of advantages to such a classification of insubordination. First of all, it offers a heuristic for delimiting insubordination from subordination on the basis of relatively clear-cut syntactic criteria, while still allowing for some internal differentiation of the class. Moreover, although essentially synchronic in nature, the proposed classification is highly compatible with a diachronic perspective owing to its usage-based perspective which assumes a close link between usage and structure in the process of language change. The proposed identification of insubordination in strictly syntactic terms also has the advantage of disentangling the concept from its mode of use, such as dyadic or monologic. Although dyadic uses may play an important role in the diachronic development of insubordination (as noted in Section 3.3), it is only by clearly distinguishing between the two concepts that we can trace a potential link between them.

A further advantage of the proposed identification of insubordination in terms of syntactic independence is that it enables us to unite under one umbrella term linguistic categories that are often treated separately in the literature. As discussed in Section 4, it includes also parenthetical uses of subordinate clauses and various other categories which are often seen as unrelated. The criterion of syntactic independence thus highlights the commonality with other linguistic constructions not integrated into the structure of the clause. This allows us to see insubordinate clauses not as an isolated, somewhat unusual category, but as part of a larger family of extra-clausal constituents or theticals.

The last section of the paper (Section 5) has been devoted to the rather special case of semi-insubordination, which was included as a subtype of insubordination by Van linden and Van de Velde (2014). It was argued that semi-insubordination is best excluded from the category of insubordination as its internal syntax contains a clearly identifiable subordinate clause (with a matrix predicate) and it may also accommodate non-clausal elements. It does, however, share with insubordination its syntactic independence and a similar subjectivising function, which can be accounted for by the inclusion of both in the larger category of theticals.

References

Aarts, Bas. 2007. *Syntactic gradience. The nature of grammatical indeterminacy*. Oxford: Oxford University Press.
Biber, Douglas, Stig Johansson, Geoffrey Leech, Susan Conrad & Edward Finegan. 1999. *Longman grammar of spoken and written English*. London: Longman.
Bolinger, Dwight L. 1977. *Meaning and form*. London: Longman.
Bowie, Jill & Bas Aarts. 2016. Clause fragments in English dialogue. In María José López-Couso, Belén Méndez-Naya, Paloma Núñez-Pertejo & Ignacio M. Palacios-Martínez (eds.), *Corpus linguistics on the move: Exploring and understanding English through corpora*, 259–288. Amsterdam & New York: Brill/Rodopi.
Boye, Kasper & Peter Harder. 2007. Complement-taking predicates: Usage and linguistic structure. *Studies in Language* 31. 569–606.
Burton-Roberts, Noel. 1999. Language, linear precedence and parentheticals. In Peter Collins & David Lee (eds.), *The clause in English*, 33–52. Amsterdam & Philadelphia: Benjamins.
Bybee, Joan. 2010. *Language, usage and cognition*. Cambridge: Cambridge University Press.
Collins, Peter. 1994. Extraposition in English. *Functions of Language* 1 (1). 7–24.
D'Hertefelt, Sarah & Jean-Christophe Verstraete. 2014. Independent complement constructions in Swedish and Danish: Insubordination or dependency shift? *Journal of Pragmatics* 60. 89–102.
D'Hertefelt, Sarah. 2015. *Insubordination in Germanic: A typology of complements and conditional constructions*. Leuven: University of Leuven dissertation.
D'Hertefelt, Sarah. 2018. Insubordination in Germanic: A typology of complements and conditional constructions. Berlin: De Gruyter.
Dancygier, Barbara & Eve Sweetser. 2005. *Mental spaces in grammar: Conditional constructions*. Cambridge: Cambridge University Press.
Dancygier, Barbara. 1998. *Conditionals and prediction. Time, knowledge, and causation in conditional constructions*. Cambridge: Cambridge University Press.
Davies, Mark. 2004. *BYU-BNC*. (Based on the British National Corpus from Oxford University Press). http://corpus.byu.edu/bnc/.
Davies, Mark. 2008. *The Corpus of Contemporary American English: 425 million words, 1990-present*. http://corpus.byu.edu/coca.
Dik, Simon C. 1997. *The Theory of Functional Grammar. Part 2: Complex and derived constructions*. Berlin & New York: Mouton de Gruyter.

Du Bois, John W. 1985. Competing motivations. In John Haiman (ed.), *Iconicity in syntax*, 343–365. Amsterdam: Benjamins.

Espinal, Teresa M. 1991. The representation of disjunct constituents. *Language* 67 (4). 726–762.

Evans, Nicholas. 2007. Insubordination and its uses. In Irina Nicolaeva (ed.), *Finiteness: Theoretical and empirical foundations*, 366–431. Oxford: Oxford University Press.

Fabb, Nigel. 1990. The difference between English restrictive and nonrestrictive relative clauses. *Journal of Linguistics* 26. 57–78.

Ford, Cecilia E. & Sandra A. Thompson. 1986. Conditionals in discourse: A text-based study from English. In Elizabeth Closs Traugott, Alice ter Meulen, Judith Snitzer Reilly & Charles A. Ferguson (eds), *On conditionals*, 353–372. Cambridge: Cambridge University Press.

Gentens, Caroline, Ditte Kimps, Kristin Davidse, Gilles Jacobs, An Van linden & Lieselotte Brems. 2016. Mirativity and rhetorical structure: The development and prosody of disjunct and anaphoric adverbials with 'no' wonder. In Gunther Kaltenböck, Evelien Keizer & Arne Lohmann (eds.), *Outside the clause: form and function of extra-clausal constituents*, 125–156. Amsterdam: Benjamins.

Gras, Pedro & María Sol Sansiñena. 2015. An interactional account of discourse-connective que-constructions in Spanish. *Text & Talk* 35 (4). 505–529.

Gras, Pedro. 2012. Entre la gramática y el discuro: Valores conectivos de *que* inicial átono en español. In Daniel Jacob & Katja Ploog (eds.), *Autour de Que. El Entomo de Que*, 89–112. Frankfurt: Peter Lang.

Gras, Pedro. 2016. Revisiting the functional typology of insubordination: *que*-initial sentences in Spanish. In Nicholas Evans & Honoré Watanabe (eds.), *Dynamics of Insubordination*, 113–144. Amsterdam & Philadelphia: Benjamins.

Green, Georgia M. 1976. Main clause phenomena in subordinate clauses. *Language* 52 (2). 382–397.

Günthner, Susannne. 1996. From subordination to coordination? Verb-Second position in German causal and concessive constructions. *Pragmatics* 6 (3). 323–371.

Haegeman, Liliane. 1984. Pragmatic conditionals in English. *Folia Linguistica* 18. 485–502.

Haegeman, Liliane. 2003. Conditional clauses: external and internal syntax. *Mind and Language* 18 (4). 317–339.

Haiman, John. 1994. Ritualization and the development of language. In William Pagliuca (ed.), *Perspectives on Grammaticalization*, 3–28. Amsterdam: Benjamins.

Harder, Peter. 2003. The status of linguistic facts: Rethinking the relation between cognition, social institution and utterance from a functional point of view. *Mind and Language* 18 (1). 52–76.

Heine, Bernd, Gunther Kaltenböck & Tania Kuteva. 2016. On insubordination and cooptation. In Nicholas Evans & Honoré Watanabe (eds.), *Dynamics of Insubordination*, 39–64. Amsterdam & Philadelphia: Benjamin.

Heine, Bernd, Gunther Kaltenböck, Tania Kuteva & Haiping Long. 2017. Cooptation as a discourse strategy. *Journal of Linguistics* 55 (4). 813–855.

Heine, Bernd, Gunther Kaltenböck, Tania Kuteva & Haiping Long. 2013. An outline of discourse grammar. In Shannon Bischoff & Carmen Jany (eds.), *Functional Approaches to Language*, 155–206. Berlin: Mouton de Gruyter.

Hilpert, Martin. 2015. Kollaborative insubordination in gesprochenem English: Konstruktion oder Umgang mit Konstruktionen? In Alexander Ziem & Alexander Lasch (eds.),

Konstruktionsgrammatik IV. Konstruktionen als soziale Konventionen und kognitive Routinen, 25–40. Tübingen: Stauffenburg

Hooper, Joan B. & Sandra Thompson. 1973. On the acceptability of root transformations. *Linguistic Inquiry* 4 (4). 465–497.

Huddleston, Rodney & Geoffrey K. Pullum. 2002. *The Cambridge grammar of the English language*. Cambridge: Cambridge University Press.

Huddleston, Rodney. 1984. *Introduction to the grammar of English*. Cambridge: Cambridge University Press.

Kac, Michael B. 1972. Clauses of saying and the interpretation of *because*. *Language* 48 (3). 626–632.

Kaltenböck, Gunther. (in preparation). Semi-insubordination in English: form and function.

Kaltenböck, Gunther, Bernd Heine & Tania Kuteva. 2011. On thetical grammar. *Studies in Language* 35 (4). 848–893.

Kaltenböck, Gunther. 2003. On the syntactic and semantic status of anticipatory *it*. *English Language and Linguistics* 7 (2). 235–255.

Kaltenböck, Gunther. 2007. Spoken parenthetical clauses in English. In Nicole Dehé & Yordanka Kavalova (eds.), *Parentheticals*, 25–52. Amsterdam & Philadelphia: Benjamins.

Kaltenböck, Gunther. 2016. On the grammatical status of insubordinate *if*-clauses. In Gunther Kaltenböck, Evelien Keizer & Arne Lohmann (eds.), *Outside the clause: form and function of extra-clausal constituents*, 341–377. Amsterdam: Benjamins.

Kiparsky, Paul & Carol Kiparsky. 1970. Fact. In Manfred Bierwisch & Karl E. Heidolph (eds.), *Progress in Linguistics*, 143–173. The Hague: Mouton.

Lakoff, George. 1974. Syntactic amalgams. *Chicago Linguistic Society* 10. 321–44.

Langacker, Ronald W. 2000. A dynamic usage-based model. In Michael Barlow & Suzanne Kemmer (eds.), *Usage-Based Models of Language*, 1–63. Stanford: CSLI Publications.

Laury, Ritva. 2012. Syntactically non-integrated Finnish *Jos* 'If'-conditional clauses as directives. *Discourse Processes* 49 (3–4). 213–242.

Lindström, Jan, Camilla Lindholm & Ritva Laury. 2016. The interactional emergence of conditional clauses as directives: Constructions, trajectories and sequences of action. *Language Sciences* 58. 8–21.

Lombardi Vallauri, Edoardo. 2004. Grammaticalization of syntactic incompleteness: Free conditionals in Italian and other languages. *SKY Journal of Linguistics* 17. 189–215.

Lombardi Vallauri, Edoardo. 2010. Free conditionals. *Linguisticæ Investigationes* 33 (1). 50–85.

Mato-Míguez, Beatriz. 2014. *If you would like to lead*: on the grammatical status of directive isolated *if*-clauses in spoken British English. In Alejandro Alcaraz-Sintes & Salvador Valera-Hernández (eds.), *Diachrony and synchrony in English corpus linguistics*, 259–283. Bern: Peter Lang.

Michaelis, Laura A. 2001. Exclamative constructions. In Martin Haspelmath, Ekkehard König, Wulf Oesterreicher & Wolfgang Raible (eds.), *Language Typology and Language Universals*, 1038–1050. Berlin: Walter de Gruyter.

Mithun, Marianne. 2008. The extension of dependency beyond the sentence. *Language* 84 (1). 69–119.

Nelson, Gerald, Sean Wallis & Bas Aarts. 2002. *Exploring Natural Language. Working with the British Component of the International Corpus of English*. Amsterdam & Philadelphia: John Benjamins.

Ono, Tsuyoshi & Elizabeth Couper-Kuhlen. 2007. 'Incrementing' in conversation. A comparison of practices in English, German and Japanese. *Pragmatics* 17 (4). 513–552.

Quirk, Randolph, Sidney Greenbaum, Geoffrey Leech & Jan Svartvik. 1985. *A Comprehensive Grammar of the English Language*. London: Longman.

Rutherford, William W. 1970. Some observations concerning subordinate clauses in English. *Language* 46 (1). 97–115.

Sansiñena, María Sol, Hendrik De Smet & Bert Cornillie. 2015. Between subordinate and insubordinate. Paths toward complementizer-initial main clauses. *Journal of Pragmatics* 77. 3–19.

Sansiñena, María Sol. 2015. The multiple functional load of *que*. An interactional approach to insubordinate complement clauses in Spanish. Leuven: University of Leuven dissertation.

Schwenter, Scott A. 2016. Independent *si*-clauses in Spanish: Functions and consequences for insubordination. In Nicholas Evans & Honoré Watanabe (eds.), *Dynamics of insubordination*, 89–112. Amsterdam: Benjamins.

Stenström, Anna-Brita. 1998. From Sentence to Discourse. *Cos (because)* in Teenage Talk. In Andreas H. Jucker & Yael Ziv (eds.), *Discourse markers: Descriptions and theory*, 127–146. Amsterdam: Benjamins.

Stirling, Lesley. 1998. Isolated *if*-clauses in Australian English. In Peter Collins & David Lee (eds.), *The clause in English: In honour of Rodney Huddleston*, 273–294. Amsterdam: Benjamins.

Sweetser, Eve E. 1984. *Semantic structure and semantic change: a cognitive linguistic study of modality, perception, speech acts, and logical relations*. Berkeley: University of California dissertation.

Torres Cacoullos, Rena & James A. Walker. 2009. On the persistence of grammar in discourse formulas: a variationist study of that. *Linguistics* 47 (1). 1–43.

Van linden, An & Freek Van de Velde. 2014. (Semi-)autonomous subordination in Dutch: Structures and semantic-pragmatic values. *Journal of Pragmatics* 60. 226–250.

Verstraete, Jean-Christophe & Sarha D'Hertefelt. 2016. Running in the family: Patterns of complement insubordination in Germanic. In Nicholas Evans & Honoré Watanabe (eds.), *Insubordination*, 65–87. Amsterdam & Philadelphia: John Benjamins.

Verstraete, Jean-Christophe, Sarah D'Hertefelt & An Van Linden. 2012. A typology of complement insubordination in Dutch. *Studies in Language* 36. 123–153.

Verstraete, Jean-Christophe. 2007. *Rethinking the coordinate-subordinate dichotomy: Interpersonal grammar and the analysis of adverbial clauses in English*. Berlin: Mouton de Gruyter.

Verstraete, Jean-Christophe. 2008. The status of purpose, reason, and intended endpoint in the typology of complex sentences: implications for layered models of clause structure. *Linguistics* 46 (4). 757–788.

María Sol Sansiñena

6 Patterns of (in)dependence

Abstract: Complementizer *que* 'that' has a multiple functional load in that it not only marks the finiteness of the clause but also signals a pragmatic meaning to the speech participant when it is used without a matrix verb. This study discusses the interconnectedness of some diverse functions associated with *que* by addressing the phenomenon of 'semi-insubordination' (Van linden and Van de Velde 2014) in Spanish, discussing it against the pattern <preface + *que*-clause> and the case of 'causal' *que*. Specifically, this chapter focusses on the diverse relations that are established between *que*-clauses and immediately preceding elements in the turn, as well as what types of premodifying elements contribute to the interpretation of the *que*-clause. Based on the interactional-constructional analysis of real conversational data, and mainly taking into account the structure of the turn-intervention, it will be argued that the relation between the *que*-clause and the preceding element is essentially different depending on whether they constitute two turn-constructional units (TCUs) or only one. Moreover, the preceding element is classified according to its function in discourse, either as preface, element with illocutionary force or modal element.

1 Introduction

Spanish *que*-constructions can function as syntactically independent sentences, i.e. as *insubordinate constructions* (see Evans 2007, Evans and Watanabe 2016).[1] However, the empirical evidence shows that there are types and degrees of (in)dependence available for constructions formally marked as subordinate (see D'Hertefelt 2018 for Germanic languages and Sansiñena 2015 for Spanish). Between the traditional 'dependent' use of a subordinate clause, i.e. as part of a complex sentence, and the 'main clause' use of a formally subordinate clause, i.e. insubordination, there are different intermediate degrees of (in)dependence, including various types of *dyadic* dependence[2] (see Sansiñena et al. 2015) and

---

[1] See Gras (2011, 2013, 2016), Gras & Sansiñena (2015) and Sansiñena (2015) for discussions on insubordinate complement constructions in Spanish.

[2] Dyadically dependent clauses have the complementizer *que* in sentence-initial position and lack an explicit matrix, but can be construed as dependent on a matrix from the previous turn.

María Sol Sansiñena, University of Leuven

https://doi.org/10.1515/9783110638288-007

semi-insubordination (see Van linden and Van de Velde 2014 as well as other chapters in this volume).

Furthermore, there are also different levels upon which a structure might be dependent (e.g. functional vs. syntactic). Gras & Sansiñena (2015) and Sansiñena (2015), for example, discuss constructions introduced by *que* in Spanish which are not syntactically dependent on any main clause element but are 'pragmatically' dependent (in the sense of Lindström and Londen 2008) on preceding discourse. Verstraete et al. (2012) and D'Hertefelt & Verstraete (2014) discuss 'that'-constructions in Dutch and in Swedish and Danish, respectively, which also have a wide or discursive scope.[3]

This paper deals with *que*-constructions in Spanish that, in different ways, relate to a previous element in the speaker's turn, and discusses the wealth of semantic relations found between *que*-clauses and the various types of preceding elements, as well as the syntactic status of these constructions within the gradient from syntactic dependence to insubordination.

The term 'semi-insubordination' has been coined by Van linden and Van de Velde to refer to a construction type in Dutch in which the *dat*-clause is preceded by one single element which "seems to function at matrix clause level" (Van linden and Van de Velde 2014: 231), as in (1). This preceding element can be adverbial, adjectival or nominal.

(1) *misschien* **da**'k *als bob*   *stomdronken toch*
     maybe   CONJ.I as   designated.driver dead.drunk nevertheless
     binnen zal   mogen : -)))
     inside will may
     'Maybe [that], as a designated driver I will nevertheless be allowed to get in dead drunk *smile*.'
     (CONDIV, IRC, Brug 1; cited in Van linden and Van de Velde 2014: 231)

Semi-insubordinate constructions are also found in Spanish, as exemplified in (2) to (4). In these constructions, the *que*-clause functions as the propositional content of a modal element and the pattern <element + *que*-clause> constitutes one turn-constructional unit (henceforth abbreviated as TCU).[4] In (2), B's first

---

3 See Mithun (2008, 2016) for a description and discussion of other types of discourse-organizing constructions in languages indigenous to North America and the process of extension of dependency from sentence to discourse domain.

4 A turn-constructional unit (TCU) is the smallest unit which can form a turn at talk (See Sacks, Schegloff and Jefferson 1974; Ford and Thompson 1996; Schegloff 1996).

TCU is headed by the evidential adverb *obviamente* 'obviously', which intensifies the strength of the assertion.

(2) [Two senators discuss a law of public ethics at an ordinary session of the Senate]

A: *Quizás, obviamente, usted no lo ignora, señor senador, pero la ley de ética pública que hemos sancionado permite el acceso a cualquier ciudadano a las declaraciones de bienes que hacemos todos los funcionarios públicos.* [. . .]

B: *Obviamente **que** no me refiero a la declaración de bienes.*[5] *Eso lo sabemos todos, porque todos hemos sancionado la ley de ética pública.*

'A: Maybe, obviously, you do not ignore it, Mr. Senator, but the law of public ethics that we have passed allows any citizen to have access to the asset declarations that all civil servants do. [. . .]

B: Obviously [that] I do not mean the declaration of assets. We all know that, because we have all sanctioned the law on public ethics.'
(CREA oral, Reunión 65, sesión ordinaria 32, Senado de la Nación, Argentina)

In (3), the adjectival adverb[6] *claro* 'clearly, of course' expresses confidence about the propositional content of the *que*-clause, i.e. the fact that somebody will check whether the IDs of people who signed the petition are real.

(3) [A group of friends talk about signing a petition]
G03: *es una recogida de firmas para evitar que demuelan unos edificios por aquí*
[. . .]
G03: *eso no lo comprueban (.) o sea si me invento un DNI ahora no lo comprueban no/*
G04: *[nada tú firma ahí]*
G02: *[claro **que** lo comprueban Lucas]*

---

5 For the sake of clarity, semi-insubordinate constructions will be completely underlined. Whenever discussing another type of pattern, only the element or structure preceding the *que*-clause is underlined.

6 The so-called *adjectival adverbs* or short adverbs often alternate with the corresponding forms in *-mente*, as in *llegar {rápido ~ rápidamente}* 'to arrive fast'; *hablar {claro ~ claramente}* 'to speak clearly'.

'G03: it's a petition to collect signatures to prevent some nearby buildings
to be demolished
[. . .]
G03: they don't check it (.) I mean if I make up an ID now
they will not check it right/
G04: [nothing you sign there]
G02: [of course [that] they check it Lucas]'
(MAESB2-02, COLA M)

Finally, the interjection derived from the noun *lástima* 'pity' used in (4) preceding a *que*-clause in the subjunctive mood develops a factive or evaluative component. This use of *lástima* is created from the structure <*ser una lástima que* + subjunctive> 'to be a pity that + subjunctive', in which the attribute *una lástima* 'a pity' imposes the subjunctive mood to the subordinate noun clause acting as the subject of the sentence (RAE-AALE 2009: §25.14t).

(4) [Two journalists comment on a football match]

A: *¿Lo ha visto animado, ahora?*
B: *Sí sí sí sí. Está muy animado y y muy esperanzado ya pensando en el partido del domingo, que % muy bien.*
A: *Lástima **que** Ronaldo fallara esos dos goles, aunque también marcó uno y otro.*
B: *Sí, además uno muy difícil. El gol de cabeza para mí ha sido muy espectacular y muy bonito.*

'A: Have you seen him lively, now?
B: Yes yes yes yes. He's very lively and and very hopeful already thinking about the Sunday match, that % very well.
A: Too bad [that] Ronaldo missed those goals, although he did score one and another one.
B: Yes, besides a very difficult one. The headed goal has been to me very spectacular and very nice.'
(CREA oral, *Supergarcía*, Cadena COPE, Spain)

The purpose of this chapter is to account for the distribution and functional properties of the semi-insubordinate construction <element + *que*-clause>, as in (2)–(4), and to disentangle this construction from other related, but different constructions, such as discourse-connective *que*-clauses preceded by prefaces, as in (5) below, and the so-called 'causal *que*', as in (6) below. In the latter use, the relation linking the two component clauses has been referred to as either 'subordination' (see RAE-AALE 2009: §46.6) or 'parataxis' and 'sociation', a concept used by Lehmann (1988) to refer to relations closer to the left pole of the continuum of hierarchical downgrading (see Aliaga García and Bustos Guadaño 1997; Iglesias Recuero 2000). [7]

(5) [An adolescent has fallen in the mud]

> J01: _tronco_ **que** _me da vergüenza ajena_
> G01: _qué/_
> J01: _que se ha caído en todo en el barro_

> 'J01: dude [QUE] I fell embarrased for him/her
> G01: what/
> J01: that (s)he has fallen in the mud'
> (MABPE2-07, COLA M)

(6) [An adolescent realizes it is getting late]

> J02: _qué hora es_ **que** _yo me voy_

> 'J02: what time is it [QUE] I'm leaving'
> (MAMTE2-02B, COLA M)

The questions to be resolved are the following: First, what is the relation between the preceding element and the _que_-clause? Second, by virtue of those relations, what types of elements can precede the _que_-clause? To answer these questions, it will be necessary to clarify whether the combination of the procedural meaning of _que_ with the meaning of a preceding modal element has a compositional or unitary structure. To this end, the analysis will make use of formal and semantic criteria which will be described in Section 3.

The rest of this chapter is organized as follows. Section 2 discusses the phenomenon of semi-insubordination (Van linden and Van de Velde 2014) in more

---

7 Lehmann considers the parameter of 'hierarchical downgrading' when discussing clause linkage across languages. He argues that at the "starting pole of the continuum, there is no hierarchical relation between the two clauses forming the complex sentence. This is the situation which we call parataxis. At the end pole, there is a clear hierarchical relation between them, the subordinate clause being downgraded to a particular, well-defined constituent within the main clause. This is the situation we call embedding. Between the poles, there are various constructions in which the subordinate clause is ever more downgraded" (Lehmann 1988:184–185).

detail. The discussion draws on the evidence attested in some European languages but then homes in on semi-insubordination in Spanish. Section 3 describes the data and methodology followed. Section 4 presents the analysis of *que*-constructions in non-initial turn types preceded by one element which does not have scope over the *que*-clause, i.e. cases of <preface + discourse connective *que*-construction> and cases of 'causal *que*'. Section 5 discusses the results of the analysis of semi-insubordinate constructions in the corpus data, and presents a classification of different types of elements being the end result of the analysis. Finally, Section 6 presents the final conclusions.

2 Semi-insubordination

This section discusses the phenomenon of semi-insubordination in Spanish and proposes a classification of the preceding element according to the criterion of whether the element forms a separate speech act with its own speech functional value. In turn, a further classification scheme will be presented for the cases in which the *que*-clause and its preceding element constitute two separate TCUs, according to the type of relation linking the two.

2.1 Semi-insubordination as a cross linguistic phenomenon

Van linden and Van de Velde (2014) discuss a range of constructions in Dutch referred to as 'semi-autonomous subordination' which include proper insubordinate constructions, semi-insubordinate ones, 'cleft-like' constructions, and a 'clause-less' type which has no full subordinate clause following the *dat*-subordinator. They argue that all these types share the common property of expressing interpersonal meaning. This shared property, they suggest, can be accounted for by drawing on Croft's (2000) concept of 'hypoanalysis' or 'underanalysis':

> In hypoanalysis, the listener reanalyses a contextual semantic/functional property as an inherent property of the syntactic unit. In the reanalysis, the inherent property of the context [...] is then attributed to the syntactic unit, and so the syntactic unit in question gains a new meaning or function. (Croft 2000: 126–127)

As such, Van linden and Van de Velde's (2014: 229) hypoanalysis proposal is complementary to Evans' (2007) pathway of change involving diachronic ellipsis, but disagrees with Aelbrecht's (2006) synchronic ellipsis account of semi-insubordinate construction in that there is no textual evidence that a main clause is present in synchrony in an underlying deep structure. Their study proposes a plausible explanation for the development of semi-insubordinate constructions, explaining its mechanism of change while accounting for the reasons why speakers might have opted to leave the main clause aside. For the semi-insubordinate construction type in particular, they propose a classification of formal subtypes including adverbial, adjectival and nominal subtypes. At the same time, they argue that the semantic nature of the subtypes can be epistemic, evaluative or affective.[8] In sum, in Dutch the element preceding the *dat*-clause always expresses the speaker's attitudinal assessment of the content of the *dat*-clause.

Aelbrecht (2006) takes a different approach to the phenomenon, arguing that the semi-insubordinate construction in Belgian dialects of Dutch involves IP-ellipsis. She proposes an analysis of the construction <X + *that*-clause> in which X stands for an adverbial or adjectival phrase. Her analysis of the preceding element is based on Cinque's (1999) hierarchy of 'higher' and 'lower' adverbs, and supports the idea that the adverbs attested in the semi-insubordinate construction are the ones found in the 'higher Mod-nodes' – Mod$_{epistemic}$, Mod$_{irrealis}$ and Mod$_{necess.ty}$ – (Aelbrecht 2006: 3). Yet, her analysis does not seem to uncover the functional motivations for speakers to use the semi-insubordinate construction instead of the complex construction. Moreover, the synchronic ellipsis account is contentious, as pointed out by Van linden and Van de Velde (2014).

Adverbial semi-insubordination has been attested in several European languages, such as Swedish (*kanske att* 'maybe that'), French (*peut-être que* 'maybe that') and Spanish (*tal vez que* 'maybe that', *por supuesto que* 'certainly that') (cf. Ramat and Ricca 1998; Van linden and Van de Velde 2014: 247). Aelbrecht (2006) also points out the existence of semi-insubordinate constructions in French – restricted to the adverbial subtype – and Beijering (2016) and Beijering & Norde (this volume) have also attested instances of the construction in Norwegian (*bra at* 'good that', *flaks at* 'luck that') and Swedish (*måhända att* 'perhaps that'), respectively. Kaltenböck (this volume) offers a discussion on semi-insubordination in contemporary English and argues that insubordination and semi-insubordination should both be treated as a category of theticals. The following subsection presents some previous accounts of the <element + *que*-clause> construction in Spanish.

---

8 Note that for the formal 'adverbial' subtype there is no semantic 'affective' subtype available, while for the formal 'adjectival' subtype there is no semantic 'epistemic' subtype available.

2.2 Semi-insubordinate constructions in Spanish

Semi-insubordinate constructions in Spanish are constructions in which the *que*-clause is preceded by one element that is not a full matrix clause, i.e. the *que*-clause occurs without a full main clause, but in combination with a complement-taking predicate. For Spanish, there is still no clear description of what type of elements can precede a *que*-clause in a semi-insubordinate construction.[9] Moreover, there is still no account that satisfactorily explains what determines the presence of *que* in those constructions and whether its presence is required by formal features – such as the selection of a lexical piece like *ojalá* –, semantic features, – such as the expression of evidentiality –, or pragmatic features, – such as a formal or informal register. As is discussed below, most previous studies account for the semi-insubordinate construction from a syntactic approach and take as the maximum unit of analysis an extended projection of the sentence, i.e. the left periphery. However, little attention is directed to the functioning of the construction <element + *que*> in talk-in-interaction.

Rodríguez Ramalle (2008b) presents an analysis of so-called derived interjections such as *anda* lit. 'go', *vaya* lit. 'go' and *mira* lit. 'look', which admit a following clause introduced by the conjunction *que*. According to her, these interjections express a degree reading when they appear in a sentence together with a noun, adjective or verb susceptible to being measured on a scale. Rodríguez Ramalle (2011) compares the construction <interjection + *que*-clause>, such as in *mira que* lit. 'look that', to the construction <evidential adverb + *que*-clause>, as in *naturalmente que* lit. 'naturally that', and argues that although the first one has a broader range of uses, in some cases, both constructions are used to perform an emphatic reaction. Rodríguez Ramalle contends that whenever the interjection is combined with – occurs immediately before – *que*, "it cannot be separated from it" (2011: 215). However, as will be shown, interjections such as *mira* are attested in the corpus data preceding *que* both (i) as a separate TCU (see example (9) below) and (ii) in constructions expressing a degree reading (see example (10) below).

Demonte and Fernández Soriano (2013) argue that in the cases in which the so-called 'interjection' forms a unit with the *que*-clause, the first element actually functions as an adverbial phrase, similar to the cases of *Bien que* lit. 'well that' and *Sí que* lit. 'yes that' discussed by Hernanz (2007) and Pons (1998).

---

9 See Rodríguez Ramalle (2007, 2008a, 2008b, 2011) on the use of interjections and evidential adverbs preceding *que*-clauses.

In line with Hernanz (2007), Demonte and Fernández Soriano support the idea that the adverbs occupy the position of specifiers and "typify the sentence as declarative, in relation with a previous speech act" (Demonte and Fernández Soriano 2013: 60).

Following a pragmatic approach, Pons (1998) works on the basis of empirical evidence from corpus data and proposes the label *que soldador* 'welder *que*' to refer to the *que* which joins one word to the rest of the utterance, as in the case of *claro que* lit. 'clear that', *bien que* lit. 'well that', *sí que* lit. 'yes that'. He suggests that the *que soldador* is related to lexicalization processes that may lead to formal fixation of *que* together with the form which it used to previously 'weld' to the rest of the utterance. Pons argues that by means of the *que soldador* units can change from being parenthetical, located to the left of an utterance, to being integrated. This process, according to Pons (1998), involves a reanalysis that in turn implies a categorical change, in line with insights from grammaticalization studies. His account takes into consideration a wide range of elements with a very different syntactic and semantic nature – such as adverbs, adjectives, conjunctions and conjunctive phrases and other expression types – which are analysed according to whether they constitute a discourse unit and what kind of unit. However, he is not particularly concerned with delimiting instances of use of the '*que* soldador' from cases of the so-called 'causal *que*'.[10]

These and other previous studies (see Etxepare 2008, 2010; Serret Lancharez 2012, among others) provide a valuable general characterization of some of the elements that appear in first position in the semi-insubordinate construction. However, they do not explicitly distinguish between cases in which the *que*-clause and the preceding element constitute one construction from cases in which the *que*-clause and the preceding element constitute two TCUs and, therefore, enter into a different discourse relation. This paper aims at filling such a gap.

3 Data and methodology

The linguistic data used in this study come from the COLA (*Corpus Oral del Lenguaje Adolescente*) and from the spoken section from Spain of the CREA

---

10 Pons (1998) provides an example of use of 'causal *que*' and comments that in some cases it is difficult to differentiate the '*que soldador*' from the '*que inespecífico*', which coordinates two sequences between which a specific syntactic relation cannot be established.

(*Corpus de Referencia del Español Actual*). The COLA contains conversations among adolescents of both sexes who are native speakers of Spanish from Madrid (Spain), Santiago de Chile (Chile), and Buenos Aires (Argentina). The informants carry minidiscs and record spontaneous interactions among friends, classmates and family members in diverse settings. The original transcripts in the COLA were revised and compared to the original recordings, and the transcripts were adjusted when they did not match the recordings.

The instances of semi-insubordinate constructions under examination were collected by querying the components of the COLA for *que*-clauses constructed with verbs in both subjunctive and indicative mood in non-initial position in the turn, manually selecting the cases with preceding elements (1 or 2 words preceding *que*), and filtering out the noise.[11] Some instances of combinations of *que*-clauses with preceding elements are mentioned in the literature but were not attested in the COLA. For these patterns, examples were collected by querying the oral component of the CREA.

The analysis presented here makes use of certain formal and semantic criteria. Attention is paid to the meanings expressed by semi-insubordinate constructions, their near equivalence to plain *que*-clause alternatives – if any –, the restrictions on the meaning of the *que*-clause imposed by the preceding element, the potential for an intonation break between the *que*-clause and the element that precedes it, and the type of syntactic relation between the *que*-clause and the preceding element.

A classification of the type of preceding element was established according to (i) whether the element forms a separate speech act and, therefore, whether it constitutes a separate TCU, as in (6), repeated here as (7), and (ii) taking into account the functional value of the element. These cases are not regarded as instances of semi-insubordination.

(7) [An adolescent realizes it is getting late]

> J02: *qué hora es **que** yo me voy*

> 'J02: <u>what time is it</u> [QUE] I'm leaving'
> (MAMTE2-02B, COLA M)

Contrariwise, cases in which the <element + *que*-clause> constitute one TCU, as in (3) above, repeated here as (8), are considered instances of semi-insubordination

---

11 Noise here includes complex sentences such as *Sabía que allí abajo había dos* 'I knew that there were two down there' (MAESB2-03, COLA M).

and are classified in semantic subtypes. These cases will be dealt in detail in Section 5.

(8)   [A group of friends talk about signing a petition]

    G03: *es una recogida de firmas para evitar que demuelan unos edificios por aquí*

    [...]

    G03: *eso no lo comprueban* (.) *o sea si me invento un DNI ahora no lo comprueban no/*

    G04: [*nada tú firma ahí*]

    G02: [*claro **que** lo comprueban Lucas*]

    'G03: it's a petition to collect signatures to prevent some nearby buildings to be demolished

    [...]

    G03: they don't check it (.) I mean if I make up an ID now they will not check it right/

    G04: [nothing you sign there]

    G02: [of course [that] they check it Lucas]'

    (MAESB2-02, COLA M)

The present study takes an interactional perspective, mainly taking into account the structure of the turn-intervention and type of turn, and presents an inventory of types of combinations between a *que*-clause and a preceding element. This interactional analysis also integrates other features that contribute to the identification of the structure of the turn, such as intonation breaks and the grammatical category of the preceding element.

First, instances of <X + *que*-clause> are divided according to whether they constitute one or two TCUs, as they reflect different syntactic and discourse relations. Whenever there are two TCUs, the first one can be constituted by (i) a preface which expresses different attitudinal, interpersonal and metadiscursive values, followed by the main component – constituted by the *que*-clause – or (ii) an element with illocutionary force – usually, but not necessarily, directive force – followed by a justification. In the case of <preface + *que*-clause> I will consider the second TCU to be a discourse-connective *que*-construction.[12]

---

12 In discourse-connective *que*-constructions, as (a), the complementizer *que* lacks an accompanying matrix clause and it connects the clause it introduces with preceding discourse (see Gras and Sansiñena 2015):

In the case of <element with illocutionary force + *que*-clause> the relation between the two components resembles reason clauses in some respects and 'sociation' (in the spirit of Lehmann 1988) in others.[13] Whenever there is only one TCU, the first position in the unit is occupied by a modal element which resembles a finite modal predicate. In the case <modal element + *que*-clause>, I consider the construction to be semi-insubordinate.

One methodological side-note is in order at this point. Some elements can appear in more than one of the three patterns just discussed, with changes in meaning. *Mira*, for example, has been attested in multi-unit turns (Ford, Fox and Thompson 1996; Ford and Thompson 1996; Ford, Fox and Thompson 2002), functioning as a preface to a *que*-clause, but also introducing a *que*-clause over which it has scope, in a single TCU within the turn. When it is not used as a full verb, *mira* is an interjection derived from the imperative of the perception verb *mirar* 'to look'. It shows a lower degree of lexicalization than other interjections derived from imperative verbs such as *toma* 'take' or *venga* 'come' and therefore it admits some variation in form – *mirá; mire* – (RAE-AALE 2009: 2501).

In (9), for instance, *mira* functions as a preface in a multi-unit turn and is used to maintain and to reinforce the interlocutor's attention, i.e. with a phatic function. It has an independent status with regard to the *que*-clause. The *que* in (9) introduces a clause in the subjunctive mood with directive meaning. In (10), however, *mira* introduces a *que*-clause in the indicative mood and takes the role of external quantifier of an internal component of the predicate. There is

---

(a) [Two friends talking about their weight]

J02: *he engordado (.) es que yo me siento más gorda es que es verdad*
J01: *[**que** yo no te veo más gorda (.) yo te veo perfecta tía como antes]*
J02: *[no he engordado]*

'J02: I've put on weight (.) it's like I feel fatter it's true
J01: [[QUE] you don't look fatter to me (.) you look perfect to me pal like before]
J02: [no I've put on weight]'
(MABPE2-01B, COLA M)

13 The relation between preface and *que*-clause on the one hand and element with illocutionary force and *que*-clause on the other can be explained within the frame of the Val.Es.Co.'s (2014) theory of discourse units, using the notions of *substantive* and *adjacent subacts*. A subact is an immediate constituent of the act which counts as an informative segment, usually identifiable by semantic and prosodic marks (Val.Es.Co. 2014: 55), and which combines with other subacts to convey full propositional meaning (Cabedo Nebot 2014: 163). Substantive subacts convey propositional content while adjacent subacts do not convey propositional content.

a short intonation break between *mira* and the *que*-clause in (9), while there is no intonation break in (10), what nicely reflects two different patterns. The uses of elements as prefaces in multi-unit turns and as introductory elements in a single TCU will be discussed in Sections 4 and 5, respectively.

(9) [A group of friends watching TV and smoking marijuana]

> J01: *ah cállate Pepa y Miguel por favor vete que me duele la cabeza eh/*
> G03: *vuela*
> G02: *bueno si a ti te duele la cabeza es que*
> 1[*a mí imagínate*]
> J01:1[*mira* (.) **que** *te pires tronco*]
> G02: 2[*eh/*]
> J01: 2[*que te pires que te pires*]

> 'J01: oh shut up Pepa and Migue͟ please go away [QUE] my head aches eh/
> G03: fly away
> G02: right if you have a headache it's like
> 1[imagine how I feel]
> J01: 1[look (.) [QUE] go away man]
> G02:2[eh/]
> J01: 2[[QUE] go away [QUE] go away]'
> (MALCC2-07, COLA M)

(10) A: *Hola, ¿qué hacéis cavernícolas?*
> B: *Hemos inventado la rueda.*
> C: *Hemos inventado la rueda.*
> D: *Hemos inventado la rueda.*
> A: *Mira* **que** *sois tontícolas.*

> 'A: Hi, what are you doing cavemen?
> B: We've invented the wheel.
> C: We've invented the wheel.
> D: We've invented the wheel.
> A: You are so silly!'
> (CREA Oral, Magacines, Tariro, tariro, Spain)

According to RAE-AALE (2009), *mira* functions in contexts like (10) as an 'emphatic particle' which does not inflect for person or number, i.e. it is strongly grammaticalized, and it cannot introduce a direct complement, which implies the *que*-clause does not function as direct complement either. *Mira* assumes the grammatical role of quantifier and affects the internal components of the predicate, so that '*Mira que sois tontícolas*' means 'You are very silly!'. Sánchez López (2017) argues that *mira* in this construction is a mirative marker which expresses an intensified quantity and denotes a stronger presence of the expression of the speaker's subjectivity than in its use as the imperative form of verb *mirar* 'to look'. In examples like (10) *mira* is indeed used to weigh a fact or event.

4 Two turn-constructional units

This section presents the analysis of *que*-clauses which appear in multi-unit turns preceded by other linguistic elements such as vocatives, primary interjections or expressions derived from lexicalized forms. Any type of *que*-clause, constructed with a verb either in the subjunctive or indicative, can be used in these complex turns preceded by another element which contributes to the interpretation of the *que*-clause, but does not have scope over it.

4.1 Preface + *que*-clause: Attitudinal, interpersonal and metadiscursive values

The preceding elements that express attitudinal, interpersonal and metadiscursive values are address terms (vocatives), interjections, and expressions derived from lexicalized forms. These elements are not syntactically integrated with the following turn-constructional unit, i.e. the *que*-clause, and they differ greatly in their semantic and functional import. Moreover, they can occur in different positions in the turn, such as turn-initial or turn-medial , but also in different positions in the conversational sequence, i.e. in initiating, responsive or closing position, showing diverse functional significance. The following subsections provide an analysis of each type of preceding elements.

4.1.1 Vocative expressions

Vocative expressions can be personal names and nicknames, nouns, pronouns and nominal groups that are used to address somebody or to call somebody else's attention[14] in order to initiate a conversational sequence and to address a question, a greeting, an order, a request, an apology or a warning to somebody. They are usually constructed without a determiner and are directed to the addressee to elicit a response or reaction (see RAE-AALE 2009: 2485; 3200).

Vocatives attested in the corpus data include names and nicknames (Cris, Pepe, etc.), and many nouns such as *gilipollas* 'asshole', *huevón* 'jerk', *chaval* 'kid', *hijo/a* 'son/daughter', *madre* 'mother', *tío/a* 'uncle/aunt', *tronco/a* 'friend', *macho* 'man', *colega* 'friend'. They function as prefaces in complex turns and they can appear initiating first (11) or second (12) parts of adjacency pairs.

(11) [An adolescent cannot hear his friend talking]

> J02: *pero parecéis gilipollas los dos*
> [*es que me río de vosotros*]
> G01: [venga ahora]
> venga quítasela
> J01: *tío **que** no te escucho habla un poco más alto*
> G02: *no*
>
> 'J02: but you both seem like assholes
> [it's like I laugh at you]
> G01: [come on now]
> come on take it away from her
> J01: dude [QUE] I can't hear you speak a bit louder
> G02: no'
> (MAMTE2-06A, COLA M)

(12) [A group of friends learning how to die somebody's hair]

> J03: *que no sé pintarle el pelo* (.) *o cómo lo lleva*
> [. . .]
> J03: *haces así/*
> J04: *gilipollas **que** es fácil haces así luego para allá*
>
> 'J03: [QUE] I don't know how to dye her hair (.) or how she wears it
> [. . .]
> J03: you do like this/
> J04: moron [QUE] it's easy you do like this then to that side'
> (MALCE2-04A, COLA M)

---

14 They can also be directed to animals or personified things.

4.1.2 Interjections

Interjections can be classified into 'primary' and 'secondary'[15] according to their grammatical nature, as proposed by Ameka (1992) (see also Nübling 2004 and Norrick 2007, among others). Primary interjections such as *epa* 'whoops' or *oh* 'oh' are only used as interjections[16] and, as Norrick (2007) points out, show little association with a specific pragmatic function. Secondary interjections are derived from nominal (*ojo,* lit. 'eye'), verbal (*venga,* lit. 'come'), adverbial (*fuera,* lit. 'out') or adjectival (*claro,* lit. 'clear') content words. The polyvalent character of interjections makes it possible for them to be used in a wide range of contexts and gives rise to many interpretations which are not always accounted for in reference grammars or dictionaries of the language. In this section, a distinction will be made between primary interjections and secondary interjections, which include one-word expressions and multiword expressions.

The primary interjections that precede *que*-clauses in the COLA data are *ah, ay, eh, hey, ja, je, ji, jo, oh, uf, uh* and *uy.* These are syntactically independent, and can be classified in emotive, cognitive and conative classes according to whether they primarily (i) express emotion, (ii) convey the speaker's mental state without expressing feeling or wanting or (iii) are used to attract the interlocutor's attention (see Ameka 1992). Those meanings are largely determined by intonation and context.

In (13), for example, *hey* signals surprise at the fact that the speaker had not noticed the presence of the interlocutor at the party, while in other contexts it is used as a truly conative interjection, to appeal to the addressee.

(13) [Adolescents leaving a party]

> J04: *bueno vamonos*
> J01: *sí* (.) *hasta luego Clara*
> <background noise>
> J01: <u>*hey*</u> **que** *no te vi* (..) *qué haces aquí*
> <pause>
> *gorroneando eh de fijo porque tienen todos aquí palmera*
>
> 'J04: ok let's go
> J01: yes (.) see you later Clara

---

15 These categories also correspond to the classes of *interjecciones propias* and *interjecciones impropias* (Alcina & Blecua 1975, RAE-AALE 2009).
16 Besides their nominalized uses (RAE-AALE 2009), such as in *el olé profundo 'the deep olé'.*

<background noise>
J01: <u>hey</u> [QUE] I didn't see you (..) what are you doing here
<pause>
scrounging eh for sure because everybody here has money'
(MALCE2-01, COLA M)

In (14) *uf* expresses annoyance at the fact that the person who is supposed to answer the phone is taking a long time to do so. In a different context *uf* is used to signal fatigue.

(14) [An adolescent trying to make a phone call]

> J03: *estoy muy inquieta estoy aburrida*
> J01: *dale más*
> <background music>
> *uf* **que** *se demora en contestar*

> '*J03: I'm very restless I'm bored
> J01: turn it up
> <background music>
> <u>ugh</u> [QUE] (s)he takes so long to answer'
> (SCACB8-01, COLA S)

In (13) and (14) the interjections contribute to signal the focus status of the propositional content of the *que*-clause. Primary interjections can also precede optative *que*-clauses, evaluatives, and other discourse connective *que*-clauses (see Sansiñena 2015).

The use of <interjection + vocative + *que*-clause> was also attested in the corpus data, e.g. (15). This type constitutes complex or multi-unit turns, in which each element contributes to the interpretation of the turn. In (15) the iterative use of *eh* expresses a singular value, different from the one that a single *eh* conveys. The repeated interjection is used by the speaker to warn the other discourse participants that they should be careful with what they talk about – given that the recording has already started –, but also to reprehend speaker J01. The single use of *eh* in the corpus data usually signals that the speaker just wants to call the interlocutor's attention.

(15) [A group of classmates talking about the minidisk recorder]

> J02: *quién lo ha traído/ eso de quién es/*
> 1[*del colegio/*]

J01: 1[noruegas]
J03: *eh eh eh tía* (.) **que** *ya está grabando*

'J02: who has brought it/ whose is that/
1[the school's/]
J01: 1[norwegians]
J03: eh eh eh girl (.) [QUE] it's already recording'
(MAORE2-08, COLA M)

Secondary interjections are derivative uses of other words or locutions which have lost their original conceptual meanings – a process known as semantic bleaching (see Traugott 1988, 2003; Hopper and Traugott 2003, among many others). The secondary interjections that act as prefaces to *que*-clauses in the COLA data are the ones derived from grammaticalized imperative verbs or adjectives. The attested instances include *anda* lit. 'go', *mira* lit. 'look', *vaya* lit. 'go' and *venga* lit. 'come', as in (16), and *bueno* lit. 'good', as in (17). Again, these interjective expressions form utterances on their own and the meanings that they express change according to the context in which they appear.

In (16) speakers A and B take each other's leave. The first move is a coherent reaction to the previous turn while the second move is an additional expression of a good wish.

(16) [A presentation on TV greets a colleague]

A: *Nos vemos. ¡Venga!*
B: *¡Venga!, **que** pases una velada sencilla.*

'A: See you. ¡Come on!'
B: ¡Come on!, have an easy going evening.'
(CREA oral, Sorteos y concursos, *Un, dos, tres, Madrid*, Spain)

In (17) *bueno* signals that it is what follows in the turn – the warning or admonition – which should be taken into account in the continuation of the interactional sequence (see Portolés 1998).[17]

(17) [A group of friends singing and playing around]

G05: *pero es que el mono lo puedo hacer rapeando*

---

17 Portolés (1998) points out that *bueno, claro* and *hombre* do not have the same distribution in written texts as in conversations.

<noise of somebody rapping>
J01: *ese es Jorge*
G01: *bueno* (.) ***que*** *quede claro que ese era Jorge eh que no era yo* <laughter>

'G05: but I can do the monkey rapping
<noise of somebody rapping>
J01: that's Jorge
G01: okay (.) let it be clear that that was Jorge eh that it wasn't me <laughter>'
(MALCC2-01b, COLA M)

Interjective phrases which constitute a single lexical unit have been attested in only very few cases in the COLA. However, some instances of use have been found in the oral component of the CREA. These multiword expressions include discourse markers such as *a ver*, lit. 'to see' used as 'let's see' (18) and *en fin*, lit. 'in end' with the meaning of 'in short' (19).

(18) [A boy talks to his sister and mother about a problem he has with a classmate]

J01: *qué te hace/*
G01: *pues ya lo he dicho que me hace una cosa que me molesta*
[. . .]
J01: *mamá no le enseñes a ser chivato al pobre*
V02: *chivato no* (.) *pero si te molesta díselo*
J01: *cuéntanoslo a nosotras que nosotras*
[*no se lo decimos a nadie*]
V02: [*a ver* (.) ***que*** *yo se lo digo a] a a a*
J01: *tú no le dices nada*
V02: *a a él*

'J01: what does he do to you/
G01: well I already said it that he does a thing that bothers me
[. . .]
J01: mom don't teach the poor guy how to be a snitch
V02: snitch no (.) but if it bothers you tell him
J01: tell it to us that we
[don't tell it to anyone]
V02: [let's see (.) [QUE] I tell it to] to to to
J01: you don't tell him anything
V02: to to him'
(MAESB2-06B, COLA M)

(19) A: *Aprovecho para decir que tanto que habláis del Zaire, que los problemas*
del Zaire no se van a acabar con esto y van a seguir y seguirán siempre, por-
que la gente la gente del Zaire tiene un tiene todavía una organización
tribal. Se comportan tal y como se comportaban hace un siglo, ¿no? O sea,
*las etnias, el odio, el odio por simple odio. En fin, **que** son organizaciones*
tribales que no han avanzado [. . .].
'A: I take this opportunity to say that you speak so much about Zaire, that
Zaire's problems are not going to end with this and are going to continue
and will always continue, because the people the people of Zaire still have
a tribal organization. They behave as they behaved a century ago, right?
I mean, ethnic groups, hatred, hatred simply for the sake of hatred. In
short, [QUE] they are tribal organizations that have not advanced [. . .].'
(CREA oral, Grupo G 12: *Biológicas*, Spain)

The interjective phrase *en fin* occupies an internal position within the turn. In (19)
it precedes a *que*-clause which functions as a turn increment after a transition-
relevance place. Discourse-connective *que*-constructions can occupy non-initial
positions in the turn, functioning as increments (see Gras and Sansiñena 2015,
2017). The *que*-clause summarizes and restates the main point put forward before,
so it needs to be interpreted in close connection to the preceding discourse. The
use of *en fin* is consistent with this recapitulation (see Portolés 1998).

4.2 'Causal' que

The so-called 'causal' *que* appears in incremental *que*-constructions used to justify the speaker's previous utterance within the same turn. These incremental
que-constructions occur in multi-unit turns in which the first TCU can be a directive speech act (20)-(22) or a desiderative utterance (23), an interrogative utterance (24), or a declarative utterance (25).[18]

---

18 This class includes declarative proforms, as in (a):

(a) [Two friends cooking. One of them wants the other one to try the ketchup]
G01: *toma mira prueba*
J02: *no no no **que** estoy comiendo chicle Pablo*

'G01: take it look try
J02: no no no [QUE] I'm chewing gum Pablo'
(MABPE2-01, COLA M)

The lexicalized form *venga* (20) has lost its referential content and its modality/illocutionary force is its most prominent feature. By using *venga* in (20) G01 expresses not only acceptance and compliance with J01's offer, but also urges her to perform the act of telling the next joke. The *que*-clause adds a motivation for the first move.

(20) [An adolescent is telling jokes to a group of friends]

> J01: *vale* (.) *oye os cuento* \
> 1[*os cuento otro/*]
> J03: 1[*je je je je je*]
> J01: 2[*os cuento otro/*]
> J03: 2[*coño*]
> G01: *venga* **que** *esto ya está aporreándose*
> G02: *esa es la cagada*

> 'J01: ok (.) hey shall I tell you\
> 1[shall I tell you another one/]
> J03:1[he he he he he]
> J01: 2[shall I tell you another one/]
> J03: 2[fuck]
> G01: come on [QUE] this is dying out
> G02: that's the shit'
> (MAESB2-03, COLA M)

The hearer-oriented interjections *cuidado* lit. 'care' (21) and *ojo* lit. 'eye' (22), derived from nouns, are used to express warnings. The *que*-clause justifies such an action.

(21) G01: *cuidado* (.) **que** *se cae*

> 'G01: be careful, [QUE] it will fall'
> (MAESB2-01C, COLA M)

(22) ¡*Ojo*, **que** *ya vi yo como le cogieron a alguien la cartera!*

> 'Be careful, [QUE] I already saw somebody's bag being stolen.'
> (CREA oral, interview CSC009, Spain)

(23) [Two skiing enthusiasts talking about a ski resort]

> Astur-Con: *En pajares, me comentan que estaba una máquina trabajando en el tubo* [...]

PUTHAM: *Ojalá, **que** ya estoy harto de esquiar sólo en el valle.*

'Astur-Con: In Pajares, they tell me that there was a machine working on the tube [. . .]
PUTHAM: Hopefully, [QUE] I'm tired of skiing only in the valley.'
(Forum nevasport, Valgrande-Pajares, Spain)

(24) [An adolescent realizes it is getting late]

J02: <u>*qué hora es*</u> (.) ***que** yo me voy*

'J02: <u>what time is it</u> (.) [QUE] I'm leaving'
(MAMTE2-02B, COLA M)

(25) [An adolescent in a hurry to leave]

J03: <u>*me voy*</u> (.) ***que** son menos cuarto*

'J03: <u>I'm leaving</u> (.) [QUE] it's quarter to the hour'
(MABPE2-01C, COLA M)

In these cases, speakers support their actions by pointing to some evidence that can be observed or inferred from the situational context, e.g. the fact that something is falling or might fall (21), the fact that there are burglars around (22) or the fact that it is late (25). These incremental *que*-constructions are used as a device to justify speaker decisions by means of making explicit a piece of evidence that can be easily accessed from contextual observation (see Gras and Sansiñena 2015, 2017). Constructions like these have been traditionally treated as causal subordinate clauses in Spanish reference grammars (see, for instance, RAE-AALE 2009: §46.6). As subordinate causal clauses, incremental *que*-constructions describe the justification for uttering a previous clause. However, unlike subordinate reason clauses, they cannot be clefted, since they are not syntactic adjuncts of the previous clause (see Verstraete 1998).

Iglesias Recuero (2000: 337–340) points out that the construction *p que q* is formed by two utterances with different illocutionary values and that the value of justification is not associated to *que* but to discourse properties, i.e. to the illocutionary and interactive values of the utterances. In this sense, the relation established between *p* and *q* does not correspond to traditional conceptions of subordination, given that *q* is never a constituent of *p*. Iglesias Recuero also suggests that in order to account for the cases of 'causal' *que*, it is necessary to adopt a broader and more "gradual conception of the relation of subordination" (2000: 341), as is clearly the case in (24) above. She follows Aliaga García and Bustos Guadaño (1997) in describing the relation between both sentences in terms of parataxis or 'sociation'. It is argued here that the case of causal *que* can be understood in connection w_th the mechanism of *dependency shift*, which describes cases "in which conjunctions that typically mark subordinate dependency on the propositional level can also come to express dependencies on the discursive level" (D'Hertefelt and Verstraete 2014: 97).

4.3 Summary

Whenever there are two TCUs, there is no semi-insubordination. The cases can be classified as either <preface + *que*-clause> or <separate speech act + *que*-clause>.

The meanings expressed by the prefaces or separate speech acts have to do with (i) attention getting, (ii) the expression of speaker's attitude or (iii) discourse organization. Each move would be possible without the other and the preceding TCU is not scoping over the *que*-clause. Tables 1 and 2 summarize the findings for the patterns corresponding to two TCUs.

Table 1: Pattern <preface + *que*-clause>.

Phenomenon	Insubordination
TCU	Two TCUs
Pattern	**<preface + *que*-clause>**
Types of prefaces	Vocative expressions
	Interjections (primary, secondary, and interjective phrases)
	Interjection + vocative expression

Table 2: Pattern <speech act + *que*-clause>.

Phenomenon	Causal *que*
TCU	Two TCUs
Pattern	**<speech act + *que*-clause>**
Types of speech acts (elements with illocutionary force)	Imperative utterance
	Desiderative utterance
	Interrogative utterance
	Declarative utterance

5 One turn-constructional unit: Semi-insubordination

This section discusses the cases which can truly be considered as instances of the phenomenon of semi-insubordination, i.e. constructions introduced by an element which has scope over the *que*-clause and which involves some kind of modal qualification of a proposition. These elements can be classified into two broad semantic categories: the ones that express subjective evaluation and imply presuppositionality, and the ones that express epistemic and evidential qualification of a proposition.

5.1 Subjective evaluation, implied presuppositionality

The first semantic category encompasses elements that express a subjective evaluation on the part of the speaker. This evaluation is concerned with the presupposed propositional content of the *que*-clause. The elements in this class are secondary interjections which consist of one-word elements and multi-word elements. One-word interjections are derived from grammaticalized imperative verbs and from nouns, and multi-word interjective expressions are derived from lexicalized forms.

5.1.1 Secondary interjections

As was pointed out in Section 2.2 some of the same elements that can occur in the two-TCUs pattern also occur in the one-TCU pattern. This is the case for secondary interjections, including one-word and multi-word expressions. In the semi-insubordinate construction, *anda* 'go', *mira* 'look', *vaya* 'go'[19] preceding a *que*-clause express degree evaluation related to counterexpectation, as in (26)–(27). It has been pointed out (see RAE-AALE 2009; Rodríguez Ramalle 2008b) that constructions such as (26) – which contains a grammaticalized perception verb and a complement clause – do not admit a degree adverb to mea-

---

19 See Octavio de Toledo y Huerta (2001–2002) on the grammaticalization of *vaya* as marker and quantifier.

sure the quality expressed in the adjective. Sánchez López (2017) considers *mira* a mirative marker which plays a significant role in the exclamative value of the *que*-clause (see Gras and Sansiñena 2017).

(26) [A group of friends having a drink]

> J02: *bueno si pues mañana estáis por la plaza por la tarde*
> <burp>
> G01: *joder* <u>*mira*</u> **que** <u>*eres cerda tronca*</u> *no tires las cosas*

> 'J02: well if tomorrow you are at the square in the afternoon
> <burp>
> G01: fuck <u>you are so dirty girl</u> don't throw away the things'
> (MABPE2-01C, COLA M)

(27) [A group of friends talking about a scout organization]

> J03: *qué coño es eso exactamente*
> J04: 1[*una organización*]
> J01: 1[*es una cosa*] *es como tipo scouts solo que internacional*
> J03: 2[*ah y va de todo el mundo y como habláis/*]
> J01: 2[*y van a campamentos de gente y eso*]
> J04: *en inglés*
> J03: *uy las dos qué guay no/*
> J01: *Ana es que está con % está sola de seminar que son en plan*
> *con gente de dieciocho años eso todos ahí*
> J03: <u>*anda*</u> **que** <u>*no sabes*</u>

> 'J03: what the fuck is that exactly
> J04: 1[an organization]
> J01: 1[it's a thing] it's like scouts but just international
> Jo3: 2[oh and there's people from all over the world and how do you talk to
> each other/]
> J01: 2[and they go camping with people and that]
> J04: in English
> J03: wow both of you how cool right/
> J01: Ana is the one who is with % is alone at a seminar which is like with
> people who are eighteen years old that all of them there
> J03: <u>You know so much!</u>'
> (MAESB2-06A, COLA M)

In (27) the *que*-clause is selected by *anda*. They form a complex construction whose value is that of degree quantification.[20] Rodríguez Ramalle (2008b) argues that in this construction the adverb *no* 'no' does not negate, but functions as an emphatic polarity element which reinforces the speaker's assertion. In this sense, it can be understood as a case of 'expletive' negation.[21]

A special case is the form *ojalá* 'I wish', which is considered by some linguists to be an interjection and by others to be an adverb (see Bosque and Demonte 1999: § 32.3.2.3; RAE-AALE 2009: §35.5o-r), given that it shares properties with both interjections and adverbs. With adverbs it shares the property of introducing the subjunctive mood, as illustrated in (28).

(28) [Adolescents talking about their plans for the weekend]

> J02: *yo no sé qué voy a hacer* (.) *el sábado*
> <sound of bell>
> J02: *ajj ajj ajj ajj* (.) *ojalá* **que** *vengan todos a* XXX

> 'J02: I don't know what to do (.) on Saturday
> <sound of bell>
> J02: ajj ajj ajj ajj (.) I wish everyone comes to XXX'
> (BABS2-10, COLA BS)

The form *ojalá* comes from the Hispanic Arabic *law sha'a Allah* 'God willing' or 'if Allah wills'. When it introduces a sentence, it admits the conjunction *que*, which is optional, a feature shared by only a few verbs, such as *demandar* 'demand' or *pedir* 'ask' (RAE-AALE 2009: §43b-j). The *que*-clause that follows *ojalá* in semi-insubordinate constructions expresses the content of what is desired. Its particular historical development – the fact that it derives from an optative sentence – explains the special features of this form.

The secondary interjections derived from nouns have not been attested in the COLA data in semi-insubordinate constructions. However, two of them are attested in the oral component of the CREA: *lástima* 'pity' (4, repeated here as 29) and *suerte* 'luck' (30). A similar analysis to the one suggested above for *lástima* + *que*-clause (see Section 1) applies to *suerte* + *que*-clause: this use of *suerte* is created from the structure <*ser una suerte que* + subjunctive> lit. 'to be

---

20 These cases have been discussed in Sansiñena (2015) and Gras and Sansiñena (2017) in relation to an insubordinate indicative evaluative construction found in Chilean Spanish.
21 The term 'expletive negation' is often used for a negative marker that has no negative meaning. For a discussion on 'expletive' negation in Romance languages, see Muller (1978), Nocentini (2003) and Pons & Schwenter (2005).

a luck that + subjunctive', in which the attribute *una suerte* 'a luck' imposes the subjunctive mood to the subordinate noun clause.

(29) [Two journalists commenting a football match]

A: *¿Lo ha visto animado, ahora?*
B: *Sí sí sí sí. Está muy animado y y muy esperanzado ya pensando en el partido del domingo, que % muy bien.*
A: *Lástima **que** Ronaldo fallara esos dos goles, aunque también marcó uno y otro.*
B: *Sí, además uno muy difícil. El gol de cabeza para mí ha sido muy espectacular y muy bonito.*

'A: Have you seen him lively, now?
B: Yes yes yes yes. He's very lively and and very hopeful already thinking about the Sunday match, that % very well.
A: Too bad **that** Ronaldo missed those goals, although he did score one and another one.
B: Yes, besides a very difficult one. The headed goal has been to me very spectacular and very nice.'
(CREA oral, *Supergarcía*, Cadena COPE, Spain)

(30) [A reporter talking about the Spanish athlete Antonio Prieto]

A: *En enero de mil novecientos ochenta y seis se operó, y no pudo volver a los entrenamientos hasta el mes de abril. Suerte **que** Antonio se toma la vida con optimismo. Él dice que los dos años de lesión en el fondo le han venido bien para que el organismo haya podido regenerarse.*

'A: In January nineteen eighty six he had a surgery, and he couldn't come back to training until April. Luckily [QUE] Antonio faces life with optimism. He says the two years of injury in essence have been good for the body to be able to regenerate.'
(CREA oral, *Estadio dos*, TVE 2, Spain)

Only one interjective expression derived from a lexicalized form has been attested in the COLA data. It is the complex secondary interjection *menos mal* 'luckily' (31)–(32), which expresses the speaker's subjective evaluation of the propositional content. In (31) the speaker is glad and relieved that she is going to see her friend on the same day given that she misses her, while in (32) the speaker is relieved that they do not have to run on that day, given that she has stiff legs.

(31) [A girl talking on the phone]

> J05: *menos mal **que** hoy ya te veo* (.) *no sé lo que haría sin ti* (.)
> *en serio te quiero mazo*

> 'J05: <u>luckily [QUE] I see you today</u> (.) I don't know what I would do without
>   you (.) seriously I love you a lot'
> (MAORE2-12C, COLA M)

(32) [A group of classmates at school]

> G01: *me voy a tomar un agua con azúcar chavaal* (.) *porque tengo unas*
>   *agujetas*
> G03: *Pilar*
> G01: *menos mal **que** hoy no corremos*

> 'G01: I'm going to drink water with sugar man (.) because I have such
>   soreness
> G03: Pilar
> G01: <u>luckily [QUE] we don't run today</u>'
> (MALCE2-07B, COLA M)

5.2 Epistemic and evidential qualification of a proposition

The second broad class of elements preceding *que*-clauses in semi-insubordinate constructions encompasses sentential adverbs and adverbials expressing epistemic and evidential values. These will be presented in the following subsections: interjective expressions derived from lexicalized forms, affirmative adverbs, adverbs of doubt/uncertainty and evidential adverbs.

5.2.1 Interjective expressions derived from lexicalized forms

The only complex secondary interjection attested in the COLA data is *de verdad* 'truly' (33), but *sin duda* 'no doubt' (34) has also been attested in the spoken component of the CREA.[22] In (33) speaker G02 has already said that he has not scored

---

22 Even though *sin duda* 'no doubt' has traditionally been classified by scholars as an epistemic marker expressing varying degrees of certainty (See Simon-Vandenvergen 2007, among

a goal in two previous turns. The first time he repeats his utterance he uses an insubordinate complement construction introduced by *que* to signal repetition. The second time he repeats his utterance, he uses a semi-insubordinate construction introduced by *de verdad* to strengthen his assertion.

(33) [A group of friends playing football]

> G01: *tú has marcado un gol*
> G02: *yo no he marcado*
> G01: *sí has marcado un gol*
> G02: *je je que yo no he marcado*
> G01: *habéis empezado otro/*
> G04: *tú estás gilipollas*
> G02: 1[*de verdad* **que** *no lo he marcado*]
> G03: 1[*va por el ochenta y siete*]
> G01: *pero él no no me%* (.) *yo juraría que he visto que ha metido un gol el Luis*

> 'G01: you have scored a goal
> G02: I haven't scored a goal
> G01: yeah you have scored a goal
> G02: hehe [QUE] I haven't scored
> G01: have you started another one/
> G04: you are silly
> G02: 1[I really haven't scored it]
> G03: 1[he's scoring the eighty seventh]
> G01: but he didn't didn't sco% (.) I would swear that I've seen Luis score
>   a goal'
> (MALCE4-06, COLA M)

(34) A: *Ser su alumno era realmente un privilegio. Sin duda* **que** *exigía, pero sin llegar nunca a la exageración.*

> 'A: Being her students was really a privilege. No doubt [QUE] she demanded, but without ever getting to exaggerate.'
> (CREA oral, session of the Senate, Chile)

---

many others), it has also been assimilated to one class of evidential adverbs, in that it intensifies the strength of the assertion (see RAE-AALE 2009: §30.11o).

5.2.2 Sí 'Yes'

The sentential adverb *sí* 'yes' has been attested in semi-insubordinate constructions in the COLA data from different varieties of Spanish, showing different values in different contexts. In (35) it is used to intensify the assertion, as an adverb with *informative* focus or an emphatic adverb, while in (36) it functions as an adverb of *contrastive* focus, which requires a previous negation in the discourse context: *no tenemos a Paco Porras* 'we don't have Paco Porras', *sí que tenéis* 'indeed you have it'.

(35) A: *Otra falta personal. ¡Qué poquito habrá hecho en favor del baloncesto este encuentro!*
　　　B: *Sí **que** es verdad, en esto coincido.*

　　　A: 'Another personal foul. How little will this encounter have done for b asketball!
　　　B: Indeed [QUE] it is true, I agree on that.'
　　　(CREA oral, *Televisión*, Madrid, 02/91 F, Spain)

(36) [A girl wants to watch a film of a popular puppeteer at home]
　　　G01: *puedes poner otra peli que no sea Harry*
　　　J01: *vale cuál quieres/* <steps> (.)
　　　1[*pareces un pescadero*]
　　　V02: 1[*Paco Porras*]
　　　V01: *eh/*
　　　V02: *Paco Porras/*
　　　2[*no tenemos a Paco Porras*]
　　　J01: 2[*Paco Porras ja ja*]
　　　G01: *sí **que** tenéis*
　　　V02: *dónde está Paco Porras/*

　　　'G01: can you play another movie that is not Harry
　　　J01: ok which one do you want/ <steps> (.)
　　　1[you look like a fisherman]
　　　V02: 1[Paco Porras]
　　　V01: eh/
　　　V02: Paco Porras/
　　　2[we don't have Paco Porras]
　　　J01: 2[Paco Porras ha ha]
　　　G01: indeed [QUE] you have it

V02: where is Paco Porras/'
(MAESB2-06B, COLA M)

5.2.3 Adverbs of doubt (uncertainty)

Epistemic modal adverbials are associated with trustworthiness, possibility and uncertainty (see Kärkkäinen 2003; Simon-Vandenbergen 2007; Simon-Vandenbergen and Aijmer 2007a, 2007b; Cornillie 2010, among many others). The so called 'adverbs of doubt' are contained within this class. The only adverb of doubt attested in the corpus data in a semi-insubordinate construction is *capaz* 'maybe, possibly', which appears in the data from both Buenos Aires (37) and Santiago de Chile (10 hits in total). *Quizás* 'maybe', the functional near-equivalent to *capaz* used in Peninsular varieties of Spanish,[23] has not been attested in semi-insubordinate constructions in the COLA and (38) is an *hapax legomenon* in the oral component of the CREA, which suggests that *quizás* + *que*-clause is really odd in Spanish.[24]

(37) [A group of classmates going back to the classroom after recess]

> G01: *ahora hay que correr* (..) *correr*
> G03: *ja ja ahora hay que correr*
> J01: *sí* (.) *capaz **que** corro hoy*

> 'G01: now we have to run (..) run
> G03: ha ha now we have to run
> J01: yes (.) <u>maybe I run today</u>'
> (BABS2-06, COLA BS)

(38) A: *Mari Carmen Quintero, de Barcelona, le pregunta qué efectos secundarios puede tener hacerse la vasectomía.*

---

23 See Espejo Muriel & Espinoza Elorza (2012) and Houle & Martínez Gómez (2011) for a discussion on the origins and grammaticalization of *quizás*.
24 I would like to thank one of the anonymous reviewers, who is a native speaker of Northern Peninsular Spanish, for pointing out that example (38) might as well be an unfinished utterance (with suspended intonation) which has been poorly transcribed from the oral recording due to the broad, orthographic transcription system employed for oral sources in the CREA.

B: *Ninguno. Bueno, ¿saben lo que es la vasectomía, en primer lugar?* <u>*Quizás*</u>
<u>*que* *aclarásemos este punto*</u>. *La vasectomía consiste en la esterilización*
del varón.

'A: Mari Carmen Quintero, from Barcelona, asks you what secondary ef-
fects can cause having a vasectomy done.
B: None. Well, do you know what a vasectomy is, in the first place? <u>Maybe</u>
<u>we should clarify that point</u>. The vasectomy consists in male sterilization.'
(CREA oral, *La Luna*, TVE 1, Spain)

Capaz was originally used as an adjective (attribute), whereas this is not the
case with *quizás*. The now adverbial expression *capaz que* can be interpreted
as a result of the deletion of the verb *ser* 'to be' in the copular construction *es*
capaz que. Note that although *capaz que* can be combined with either the indicative or subjunctive mood, the corpus data shows that speakers from
Buenos Aires tend to use the indicative mood in the construction <*capaz* +
que-clause>.

5.2.4 Evidential adverbs and adverbial phrases

Evidential adverbs and adverbial phrases either reinforce or mitigate the assertion, and present the truth or falseness of the propositional content as evident or hypothetical (see Pietrandrea 2007; Brânză and Delbecque 2008;
Cornillie 2010, among many others). Only the evidential adverbial phrases *por*
supuesto 'of course' (40) and *desde luego* 'of course' have been attested in
semi-insubordinate constructions in the COLA data, but several instances of
use of evidential adverbs in -*mente* '-ly', such as *evidentemente* 'evidently',
naturalmente 'naturally', *indudablemente* 'undoubtedly', *obviamente* 'obviously' (2, repeated here as 39) have been attested in the oral component of the
CREA. These adverbs in -*mente* belong to a more formal register than the one
represented in the COLA, which explains why they do not show up in the latter. In all cases attested in the data, the evidential adverbs intensify the
strength of the assertion of the *que*-clause and establish a direct relation to
the previous turn.

(39) A: *Quizás, obviamente, usted no lo ignora, señor senador, pero la ley de*
ética pública que hemos sancionado permite el acceso a cualquier ciuda-
dano a las declaraciones de bienes que hacemos todos los funcionarios
públicos. [...]

B: *Obviamente **que** no me refiero a la declaración de bienes.*[25] *Eso lo sabemos todos, porque todos hemos sancionado la ley de ética pública.*

'A: Maybe, obviously, you do not ignore it, Mr. Senator, but the law of public ethics that we have passed allows any citizen to have access to the asset declarations that all civil servants do. [...]
B: Obviously I do not mean the declaration of assets. We all know that, because we have all sanctioned the law on public ethics.'
(CREA oral, meeting 65, ordinary session 32, Senate, Argentina)

(40) [Adolescents discussing their plans for the day]

G03: *a qué hora va a venir la gente/*
J01: *por supuesto **que** iban a venir a las cinco y media*

'G03: what time are people going to come/
J01: of course they were going to come at half past five'
(MALCC2-08, COLA M)

Semi-insubordinate constructions introduced by an evidential adverbial tend to occur in turn-initial position of responsive turns, i.e. they function as a reply, either indirect (39) or direct (40), to the previous intervention.

From an intralinguistic perspective, a purely functional explanation is insufficient to account for the varying degrees of acceptability of adverbials + *que*. A diachronic study focusing on the origin and individual development of each form would have to explain their different behaviour in synchrony. As Beijering and Norde (this volume) point out, Ramat and Ricca (1998: 212) argue that adverbs in the semi-insubordinate construction "go against their very nature", as they function as the main predication. Ramat and Ricca propose a different diachronic account for *univerbated* adverbs, such as *peut-être* 'maybe' in French or *quizás* 'maybe' in Spanish, and *derived* adverbs, such as *probablement* 'probably' in French *claramente* 'clearly' in Spanish. They argue that univerbated adverbs have an origin in a morpheme cluster which contains a predicate that takes a subordinate clause, which is why these adverbs can also head a subordinate clause. In the case of derived adverbs, Ramat and Ricca (1998: 214) propose a process of extension of the predicative construction 'it is + ADJ + that...' to the adverbial construction 'it is + ADV + that', followed by ellipsis. Linguistic elements that are morphologically identical in their adjectival and adverbial use would, according

---

25 It is interesting to point out how speaker B mimics the lexical choice of speaker A by initiating his intervention with the adverb *Obviamente*, which could be an effect of syntactic priming.

to their proposal, function as bridging forms. This hypothesis is plausible for elements like *peut-être* and *probablement* in French (Ramat and Ricca 1998) or *claro* and *claramente* in Spanish, although the possibility of simple analogical attraction between the elements should also be considered.[26] The most appropriate explanation of the development and mechanisms of change for each (type of) adverb can only be uncovered by a detailed study of instances of use of each individual element in diachronic data.

5.3 Summary

Semi-insubordinate constructions constitute only one TCU in which the preceding element is scoping over the *que*-clause. According to their meanings, preceding elements can be classified as expressing (i) subjective evaluation of the content of the proposition and (ii) epistemic/evidential qualification of the truth of a proposition. Some subtypes express interpersonal meaning, which is in line with Van linden and Van de Velde (2014). Table 3 summarizes the findings for the pattern corresponding to one TCU.

Table 3: Pattern <modal element + *que*-clause>.

Phenomenon		**Semi-insubordination**
TCU		One TCU
Pattern		**<modal element + *que*-clause>**
Types of modal elements	Subjective evaluation; implied presuppositionality	Secondary interjections (and interjective phrases)
	Epistemic and evidential qualification of a proposition	Interjective expressions derived from lexicalized forms
		Sentential adverb *Sí*
		Adverbs of doubt
		Evidential adverbs and adverbial phrases

---

26 See Hummel (2012) for a discussion on the diachronic development, polyfunctionality and polysemy of discourse markers in Spanish.

The position of the TCU in the conversational sequence shows that it often appears as an emphatic reaction to a previous turn in direct or indirect responses occurring in turn-initial position. Finally, in order to account for the relative acceptability and optionality of *que* with adverbials, it is necessary to look at the historical development of each form. Yet, such an account exceeds the limits of this study.

6 Conclusion

This chapter sheds light on the types of relations that *que*-clauses can establish with other elements within the same turn. Three syntactic relations have been identified for cases in which a *que*-clause is preceded by one or two linguistic elements: <preface + *que*-clause>, <element with illocutionary force + *que*-clause> and <modal element + *que*-clause>. It has been put forward that it is important to distinguish between the three phenomena, namely insubordination, causal *que*, and semi-insubordination, always bearing in mind that the same element, even in the same position in the turn, may enter into more than one type of relation with a *que*-clause. Criteria to determine which of the three cases we are facing include the number of TCUs in the turn, the potential for an intonation break between the *que*-clause and the element that precedes it, and the function of the preceding element in relation to the *que*-clause. Table 4 summarizes the three broad patterns found.

Table 4: Patterns corresponding to one or two TCUs.

TCU	Two TCUs		One TCU
Phenomenon	Insubordination	Causal *que*	Semi-insubordination
Pattern	<preface + *que*-clause>	<speech act + *que*-clause>	<modal element + *que*-clause>

I described the phenomenon of semi-insubordination and discussed some of the previous studies on semi-insubordination in European languages, to then focus on Spanish. As has been shown, semi-insubordination exists in languages belonging to diverse families and shows some similarities, such as the formal adverbial, adjectival and nominal subtypes.

The phenomenon of semi-insubordination was discussed and illustrated on the basis of the interactional corpus data from the COLA and CREA. It was argued that semi-insubordination involves one TCU. The elements preceding the *que*-clause in semi-insubordinate constructions were classified in two broad classes, according to whether they express subjective evaluation of the content of the proposition – and implied presuppositionality – or evidential and epistemic qualification of the truth status of a proposition. A variety of forms was discussed and it was shown that the degree of optionality of *que* cannot be explained from a purely functional perspective and therefore the particular development of each form should be looked at. This study presents a typology that is in its own right suggestive of a gradient between some semi-insubordinates leaning close to subordination and others approximating insubordination.

I also presented and discussed the data corresponding to the two types of relation that can be established between *que*-clauses and preceding elements whenever there are two TCUs, i.e. whenever there is no semi-insubordination. For the class of prefaces documented introducing insubordinate *que*-clauses, it was argued that such elements express attitudinal, interpersonal and meta-discursive values. For the class of elements with illocutionary force which enter into the 'causal *que* construction', it was shown that they can be imperative, desiderative, interrogative, or declarative utterances. The *que*-clause in these cases justifies that previous speech act. It was also shown that the relation between the two TCUs cannot be conceived from a traditional conception of subordination. The present study considers 'dependency shift' as a complication of the notion of syntactic dependence – the relevance of the latter phenomenon, may lie especially in the cases of what is often referred to as 'sociation'.

One of the main contributions of this study is the introduction of interactional criteria in the discussion on semi-insubordination and related phenomena. In that sense, one limitation of previous studies that focus on the syntactic structure of the semi-insubordinate construction and which has been overcome here, is accounting for the differences between the types of semi-insubordinate constructions – containing elements expressing subjective evaluation or epistemic and evidential meanings – in relation to the structure of the turn they appear in and what interactional functions they perform.

List of abbreviations

Abbreviations for data sources

COLA	Corpus Oral del Lenguaje Adolescente
COLA BA	Subcorpus from Buenos Aires

COLA M	Subcorpus from Madrid
COLA S	Subcorpus from Santiago
CREA Oral	Corpus de Referencia del Español Actual, oral component

Transcription conventions

[word]	overlap (single)
1[word]	overlap (first pair)
2[word]	overlap (second pair)
XXX	unintelligible
%	truncated/cut-off word
<word>	comment
/	rising intonation contour
\	falling intonation contour
(.)	one-second pause
(..)	two-second pause
<pause>	longer, untimed pause
[. . .]	omitted excerpt
word	element or structure under analysis

Acknowledgments: The research reported in this study was supported by project GOA/12/007, funded by the Research Council of the University of Leuven. I am very grateful to Bert Cornillie, Hendrik De Smet and Pedro Gras, as well as to the two anonymous reviewers, for their useful comments and suggestions on an earlier version. I would also like to thank all the participants of the workshop '(Semi-)independent subordinate constructions', held in September 2015 at the SLE conference in Leiden, for their valuable contributions.

References

Aelbrecht, Lobke. 2006. IP-ellipsis in Dutch dialects: X + that-clause. In Jeroen Van de Weijer & Bettelou Los (eds.), *Linguistics in the Netherlands 2006*, 1–14. Amsterdam: Benjamins.

Alcina, Juan & José Manuel Blecua. 1975. *Gramática española*. Barcelona: Ariel.

Aliaga García, Francisco & Eduardo de Bustos Guadaño. 1997. Acerca de los límites entre gramática y pragmática: de nuevo sobre las oraciones causales. Paper presented at I International symposium of semantics, University of La Laguna.

Ameka, Felix. 1992. Interjections: The universal yet neglected part of speech. *Journal of Pragmatics* 18 (2). 101–118.

Beijering, Karin. 2016. Semi-insubordinate at-constructions in Norwegian: formal, semantic and functional properties. *Norsk Lingvistisk Tidsskrift* 34 (2). 161–182.

Bosque, Ignacio and Violeta Demonte (eds.), 1999. *Gramática descriptiva de la lengua española*. Madrid: Espasa Calpe.

Brânză, Mircea. D. & Nicole Delbecque. 2008. Variación modal con los adverbios de duda en español. In Alexandra Cuniță, Coman Lupu and Liliane Tasmowski (eds.), *Studii de Lingvistică și Filologie Romanică*, 58–71. Bucharest: Editura Universității București.

Cabedo Nebot, Adrian. 2014. On the delimitation of discursive units in colloquial Spanish. Val. Es.Co application model. In Salvador Pons Bordería (ed.), *Discourse Segmentation in Romance Languages*. [Pragmatics & Beyond New Series 250]. Amsterdam: John Benjamins.

Cinque, Guglielmo. 1999. *Adverbs and functional heads: A cross-linguistic perspective*. Oxford: Oxford University Press.

Cornillie, B. 2010. An interactional approach to evidential and epistemic adverbs in Spanish conversation. In Gabriele Diewald & Elena Smirnova (eds.), *The linguistic realization of evidentiality in European languages*, 309–330. Berlin and New York: Mouton de Gruyter.

Croft, William. 2000. *Explaining language change. An evolutionary approach*. Harlow: Longman.

Demonte, Violeta & Olga Fernández Soriano. 2013. El *que* citativo, otros elementos de la periferia izquierda oracional y la recomplementación: Variación inter e intralingüística. In Daniel Jakob & Katya Plooj (eds.), *Autour de que – El entorno de que*, 47–69. Frankfurt am Main: Peter Lang.

D'Hertefelt, Sarah & Jean-Christophe Verstraete. 2014. Independent complement constructions in Swedish and Danish: Insubordination or dependency shift? *Journal of Pragmatics* 60. 89–102.

D'Hertefelt, Sarah, 2018. *Insubordination in Germanic. A Typology of Complement and Conditional Constructions*. [Trends in Linguistics. Studies and Monographs 318]. Berlin: Mouton de Gruyter.

Espejo Muriel, María del Mar & Rosa María Espinosa Elorza. 2012. *Quiçab, quiçá, quizá*. In Emilio Montero Cartelle and Carmen Manzano Rovira (eds.), *Actas del VIII Congreso Internacional de Historia de la Lengua Española*. Vol. 1, 749–760. Santiago de Compostela: Meubook.

Etxepare, Ricardo, 2008. On quotative constructions in Iberian Spanish. In Ritva Laury (ed.), *Crosslinguistic studies of clause combining: The multifunctionality of conjuctions, 35–78*. Amsterdam: John Benjamins.

Etxepare, Ricardo. 2010. From hearsay evidentiality to samesaying relations. *Lingua* 120(3). 604–627.

Evans, Nicholas. 2007. Insubordination and its uses. In Irina Nikolaeva (ed.), *Finiteness: Theoretical and Empirical Foundations*, 366–431. Oxford: Oxford University Press.

Evans, Nicholas & Honoré Watanabe. 2016. *Insubordination*. [Typological Studies in Language 155]. Amsterdam: John Benjamins.

Ford, Cecilia & Sandra Thompson. 1996. Interactional units in conversation: syntactic, intonational, and pragmatic resources for the management of turns. In Elionor Ochs, Emanuel Schegloff & Sandra Thompson (eds.), *Interaction and Grammar*. [Studies in Interactional Sociolinguistics 13], 134–184. Cambridge: Cambridge University Press.

Ford, Cecilia, Barbara Fox & Sandra Thompson. 1996. Practices in the construction of turns: the 'TCU' revisited. *Pragmatics* 6. 427–454.

Ford, Cecilia, Barbara Fox & Sandra Thompson. 2002. *The language of turn and sequence*. Oxford: Oxford University Press.

Gras, Pedro. 2011. *Gramática de construcciones en interacción. Propuesta de un modelo y aplicación al análisis de estructuras independientes con marcas de subordinación en español*. Barcelona: University of Barcelona dissertation.

Gras, Pedro. 2013. Entre la gramática y el discurso: valores conectivos de que inicial átono en español. In Daniel Jacob & Katia Ploog (eds.), *Autour de que*, 89–112. Frankfurt am Main: Peter Lang.

Gras, Pedro. 2016. Revisiting the functional typology of insubordination: *que*-initial sentences in Spanish. In Nicholas Evans & Honore Watanabe (eds.), *Insubordination*. [Typological Studies in Language 155], 113–144. Amsterdam: John Benjamins.

Gras, Pedro & María Sol Sansiñena. 2015. An interactional account of discourse-connective *que*-constructions in Spanish. *Text and Talk* 35 (4). 505–529.

Gras, Pedro & María Sol Sansiñena. 2017. Exclamatives in the functional typology of insubordination: evidence from complement insubordinate constructions in Spanish. *Journal of Pragmatics* 115. 21–36.

Hernanz, Maria Lluïsa. 2007. From polarity to modality: Some (a)symmetries between bien and sí in Spanish. In Luis Eguren & Olga Fernández-Soriano (eds.), *Coreference, Modality, and Focus: Studies on the syntax–semantics interface. Linguistics Today 111*, 133–169. Amsterdam: John Benjamins.

Hopper, Paul & Elizabeth Closs Traugott. 2003. *Grammaticalization*. Cambridge: Cambridge University Press.

Houle, Leah & Rebeca Martínez Gómez. 2011. A closer look at *quizá(s)*: grammaticalization and an epistemic adverb. In Luis A. Ortiz-López (ed.), *Selected proceedings of the 13th Hispanic linguistics symposium*, 296–304. Somerville: Cascadilla Proceedings Project.

Hummel, Martin. 2012. *Polifuncionalidad, polisemia y estrategia retórica. Los signos discursivos con base atributiva entre oralidad y escritura*. Berlin: De Gruyter.

Iglesias Recuero, Silvia. 2000. Gramática de la oración frente a gramática del discurso: de Nuevo sobre el llamado que causal. In José Jesús de Bustos Tovar (ed.), *Lengua, discurso, texto: I simposio internacional de análisis del discurso. Vol.1*, 333–344. Madrid: Visor.

Jørgensen, Annette Myre (ed.). *Corpus Oral del Lenguaje Adolescente (COLA)*. http://www.colam.org/om_prosj-espannol.html.

Kärkkäinen, Elise. 2003. *Epistemic stance in English conversation: A description of its interactional functions, with a focus on I think. Vol.115. Pragmatics & beyond*. Amsterdam, Philadelphia: John Benjamins.

Lehmann, Christian. 1988. Towards a typology of clause linkage. In John Haiman & Sandra A. Thompson (eds.), *Clause Combining in Grammar and Discourse*, 181–225. Amsterdam: John Benjamins.

Lindström, Jan & Anne-Marie Londen. 2008. Constructing reasoning. The connectives *för att* (causal), *så att* (consecutive) and *men att* (adversative) in Swedish conversations. In Jaakko Leino (ed.), *Constructional Reorganization* [Constructional Approaches to Language 5], 105–152. Amsterdam: John Benjamins.

Mithun, Marianne. 2008. The extension of dependency beyond the sentence. *Language* 84 (1). 264–280.

Mithun, Marianne. 2016. Shifting finiteness in nominalization: From definitization to refinitization. In Claudine Chamoreau (ed.), *Finiteness and Nominalization*, 299–324. Amsterdam: John Benjamins.

Muller, Claude. 1978. La negation explétive dans les constructions complétives. *Langue Française* 39. 76–103.

Nocentini, Alberto. 2003. La cosidetta negazione espletiva in italiano. *Archivio Glottologico Italiano* 88. 72–90.

Norrick, Neal R. 2007. Discussion article: pragmatic markers, interjections and discourse. *Catalan journal of linguistics* 6. 159–168.

Nübling, Damaris. 2004. Die prototypische Interjektion: Ein Definitionsvorschlag. *Zeitschrift für Semiotik* 26. 11–46.

Octavio de Toledo y Huerta, Álvaro Sebastián. 2001–2002. ¿Un viaje de ida y vuelta? La gramaticalización de *vaya* como marcador y cuantificador. *Anuari de filologia F* 11–12. 47–72.

Pietrandrea, Paola. 2007. The grammatical nature of some epistemic-evidential adverbs in spoken Italian. *Italian Journal of Linguistics* 2. 39–64.

Pons, Salvador. 1998. *Conexión y conectores. Estudio de su relación en el registro informal de la lengua*. Valencia: University of Valencia.

Pons, Salvador & Scott Schwenter. 2005. Polar meaning and "expletive" negation in approximative adverbs: Spanish. *Journal of Historical Pragmatics* 6 (2). 262–282.

Portolés, José. 1998. *Marcadores del discurso*. Barcelona: Ariel.

Ramat, Paolo & Davide Ricca. 1998. Sentence adverbs in the languages of Europe. In Johan van der Auwera & Dónall P. Ó Baoill (eds.), *Adverbial constructions in the languages of Europe*, 187–273. Berlin: Mouton de Gruyter.

Real Academia Española: *Corpus de referencia del español actual* (CREA). http://www.rae.es

Real Academia Española & Asociación de Academias de la Lengua Española. 2009. *Nueva gramática de la lengua española*. Madrid: Espasa.

Rodríguez Ramalle, Teresa Maria. 2007. El complementante *que* como marca enfática en el texto periodístico. *Revista Electrónica de Lingüística Aplicada (RAEL)* 6. 41–53.

Rodríguez Ramalle, Teresa Maria. 2008a. Estudio sintáctico y discursivo de algunas estructuras enunciativas y citativas del español. *Revista española de lingüística aplicada* 21. 269–288.

Rodríguez Ramalle, Teresa Maria. 2008b. Marcas enunciativas y evidenciales en el discurso periodístico. In Inés Olza, Manuel Casado Velarde and Ramón González Ruiz (eds.), *Actas del XXXVII Simposio de la Sociedad Española de Lingüística (SEL)*, 735–744. Pamplona: Servicio de Publicaciones de la Universidad de Navarra.

Rodríguez Ramalle, Teresa Maria. 2011. La expresión de grado en las interjecciones y la función de la conjunción *que*. Verba. *Anuario Galego de Filoloxía* 38. 191–217.

Sacks, Harvey, Emanuel Schegloff & Gail Jefferson. 1974. A simplest systematics for the organization of turn-taking for conversation. *Language* 50. 696–735.

Sánchez López, Cristina. 2017. Mirativity in Spanish. The case of the particle *mira*. *Review of Cognitive Linguistics* 15 (2). 489-514.

Sansiñena, María Sol. 2015. The multiple functional load of *que*. An interactional approach to insubordinate complement clauses in Spanish. Leuven: University of Leuven dissertation.

Sansiñena, María Sol, Hendrik De Smet & Bert Cornillie. 2015. Between subordinate and insubordinate: Paths towards complementizer-initial main clauses. *Journal of Pragmatics* 77. 3–19.

Schegloff, Emanuel A. 1996. Turn organization: One intersection of grammar and interaction. In Elinor Ochs, Sandra Thompson and Emanuel Schegloff (eds.), *Interaction and Grammar*, 52–133. Cambridge: Cambridge University Press.

Serret Lancharez, Silvia. 2012. *Los adverbios oracionales y la periferia izquierda*. Master thesis: University of Barcelona.

Simon-Vandenbergen, Anne-Marie. 2007. *No doubt* and related expressions: A functional account. In Mike Hannay & Gerard J. Steen (eds.), *Structural-Functional Studies in English Grammar: In honour of Lachlan Mackenzie*. [Studies in Language Companion Series 83], 9–34. Amsterdam and Philadelphia: John Benjamins.

Simon-Vandenbergen, Anne-Marie & Karin Aijmer. 2007a. The discourse functionality of adjectival and adverbial epistemic expressions: Evidence from present-day English. In Christopher S. Butler, Raquel Hidalgo Downing & Julia Lavid (eds.), *Functional Perspectives on Grammar and Discourse· In honour of Angela Downing*. [Studies in Language Companion Series 85], 419–446. Amsterdam and Philadelphia: John Benjamins.

Simon-Vandenbergen, Anne-Marie & Karin Aijmer. 2007b. *The semantic field of modal certainty. A corpus-based study of English adverbs*. [Topics in English Linguistics 56]. Berlin and New York: Mouton de Gruyter.

Traugott, Elizabeth Closs. 1988. Pragmatic strengthening and grammaticalization. In Shelley Axmaker, Annie Jaisser & Helen Singmaster (eds.), *Proceedings of the fourteenth annual meeting of the Berkeley Linguistics Society*, 406–416. Berkeley: Berkeley Linguistics Society.

Traugott, Elizabeth Closs. 2003. Constructions in grammaticalization. In Brian D. Joseph & Richard D. Janda (eds.), *The Handbook of Historical Linguistics*, 624–647. Oxford: Blackwell.

Val.Es.Co. Research Group. 2014. Las unidades del discurso oral. La propuesta Val.Es.Co. de segmentación de la conversación (coloquial). *Estudios de Lingüística del Español* 35 (1). 13–73.

Van linden, An & Freek Van de Velde. 2014. (Semi-)autonomous subordination in Dutch: structures and semantic-pragmatic values. *Journal of Pragmatics* 60. 226–250.

Verstraete, Jean-Christophe. 1998. A semiotic model for the description of levels in conjunction: external, internal-modal and internal-speech functional. *Functions of Language* 5. 179–211.

Verstraete, Jean-Christophe, Sarah D'Hertefelt & An Van linden. 2012. A typology of complement insubordination in Dutch. *Studies in Language* 36 (1). 123–153.

Wendy Elvira-García

7 Two constructions, one syntactic form: Perceptual prosodic differences between elliptical and independent <*si* + V indicative> clauses in Spanish

Abstract: This work examines Spanish speakers' preferences to interpret a grammatical construction as elliptical or insubordinate depending on its prosody. Spanish <*si* + indicative> clause can be either an elliptical clause or an insubordinate clause expressing refutation and earlier work has claimed that they differ in intonation (Montolío 1999a; Gras 2011; Schwenter 1998; Schwenter 2015). Specifically, refutative insubordinate constructions show falling final intonation contours (L+H*L%) whereas elliptical clauses show rising (non-final) contours (H* H%) (Elvira-García, Roseano and Fernández-Planas 2017).

This study uses two perceptual forced-choice discrimination tests in order to show that listeners chose continuation rise contours for elliptical contexts (86.9%) and rising falling contours for insubordinate contexts L+H*L% (93.2%). The distribution is significant χ^2 (1, n=1600, 35,519,p<.01) when exposed to natural stimuli. A second experiment conducted with manipulated stimuli confirms that intonation (not speech rate or intensity) intonation is the main cue to categorize constructions that are segmentally identical as elliptical or insubordinate χ^2 (1, N= 1600, 70.866, p<.01).

1 Introduction

This chapter sheds light on Spanish speakers' preferences to interpret a grammatical construction as elliptical or independent depending on its prosody. Earlier work has claimed that Spanish <*si* + indicative> clause can be either an elliptical clause or a syntactically independent clause expressing refutation depending on the intonation with which it is produced (Montolío 1999a; Gras 2011; Schwenter 1998; Schwenter 2015), hence speakers could use intonation to process functional differences in the constructions. The aim of this chapter is to show that intonation is the main cue listeners use in order to process an

Wendy Elvira-García, Universidad Nacional de Educación a Distancia

https://doi.org/10.1515/9783110638288-008

utterance as elliptical or insubordinate. As such, intonation could be understood as a cue for the level of syntactic dependency of a construction.

Construction Grammar assumes that prosody plays a role in the construction since the general assumption is that a construction is a pair of form and meaning (Kay and Fillmore 1999), however most studies focus on the morphosyntactic features of constructions, as will be discussed in Section 2.

In the case of the Spanish <si + indicative> clause previous research shows that the same segmental content e.g. *Si no viene Juan* 'SI John does not come' is produced with different intonations patterns depending on the context (Elvira-García, Roseano and Fernández-Planas 2017). A suitable context for a non-final intonation contour (H*H%) would be (1) where Juan/John is speaker B's former boyfriend and B states that she would only go to the party if John is not there. A final contour (L+H* L%), on the other hand, would be chosen by speaker B in (2), where John is a vegetarian and B states that A's question: *What's he going to eat in the barbecue*" is inappropriate given that he is not coming.

(1) A: *¿Vienes a la fiesta?*
       'Are you coming to the party?'
     B: *Si no viene Juan*
       'SI John is not coming'

(2) A: *¿Qué va a comer Juan en la barbacoa?*
       'What will John eat in the barbacue?'
     B: *Si no viene Juan*
       'SI John is not coming'

In order to test if these production differences have an effect on perception, this chapter presents two perceptual forced-choice discrimination tests. Our hypothesis is that the differences attested in production would have an impact in the processing of the constructions, resulting in refutative interpretations for rising-falling contours and elliptical interpretations for rising contours.

The rest of the chapter is organized as follows. Section 2 stablishes the role of intonation in the study of Construction Grammar and 3 introduces the object of study, Spanish *si*-clauses. Section 4 deals with the previous work in the intonation of *si*-clauses. Section 5 states the goals and hypotheses of the paper. In Section 6 the methodology of the perceptual test conducted is detailed. Section 7 explains the results, which are divided by the type of stimuli (manipulated or non-manipulated) used in the test. Section 8 provides a discussion of the results and section 9, finally, states the conclusions based on the experiments conducted.

2 The role of intonation in the study of constructions

Prosody plays a central role in Construction Grammar since the general assumption is that a construction is a pair of form and meaning (Kay and Fillmore 1999). However, most constructionist work focuses on grammatical form, leaving intonation to the phonologists.

And there is little investigation on how exactly prosody can affect a construction. General studies about constructions do not include prosody in the parameters that they study, and, even when they do, they provide impressionistic notes on intonation. The scarce mentions of intonation usually deal with phrasing (i.e. prosodic units) (Croft 2001) or stress and deaccentuation. On the other hand, from the perspective of intonational studies, papers very rarely assume a constructional point of view. In Romance languages the only intonation study that takes a constructional approach is Vanrell, Armstrong and Prieto (2014).

When intonation is taken into account, two different perspectives are possible. In the first one, intonation is treated as an attribute of the construction. The construction is defined by its grammatical form and intonation is only a feature that accompanies the construction but does not provide additional information about its meaning (Fried & Östman 2005; Michaelis & Lambrecht 1996). The same perspective has been assumed by intonation studies which argue that constructions are stored together with their possible intonation contours (Calhoun and Schweitzer 2012). Specifically, it has been argued that prosody can be lexicalised in a specific construction given that some words and short phrases often occur with the same discourse meaning, making possible pairings between lexical material and pitch contour. These results are congruent with frequency-based collocations grammar defended in Bybee & Eddington (2006).

This latter perspective argues that intonation pairs directly with the meaning of the construction. In other words, it understands a contour as a construction in itself that pairs the prosodic form with the pragmatic meaning (Marandin 2006; Sadat-Tehrani 2004). That is also what seems more plausible from the point of view of intonational phonology (Liberman & Sag 1974).

However, intonational phonologists from the last decades have followed an approach that has very little to do with Construction Grammar. In fact, the theoretical framework most used is ultimately an heir of the principles of Generativism (e.g. Chomsky 1969), and that makes it difficult to apply the research in the field of phonology to cognitivist frameworks. This applies particularly to Autosegmental Phonology (Goldsmith 1976; Liberman 1975), which defends the existence of a surface and a deep structure, for example. For prosody the present study adopts the Autosegmental-Metrical model, henceforth AM (Pierrehumbert 1980). AM assumes that the phonological level and the syntactic one are completely independent. This means that a simple one-word utterance like *Marina* can be produced with any prosodic contour available in the language inventory. But from the perspective of constructions this has been shown not to be true, given that there are multiple constructions that are only possible with one pitch contour, for example the *si*-clause that we will be dealing with in this paper.

In the study of insubordination,[1] the first approach, which takes intonation as a feature of the construction, is usually adopted. It has been usually noted that intonation is a distinctive parameter (Evans 2007; Schwenter 2015; Kawanachi 2010; Kaltenböck 2016) in several constructions and, thus, needs to be included with the rest of formal features of the construction. In Elvira-García, Roseano & Fernández-Planas (2017) the integration of prosody goes a step further: they describe not a prosodic pattern for each type of construction but a set of constructions that share the same contour. In their opinion, this is due to the fact that they share the same discursive function. But this claim is not new in prosody studies. From the point of view of intonational phonology, a change in intonation (prosodic form) conveys a change in meaning (Bolinger 1989), therefore, analysing the prosodic form could help to distinguish between constructions.

3 Object of study: si-clauses

Specifically, this chapter deals with the intonation of two constructions that have the same segmental content but different prosodic properties in Spanish <*si* + V indicative>.

Si 'if' is the main subordinate conditional conjunction in Spanish. Spanish conditionals, as it happens in other languages, can appear in discourse as subordinate clauses but also as a free standing main clause.

Gras (2011) has described two constructions that can appear when the *si*-clause acts as a free clause. Both constructions can share the same grammatical form <*si* + V indicative> but differ in their degree of dependency (elliptical versus independent) and their discursive function. Examples (3) and (4) illustrate an elliptical and an independent *si*-clause in Spanish respectively

---

1 According to Evans (2007) an insubordinate construction is a syntactic independent construction with subordination marks.

(3)   A: *¿Vas a ir a la reunión de esta tarde?*
      'Are you going to the meeting this afternoon?'
      B: *Si tú vas...*
      'If you are going...'

The example in (3) illustrates an elliptical construction. The elliptical *si*-construction consists of a finite clause in indicative or subjunctive (Montolío 1999b). The elided material can be recovered by means of a conversational inference, the recovered clause can be any clause that is a possible continuation of the first one. Therefore, the discursive function of an elliptical clause is context dependent, but it has been related to courtesy and doubt, among others. In (3) A asks if its interlocutor is going to the meeting and speaker B answers with the elliptical clause *Si tú vas...* 'If you are going...'. The second part of the conditional subordinate, "I will go to the meeting", is supposed to be inferred by the interlocutor.

(4)   A: *¿Vas a ir a la reunión de esta tarde?*
      'Are you going to the meeting this afternoon?'
      B: *¡Si es mañana!*
      'But the meeting is tomorrow'[2]

The example in (4) illustrates an insubordinate (i.e. independent) construction. In fact, Spanish independent *si*-clauses have been taken as a prototypical example of insubordination (Evans 2007). The independent *si*-clause consists of a *si* marker (formerly a conditional conjunction)[3] followed by a finite clause in indicative (Montolío 1999a; Schwenter 2015; Gras 2011; Almela Pérez 1985; Bello 1988). So, while elliptical clauses can accept verbs in indicative and subjunctive, independent clauses have a mood restriction. Furthermore, its discursive function is also restricted. *Si*-clauses are used in Spanish as is a counter-argumentative construction, which has been called refutative (Schwenter 2015). In the example, speaker A asks the same question than in (3) but, in this case, speaker B uses the clause to reject the previous intervention. In this case, it is not even used to reject the propositional content of the intervention but the speech act itself. B believes that the question expressed by A is not appropriate given that the meeting is not today but tomorrow.

---

2 Despite *but* not being a perfect translation of *si* in *si*-clauses, it is used here for the sake of clarity.
3 See Schwenter (2015) for a discussion on the grammatical status of *si*.

Besides differences in use and function, earlier grammatical studies on these constructions have claimed that elliptical and insubordinate clauses differ in intonation (see Section 4), hence speakers could use intonation to process functional differences in the constructions. The aim of this chapter is to prove that intonation is the main cue listeners use in order to process an utterance as elliptical or insubordinate.

The rest of the chapter is organized as follows. Section 4 deals with the previous work in the intonation of si-clauses. Section 5 states the goals and hypothesis of the paper. In Section 6 the methodology of the perceptual test conducted is detailed. Section 7 explains the results, which are divided by the type of stimuli (manipulated or non-manipulated) used in the test. Finally, Sections 8 and 9 state the conclusions based on the experiments conducted.

4 Previous work on the intonation of *si*-clauses

A previous phonetic acoustic study (Elvira-García, Roseano and Fernández-Planas 2017) showed that in Spanish insubordinate constructions showed falling final intonation contours, while elliptical clauses showed rising contours, probably linked with the notion of continuation rise (Pierrehumbert and Hirschberg 1990; Beckman et al. 2002; Frota et al. 2007).

In the particular case of *si*-clauses the following patterns have been attested. For elliptical *si*-clauses the attested patterns agree with those described as typical continuation rises contours (Frota et al. 2007). A rising stressed syllable until the end of the intonational group (L+H*H%), a low stressed syllable and a final rising (L*H%) and a rising stressed syllable a slight falling and final rise (L+H*!HH%) (Roseano et al. 2015). Moreover, the so-called suspended pattern (Navarro Tomás 1944; Sosa 1999) has also been found and it is the most characteristic and usual pattern (H*H%).

The independent *si*-clause, which has been described as refutational, adversative, counterargumentative or mirative (Gras 2011; Schwenter 2015; Schwenter 1998; Montolío 1999a; Almela Pérez 1985; Moliner 1966) has been usually claimed to have a specific intonation. Moliner (1966) was the first providing an accurate description of the intonation of refutational *si*-clauses. She stated that independent *si*-clauses, when used in a context of surprise, had an exclamatory intonation. This claim, despite being made analyzing intonation "by ear", is accurate, since, phonetically, the contour used in Spanish in exclamations is the same as in narrow focus, which has been proved to be the most frequent pattern in these constructions (Elvira-García, Roseano and Fernández-Planas 2017).

Later, Montolío Durán (1999) stated that the typical intonation for refutational *si*-clauses was a rise in the stressed syllable and final falling. Elvira-García (2012) carried out an acoustical analysis of 200 clauses using the Sp_ToBI framework,[4] which showed that, besides the exclamative/narrow focus intonation (L+H*L%), the construction could also have a different pattern, a low stressed syllable and high-falling boundary tone (L*HL%) related to statements of the obvious in the literature (Estebas-Vilaplana and Prieto 2008). Schwenter (2015) also used Sp_ToBI conventions and noticed that L+H*L% is the most typical contour of refutative *si*-clauses, while elliptical *como*-conditionals and elliptical *si*-clauses could show an L+H*H% contour. Furthermore, Schwenter (2016) states the non-rising contour (L+H*L%) becomes a problem for defending that the refutative *si*-clauses are diachronically related to independent *si*-clauses found in other languages like Italian, given that those have been described as rising (Lombardi Vallauri 2004).

Recent findings, based on an experimental corpus of 954 *si*-clauses from four varieties of Peninsular Spanish, have shown that independent *si*-clauses can be produced with any intonational contour as long as the intonation matches the discursive function of the construction in the context in which it is produced, i.e. refutation (Elvira-García 2016). However some patterns are more frequent than others, refutative *si*-clauses appear mostly with the Spanish contour for narrow/contrastive focus, L+H*L%, and the contour of statements of the obvious, L*HL%. Alternatively, the construction can be produced with any dialectal patterns that express contrast in their varieties. That is the case of ¡H*L%, a refutational pattern used in Seville, or H+L*L%, used in Seville and in Barcelona, which has been described as categorical statement. Figure 1 depicts the intonational patterns found in Elvira-García (2016) for elliptical (left) and independent (right) *si*-clauses.

As can be noticed, the literature has focused on the nuclear configuration of the constructions (i.e. the pitch contour from the last stressed syllable of the sentence until the end). The main reason for that is that Spanish is a language that has the prosodic nucleus at the end of the utterance, meaning that the last part of the sentence (*toneme*) is enough to identify correctly the pragmatic function of the contour. However, in the case of the nuclear configuration H*H%, the pretoneme is as important as the nucleus given that these utterances are

---

4 Sp_ToBI (Spanish Tones and Break Indices) is a system of notation conventions for Spanish prosody, the system is largely based on Pierrehumbert's Autosegmental Metrical model (Pierrehumbert 1980) and, in its last version, establishes four levels of tonal height: high (H), low (L), mid (!H) and extrahigh (¡H) (Hualde and Prieto 2015). It marks stressed syllables with a star (*) and final boundary tones with a percentage (%) (Beckman and Hirschberg 1994). There are analogous ToBI systems for many languages (Jun 2014; Jun 2005).

Elliptical clauses		Insubordinated clauses	
Pitch contour	Transcription	Pitch contour	Transcription
	L+H*H%		L+H*L%
	H*H%		L*HL%
	L*H%		L*L%
	LH*!HH%		H+L*L%
			¡H*L%

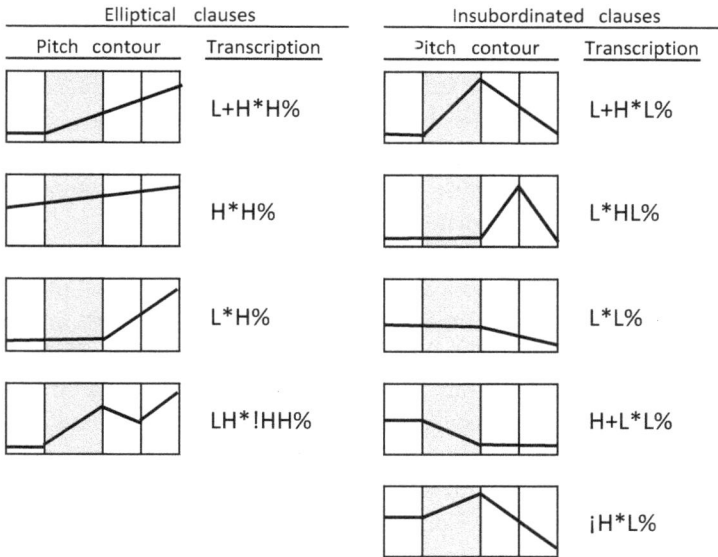

Figure 1: Schematic representations of prosodic patterns attested for elliptical (left) and insubordinate (right) constructions. The figure has been adapted from (Elvira-García 2016).

characterized by a sustained (and slightly rising) high plateau from the beginning of the sentence. It is specially worthy noticing that, whereas most of the nuclear configurations that are illustrated in Figure 1 can appear in first clauses of subordinate clauses, the sustained pitch (here transcribed as H*H%) only occurs in elliptical clauses.

The classification of contours based on its nuclear configuration allows us to generalize the patterns into two categories. Contours that are related to continuation rises (i.e. non-terminal contours) and hence related to elliptical clauses and contours that are not (i.e. terminal contours). This classification has served to prove that the intonation of a grammatical construction is a cue to its level of dependency (Elvira-García, Roseano and Fernández-Planas 2017). More specifically, it has been argued that continuation rise is used in Spanish, as it happens in other languages, to trigger a conversational inference that allows us to explain its pragmatic function, hence continuation rise is necessary in order to trigger that inference in elliptical clauses. By contrast, in independent clauses its function is more fixed. Their syntactic form is a cue to the type of speech act that they accomplish. And in this kind of construction their prosody reflects their pragmatic function. Therefore, the intonation of Spanish refutative *si*-clauses is the typical intonation in Spanish for expressing contrastive statements.

5 Hypothesis

The previous section has shown that intonation of elliptical and independent *si*-clauses differs systematically in speech production, meaning that none of the contours of elliptical sentences appear in independent clauses and independent clauses cannot be produced with the contours that appear in elliptical clauses. However, these findings have not been validated perceptually.

According to acoustic results presented in Section 4, a change in intonation should be enough in order to process a *si*-clause as insubordinate or elliptical. Specifically, *si*-clauses with rising intonation should be processed as elliptical, while *si*-clauses with falling or rising-falling intonation should be processed as refutative. Therefore, it is expected that most speakers of Spanish use intonation in order to disambiguate a construction when its segmental form could correspond to either an elliptical or an insubordinate structure.

The general assumption in current phonological studies of Spanish (Hualde and Prieto 2015) establishes that all the attested contours in Section 3 are phonologically (and thus perceptually) different. Consequently, a categorical perception paradigm is useless in this study, given that all the contours presented in 2 are phonologically different.

In fact, the goal of the experiment is not to tell whether the intonation of these two constructions is different (we know that already thanks to the acoustic results) but how listeners decide on the function of the construction using its prosody. In other words, given two possible contours, will the listeners really choose continuation rise contours for elliptical sentences and falling for independent sentences?

6 Methodology

In order to test the hypothesis, two perceptual forced-choice discrimination tests have been conducted. The experimental design of the tests has been inspired by a conjunction of classical discrimination perception tests (Liberman et al. 1957) and acceptability (or grammaticality) judgment tests that use prosody (Berndt et al. 1988; Linebarger, Schwartz and Saffran 1983).

The tests are designed as acceptability tests where the listener is given a context and has to choose between the two sounds: a <*si* + V indicative> clause with rising intonation and a <*si* + V indicative> clause with rising-falling intonation. Each context was compatible with only one discursive function, either refutation or ellipsis (see Appendix).

The tests differ in the stimuli (natural or synthetic) they used but the procedure was the same. The imperative of using two different tests is related to the impossibility of knowing which of the acoustic features in the utterance listeners are using in order to process the meaning of a sentence. In a natural stimulus, extracted from its natural context, the functional load of the construction can be encoded in grammar and lexis (which have been neutralized in these experiments given that we use constructions with the same segmental content) and in suprasegmental features.

However, suprasegmental features do not only include intonation, which is a controlled variable in this experiment, but also speech rate and voice quality (e.g. creaky voice). These two features (creaky voice and lower speech rate) cannot be controlled in natural speech and yet they have been reported as characteristic in doubtful utterances (Vanrell et al. 2011). Likewise, doubt and courtesy are possible situated meanings in elliptical clauses (Narbona 1990). Therefore, when analyzing intonation as a cue for ellipsis, speech rate and voice quality need to be neutralized. The second experiment has manipulated the stimuli in order to verify that intonation is the main feature that listeners use in order to distinguish between independent and elliptical *si*-clauses (see Section 6.2.2).

6.1 Participants

The participants were 100 speakers of Peninsular Spanish, 72 percent female, 28 percent male aged between 18 and 60. All the listeners filled in a sociolinguistic survey where they were asked for the following variables L1, place of birth and residence, musical studies and possible hearing impairment. It is also noticeable that 51 percent of the participants had a linguistics-related degree. However, this did not influenced their answers ($F[1600,1]= 0.06$ p=0.807). All participants took part in both tests allowing for a comparison of their answers using statistical tests for paired samples.

6.2 Materials

6.2.1 Test 1: Natural stimuli

In order to allow any Peninsular Spanish speaker to do the test, the contours used as stimuli in the test needed to be attested in as many Peninsular Spanish dialects as possible. That is why the chosen patterns were: L+H*L% for independent constructions and the suspended pattern (with nuclear configuration H*H%) for elliptical constructions.

L+H*L%, a pitch contour consisting of a rise in the last stressed syllable and a final boundary tone, has been attested in 4 different Peninsular prosodic varieties, Castilian Spanish, northern Castilian Spanish, Andalusian Spanish and in the bilingual area of Catalonia. Furthermore, this pattern is used in the standard variety and it is a widespread pattern for realizing narrow focus, not only in the Peninsular Spanish but also in American varieties (Prieto and Roseano 2010).

H*H%, which consists of a sustained high pitch (*plateau*) from the first stressed syllable of the utterances, also has been attested in Castilian Spanish, Andalusian Spanish, etc. and it is used in the Standard variety.

The stimuli were recorded in their natural context. All the selected clauses can appear with both pitch contours in the adequate context. In order to elicit the clauses with both contours, a discourse completion task was used (Blum-Kulka 1982). All the stimuli were produced by the same woman, who had knowledge of prosody. This made it possible to produce every elliptical clause with the same intonation pattern. Therefore, all elliptical constructions had the suspended pattern (H*H%) and all insubordinate constructions had the pattern L+H*L% (Figure 2).

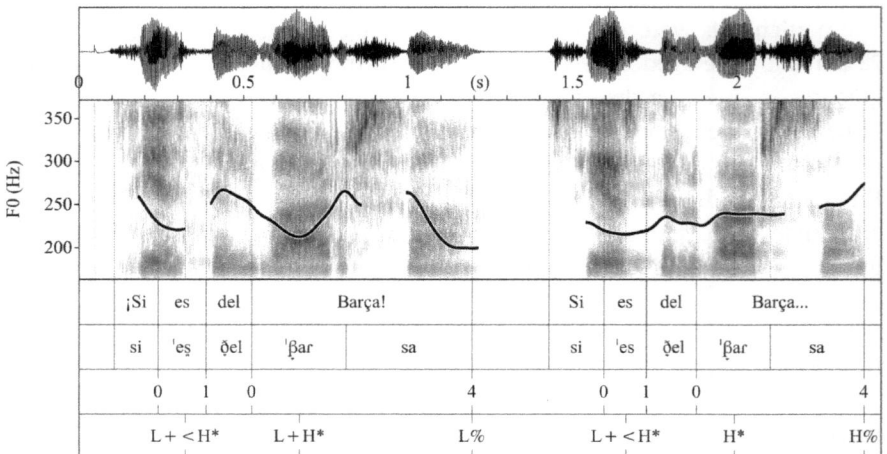

Figure 2: Example of stimuli. Waveform, spectrogram and F0 curve of the construction "Si es del Barça" produced in a refutative context 'But he is a FC Barcelona supporter' (left) and in an elliptical context 'If he is a FC Barcelona supporter. . .' (right).

The recordings were made in an anechoic chamber by means of a Marantz PDM60 recorder and a SHURE SM58 microphone. The files were digitalized with a sampling rate of 44,100 Hz encoded in a format without compression (wav) and later converted to mp3 in order to match the software requirements.

6.2.2 Test 2: Synthetic stimuli

As has been previously said, elliptical clauses can be produced with a doubtful attitude. Likewise, doubt has been claimed to be encoded prosodically through speech rate and creaky voice. Therefore, in order to assure that listeners were relating only intonation to the construction, the stimuli needed to lack those features. To achieve such stimuli it was necessary to manipulate the original utterances. There are two ways of achieving these kinds of stimuli and both include speech synthesis.

The first option consists in creating synthetic stimuli that have their speech rate and quality normalized. This means that any kind of synthesis that uses real speech, like concatenative speech synthesis, will not be methodologically accurate. Instead some kind of articulatory synthesis will be needed (e.g. Klatt synthesis). However, articulatory synthesis is far from perfect and it sounds unnatural and mechanical. Listeners notice that it is an artificial voice and their performance diminishes (Pisoni 1997).

The second option consists in using natural voice and manipulate the stimuli in order to match the requirements. This is the method used in this experiment. The result of this synthesis is more similar to human voice and causes less surprise in the listener but it is far from perfect.

The natural voice stimuli described in 6.2.1 were used as source. And for each stimulus its pitch contour was substituted with the pitch contour of its pair counterpart. For example, the pitch of the original elliptical clause was substituted by the pitch of the refutative clause. As a result, we obtained refutative *si*-clauses with the pitch contour of an elliptical *si*-clause and elliptical *si*-clause with the pitch contour of a refutative *si*-clause. We obtained, hence, incongruous stimuli.

The F0 contour of the stimuli was extracted and by means of Praat (Boersma and Weenink 2015) and PSOLA (Moulines and Charpentier 1990) synthesis method was used in order to achieve the non-congruent stimuli. PSOLA is a method for manipulating the F0 and duration of a speech signal. This kind of synthesis can modify the intonation of a sentence until it matches a given contour (i.e. the intonation of other sentence). It works by slicing the waveform in little pieces and then moving these pieces apart to decrease the pitch or moving them closer in order to get a higher pitch. This way, the intonation of elliptical clauses can be transposed to refutative and vice versa.

As an illustration, Figure 3 shows a construction with its acoustical content and the original F0 contour in black, the grey line depicts the manipulated pitch contour. It can be noticed that the transposition is of the complete contour and not only the nuclear region, since the so-called suspended contour, does not only consist in the nuclear configuration H*H% but in a sustained H tone from the first stressed syllable until the end of the sentence.

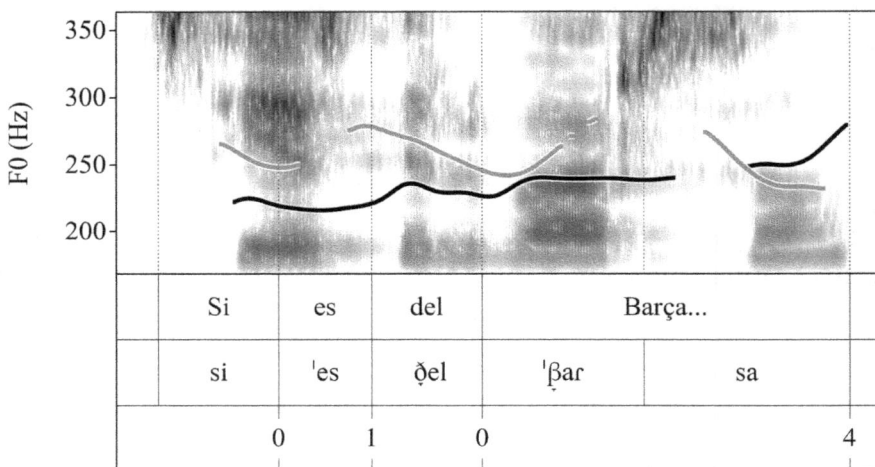

Figure 3: Illustration of the manipulation process. The original pitch contour (drawn in black) corresponding to an elliptical clause was substituted with the grey pitch contour corresponding to a refutative clause.

Therefore, previously elliptical clauses, with all the features of elliptical clauses like speech rate and voice quality, now had the intonation of insubordinate clauses. The files resulting of the manipulation were correct in terms of their prosody but they sounded mechanical as most of PSOLA manipulations. Seventeen experts were asked to assess the "naturalness" of the stimuli compared to natural and to robot-like stimuli, grading the stimuli from 0 to 10 (where 0 represents completely robot-like and 10 completely natural). They graded natural stimuli from 3 to 10 (x= 8.6); robot-like stimuli from 0 to 8 (x=1.3) and the stimuli used in this work from 0 to 9 (x= 3.25).

6.3 Procedure

The task performed by the listeners consisted in choosing the most suitable stimulus in a given context. Contexts were designed to be congruent only with either the elliptical construction or the independent construction. For example, given the previous interaction *Juan se ha comprado una camiseta del Real Madrid* 'Juan has bought a Read Madrid T-shirt' the listeners need to choose between the construction *Si es del Barça* 'SI he is a Barcelona supporter' with rising intonation or rising-falling intonation.

Both tests consisted of four contexts congruent with elliptical constructions and four contexts congruent with insubordinate constructions (see Appendix). The contexts try to include as many situated meanings of the constructions as possible. For example, for the independent constructions there are adversative contexts but also mirative contexts.

The test also included 50 percent of distractors. Each context was tested twice with the answer stimulus in different order to test for participants' consistency. The tests were conducted by means of the on-line tool SurveyGizmo, which allows for the monitoring of listeners' performance and track their IP-addresses in order to check the location of the listeners when they are doing the test.

7 Results

This section details the perception results of 100 listeners of Peninsular Spanish. It comprises the eight contexts in which they had to decide which utterance was more accurate for the given context. The section is divided in 7.1 results with natural stimuli, 7.2 results with synthetic stimuli and 7.3 manipulation effects on listeners' performance.

7.1 Results of test 1: Natural stimuli

The results of the first test reveal a high level of agreement with the hypothesis. When choosing between two non-manipulated stimuli, speakers chose for elliptical the suspended contour (H*H%) in 91 percent of the cases, whereas they chose the rise-falling contour in 9 percent of the trials. In the case of independent contexts, they chose the expected pattern L+H*L% in 98 percent of the cases and the suspended pattern in 2 percent (Table 1).

Table 1: Results for non-manipulated stimuli split by type of context.

		N cases	%
Elliptical	Non expected	74	9%
	Expected	726	91%
Independent	Non expected	17	2%
	Expected	783	98%

If the data are categorized only as expected and not expected disregarding the type of context, expected answers represent 94.3 percent of the cases. The distribution of the patterns is significant (χ^2[1, n=1600, 35,519,p<,01]) meaning that each context has an associated contour. Furthermore, the high level of recognition suggests that the contexts cannot accept other solutions.

7.2 Results of test 2: Manipulated stimuli

The results of the second test are also in high agreement with the hypothesis. In elliptical contexts the listeners chose suspended intonations in 83 percent of the cases and rising-falling contours (L+H*L%) in 17 percent of the trials. In refutational contexts, listeners preferred rising-falling contours (L+H*L%) for 89 percent of the trials and suspended patterns for 11 percent of the cases. Without taking into account the type of context, the expected answers account for 85.75 percent (Table 2).

Table 2: Results for manipulated stimuli split by type of context.

		N cases	%
Elliptical	Non expected	136	17%
	Expected	664	83%
Independent	Non expected	92	11%
	Expected	708	89%

It can be noticed that results obtained with manipulated stimulus are slightly worse that those presented in the previous section. Section 7.3 deals with these differences and tries to explain to what are they due.

7.3 Manipulation effects

Having the same questions and listeners for manipulated and non-manipulated stimuli allowed for checking the manipulation effects in the correctly assigned contours with the help of the McNemmar test for paired samples. Although, as seen in Section 7.2 recognition is good in both cases, listeners' performance is worse when exposed to manipulated stimuli (χ^2 [1, N= 1600, 70,866, p<,01]) (Figure 4).

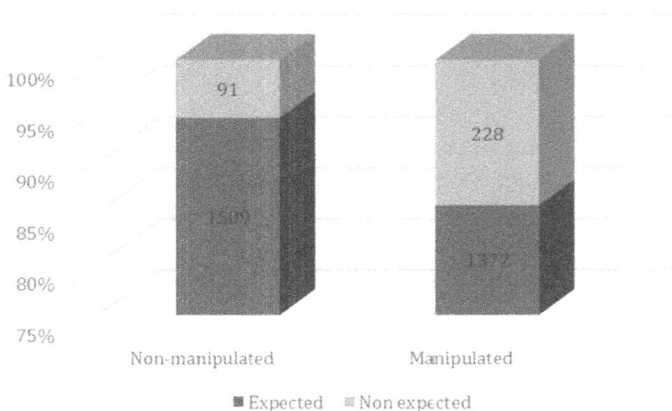

Figure 4: Performance differences between test 1 (left) and 2 (right), which used natural and synthetic stimuli.

This can be due to the influence of speech rate and other suprasegmental features. The stimuli resulting from the manipulation were incongruous, they had the intonation of a refutative clause but the rest of suprasegmental cues were those of an elliptical clause. It is possible that some speakers have used speech rate in order to categorize the stimulus function, however the vast majority of listeners have used intonation as the main cue. Despite having some effect, speech rate is not a definitive parameter and the function of intonation prevails.

This notwithstanding, manipulated stimuli are always more difficult to classify. It has been noted in the literature that synthetic voices entail a greater cognitive load, which affects short-term memory (Luce, Feustel and Pisoni 1983).

Thus, the drop in performance could have two main causes: the stimuli were not congruent, and manipulation always adds noise and some weirdness to the sound. However, seeing Figure 4 it is clear that the recognition rate is good and therefore the listeners attribute H*H% to the elliptical *si*-clause and L+H*L% to the insubordinate clause in most cases even when dealing with manipulated stimuli.

8 Discussion

Results indicate that speakers tend to interpret formally similar constructions differently depending on their intonation. Specifically, they connect the contours with different degrees of independence (i.e., ellipsis and insubordination). On one hand, they link rising boundary tones (H%) with adverbial elliptical clauses. On the other hand, they have chosen the narrow focus contour for the insubordinate construction.

It is worth noting that the contour chosen for elliptical clauses appears also in the non-final clauses of complex sentences, whereas the pattern used for insubordinate clauses appears in final clauses. Therefore, the listeners are using intonation as a formal feature that can distinguish insubordinate clauses from other semi-dependent clauses. Specifically, in Spanish, intonation is a formal difference between insubordinate and adverbial, elliptical clauses. Since prosody is the only feature that allowed distinguishing between the constructions, this could be taken as an indication that the prosody-meaning pair forms a construction by itself. However, this is a hypothesis that needs to be confirmed.

Intonation can also shed light about the emergence of insubordinate constructions. In Evans' (2007) definition of insubordination, he states that a subordinate clause is: "the conventionalized main clause use of what, on prima facie grounds, appear to be formally subordinate clauses" (Evans, 2007:367). In Spanish, insubordinate clauses only share formal, lexical markers with subordinate clauses, but do not share intonation, given that insubordinate clauses can differ prosodically from their subordinate counterparts. Thus, whereas subordinate and elliptical clauses use intonation as a syntactic marker in the form of a continuation rise, in insubordinate clauses intonation needs to be understood both as a syntactic marker and a pragmatic marker. Figure 5 extracted from Elvira-García, Roseano & Fernández-Planas (2017) gives a correlation between the independency level of a construction in Evans' diachronic scheme and its expected prosody in speech production. The present study has shown that this hypothesis also works perceptually.

It has previously been noted that listeners use continuation rises as a trigger for conversational inferences (Safarova 2006) and that this can explain why it occurs up in elliptical clauses. However, the insubordinate *si*-clause also

Dependency stage	Subordinate first clause	Elliptical clause	Insubordinate clause
Intonational pattern	T* H-	T* H%	T* L%

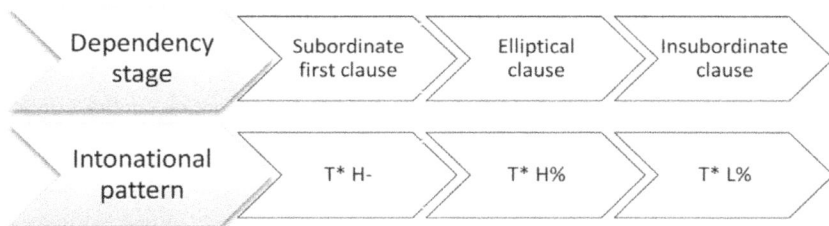

Figure 5: Evans (2007) insubordination scherr a and attested prosodic behaviour. T stands for any possible tone (extracted from [Elvira-García, Roseano & Fernández-Planas 2017]).

implies an inference (a presupposition), so a possible question would be why listeners do not need a continuation rise in order to trigger the inference in this case. An explanation would be that those rises only appear in constructions where the elided clause can be recovered, or in Pierrehumbert & Hirschberg's (1990: 284) words, when there is "more to come". Since the possibility of recovering the second clause has been described as evidence of syntactic dependency (Evans, 2007), the intonation of a sentence can be understood as an indicator of its degree of (in) dependence. In this context, describing continuation rises as markers of syntactic dependency give a more accurate picture of their implications for both syntax and pragmatics.

The perceptual tests show that listeners use intonation as a cue for syntactic dependency insofar as changes in dependency imply changes in the intonational contour. However, these results also provide additional support for Evans' (2007) insubordination theory in terms of ellipsis: Given that complex sentences typically have two minor intonational groups (intermediate phrases) (Bolinger 1984; Navarro Tomás 1944 for Spanish), which correspond to their clauses (main and subordinate respectively), it is to be expected that the intonation of the first clause is a continuation rise. According to Evans (2007), the following stage is the ellipsis of the main clause. Thus, it seems reasonable that the elliptical clause keeps the prosodic features of the subordinate clauses, in this case, in the form of a continuation rise. However, a conclusion about the relationship between the elliptical and insubordinate clauses cannot be drawn from this study. Whereas the results of this study do not contradict the ellipsis theory, alternative pathways to the development of insubordinate clauses remain possible.

Several diachronic paths from subordination to insubordination have been proposed (Mithun 2008; Van de Velde, De Smet & Ghesquière 2013). Even within the same language, different constructions might have followed different paths to achieve syntactic independence. For example, in Spanish, the independent *si*-clause (included in this study) has traditionally been described as a perfect example of the ellipsis theory, given that a presupposition is needed in order to understand the construction (Evans, 2007; Gras, 2011; Schwenter, 2015). However, the independent *que*-initial clause has been described as a discourse-connective clause that would rely on contextual dependency (Gras & Sansiñena 2015) and it may have originated from dyadically dependent clauses (Sansiñena, De Smet & Cornillie 2015).

It must be noted that the prosodic schema that I have put forward in this chapter would only be congruent for the first case mentioned, that is cases where Evans' (2007) ellipsis-based pathway can be applied. In other words, only insubordinate clauses where there is a presupposition involved in the correct understanding of the sentence, would have shown an intonational rise in a previous stage of development, given that only constructions relying on a presupposition would need a continuation rise in order to be processed appropriately.

9 Conclusions

Grammarians have often drawn attention to the intonation of grammatical constructions. From the perspective of intonational studies, laboratory phonology (Pierrehumbert, Beckman and Ladd 2000) has been pointing out for years the importance of empirical work in phonetics and its relevance for intonation studies. In this sense, this work does not want to be an exception but a new imperative, since working with empirical approaches in insubordination can enrich both insubordination studies and intonational studies.

In many studies Independent and elliptical *si*-clauses in Spanish have been taken as prototypical cases of two different stages of the insubordination process (i.e. elliptical and insubordinate) proposed by Evans (2007): The first stage being an elliptical clause and the fourth the insubordinate clause. Many studies have also claimed that the two constructions differ in their intonation patterns. In particular, the independent *si*-clause has been claimed to have a characteristic intonation in these works that makes it different from its elliptical counterpart but also forms a broad focus declarative (Montolío 1999a; Schwenter 2015). Mainly, it is claimed to appear with contours related to contrastive focus and statements of the obvious, while its elliptical counterpart shows continuation rises.

The results of the present study highlight that <*si* + V indicative> construction, which is an ambiguous form, since it can correspond to the independent *si*-clause which has a refutational meaning or to the elliptical *si*-clause, is processed by listeners as elliptical when it shows a pitch contour consistent with a continuation rise and as insubordinate when it shows a contrastive focus pitch contour. The contours that were tested in the experiment were H*H% (Spanish suspended pattern) for continuation rise patterns and L+H*L% for narrow focus; both of them are used in most Spanish varieties and especially in Castilian Spanish. The recognition rate surpasses 80 percent even when tested with synthetic incongruous stimuli.

In sum, elliptical and independent *si*-clauses in Spanish can share their syntactic form and lexis content but differ formally in their intonation. Therefore, in order to provide a complete description, prosody needs to be included since it is a determinant feature of its form that gives a cue as to ts level of syntactic independency (elliptical or insubordinate). It has already been shown that the distinction between elliptical and insubordinate clauses can be performed using the acoustic prosodic features of the constructions (Elvira-García, Roseano and Fernández-Planas 2017) and the present study shows that the same distinction can be detected perceptually.

Acknowledgements: I would like to thank both reviewers for their careful reading and insightful and constructive comments. Also, I would like to thank the following colleagues for assessing the "naturalness" of the synthetic stimuli: Albert Ventayol (Cambridge University); Macarena Céspedes (Universidad Alberto Hurtado); Mauricio Figueroa (Universidad de Concepción); Paolo Roseano (University of South Africa); Santiago González-Fuentes (Universitat Pompeu Fabra); Karina Cerda (Pontificia Universidad Católica de Chile); Giane Santos (Universidade Federal do Pampa); Sebastián Zepeda (Pontificia Universidad Católica de Chile); Diana Muñoz (Pontificia Universidad Católica de Chile); Ana Ma. Fernández Planas (Universitat de Barcelona), Juanma Garrido (Universitat de Barcelona); Francisco Nocetti (Universidad de Concepción) Joaquín Miranda Puentes (Pontificia Universidad Católica de Chile); Rafèu Sichel-Bazin (Université Toulouse 2 – Jean Jaurès) Ingo Feldhausen (Goethe-Universität Frankfurt) and 7 anonymous phoneticians.

References

Almela Pérez, Ramón. 1985. El si introductor de oraciones independientes en español. *LEA. Lingüística española actual* 7(1). Madrid Centro Iberoamericano de Cooperación. 5–14.
Beckman, Mary E., Manuel Díaz-Campos, Julia Tevis McGory & Terrell A. Terell A. Morgan. 2002. Intonation across Spanish, in the Tones and Break Indices framework. *Probus* 14 (1). 9–36. doi:10.1515/prbs.2002.008. http://www.degruyter.com/view/j/prbs.2002.14. issue-1/prbs.2002.008/prbs.2002.008.xml (30 June, 2016).

Beckman, Mary & Julia Hirschberg. 1994. The ToBI annotation conventions. *Ohio State University*. http://web3.cs.columbia.edu/~julia/courses/CS4706/hw/tobi/tobi_convent. pdf (13 July, 2014).

Bello, Andrés. 1988. *Gramática de la lengua castellana destinada al uso de los americanos*. 1st ed. 18. Madrid: Arco/Libros.

Berndt, Rita Sloan, Aita Salasoo, Charlotte C. Mitchum & Sheila E. Blumstein. 1988. The role of intonation cues in aphasic patients' performance of the grammaticality judgment task. *Brain and Language* 34(1). 65–97. doi:10.1016/0093-934X(88)90125-3.

Blum-kulka, Shoshana. 1982. Learning to say what you mean in a second language: A study of the speech act performance of learners of hebrew as a second language. *Applied Linguistics* 3 (1). Oxford University Press. 29–59. doi:10.1093/applin/III.1.29. http://applij. oxfordjournals.org/cgi/doi/10.1093/applin/III.1.29 (30 June, 2016).

Boersma, Paul & David Weenink. 2015. Praat: doing phonetics by computer. http://www. praat.org/.

Bolinger, Dwight. 1984. Intonational Signals of Subordination. *Proceedings of the Annual Meeting of the Berkeley Linguistics Society*, vol. 10, 401–403. doi:10.3765/bls.v10i0.1941. http://journals.linguisticsociety.org/proceedings/index.php/BLS/article/view/1941 (16 May, 2015).

Bolinger, Dwight. 1989. *Intonation and its uses: Melody in grammar and discourse*. Standford, California: Stanford University Press.

Bybee, Joan L & David Eddington. 2006. A Usage-based Approach to Spanish Verbs of "Becoming." *Language* 82(2). 323–355. doi:10.1353/lan.2006.0081. http://muse.jhu. edu/content/crossref/journals/language/v082/82.2bybee.pdf.

Calhoun, Sasha & Antje Schweitzer. 2012. Can Intonation Contours be Lexicalised? Implications for Discourse Meanings. In G. Elordieta & P. Prieto (eds.) Prosody and Meaning (Interface Explorations 15, pp. 271–328), Berlin: De Gruyter Mouton.

Chomsky, N. 1969. Deep structure, surface structure, and semantic interpretation. https:// scholar.google.es/scholar?q=chomsky+deep+surface+semantic+chomsky&btnG=&hl= es≈sdt=0%2C5#0 (20 July, 2015).

Croft, William. 2001. *Radical construction grammar: Syntactic theory in typological perspective*. Oxford: Oxford University Press on Demand.

Elvira-García, Wendy. 2012. Análisis pragmaprosódico de las oraciones replicativas de "si" en español. Barcelona: Universitat de Barcelona.

Elvira-García, Wendy. 2016. La prosodia de las construcciones insubordinadas conectivo argumentativas del español. Barcelona: University of Barcelona dissertation.

Elvira-García, Wendy, Paolo Roseano & Ana Ma. Fernández-Planas. 2017. Prosody as a cue for syntactic dependency. Evidence from dependent and independent clauses with subordination marks in Spanish. *Journal of Pragmatics* 109. 29–46. doi:10.1016/j. pragma.2016.12.002.

Estebas-Vilaplana, Eva & Pilar Prieto. 2008. La notación prosódica del español: una revisión del Sp-ToBI. *Estudios de fonética experimental* 17. 264–283. http://www.raco.cat/index. php/EFE/article/view/140072/0 (5 April, 2016).

Evans, Nicholas. 2007. Insubordination and its uses. In Irina Nikolaeva (ed.), *Finiteness: theoretical and empirical foundations*. Oxford: Oxford University Press.

Fried, M. & J. O. Östman. 2005. Construction Grammar and spoken language: The case of pragmatic particles. *Journal of Pragmatics* 37(11). 1752–1778. https://www.sciencedirect. com/science/article/pii/S0378216605000858 (23 April, 2018).

Frota, Sónia, Mariapaola D'Imperio, Gorka Elordieta, Pilar Prieto & Marina Vigário. 2007. The phonetics and phonology of intonational phrasing in Romance. In Pilar Prieto, Joan Mascaró & Maria-Josep Solé (eds.), *Segmental and Prosodic Issues in Romance Phonology*, 131–153. Amsterdam/Philadelphia: John Benjamins Publishing Company.
Goldsmith, John Anton. 1976. Autosegmental phonology. Cambridge MA: Massachusetts Institute of Technology (MIT).
Gras, Pedro. 2011. Gramática de Construcciones en Interacción. Propuesta de un modelo y aplicación al análisis de estructuras independientes con marcas de subordinación en español. Barcelona: University of Barcelona dissertation. http://www.tdx.cat/TDX-0308111-094423.
Gras, Pedro & María Sol Sansiñena. 2015. An interactional account of discourse-connective que-constructions in Spanish. *Text & Talk* 35(4). 505–529. doi:10.1515/text-2015-0010. http://www.degruyter.com/view/j/text.2015.35.issue-4/text-2015-0010/text-2015-0010.xml (30 June, 2016).
Hualde, José Ignacio & Pilar Prieto. 2015. Intonational variation in Spanish: European and American varieties. In Sónia Frota & Pilar Prieto (eds.), *Intonational Variation in Romance*, 350–391. Oxford: Oxford University Press.
Jun, Sun-Ah. 2005. *Prosodic typology: the phonology of intonation and phrasing*. Oxford: Oxford University Press.
Jun, Sun-Ah. 2014. *Prosodic Typology II: The Phonology of Intonation and Phrasing*. Oxford: Oxford University Press.
Kaltenböck, Gunther. 2016. On the grammatical status of insubordinate if-clauses. In Gunther Kaltenböck, Evelien Keizer & Arne Lohmann (eds.), *Outside the clause: Form and function of extra-clausal constituents*, 341–378. Amsterdam: Benjamins Publishing Company.
Kawanachi, Kazuhiro. 2010. Pitch Accent Patterns and Meanings of Full and Insubordinated Conditional Constructions in Sidaama. *Symposium "Dynamics of Insubordination."*
Kay, Paul & Charles J. Fillmore. 1999. Grammatical Constructions and Linguistic Generalizations: The What's X Doing Y? Construction. *Language* 75 (1).Linguistic Society of America. 1–33. http://www.jstor.org/stable/417472.
Liberman, Alvin M., Katherine Safford Harris, Howard S. Hoffman & Belver C. Griffith. 1957. The discrimination of speech sounds within and across phoneme boundaries. *Journal of Experimental Psychology* 54 (5).American Psychological Association. 358–368. doi:10.1037/h0044417. http://content.apa.org/journals/xge/54/5/358 (30 September, 2016).
Liberman, Mark. 1975. The intonational system of English. *PhD Thesis, MIT. Liberman, Mark and Alan Prince* 8. 249–336.
Liberman, Mark & Ivan Sag. 1974. Prosodic form and discourse function. *Chicago Linguistics Society (CLS)* 10. 416–427.
Linebarger, Marcia C., Myrna F. Schwartz & Eleanor M. Saffran. 1983. Sensitivity to grammatical structure in so-called agrammatic aphasics. *Cognition* 13(3). 361–392. doi:10.1016/0010-0277(83)90015-X.
Lombardi Vallauri, Edoardo. 2004. Grammaticalization of syntactic incompleteness: free conditionals in Italian and other languages. *Sky Journal of Linguistics* 17. 189–215.
Luce, Paul, Timothy Feustel & David Pisoni. 1983. Capacity Demands in Short-Term Memory for Synthetic and Natural Speech. *Human Factors: The Journal of the Human Factors* and Ergonomics Society 25(1). 17–32. doi:10.1177/001872088302500102. http://www.ncbi.nlm.nih.gov/pubmed/6840769 (2 October, 2016).
Marandin, Jean-Marie. 2006. Contours as constructions. *Constructions* SV1(10).

Michaelis, Laura A. & Knud Lambrecht. 1996. Toward a Construction-Based Theory of Language Function: The Case of Nominal Extraposition. *Language* 72 (2).Linguistic Society of America. 215. doi:10.2307/416650. https://www.jstor.org/stable/416650?origin= crossref (23 April, 2018).

Mithun, Marianne. 2008. The Extension of Dependency Beyond the Sentence. *Language* 84 (1).Linguistic Society of America. 69–119. doi:10.1353/lan.2008.0054. http://www.jstor. org/stable/40071012 (7 September, 2015).

Moliner, María. 1966. *Diccionario de uso del español.*. Vol. 2a. Madrid: Gredos.

Montolío, Estrella. 1999a. ¡Si nunca he dicho que estuviera enamorada de él! Sobre construcciones independientes introducidas por si con valor replicativo. *Oralia: análisis del discurso oral* 2. Madrid: Arco/Libros. 37–70.

Montolío, Estrella. 1999b. Las construcciones condicionales. In Ignacio Bosque & Violeta Demonte (eds.), *Gramática descriptiva de la lengua española*, vol. 3, 3643. Madrid: Espasa.

Moulines, Eric & Francis Charpentier. 1990. Pitch-synchronous waveform processing techniques for text-to-speech synthesis using diphones. *Speech communication* 9(5). 453–467. http://www.sciencedirect.com/science/article/pii/016763939090021Z (7 July, 2015).

Narbona, A. 1990. *Las subordinadas adverbiales impropias. II. Causales y finales, comparativas y consecutivas, condicionales y concesivas*. Málaga. Ágora.

Navarro Tomás, Tomás. 1944. *Manual de entonación española*. 1974th ed. Madrid: Guadarrama.

Pierrehumbert, Janet. 1980. The Phonology and Phonetics of English Intonation. Cambridge, Massachusetts: MIT.

Pierrehumbert, Janet, Mary E. Beckman & D. Robert Ladd. 2000. Conceptual foundations of phonology as a laboratory science. *Phonological knowledge: Conceptual and empirical issues*. Oxford University Press, USA. 273–304.

Pierrehumbert, Janet & Julia Hirschberg. 1990. The meaning of intonational contours in the interpretation of discourse. In P- Cohen, J. Morgan & M. Pollack (eds.), *Intentions in communication*, 271–311. Cambridge MA: Bradford Books, MIT Press. http://www.citeu like.org/group/220/article/874144 (27 April, 2015).

Pisoni, DB. 1997. *Perception of synthetic speech. Progress in speech synthesis*. New York, NY: Springer New York. doi:10.1007/978-1-4612-1894-4_43. http://link.springer.com/10. 1007/978-1-4612-1894-4_43 (2 October, 2016).

Prieto, Pilar & Paolo Roseano (eds.). 2010. *Transcription of Intonation of the Spanish Language*. München: Lincom Europa.

Roseano, Paolo, Ana Ma. Fernández Planas, Wendy Elvira-García & Eugenio Martínez Celdrán. 2015. Els tons de continuació en parla espontània: Descripció i transcripció. *VII Workshop sobre la prosòdia del català*.

Sadat-Tehrani, Nima. 2004. An Intonational Construction. *Constructions* 3 1–13. https:// journals.linguisticsociety.org/elanguage/constructions/article/view/67.html (23 April, 2018).

Safarova, M. 2006. Rises and falls: studies in the semantics and pragmatics of intonation. Universiteit van Amsterdam. http://dare.uva.nl/document/33638 (1 April, 2015).

Sansiñena, María Sol, Hendrik De Smet & Bert Cornillie. 2015. Between subordinate and insubordinate: Paths towards complementizer-initial main clauses. *Journal of Pragmatics* 77. 3–19.

Schwenter, Scott. 1998. Sobre la sintaxis de una construcción coloquial. *Anuari de Filologia. Secció F, Estudios de lengua y literatura españolas*(9). Barcelona: Universitat de Barcelona. 87–100.

Schwenter, Scott. 2015. Independent si clauses in Spanish: Functions and Consequences for Insubordination. In Nicholas Evans & Honoré Watabe (eds.), *Dynamics of Insubordination*, 1–19. Amsterdam: Benjamins Publishing Company.

Schwenter, Scott A. 2016. Meaning and interaction in Spanishindependent si-clauses. *Language Sciences*. doi:http://dx.doi.org/10.1016/j.langsci.2016.04.007.

Sosa, Juan Manuel. 1999. *La entonación del español: su estructura fónica, variabilidad y dialectología*. Madrid: Cátedra.

Vanrell, Maria del Mar, Meghan E. Armstrong & Pilar Prieto. 2014. The role of prosody in the encoding of evidentiality in Catalan. *Speech Prosody*(5). Dublin, Ireland. 1222–1226.

Vanrell, Maria del Mar, Joan Borràs-Comes, Paolo Roseano & Pilar Prieto. 2011. Prosodic cues of confidence and uncertainty in Catalan. *Phonetics & Phonology in Iberia (PaPI)*. Tarragona: Universitat Rovira i Virgili, poster session. http://wwwa.urv.cat/deaa/PaPI2011/poster_session_T_files/Prosodic cues of confidence and uncertainty in Catalan.pdf.

Velde, F. Van de, H. De Smet & L. Ghesquière. 2013. On multiple source constructions in language change. *Studies in Language. International Journal sponsored by the Foundation "Foundations of Language,"* vol. 37, 473–489. doi:10.1075/sl.37.3.01int. http://www.jbe-platform.com/content/journals/10.1075/sl.37.3.01int (3 July, 2018).

Appendix

This appendix contains the dialogues used and context and the answer-stimuli used in the perception test. In the codification of contexts and answers (i) stands for insubordinate and (e) for elliptical.

Contexts where the expected answer is the independent clause

1i Carla no ve a María desde el instituto. Un día mientras pasea con su madre, la ve y dice: [Carla has not seen María since high school. One day, while she is walking with her mother, sees her and says]
1ii ¡Si es María! [SI she is María]
1ih Si es María. . . [If she is María]

2i Lorena ha empezado a salir con Paco [Lorena is dating Paco]
2ii ¡Si está casado! [But he is married]
2ih Si está casado. . . [If he is married]

3i Yo el lunes tengo que llegar a la oficina a las 8 [I need to be in the office at 8 on Monday]
3ii -¡Si el lunes es fiesta! [BUT Monday is bank holiday]
3ih -Si el lunes es fiesta. . . [If Monday is bank holiday]

4i - Paco se ha comprado una camiseta del Real Madrid
4ii - ¡Si es del Barça! [BUT he is a Barcelona supporter]
4ih - Si es del Barça. . . [If he is a Barcelona supporter]

Contexts where the expected answer is the elliptical clause

5e La vida es bella. [Life is beautiful]
5ee Si tú lo dices. . . [If you say so]
5ei ¡Si tú lo dices! [SI you say so]

6e ¿Vamos a la playa? [Shall we go to the beach?]
6ee Si hace bueno. . . [If the weather is nice]
6ei ¡Si hace bueno! [But the weather is nice]

7e Mi marido no va nunca a ver a sus padres [My husband never visits his parents]
7eh Si no le apetece. . . [If he does not feel like going]
7ei ¡Si no le apetece! [SI he does not feel like going]

8e ¿Vas a ir comprar entradas para el concierto? [Are you buying the concert tickets?]
8e Si he cobrado. . . [If my wage has been paid]
8ei ¡Si he cobrado! [But my wage has been paid]

Sophie von Wietersheim and Sam Featherston

8 Does structural binding correlate with degrees of functional dependence?

Abstract: In German and English, the connector *während/while* can introduce two formally identical but functionally different adverbial clauses. In the example *Jeder Läufer_i hört Musik, während er_i durch den Park joggt* ('Every runner_i listens to music while he_i jogs through the park.') the connector *während* has a temporal sense and introduces a dependent clause which modifies the event in the matrix clause. In *Jeder Athlet_i geht morgens joggen, während er_i abends schwimmen geht* ('Every athlete_i jogs in the morning, while he_i swims in the evening.'), by contrast, *während* introduces an equally subordinate but functionally more independent event which stands in contrast to the matrix clause event.

While both clauses are clearly subordinate, different degrees of structural integration may be identified between them in phenomena such as binding (Reis 1997; Haegeman 2004; Frey 2011). Authors have used evidence from binding as a test of integration. However, this data contains a number of complicating factors and can require fine judgements. The work reported here examines these phenomena in carefully controlled conditions.

Our research aim is to explore whether binding data provides reliable empirical support for current models of interclausal relations. We have conducted a series of experiments testing variable binding in a range of adverbial clauses of varying degrees of structural integration, like temporal and adversative clauses with *während*.

Our results show that binding relations can provide very robust evidence for the integration status of even very closely related types of subordinate clauses. Our participants clearly distinguished between the binding possibilities of the different types. We conclude first, that this evidence type is a very sound evidential basis for syntax work in this area, and second, that the theoretical work distinguishing different types of adverbial clauses is on the right track, in that it builds upon differentiations which are verifiably psychologically real.

Sophie von Wietersheim, Sam Featherston, University of Tübingen

https://doi.org/10.1515/9783110638288-009

1 Introduction

This paper focuses on two types of adverbial clauses and their formal and functional relationship towards matrix clauses. While some adverbial clauses are both formally and functionally dependent on their associated clause, some seem to be either only formally or only functionally connected to them, and some adverbial clauses are fully independent (cf. Freywald 2014). In German, formal dependence of a clause is usually (but not obligatorily) reflected in the presence of a conjunction introducing this clause, and in the location of the finite verb in the final position of the clause – as opposed to the finite verb in the first or second position of an unintroduced independent (main) clause. Functional dependence will here be understood in the sense of whether the adverbial clause proposition is part of the matrix clause proposition or not (cf. Freywald 2014).

The German conjunction *während* 'while' can be used to introduce two different kinds of adverbial clauses, one temporal, and one adversative. They differ from one another in that formally they both seem to be dependent clauses, but functionally only the temporal adverbial clause is dependent on its matrix clause.

(1) a. *Marie liest   Zeitung,   während sie   morgens   Kaffee trinkt.*
Mary   reads   newspaper while   she in the morning coffee   drinks
'Mary reads the newspaper while she drinks coffee in the morning.'

  b. *Marie trinkt   abends   Tee,*
Mary   drinks   in the evening tea
während sie   morgens   Kaffee trinkt.
while   she in the morning coffee   drinks
'Mary drinks tea in the evening, while she drinks coffee in the morning.'

In example (1a), the temporal adverbial clause introduced by *während* 'while' directly modifies the matrix clause event by defining its temporal frame. The adversative clause in (1b) shows the same formal features – the introducing conjunction *während* 'while, whereas', and the finite verb in the clause-final position – but it has a different function: it does not modify the proposition of the associated clause but adds another, contrasting proposition. Interestingly, and as already evident in the English translation of German *während* in (1), English *while* can also introduce a temporal and an adversative adverbial clause; Haegeman (2003, 2004, 2006) organizes these two kinds of English adverbial clauses into two different groups: central adverbial clauses (*CACs*) and peripheral adverbial clauses (*PACs*). CACs "structure the event expressed in the associated clause and [...] [PACs] structure the discourse" (Haegeman 2004: 61). Frey (2011) adopts Haegeman's classification of English adverbial clauses and applies it to German adverbial clauses; thus, both temporal English *while* and temporal German *während* fall into the group of CACs, whereas adversative English *while* and adversative German *während* are PACs.

Although the adverbial clauses in (1) show the same dependent-clause form, they are assumed to occupy different structural positions within their matrix clause, which reflects their different functions. The CAC in (1a) presumably occupies a position in the matrix VP, or at least below IP; the PAC in (1b) on the other hand could be attached as an adjunct to (or within) CP (Haegeman 2004; Frey 2011). CACs thus show formal and functional dependence on their matrix clause being structurally fully integrated[1] into it. The higher attachment position for the PACs reflects that they are functionally more independent of their matrix clause and less integrated. Nevertheless, they are still formally dependent (cf. Pauly 2014 on functional and formal (non)integration of adversative *während* 'while, whereas').

In the literature, there are various tests used to distinguish CACs and PACs; we will only present two of them here a negative expression should be able to scope into a CAC (2a) but not into a PAC (2b), and CACs should allow variable binding[2] into them (3a), while PACs are not supposed to (3b) (Frey 2011).

(2) a.

Marie	liest	**nicht**	die	Zeitung,
Mary	reads	not	the	newspaper
während	sie	morgens	Kaffee	trinkt,
while	she	in the morning	coffee	drinks
sondern	während	sie	morgens	
but	while	she	in the morning	
auf	den	Bus	wartet.	
for	the	bus	waits.	

'Mary doesn't read the newspaper while she drinks coffee in the morning, but while she waits for the bus in the morning.'

---

1 An integrated clause is a dependent clause, while a dependent clause is not necessarily an integrated clause (Reich and Reis 2013: 541).

2 We assume that binding takes place here when the interpretation of the pronoun as a variable is possible. For example, in (i) we understand *her* not to refer to a specific mother but to any mother the reader might choose (e.g. Büring 2005):

(i) *Every mother$_i$ wants her$_i$ son to succeed.*

This bound-variable reading is much more difficult to get in an example such as (ii):

(ii) *Her$_{*i/j}$ son disappoints every mother$_i$.*

b.
*Marie	trinkt	abends	**keinen**	Tee,
Mary	drinks	in the evening	no	tea
während	sie	morgens	Kaffee	trinkt,
while	she	in the morning	coffee	drinks
sondern	während sie	morgens	Saft	trinkt.
but	while she	in the moning	juice	drinks

'Mary doesn't drink tea in the evening, while she drinks coffee in the morning, but while she drinks juice in the morning.'

(3) a.
Jeder	Hotelgast$_i$	las	heute	Morgen	Zeitung.
every	hotel guest	read	today	morning	newspaper
während	er$_i$		Kaffee	trank.	
while	he		coffee	drank	

'Every hotel guest$_i$ read the newspaper this morning while he$_i$ drank coffee.'

b.
*Jeder	Hotelgast$_i$	trank	heute	Morgen	Tee,
every	hotel guest	drank	today	morning	tea
während	er$_i$	gestern	Kaffee	trank.	
while	he	yesterday	coffee	drank	

'Every hotel guest$_i$ drank tea this morning, while yesterday he$_i$ drank coffee.'

These tests seem to support the idea that CACs are more integrated into their matrix clauses than PACs because both negative scope and variable binding require the structural relation of c-command between matrix clause and adverbial clause. A CAC is thus attached deeply enough within the matrix clause for the matrix subject, in specIP or specCP, to c-command into it, while the attachment point of a PAC is above the subject position and therefore blocks c-command.[3]

However, in the literature, there is no clear agreement on whether a clause fails or passes these tests. Contra Frey (2011), Pauly (2014) argues that variable binding cannot be seen as a reliable test to differentiate between CACs and PACs, since there are examples that allow variable binding into PACs. He offers

---

3 Note that our work is based on a formal approach to clause combining; however, a functionalist approach could also support a categorization of clause types along the lines of CACs and PACs (cf. Verstraete 2007). For example, Verstraete (2007: 144) proposes to use a scope parameter to distinguish different types of subordinate clauses, which essentially groups them into clauses that are part of the matrix clause proposition and clauses that are not.

example (4) as one of his (rather complex) examples for adversative *während* 'while, whereas' and successful binding[4]:

(4) | *Für* | *[jeden* | *der* | *Beobachter]$_i$* | *bewegt* | *sich* | *das* | *andere* |
|---|---|---|---|---|---|---|---|
| for | every of | the | observers | moves | itself | the | other |
| *System,* | *während* | *er$_i$* | *sich* | *relativ* | *zu* | *seinem* | *System* |
| system | while | he | himself | in relation | to | his | system |
| *in* | *Ruhe* | *befindet.* | | | | | |
| at | rest | situated | | | | | |

'For [each of the observes]$_i$ the other system is moving while he$_i$ is motionless in relation to is system.'
(Pauly 2014: 189, (235e); translation added and example modified by authors)

In addition to adversative adverbial clauses introduced by *während* 'while, whereas', Frey (2011) also classifies concessive adverbial clauses introduced by *obwohl* 'although' as PACs, which means that they should not allow variable binding into them. Freywald (2014), however, gives example (5) among others to show that some *obwohl* clauses do allow binding.

(5) | *Aber* | *bei* | *all* | *den* | *kulinarischen* | *Delikatessen* | *war* | *es* |
|---|---|---|---|---|---|---|---|
| but | with | all | the | culinary | deli.food | was | it |
| *auch* | *kein* | *Wunder,* | *dass* | *jeder$_i$,* | *obwohl* | *er$_i$* | *bereits* |
| also | no | wonder | that | everyone | although | he | already |
| *schon* | *zu* | *Abend* | *gegessen* | *hatte,* | *sich* | *noch* | *einmal* |
| to | | evening | eaten | had, | himself | once | again |
| *Nachschlag* | *holte.* | | | | | | |
| refill | fetched | | | | | | |

'But with all the culinary deli food it was no surprise that everyone$_i$ got themselves a refill, although they$_i$ had eaten dinner already.'
(Freywald 2014: 143, (13b); translation added and example modified by authors)

---

4 We agree with a reviewer, who comments that this example might contain additional factors supporting a bound-variable reading, e.g. information structure. The topicalized position of the quantifier expression could make the bound-variable reading more accessible than a lower structural position. However, authors using the binding test prefer this position (SpecCP) for the quantifier phrase: if binding into an adverbial clause is impossible from this position, one can conclude that the adverbial clause should be attached above the CP of the matrix clause. See also footnote 17.

Note that Freywald (2014) divides adverbial clauses introduced by *obwohl* 'although' into four different types of categories, two of which are CACs and PACs (we will not go into detail on the other two categories here). Freywald (2014: 142) concedes that in general *obwohl* clauses tend to be peripheral and do not allow binding, but that there are *obwohl* clauses that do show successful variable binding and can be analysed as CACs.[5] Frey (2016a, 2016b) argues that concessive *obwohl* clauses cannot be CACs but only PACs, or even less integrated into their matrix clause. He suggests that Freywald's (2014) successful binding examples for these adverbial clauses are rather interpreted as concessive conditionals than as purely concessive clauses. He gives example (6) to show that if the concessive conjunction *obwohl* 'although' in (5) is replaced with the concessive conditional conjunction *auch wenn* 'even if' then binding is clearly possible because concessive conditionals can be CACs.

(6) | *Aber* | *bei* | *all* | *den* | *kulinarischen* | *Delikatessen* | *war* | *es* |
|---|---|---|---|---|---|---|---|
| but | with | all | the | culinary | deli.food | was | it |
| *auch* | *kein* | *Wunder,* | *dass* | *jeder$_i$,* | ***auch*** | ***wenn*** | *er$_i$* |
| also | no | wonder | that | everyone | even | if | he |
| *bereits* | *schon* | *zu* | *Abend* | *gegessen* | *hatte,* | *sich* | *noch* |
| already | | to | evening | eaten | had, | himself | once |
| *einmal* | *Nachschlag* | *holte.* | | | | | |
| again | refill | fetched | | | | | |

'But with all the culinary deli food it was no surprise that everyone$_i$ got themselves a refill, **even if** they$_i$ had eaten dinner already.'
(Frey (2016a), originally from Freywald (2014: 143, (13b)); translation added and slightly modified by authors)

It is not completely clear what triggers this concessive-conditional interpretation of an *obwohl* clause; especially since this interpretation differs from that of a purely concessive interpretation: in the concessive example in (5) everyone has had a full dinner already but still gets a refill; in the concessive-conditional example in (6) not necessarily everyone has had a full dinner yet. Perhaps speakers adopt the different but nevertheless closely related concessive-conditional

---

5 Even though adverbial clauses introduced by *obwohl* 'although' are CACs in Freywald's (2014) analysis and allow variable binding, they do not fulfil all of the other characteristics of CACs, e.g. they cannot be scoped over by a negative expression in the matrix clause (Freywald 2014: 142).

interpretation in the concessive cases in order to repair the otherwise impossible binding and avoid a complete failure of interpretation.

There is thus obviously no clear consensus on whether adverbial clauses with adversative *während* 'while, whereas' and concessive *obwohl* 'although' allow binding into them or not. We therefore wanted to test exactly these two adverbial clauses and their binding behaviour experimentally to see whether Frey's (2011) claim that they should not allow variable binding can be supported empirically. Together with these two clauses, which we will categorize as PACs following Frey (2011, 2016a, 2016b), we also tested two CACs in order to contrast their binding results with those of the PACs. The two CACs are introduced by the temporal conjunction *während* 'while' and another temporal conjunction *nachdem* 'after'. Using the conjunction *während* 'while' in its two functions allows us a direct comparison of two different kinds of adverbial clauses without a possible interference of lexical differences.

In this paper, we will present our study on the binding behaviour of four German adverbial clauses, two CACs, two PACs. This experiment is part of an extensive studies series (parts of which are reported in von Wietersheim & Featherston 2016 and von Wietersheim 2016) centred around the temporal CAC and the adversative PAC both introduced by one and the same conjunction *während* 'while'.

We will first introduce our study on variable binding into two CACs and PACs presenting our experimental method, including the sentence material and our predictions. Then we will report the results of our empirical investigation and show that they offer an interesting picture which demands careful analysis. We will demonstrate that the experimental data on binding is much more detailed and not as clearly black-and-white as might be assumed. To conclude we will sum up and interpret our findings.

2 CACs and PACs – experiment

The aim of the experiment reported in this paper was to empirically investigate whether variable binding as a test of structural integration of clauses would yield clear behavioural differences between CACs and PACs. We concentrated on the German conjunction *während* 'while' and its temporal and adversative usages, and added a second CAC – introduced by temporal *nachdem* 'after' – and a second PAC – introduced by concessive *obwohl* 'although' – as a controls.

In order to test the behaviour of CACs and PACs under variable binding, we chose the universal quantifier expression *jede NP* 'every NP' as the binder, which according to Pauly (2014: 107–108) should be preferred to test for c-command relations and structural binding.[6]

We compared the binding behaviour of CACs and PACs focusing on two aspects: the first one is the linear order of matrix clause and adverbial clause,[7] such that the adverbial clause either precedes or follows the matrix clause; the second one is the relative position of the quantifier expression either in the matrix clause or in the adverbial clause. Combining these two binary parameters in a two-by-two design, we had four conditions in which each type of adverbial clause was tested. Note that the two parameters interact with one another: for example, if the matrix clause precedes the adverbial clause and the quantifier expression is positioned within the matrix clause, then the quantifier expression as the binder also precedes the variable as the bindee in the adverbial clause. Depending on the combination of the two factors of linear order of clauses and position of quantifier expression, the order of binder and bindee is affected as well. These two parameters together thus yield both cases for which variable binding is generally predicted to be successful, and cases for which variable binding is expected to be unsuccessful. This allows us to compare the effects of the structural difference of PACs and CACs on their binding behaviour empirically. Since the important binding requirement of c-command is possible from the matrix clause into a CAC but not into a PAC, we expect to see clear binding effects for CACs, and less or no effects for PACs.

2.1 Method

We presented our four types of adverbial clauses in the four syntactic conditions resulting from the two binary parameters, thus varying in the linear order of matrix clause and adverbial clause and in the position of the quantifier expression. This results in 16 conditions which occurred in eight different items,

---

6 Pauly (2014) also assesses the negative quantifier expressions *keiner* 'nobody'/ *keine NP* 'no NP' as preferable binders to test for syntactic relations. He nevertheless claims that there is no absolutely reliable way to test for real structural variable binding. In our studies series we found that negative quantifier expressions have to be used with care when employed in tests of variable binding: possible effects of the negation need to be separated from those of the quantification, since the two might add up and thus alter the results (von Wietersheim 2016).

7 A reviewer comments that prosodic contours could affect the accessibility of binding in our examples and these could vary with the linear ordering of the clauses. This is no doubt true, but we assume that our experimental design should control this factor. Our experiments show that participants always assume the prosody of the most accessible reading, which is also specified by our "reference clarifications" (see below).

i.e. lexical variants. We carefully tried to keep the lexical material as comparable as possible across the four types of adverbial clauses. The lexical content and form of the adverbial clauses is nearly identical, and only the matrix clauses vary to match the specific semantics of each adverbial clause.

Some of the tested conditions are less natural cases of variable binding so that in these cases participants might adopt a reading in which the variable refers to a third party in order to make the sentence more natural again. However, we had to ensure that participants always understood the variable as related to the quantifier expression, even if this resulted in a very unacceptable interpretation. We therefore added a short text to each target sentence which clarified the relationship between quantifier expression and variable, thus enforcing the bound variable reading. It also made the semantic relationship between matrix clause and adverbial clause clear. The simple example in (7) illustrates this; the pronoun must refer to *every business woman*:

(7) **reference clarification**: Every business woman is drinking coffee. At the same time, every business woman is reading the newspaper.
target sentence: Every business woman reads the newspaper while she drinks coffee in the morning

The four conditions varying the linear order of matrix clause and adverbial clause and the position of the quantifier expression are labelled as shown in the following table, e.g. *MqAv* stands for *matrix clause & quantifier > adverbial clause & variable*, and *AvMq* for *adverbial clause & variable > matrix clause & quantifier*.

Table 1: Experimental conditions: *MqAv, MvAq, AqMv, AvMq* (table taken from von Wietersheim 2016: 329).

	MqAv	MvAq	AqMv	AvMq
Matrix clause > Adverbial clause	+	+		
Adverbial clause > Matrix clause			+	+
quantifier > variable	+		+	
variable > quantifier		+		+

In examples (8), (9), (10), and (11) we show the four types of adverbial clauses in one of our items and in the four conditions together with the reference clarification; first the two CACs introduced by temporal *während* 'while' (*WT*) and temporal *nachdem* 'after' (*N*), and then the two PACs, introduced by adversative *während* 'while, whereas' (*WA*) and concessive *obwohl* 'although'(*O*).

(8) **während temporal (WT) – reference clarification:**
Damals im Marienklinikum stand jeder Chirurg nachts im OP. Gleichzeitig flirtete jeder Chirurg mit der Krankenschwester.
'Back in the days at St. Mary's hospital, every surgeon stood in the operating theatre at night. At the same time, every surgeon flirted with the nurse.'

a. **WT-MqAv**
Jeder Chirurg$_i$ flirtete mit der Krankenschwester, während er$_i$ nachts im OP stand.
'Every surgeon$_i$ flirted with the nurse while he$_i$ stood in the operating theatre at night.'

b. **WT-MvAq**
Er$_i$ flirtete mit der Krankenschwester, während jeder Chirurg$_i$ nachts im OP stand.
'He$_i$ flirted with the nurse while every surgeon$_i$ stood in the operating theatre at night.'

c. **WT-AqMv**
Während jeder Chirurg$_i$ nachts im OP stand, flirtete er$_i$ mit der Krankenschwester.
'While every surgeon$_i$ stood in the operating theatre at night he$_i$ flirted with the nurse.'

d. **WT-AvMq**
Während er$_i$ nachts im OP stand, flirtete jeder Chirurg$_i$ mit der Krankenschwester.
'While he$_i$ stood in the operating theatre at night every surgeon$_i$ flirted with the nurse.'

(9) **nachdem temporal (N) – reference clarification:**
Damals im Marienklinikum stand jeder Chirurg nachts im OP. Dann war jeder Chirurg erschöpft.
'Back in the days at St. Mary's hospital, every surgeon stood in the operating theatre at night. Afterwards, every surgeon was exhausted.'

a. **N-MqAv**
Jeder Chirurg$_i$ war erschöpft, nachdem er$_i$ nachts im OP gestanden war.
'Every surgeon$_i$ was exhausted after he$_i$ had stood in the operating theatre at night.'

b. **N-MvAq**
Er$_i$ war erschöpft, nachdem jeder Chirurg$_i$ nachts im OP gestanden war.
'He$_i$ was exhausted after every surgeon$_i$ had stood in the operating theatre at night.'

c. **N-AqMv**

Nachdem jeder Chirurg_i nachts im OP gestanden war, war er_i erschöpft.

'After every surgeon_i had stood in the operating theatre at night he_i was exhausted.'

d. **N-AvMq**

Nachdem er_i nachts im OP gestanden war, war jeder Chirurg_i erschöpft.

'After he_i had stood in the operating theatre at night every surgeon_i was exhausted.'

(10) *während* **adversative (WA) – reference clarification:**

Damals im Marienklinikum stand jeder Chirurg nachts im OP. Aber jeder Chirurg schlief tagsüber.

'Back in the days at St. Mary's hospital, every surgeon stood in the operating theatre at night. But every surgeon slept during the day.'

a. **WA-MqAv**

Jeder Chirurg_i schlief tagsüber, während er_i nachts im OP stand.

'Every surgeon_i slept during the day, while he_i stood in the operating theatre at night.'

b. **WA-MvAq**

Er_i schlief tagsüber, während jeder Chirurg_i nachts im OP stand.

'He_i slept during the day, while every surgeon_i stood in the operating theatre at night.'

c. **WA-AqMv**

Während jeder Chirurg_i nachts im OP stand, schlief er_i tagsüber.

'While every surgeon_i stood in the operating theatre at night, he_i slept during the day.'

d. **WA-AvMq**

Während er_i nachts im OP stand, schlief jeder Chirurg_i tagsüber.

'While he_i stood in the operating theatre at night, every surgeon_i slept during the day.'

(11) *obwohl* **concessive (O) – reference clarification:**

Damals im Marienklinikum stand jeder Chirurg nachts im OP. Trotzdem schlief jeder Chirurg tagsüber wenig.

'Back in the days at St. Mary's hospital, every surgeon stood in the operating theatre at night. Nevertheless, every surgeon found little sleep during the day.'

a. **O-MqAv**

Jeder Chirurg_i schlief tagsüber wenig, obwohl er_i nachts im OP stand.

'Every surgeon_i found little sleep during the day, although he_i stood in the operating theatre at night.'

b. **O-MvAq**

Er$_i$ schlief tagsüber wenig, obwohl jeder Chirurg$_i$ nachts im OP stand.
'He$_i$ found little sleep during the day, although every surgeon$_i$ stood in the operating theatre at night.'

c. **O-AqMv**

Obwohl jeder Chirurg$_i$ nachts im OP stand, schlief er$_i$ tagsüber wenig.
'Although every surgeon$_i$ stood in the operating theatre at night, he$_i$ found little sleep during the day.'

d. **O-AvMq**

Obwohl er$_i$ nachts im OP stand, schlief jeder Chirurg$_i$ tagsüber wenig.
'Although he$_i$ stood in the operating theatre at night, every surgeon$_i$ found little sleep during the day.'

In order to distribute the conditions systematically in a counter-balanced pattern over the lexical items, we divided the sentence material into four experimental versions. Thus, participants did not see all conditions in all items.

We would like to point out that our sentence material might exhibit an effect of genericity, which is claimed to make binding seem possible in cases without the usual structural binding requirements (Fox and Sauerland 1995). Thus, the two PACs could show an illusion of binding because of this generic reading and therefore appear to be more acceptable than they are expected to be (e.g. Fox and Sauerland 1995). Since our aim was to keep the lexical form of all four types of adverbial clauses as similar as possible to ensure comparability, putting the finite verb in the past tense, and narrowing the event frame in the reference clarification was the closest we could get to a non-generic interpretation (see Fox and Sauerland 1995). However, if there is a clear genericity effect in the data, we expect it to hold for both PACs and CACs so that all adverbial clause types and their binding behaviour are affected by it. Thus, in direct comparison a generic CAC might be more acceptable than an episodic CAC, and a generic PAC more acceptable than an episodic PAC. We therefore regard genericity as orthogonal to our major structural concern.

In addition to our sentence material, we always include 15 *standard items* into each of the experimental versions. These have two functions: first they serve as fillers, but they are also carefully selected to form a five-point scale of acceptability and naturalness, with each scale point comprising three of these standard items. Their acceptability ranges from very acceptable to very unacceptable. This *standard scale of acceptability* (Featherston 2009) allows us to interpret our results relative to it, and also to compare data across experiments. They also occupy the full range of perceived well-formedness, so that informants have the full breadth of examples to compare the experimental sentences to.

We employ *Thermometer Judgements* (Featherston 2008) as our experimental method: native speakers are presented with our target sentences and instructed to judge their acceptability on a numerical scale. The scale is anchored by two example sentences which are the same throughout all of our experiments. The lower anchor point is exemplified by a fairly unnatural example (*Der Vater holt das frische Vollkornbrot ihm.* 'The father fetches the wholemeal bread him.') which is assigned the value 20. The upper anchor point is a more natural example (*Der Vater holt dem Kind das frische Vollkornbrot.* 'The father fetches the child the wholemeal bread.') which is alloted the value 30. The participants have to give their judgements for each of the target sentences relative to these two anchor points. A more acceptable target sentence would be expected to receive a value of around or above 30, a less acceptable one around or below 20, one that is neither very acceptable nor unacceptable might receive 25. Participants are free to use any value from below 20 to above 30. The anchoring of the scale at 20 and 30 is intended to prevent participants from needing to use numbers near zero, where distortion can occur. Each target sentence is presented one at a time, always together with its specific reference clarification[8] and the two example sentences providing the anchor points. Participants then judge the acceptability of the target sentence in relation to the two anchor points.

Before the actual experiment, participants have to fulfil two practice sessions on assigning values relative to anchor points. All our experiments on acceptability judgements are conducted online. A total of 40 native speakers of German participated in this experiment, most of them students at the University of Tübingen. As an incentive to take part, we provided four prizes of €50 each, which were distributed among the participants by lottery.

2.2 Predictions

We expect our experiment to reflect whether binding is possible or not: if binding fails, participants' acceptability judgements should be worse, if it is successful, they should be better. Classic accounts of the binding theory (e.g. Büring 2005) would suggest that structural binding will be feasible in the CAC conditions when the quantifier c-commands the variable, that is in conditions

---

8 There was no equivalent to our reference clarifications for the standard items. Participants were informed that some of the experimental examples would have reference clarifications but others not.

MqAv and *AvMq* for temporal *während* and temporal *nachdem*. Binding should fail in all other conditions, including all PAC conditions. This would then confirm assumptions of, for example, Frey (2011).

A weaker version of these predictions might suggest that only the CAC conditions *MqAv* and *AvMq* will be fully acceptable, but the other conditions might exhibit different degrees of acceptability. This would require an investigation of how these different degrees come about, and whether the binding test nevertheless distinguishes CACs and PACs.

2.3 Results

The results of our experiment can be seen below in Figure 1. The y-axis of the chart shows the acceptability judgements normalized by conversion to z-scores. The error bars show the 95% confidence intervals of the mean judgement scores by condition. The length of the error bars shows the error variance, while the marker symbol shows the mean value.

The scores of the standard items on the very right of the chart, labelled *a-e*, clearly show five different degrees of acceptability. The distribution of these five degrees is even and they form a stable standard scale of acceptability against which we can measure our target items. Level *a* of the standard items corresponds to "very acceptable", level *b* to "acceptable", level *c* to "?", level *d* to "??", and level *e* to "*". The use of these standard items thus provides us with something close to an absolute scale of perceived well-formedness, in the sense that they allow us to compare individual scores across experiments. Linguists often ask experimenters whether the results show that a structure is grammatical or not. The experimenters can usually only give an answer in relative terms, structure A is better/worse than structure B. These standard items allow us to get round this problem by providing fixed values.

Turning to the two CACs (represented by the solid square markers) we see a data pattern of one very acceptable condition (*MqAv*) at about levels *a* to *b* of the standard items, one quite unacceptable condition (*MvAq*) at levels *c* to *d*, and two middling conditions (*AqMv, AvMq*) at levels *b* to *c*. This pattern is the same for both the two adverbial clauses introduced by *nachdem* 'after' and temporal *während* 'while'.

A similar but much more compressed pattern can be found for the PACs (represented by the out-lined triangular markers). However, the data points for adversative *während* 'while, whereas' show less acceptable values than the data points for *obwohl* 'although'. The condition judged best for adversative *während* 'while' (*MqAv*) is at levels *b* to *c*, the least acceptable condition (*MvAq*)

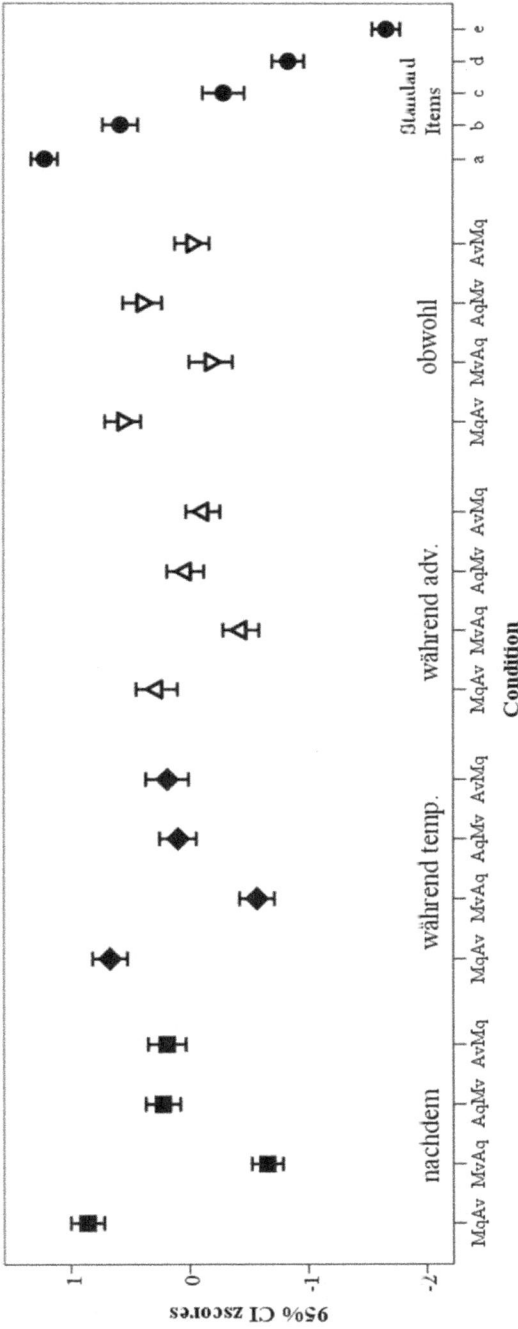

Figure 1: Experiment: error bars for 95% confidence intervals of z-scores for: the two CAC conjunctions *nachdem* 'after' (N), *während* temporal 'while' (WT), and the two PAC conjunctions *während* adversative 'while, whereas' (WA) and *obwohl* 'although' (O); each in the four syntactic conditions *MqAv, MvAq, AqMv,* and *AvMq*; standard items *a-e*.

is at about level *c*, the two intermediate conditions (*AqMv*, *AvMq*) are between levels *b* and *c*, *AqMv* being slightly better than *AvMq*. For *obwohl* 'although' the best condition *MqAv* is at level *b*, while the least acceptable condition *MvAq* is at level *c*. Condition *AqMv* is slightly below level *b*, condition *AvMq* is slightly above level *c*.

Overall the experiment yields clearly distinct results for the different conditions and adverbial clause types, which shows that the data reacts to the factors tested, and that our experimental method is valuable. The pattern of results for the CACs and for the PACs looks similar but they are nevertheless different in their degrees of acceptability and the distinctions between conditions.

2.4 Discussion

Since the results in Figure 1 are complex and require careful analysis, we will first discuss the data for the CACs, and then the PACs, and will finally compare the two groups.

2.4.1 CACs

The results for the CACs show clear distinctions between the four syntactic conditions tested. Condition *MqAv*, which clearly received the most acceptable judgements for the two CAC conjunctions *nachdem* 'after' and temporal *während* 'while', is the condition for which variable binding is expected to be possible since the quantifier is in the preceding matrix clause and can c-command the variable in the adverbial clause. The least natural condition *MvAq* on the other hand does not allow variable binding because the quantifier is in the adverbial clause. The data convincingly reflects the difference between these two conditions.

The results for the remaining two conditions *AqMv* and *AvMq* are surprising at first sight. In condition *AqMv* the quantifier expression is in the adverbial clause, unable to c-command into the matrix clause, exactly as in condition *MvAq*. The only difference between these two conditions is the linear order of matrix clause and adverbial clause: in *AqMv* the adverbial clause precedes the matrix clause, in *MvAq* the matrix clause precedes the adverbial clause. Under the assumption that preposed or postposed CACs are reconstructed to a base-generated position within IP or VP of their matrix clause for binding reasons, we would thus expect condition *AqMv* to receive as unnatural judgements as condition *MvAq*. For the other two conditions *AvMq* and *MqAv*, the order of clauses differs as well, but here the quantifier expression is in the matrix clause for both conditions, and thus able to c-command and bind the variable in the adverbial clause. Therefore, condition *AvMq* should have been judged as natural as condition *MqAv*.

What we find however is that *AqMv* is clearly more natural than *MvAq*, whereas *AvMq* is less natural than *MqAv*. This is not predicted nor accounted for by the standard accounts of structural binding and therefore we must seek other causal factors. We propose that this is due to processing and/or pragmatic effects: even though in condition *AqMv* the quantifier is in the adverbial clause unable to c-command into the matrix clause, it still linearly precedes the variable, which is not the case in *MvAq*. Participants seem to make use of this fact in order to pragmatically repair their interpretation: if they encounter the potential antecedent first, they expect a potentially associated element to follow. It thus seems that the linear ordering of quantifier before variable facilitates participants' processing of a condition which cannot allow variable binding on structural terms due to missing c-command relations. If, however, as for condition *MvAq*, both c-command and linear ordering fail to support the processing of quantifier and variable, then an interpretation is impossible, which is reflected in the least natural judgements for this condition.

A similar case of processing effects can be found between conditions *MqAv* and *AvMq*: though the quantifier expression is in the matrix clause in both cases, condition *AvMq* has been judged less acceptable. Condition *MqAv* is judged most natural, fulfilling all preconditions for successful variable binding: the matrix clause and the quantifier precede the adverbial clause and the variable, and c-command is possible from the matrix clause into the adverbial clause. Condition *AvMq* on the other hand has a change in the linear order of the clauses and thus of quantifier and variable. The variable now precedes the quantifier, and this cataphoric binding seems to demand additional processing efforts, causing *AvMq* to be judged less good than *MqAv*. This is nevertheless compatible with the structural predictions.

These pragmatic and processing effects are stable across the two CACs. A repeated measures analysis of variance (*ANOVA*) by subjects and by items shows that the contrast of *MvAq* and *AqMv*[9] on the one hand and *MqAv* and *AvMq*[10] on the other hand shows no significant difference between the two CACs.

---

9 Interaction of *N-MvAq/N-AqMv* and *WT-MvAq/WT-AqMv*: $F_1(1, 39)=3.249$, $p_1=0.079$, $F_2(1, 7)=3.756$, $p_2=0.094$.
10 Interaction of *N-MqAv/N-AvMq* and *WT-MqAv/WT-AvMq*: $F_1(1, 39)=2.162$, $p_1=0.149$, $F_2(1, 7)=2.593$, $p_2=0.151$.

While our data for the CACs thus shows one clear case of successful variable binding (*MqAv*) and one clear case of binding failure (*MvAq*), we also see that there are additional factors that lead to intermediate results for the remaining two conditions (*AqMv* and *AvMq*).

2.4.2 PACs

The two PACs introduced by adversative *während* 'while, whereas' and concessive *obwohl* 'although' show a comparable pattern of results to that of the CACs. The condition judged best for these two conjunctions is again *MqAv*, the one judged worst is *MvAq*. The two conditions *AqMv* and *AvMq* with preceding adverbial clauses are again in middling positions. We will first compare the results of the two PACs and will turn to a comparison of the CACs and the PACs in the next section.

For the two PACs the results look similar. The clear difference in naturalness between conditions *MqAv* and *MvAq* is the same for both PACs. Since c-command should not be possible from the matrix clause into a PAC, we assume that here condition *MqAv* in comparison to *MvAq* benefits from processing effects: the quantifier in the matrix clause linearly precedes the potential variable in the adverbial clause so that even without structural c-command participants are still able to get to a repaired interpretation of condition *MqAv*. For *MvAq*, however, no such mechanisms are applicable, which is why it receives the least natural values.

Condition *AqMv* is again, as for the CACs, better than *MvAq* although in both cases the quantifier is in the adverbial clause, unable to c-command into the matrix clause. Here as well we are forced to conclude that a preceding quantifier can help repair an otherwise impossible interpretation. Interestingly, what we see is that it is also important whether the preceding quantifier is positioned in the matrix clause or the adverbial clause. Both condition *MqAv* and *AqMv* seem to benefit from the order of quantifier before variable, but *MqAv* receives more natural values than *AqMv*. Thus, even though a c-command relation between a matrix clause and a PAC should not be possible, the hierarchically higher status of the matrix clause as the main proposition seems to additionally support the repairing process of a structure that should not allow variable binding.

For the difference in values between conditions *MqAv* and *AvMq*, for both of which the quantifier is in the matrix clause, we propose that participants find it much more difficult to repair a cataphoric association between variable and quantifier in *AvMq*.

The data for the PACs shows more variation than would probably have been expected by theory: if there is no c-command possible between matrix clause and PAC, then all structures aiming at variable binding should be a complete failure of interpretation. But our results suggest that participants seem to use pragmatic and processing mechanisms to improve their interpretation of such structures if possible. An absolute failure of interpretation only occurs if no such strategies can be applied any more, which seems to be the case in condition *MvAq*.

The results of the PACs show comparable behaviour of adversative *während* 'while, whereas' and *obwohl* 'although'. However, the PAC introduced by *obwohl* 'although' overall seems to have received slightly better acceptability judgements than the adversative PAC introduced by *während* 'while, whereas'. The reason might be that the adversative *während* clauses always compete with their temporal counterparts when processed. Even though the reference clarification should make the adversative reading clear for the relevant target sentence, participants might first get a temporal interpretation of *während* 'while' and need additional effort to get to the adversative meaning. This could cause the PAC with adversative *während* 'while, whereas' to be constantly judged worse than other PACs like concessive *obwohl* 'although', which do not have any other alternative meaning to compete with.

Even though the two PACs did not receive the same acceptability values in absolute terms, the differences between the conditions are very similar. Thus, the non-lexical factors in each condition, such as processing, have the same effects on the two PACs. This is supported by statistical analysis: across the two PACs there is no significant difference in the distance between conditions *MqAv* and *MvAq*,[11] as well as between *MvAq* and *AqMv*,[12] and *MqAv* and *AvMq*.[13]

2.4.3 CACs vs. PACs

In the analyses above we saw that the pattern of results for CACs and for PACs is broadly parallel: in both groups of adverbial clauses there is condition *MqAv*, which received the best acceptability judgements, and condition *MvAq*, which received the lowest judgement values. For the CACs *MqAv* is the condition with optimal variable binding: the quantifier is in the preceding matrix clause

---

11 Interaction of *WA-MqAv/WA-MvAq* and *O-MqAv/O-MvAq*: $F_1(1, 39)=0.023$, $p_1=0.881$, $F_2(1, 7)=0.041$, $p_2=0.845$.
12 Interaction of *WA-MvAq/WA-AqMv* and *O-MvAq/O-AqMv*: $F_1(1, 39)=0.571$, $p_1=0.454$, $F_2(1, 7)=0.409$, $p_2=0.543$.
13 Interaction of *WA-MqAv/WA-AvMq* and *O-MqAv/O-AvMq*: $F_1(1, 39)=1.247$, $p_1=0.271$, $F_2(1, 7)=1.452$, $p_2=0.267$.

and can c-command and thus bind into the adverbial clause. For the PACs on the other hand c-command cannot be assumed for condition *MqAv*. The syntactic account is therefore clearly not the whole story: we assume that the factors that make this condition the most natural in the PACs must therefore be pragmatic and processing effects. The least natural condition *MvAq* fails to support variable binding in any case, independent of whether the adverbial clause is a CAC or a PAC. In addition, participants do not seem to find any helpful pragmatic factors in this condition which would help them repair their failing interpretation.

We conducted our experiment to compare CACs and PACs and their binding behaviour and we indeed find the theoretically predicted difference between these two groups. We propose that the best measure of it is in the relative distance between conditions *MqAv* and *MvAq* in the CACs and in the PACs. While in the CACs the best and the worst conditions are about two standard levels apart, in the PACs there is only a distance of about one standard level. This difference between CACs and PACs is statistically highly significant.[14] We analyse this distinction as reflecting the impossibility of structural binding in the case of the PACs. The best PAC condition *MqAv* can only be interpreted by means of processing effects because there is no c-command relation supporting variable binding. Since this structural configuration is already absent in this condition, the relative difference in naturalness to the least acceptable condition *MvAq* is not very great: the poor scores of this PAC condition represent only the computational cost of attempted repair processing but nothing more. This contrasts with the CACs, where we hypothesize that the shock failure of expected syntactic binding in condition *MvAq* causes the particularly steep fall from the *MqAv* to *MvAq* conditions. Condition *MvAq* thus violates both the otherwise possible c-command relations and processing effects. This means that the greater distance of about two standard levels for the CACs reflects the possibility of structural binding, whereas the smaller distance of about one standard level for the PACs only reflects pragmatic and processing effects but no possibility of structural c-command.

Another finding in our data is that while the structural effects clearly distinguish CACs from PACs, the processing effects are almost consistent across both adverbial clause types: as described above we see that condition *AqMv* is always judged better than condition *MvAq* due to the effect of the quantifier linearly preceding the variable. Statistical analysis shows that only by items, but not by subjects, the distance between the two conditions is the same for CACs

---

14 Interaction of *CAC-MqAv*/*CAC-MvAq* and *PAC-MqAv*/*PAC-MvAq*: $F_1(1, 39)=41.754$, $p_1<0.001$, $F_2(1, 7)=38.49$, $p_2<0.001$.

and PACs.[15] However, the preference for *AqMv* is still clear in both adverbial clause types.

We also interpret the difference between *MqAv* and *AvMq* as a processing effect triggered by cataphoric binding. For this effect there is no significant difference between CACs and PACs by subjects and by items.[16] It affects CACs and PACs equally.

The results of the PACs are more compressed than those of the CACs. Additionally, it also seems as if for the PACs there is a clearer difference in naturalness between the two conditions *AqMv* and *AvMq* than for the CACs. However, considering that in the PACs the most natural condition and the worst condition are not as far apart as they are in the CACs due to absent binding configurations, we can explain this pattern: while the structural effects clearly differ for CACs and PACs and lead to a smaller difference between *MqAv* and *MvAq* in the PACs, the processing effects remain quite stable, which means that the differences between *MvAq* and *AqMv* and between *MqAv* and *AvMq* in the PACs are almost comparable to those in the CACs. Condition *AqMv* then seems to have moved up in naturalness in comparison to *AvMq*, but only because the least natural PAC condition *MvAq* and the best PAC condition *MqAv* are closer to each other than their equivalents in the CACs.

Our experiment shows that the predicted structural difference between CACs and PACs is reflected in the data. However, we also see that the results do not yield a clear black-and-white picture of successful variable binding and unsuccessful variable binding. Additional factors help participants repair their interpretations so that under certain circumstances even PACs can allow some kind of association between a quantifier and a variable. It seems plausible that when participants encounter a quantifier first they expect a variable to follow. Our data is able to show us these pragmatic effects as well.

3 Conclusion

The aim of our experiment was to see whether we could find empirical support for the theoretically predicted differences in binding behaviour between CACs

---

15 Interaction of *CAC-MvAq/CAC-AqMv* and *PAC- MvAq/PAC-AqMv*: $F_1(1, 39)=4.997$, $p_1=0.031$, $F_2(1, 7)=4.483$, $p_2=0.072$.
16 Interaction of *CAC-MqAv/CAC-AvMq* and *PAC- MqAv/PAC-AvMq*: $F_1(1, 39)=0.932$, $p_1=0.34$, $F_2(1, 7)=0.408$, $p_2=0.543$.

and PACs. CACs should allow variable binding into them because they are assumed to be attached to their matrix clauses at IP or even VP, whereas PACs are positioned much higher in the matrix clause, perhaps at CP (Haegeman 2004; Frey 2011). However, there are different opinions in the literature on whether binding into PACs should be possible or not (e.g. Frey 2011 vs. Pauly 2014). We thus hoped that our data would offer new insights into the structural differences between CACs and PACs. We therefore compared two CACs introduced by temporal *nachdem* 'after' and temporal *während* 'while', with two PACs introduced by adversative *während* 'while, whereas' and concessive *obwohl* 'although'. We tested these adverbial clauses in four syntactic conditions varying the linear order of the matrix clause and adverbial clause and the position of the quantifier in either matrix clause or adverbial clause.

Our data supports the claim that adverbial clauses categorized as PACs show a different binding behaviour than adverbial clauses that fall into the group of CACs. We found a clear difference between CACs and PACs in the distinction between the condition judged best and the condition judged worst: the difference between these conditions is greater for the CACs. This shows that for the CACs structural c-command is possible in the good condition and violating this possibility in the bad condition demands quite some costs. For the PACs however these costs are much smaller since here no structural violations can occur.

In addition to this finding, the experimental results also show a range of other interesting facts: first, we see that PACs do not completely fail an association of quantifier and variable even without the structural precondition of c-command. Participants are able to repair their interpretations when the quantifier linearly precedes the variable. This finding offers a possible explanation as to why intuitions on whether binding is possible into PACs or not differ in the literature. The association between a quantifier and a variable is best under c-command relations, but other factors can support it as well: when processing a quantifier, we expect a variable to follow. The fact that the PACs are judged better than might have been expected could lead critics to conclude that this is due to the genericity in our material, since genericity can evoke an illusion of binding (Fox and Sauerland 1995). However, be there a generic effect or not, we still find the clear difference in acceptability judgements between CACs and PACs. Since the generic effect should hold for our sentence material in total, we expect it to apply to both CACs and PACs, not only to PACs. This means that genericity is only another factor on top of the other effects we found; and these clearly show a difference in the binding behaviour between the two types of adverbial clauses.

Second, the data shows that adversative *während* 'while, whereas' and concessive *obwohl* 'although' show very similar behaviour, which would lead us to the conclusion that they belong into one group of adverbial clauses. We nevertheless see that *obwohl* 'although' received more natural values. While Frey (2011) claims that there is no binding possible into *obwohl* clauses, Freywald (2014) and Pauly (2014) would allow variable binding into them. From the acceptability judgements in our experiment we conclude that *obwohl* clauses seem to be slightly preferred by participants in contrast to adversative *während* clauses. This might be the reason why for Freywald (2014) and Pauly (2014) *obwohl* clauses seem to allow variable binding: a pragmatic association between quantifier and variable binding seems to be more easily accessible in *obwohl* clauses.

Another point visible in the data is that condition *AvMq* with the preposed adverbial clause received lower judgement values than condition *MqAv* with preposed matrix clause. This is especially interesting in the case of the CACs: if we assume that CACs are reconstructed to a base-generated position within their matrix clause for binding purposes, then we would expect them to show a comparable behaviour in both conditions. But there is a clear preference for the condition with the preposed matrix clauses. Christ (2014) discusses this phenomenon and shows that CACs do not behave the same in preposed and postposed positions: in postposed position, they show clear variable binding and Principle C violation effects due to successful c-command from the matrix clause into the adverbial clause:

(12) | *Jeder* | *Mensch$_i$* | *möchte* | *seine* | | *Ruhe,* |
| --- | --- | --- | --- | --- | --- |
| Every | human | wants | his | | peace |
| *während* | *er* | | *die* | *Sportschau* | *ansieht.* |
| while | he | | the | sports.show | watches. |

'Everyone$_i$ wants to be left alone while they$_i$ watch the sports show.'
(Christ 2014: 141, (146a); slightly modified by authors)

(13) | **Er$_i$* | *trinkt* | *eine* | *kühle* | | *Cola,* |
| --- | --- | --- | --- | --- | --- |
| He | drinks | a | cold | | coke |
| *während* | *Fritz$_i$* | *die* | *Sportschau* | *ansieht.* | |
| while | Fritz | the | sports.show | watches | |

'He$_i$ drinks a cold coke, while Fritz$_i$ watches the sports show.'
(Christ 2014: 140, (145b); slightly modified by authors)

In preposed position, variable binding is still possible, but Principle C violations do not occur anymore:

(14) *Während er$_i$*   *die*   *Sportschau*   *ansieht,*
     While   he   the   sports.show watches
     möchte   *jeder* *Mensch* *seine*   *Ruhe.*
     wants   every human his   peace
     'While they$_i$ watch the sports show everyone$_i$ wants to be left alone.'
     (Christ 2014: 141, (146a); modified by authors)

(15) *Während Fritz$_i$ die Sportschau*   *ansieht, trinkt* *er$_i$ eine kühle Cola.*
     While   Fritz the sports.show watches drinks he a   cold   coke
     'While Fritz$_i$ watches the sports show he$_i$ drinks a cold coke.'
     (Christ 2014: 141, (147c); slightly modified by authors)

In order to account for the unexpected grammaticality of example (15), Christ (2014: 145) suggests that variable binding and Principle C violation do not underlie the same structural conditions. However, if we consider the results of our experiment, we see that variable binding also does not behave completely as predicted in the preposed position: it received less natural judgements even though on structural terms it should be possible. Since it seems that c-command into a preposed adverbial clause is less readily accessible and therefore less preferred, this could in turn mean that Principle C is also less affected by a violation of c-command. Our data thus offers an account for Christ's (2014) observations such that it might be the same effects that affect variable binding and Principle C in preposed CACs.

In earlier studies on the binding behaviour of CACs and PACs we only compared the adversative PAC introduced by *während* 'while, whereas' to the temporal CAC introduced by *während* 'while, together with a second temporal CAC introduced by *nachdem* 'after', which served as control for our experimental method (von Wietersheim and Featherston 2016; von Wietersheim 2016). However, extending our research and adding a second PAC introduced by concessive *obwohl* 'although' to the experiments helped us refine our recent interpretations of the structural difference between CACs and PACs so that in this paper we offered an updated view on our data.

Our experimental method is valuable and reliably yields consistent and clear results throughout all our experiments. What becomes clear in the data is that the assumptions that PACs must be attached at a higher position within their matrix clauses than CACs can be supported: variable binding is successful into CACs, but not PACs. The latter can only benefit from pragmatic and processing repair mechanisms,[17] since their attachment positions are too high to be c-commanded into. Structural binding is thus able to reflect the different structural and thus functional statuses of CACs and PACs.

References

Büring, Daniel. 2005. *Binding theory*. Cambridge: Cambridge University Press.
Christ, Rüdiger. 2014. *Zur Satzfügung im Deutschen. Vornehmlich am Beispiel adversativer Satzgefüge*. Tübingen: Stauffenburg.
Featherston, Sam. 2008. Thermometer judgments as linguistic evidence. In Claudia Maria Riehl & Astrid Rothe (eds.),*Was ist linguistische Evidenz?*, 69–90. Aachen: Shaker Verlag.
Featherston, Sam. 2009. A scale for measuring well-formedness: Why syntax needs boiling and freezing points. In Sam Featherston & Susanne Winkler (eds.), *The Fruits of Empirical Linguistics. Vol. 1: Process*, 47–74. Berlin: de Gruyter.
Fox, Danny & Uli Sauerland. 1995. Illusive Scope of Universal Quantifiers. *North East Linguistic Society* 26. 1–15.
Frey, Werner. 2011. Peripheral adverbial clauses, their licensing and the prefield in German. In Eva Breindl, Gisella Ferraresi & Anna Volodina (eds.), *Satzverknüpfung – Zur Interaktion von Form, Bedeutung und Diskursfunktion*, 41–77. Berlin: de Gruyter.
Frey, Werner. 2016a. Zu Korrespondenzen von Lesart und Syntax bei Konzessivsätzen. Paper presented at the conference "Position und Interpretation – Syntax, Semantik und Informationsstruktur adverbialer Modifikatoren", University of Tübingen, 3–4 June. Handout.
Frey, Werner. 2016b. On some syntactic and interpretative properties of causal and concessive clauses. Paper presented at the workshop "The internal and external syntax of adverbial clauses", ZAS Berlin, 22–23 July. Handout.
Freywald, Ulrike. 2014. *Parataktische Konjunktionen. Zur Syntax und Pragmatik der Satzverknüpfung im Deutschen – am Beispiel von* obwohl, wobei, während, wogegen *und* dass. Berlin: Humboldt-Universität Berlin dissertation.
Haegeman, Liliane. 2003. Conditional Clauses: External and Internal Syntax. *Mind & Language* 18 (4). 317–339.
Haegeman, Liliane. 2004. The Syntax of Adverbial Clauses and Its Consequences for Topicalisation. *Antwerp Papers on Linguistics* 107. 61–90.
Haegeman, Liliane. 2006. Conditionals, factives and the left periphery. *Lingua* 116. 1651–1669.
Pauly, Dennis. 2014. *Grenzfälle der Subordination: Merkmale, Empirie und Theorie abhängiger Nebensätze*. Potsdam: Universität Potsdam dissertation.

---

17 As a reviewer comments, the topicalized/subject position of the quantifier phrase could make the bound-variable reading more accessible than a lower structural position. However, we would have to expect both CACs and PACs to benefit equally from the topicalization, so that this would not change our core results.

Reich, Ingo & Marga Reis. 2013. Koordination und Subordination. In Jörg Meibauer, Markus Steinbach & Hans Altmann (eds.), *Satztypen des Deutschen*, 536–569. Berlin & Boston: de Gruyter.

Reis, Marga. 1997. Zum syntaktischen Status unselbständiger Verbzweit-Sätze. In Christa Dürscheid, Karl Heinz Ramers & Monika Schwarz (eds.), *Sprache im Fokus. Festschrift für Heinz Vater zum 65. Geburtstag*, 121–144. Tübingen: Niemeyer

Verstraete, Jean-Christophe. 2007. *Rethinking the Coordinate-Subordinate Dichotomy: Interpersonal Grammar and the Analysis of Adverbial Clauses in English. Topics in English Linguistics* 55. Berlin: Mouton de Gruyter.

Wietersheim, Sophie von. 2016. Variable binding as evidence for clausal attachment. In I. Reich & A. Speyer (eds.), *Co- and Subordination in German and Other Languages. Linguistische Berichte, Sonderhefte* 21, 319–345. Hamburg: Buske Verlag.

Wietersheim, Sophie von & Sam Featherston. 2016. Violation of Principle C as evidence for structural integration. In Fernanda Pratas, Sandra Pereira & Clara Pinto (eds.), *Coordination and Subordination: Form and Meaning – Selected Papers from CSI Lisbon 2014*, 269–293. Cambridge: Cambridge Scholars Publishing.

Cristina Sánchez López

9 Optative and evaluative *que* 'that' sentences in Spanish

Abstract: Spanish main sentences introduced by *que* 'that' with a subjunctive verb such as *¡Que trabaje él mañana!* are ambiguous between an optative reading 'I wish he would work tomorrow!' and an evaluative reading 'It is annoying that he is working tomorrow!' The only way to distinguish the two readings is by intonation: the optative reading is marked with a downward final intonation whereas the evaluative reading has an upward final intonation. These two readings differ in the presuppositions they convey (anti-factive for the optative reading and factive for the evaluative reading). The evaluative reading crucially indicates a negative attitude on the part of the speaker. I propose an analysis that builds on the idea that expressive utterances, i.e. exclamatives and optatives, are main sentences with a complex left periphery. It is proposed that the main sentences with the form <*que* + V_{SUBJ}> contain an expressive operator *EX* that combines with a proposition and turns it into the expression with the speaker's emotion. The emotion is evaluated with respect to a bouletic scale that orders the proposition and all the contextually salient alternative propositions with respect to the desires of the speaker; the evaluative reading is obtained when the bouletic scale is inverted.

1 Introduction

In this paper,[1] I will try to advance the knowledge of insubordination by analyzing some prototypical cases of insubordinate sentences in Spanish: main clauses introduced by the complementizer *que* 'that' plus a verb with subjunctive mood. These sentences fulfill the commonly assumed definition of insubordinate clause, as they are used like a main clause although they have the form of a subordinate clause. The complementizer *que* 'that' is, indeed, the most common mark of subordination, and the subjunctive mood has traditionally been associated with subordination as well.

---

1 This work has been financed by the research project FFI2012-34974 funded by the MEC (Government of Spain). I thank the editors and two anonymous reviewers for their helpful comments.

Cristina Sánchez López, Complutense University of Madrid

https://doi.org/10.1515/9783110638288-010

Main sentences with the form <*que*+V$_{SUBJ}$> can receive both an optative and an evaluative reading.[2] On the one hand, they can be interpreted as optative or desiderative utterances, and express a vivid wish, desire, or hope of the speaker: the English gloss in (1a) exemplifies this reading. On the other hand, they can receive an evaluative reading and express the displeasure or discontent of the speaker: the English gloss in (1b) demonstrates this other reading. The ambiguity is solved by intonation, since a final falling intonation is associated with the optative reading, and a final rising intonation is associated with the evaluative reading, as shown in (2)[3]:

(1) *¡Que   deje   de   llover   ahora!*
      That   stops$_{subj}$ of   rain$_{inf}$ now

    a. Optative reading: 'I hope it stops raining right now!'
    b. Evaluative reading: 'It is annoying that it stops raining right now!'

(2)

    a. Optative reading: *¡Que deje de llover ahora!*
                       'I hope it stops raining right now!'

    b. Evaluative Reading: *¡Que deje de llover ahora!*
                         'It is annoying that it stops raining right now!'

In order to show the purposes and limits of this paper, let me start asking questions that an integral analysis of main <*que*+V$_{SUBJ}$> sentences should answer. Recall that some of them are common to all insubordinate sentences:

---

2 A third reading is possible, which I will ignore here. <*Que*+V$_{SUBJ}$> clauses can be interpreted as orders and have a meaning close to imperatives. Garrido Medina (1999: §60.2.1.1) says that the imperative meaning requires a certain control on the part of the speaker; he also notes that these kinds of orders are very close to optative sentences, on the one hand, and to reported speech, on the other. Sansiñena, De Smet and Cornillie (2015a) consider these sentences as displaced directives that encode a directive stance, but systematically violate one or another of the felicity conditions that normally apply to requests, orders, and commands; they posit a functional division of labor between prototypical imperatives and free-standing *que*-clauses with subjunctive mood. I will not consider the directive reading in this paper.
3 I am using the following abreviations in subindex: inf 'infinitive', subj 'subjunctive', dat 'dative', ac 'acusative', form 'formal', 3sg 'third singular person',

a) Are these sentences main clauses or are they the result of the elision of a main verb?
b) What formal properties do they have? What illocutionary force they display? How are the syntactic properties associated with the illocutionary properties?
c) What exactly do these sentences mean?
d) What relation, if any, exists between the evaluative and optative readings?
e) What role does prosody play in the interpretation of these sentences?
f) What are the discursive functions of these sentences?

The last question has received quite some attention recently. Many authors have investigated the discursive functions of main clauses introduced by *que*, although most have focused on indicative sentences rather than subjunctive sentences.[4] Some authors consider that *que* is a discourse marker that indicates the presence of the speaker (see Garrido Medina 1998; Porroche 1998; Pons 2003). However, the obligatory presence of *que* in the sentences in (1) makes it impossible to consider it a discourse marker, since it belongs to the syntactic structure of the sentence and determines its formal properties (Gras 2011: 36). From a different perspective, Sirbu-Dumitrescu (2004) relates the use of the subjunctive to the expression of wishes and politeness. However, the discursive approach will not be pursued, here. I am rather interested in discussing the basic syntactic and semantic properties of this construction, independently of the discursive uses it can have. Answering questions (a) to (e) will be necessary to discover and understand those properties.

Question (a) touches upon the very core of the insubordination phenomenon. The hypothesis that the sentence in (1) is the result of an elision process has been pointed out by traditional grammars and in recent studies. Most Spanish grammarians (Bello [1847] 1964: §995–998; Gili Gaya 1943: §219; RAE 1973: §3.13.4; Salvá 1830: 221, Alcina and Blecua 1975: §8.1.1.8; Ridruejo 1983; Garrido Medina 1999; RAE-ASALE 2009, among many others) have noted that main clauses introduced by *que* plus a subjunctive verb express not only desiderative statements but also statements with other meanings related to the optative mode in some way. Many of them assume that these sentences are the result of the ellipsis of the main predicate, in which the *que*-sentence is

---

4 The discursive values of main <*que*+indicative> sentences have been described and explained differently. See Sirbu-Dumitrescu (1994, 1998, 2004), Garrido (1998), Porroche (1998), Pons (2003), Etxepare (2008, 2010), Rodríguez Ramalle (2008a, 2008b), Gras (2011, 2013), Gras and Sansiñena (2015), Sansiñena, De Smet and Cornillie (2015b), Corr (2016), among others. Sentences with the form <*que*+V_{IND}> are excluded from this paper.

a complement. From this point of view, the ellipsis process would explain the presence of the complementizer *que* and the subjunctive morphology of the verb (Spaulding 1934; see also Rivero 1977 for a generative analysis in this line of reasoning). The ellipsis hypothesis is also important in Evans's (2007) concept of insubordination, since he proposes ellipsis to be a necessary step for explaining the origin and development of insubordinate clauses.

Although the main verb ellipsis analysis has been discussed with some pragmatic and discursive arguments (see Pons 2003: 532–533), there are analyses for which ellipsis is central. Gras (2011), for example, distinguishes *plain insubordinate*, where no elided material exists, from *suspended insubordinate*, where some elided material must be recovered. Crucially, Gras (2011) considers that the optative reading in (1a) corresponds to a plain insubordinate construction, but the evaluative reading in (2a) corresponds to a suspended insubordinate construction. In this paper, I will provide some empirical arguments against the main verb ellipsis analysis, and show that there is no difference between the evaluative and the optative readings in this respect. I will show that the sentence in (1) is actually a plain insubordinate sentence, that is, a main sentence with a marker of subordination but not matrix clause, whether it is interpreted as evaluative or optative.[5]

Question (b) is related to the grammatical status of these constructions and the way their illocutionary properties can be accounted for in a grammatical model. The cartographical approach to the sentence left periphery (see Rizzi 1997 and subsequent works) has provided a useful frame to formally analyze

---

5 As an anonymous reviewer correctly points out, question (a) can be viewed from a historical perspective as well. I am adopting here a purely synchronic perspective, without making any assumption about the historical development of these constructions. Therefore, I am using 'elision' as a synchronic process, not as a diachronic one. On the other hand, it is interesting to note that the evaluative reading of sentences with the form <*que* + V_{SUBJ}> can be traced back at least to the 16th century, as the example in (i) proves. The evaluative reading being as old as the optative reading, no historical reason supports that an use can be considered more conventionalized than the other one:

(i) | ¡Que | sea | posible, | Rey, | crueldad | | tan | grande! |
     | that | is$_{subj}$ | possible | King | cruelty | | so | big |
     | ¡Que | me | niegues | licencia | | tan | debida | a |
     | that | me$_{dat}$ | deny | permission | | so | due | to |
     | aqueste | brazo | y | a | mi | buen | deseo! | |
     | this | arm | and | to | my | good | wish | |

'Oh King, That such a big cruelty is possible! That you deny due permission to my arm and my good wish!'
(F. Lope de Vega, *Los hechos de Garcilaso*, c. 1579–1583, CORDE)

insubordinate sentences. With regard to Spanish, some authors discuss the position that *que* occupies in the sentence left periphery by focusing on the differences between <*que*+V$_{IND}$> and <*que*+V$_{SUBJ}$> sentences (Núñez Lagos 2005; Demonte and Fernández Soriano 2007, 2009, 2013, 2014; Rodríguez Ramalle 2008a, 2008b; Sánchez López 2016b, 2017). I will assume this formal approach and propose a syntactic analysis of <*que*+V$_{SUBJ}$> sentences as main sentences with a complex left periphery. Crucially, I propose that the configuration of this left periphery is responsible for the main illocutionary properties of these sentences, since the Force Phrase layer contains an expressive operator responsible for their main illocutionary properties as expressive utterances. As such, the expressive operator combines with a proposition and turns it into the expression of the speaker's emotion as it relates to the ordering of salient alternatives.

The questions (c) and (d) have received less attention in the literature. Answering these questions will be a main objective of this paper. All grammarians agree that the construction <*que*+V$_{SUBJ}$> can receive an optative or desiderative meaning, but the evaluative reading has been mostly ignored by most of them. There are, indeed, several important issues about the meaning of <*que*+V$_{SUBJ}$> sentences the literature leaves unaddressed. In my opinion, the most important issue is what relationship exists, if any, between the two readings, evaluative and optative. Gras (2011, 2013), for example, includes desideratives and evaluatives within the insubordinate sentences expressing modality, and considers that the optative reading in (1a) belongs to the deontic modality, and the evaluative reading in (1a) belongs to an exclamative-evaluative modality.[6] I will propose that the relationship between the two readings is closer than it would seem. Concretely, I will propose that they are basically optative sentences, which are interpreted with respect to a bouletic scale that orders the proposition and the relevant alternative propositions. The two readings of <*que*+V$_{SUBJ}$> sentences are the result of the type of bouletic scale, in that the evaluative reading is actually an optative reading with an inverse bouletic scale. In other words, I propose that the two readings of insubordinate sentences with the form <*que*+V$_{SUBJ}$> can be reduced to only one basic meaning, the optative.

---

6 Gras (2011) considers optative and evaluative sentences *modal insubordinates* because the speaker positions himself towards the realization of the propositional content. Gras and Sansiñena (2017) agree with Sánchez López (2014) that the two kind of sentences can be considered exclamatives. Pons (2003: 539) considers that in both desiderative and evaluative sentences, *que* and the subjunctive verb manifest the speaker's attitude towards what is said, but he doesn't explain what the speaker's attitude consists of, except for the reinforcement value shared by all the main sentences introduced by *que*.

Finally, question (e) has never been addressed.[7] The study presented here is just a starting point and focuses on the variety of Spanish spoken in Spain. In this variety, intonation is related to the different meanings of exclamative sentences with the form $<que+V_{SUBJ}>$. I will show that prosody has a semantic effect. Intonation marks the orientation of the bouletic scale according to which the sentence is interpreted: the final rising intonation marks that the sentence is interpreted according to an inverted scale whose top position is occupied by the least desirable proposition. The fact presented here demonstrates that prosody can convey a conventional meaning.

Some methodological remarks are needed here. The data have been obtained from two main sources: the Spanish data base CREA and CORDE and some grammars of Spanish language. I have also used my own competence as a speaker of Spanish for creating some minimal pairs when necessary. It goes without saying that all the generalizations have been tested with a large number of relevant data, which cannot be reproduced here.

The structure of the paper is as follows. In Section 2, I present the basic description of insubordinate sentences with the form $<que+V_{SUBJ}>$. In Subsection 2.1, I describe the main formal and syntactic properties of these sentences, which are the same regardless their reading. The optative meaning is described in Section 2.2 and the evaluative meaning is described in Section 2.3. In Subsection 2.4, I describe the prosody of the sentences, focusing on how intonation contributes to the interpretation of the sentences. Finally, some interim conclusions are presented in Subsection 2.5. Section 3 contains a formal and semantic analysis of the data that focuses on their illocutionary force, such as expressive utterances (Subsection 3.1), their syntactic structure (Subsection 3.2), their tense restrictions and the contribution of the subjunctive mood (Subsection 3.3), and the relationship between the optative meaning of the sentences and the modality of the proposition (Subsection 3.4). Section 4 presents the conclusions and some issues for further study.

---

7 The study by Elvira-García (2015) about the prosody of insubordinate sentences in Spanish includes sentences with the form $<que+V_{SUBJ}>$ which convey a directive meaning and are used to give an order or to make a suggestion. This is also the case for the study by Elvira-García, Roseano and Fernández Planas (2016). Directive utterances headed by *que* are out of the limits of this paper (see fn. 2 above).

2 Basic description of the data

In this section, I describe the main syntactic, semantic and prosodic properties of sentences with the form <*que*+V$_{SUBJ}$>. Firstly, I describe their syntactic form, focusing on the formal properties *que*-Evaluatives (henceforth *que*-Eval) and *que*-Optatives (henceforth *que*-Opt) share. Secondly, I deep on the semantics of *que*-Opt (Section 2.2) and *que*-Eval (Section 2.3). In Section 2.4, I describe the prosodic properties of both readings. Finally, some interim conclusions are presented in Section 2.5.

2.1 The syntactic form

In main sentences with the form <*que*+Vsubj>, the presence of the complementizer *que* 'that' is obligatory, and its absence results in an ungrammatical sentence[8]:

(3) a. *¡*Trabaje   él   mañana!*
         works$_{subj}$ he   tomorrow

     b. *¡*Los   empleados   trabajen mañana!*
         the   employers   work$_{subj}$ tomorrow

---

8 Optative and evaluative sentences contrast with jussive sentences with a subjunctive verb. In Spanish, the present subjunctive forms are used instead of the imperative form in some cases: a) when the speaker refers to the addressee, b) when the addressee includes the speaker, and c) when the jussive sentence expresses an order or suggestion addressed to an arbitrary referent:

(i)   *¡Vuelva   usted   mañana!*
      come$_{3.sg.subj}$-back   you$_{2.sg.formal}$ tomorrow
      'Sir, come back tomorrow!'

(ii) *¡Seamos   cuidadosos!*
      be$_{1.pl.subj}$ careful
      'Let us be careful!'

(iii) *Sea   el   conjunto de   los números naturales*
      be$_{3.sg.subj}$ the   set   of   the numbers natural
      'Let the set be of natural numbers'

I will leave aside jussive sentences in this paper, and assume that jussives and optatives are different constructions with specific formal and semantic properties. Nevertheless, this does not mean that I am not unaware of the common points between both classes of sentences. See RAE (1973: §3.2.8g), Garrido Medina (1999), Demonte and Fernández Soriano (2009), Sansiñena, De Smet and Cornillie et al. (2015a), among others.

Besides displaying subjunctive mood, these sentences display a temporal constraint: they are only possible with verbs in present and present perfect tense, and reject verbs in past and past perfect tenses. Spanish has four subjunctive tenses: present, present perfect, past and pluperfect; the examples in (4a) and (4b) show that sentences with the form $<que+V_{SUBJ}>$ are only possible with present and present perfect, but not with past and pluperfect, regardless of their optative or evaluative reading[9]:

(4) a. *¡Que ella {llegue / haya llegado} a mediodía!*
        that she arrives$_{subj}$ has$_{subj}$ arrived at noon
        'I wish she {arrives / has arrived}' at noon'
        'It is annoying that she {arrives / has arrived} at noon'

    b. **¡Que ella {*llegara / *hubiera llegado} a mediodía!*
        that she arrived$_{subj}$ had$_{subj}$ arrived at noon
        'I wish she {arrived / had arrived} at noon'
        'It is annoying that she {arrived / had arrived} at noon'

---

9 The example (4a) with a pluperfect tense could be acceptable as a jussive statement in retrospective imperatives like (iA) and (iiB) (cf. Bosque 1980 and Garrido Medina 1999). Retrospective imperatives differ from *que*-optatives in that they are restricted to pluperfect subjunctive tense and reject the presence of the complementizer, unless *que* can be interpreted as a quotative *que*, as in the last sentence of the dialog in (i). Nevertheless, a retrospective imperative preceded by *que* is possible in non reported speech context as well, as in the example (ii) provided to me by an anonymous reviewer. Jussive statements are out of the limits of this paper, but see fn.2 and 7.

(i) A: *¡Hubieras llegado a mediodía!*
          had$_{2.sg.subj}$ arrived at noon
          'You should have arrived at noon!'

      B: *¿Qué dices?*
           What say$_{2.sg}$
           'What are you saying?'

      A: *¡Que hubieras llegado a mediodía!*
           that had$_{2.sg.subj}$ arrived at noon
           '(I am saying) that you should have arrived at noon!'

(ii) A: *A Laura no le gustó mi tortilla*
          to L. not her$_{dat}$ like my omelette
          'Laura did not like my omelette'

      B: *Que la hubiese hecho ella*
          that it$_{ac}$ had$_{subj}$ done she
          'She should had done it'

The same temporal constraint operates in the evaluative reading. The examples provided in the literature (see Bello [1847] 1964: §995–998; Pons 2003; Gras 2011; Sánchez López 2014, 2016b; Gras and Sansiñena 2017, for example) display present and present perfect tenses. The corpora CREA and CORDE contain a large number of examples of the construction <*que*+V$_{\text{SUBJ}}$> with evaluative meaning, some of them reproduced in (5); I have not found any examples with past or pluperfect tense in these corpora.[10]

(5) a. *"¡Que   tenga   yo   un   sobrino   tan   salvaje!"*,
       that   have$_{\text{subj}}$ I a   nephew so   savage
       clamó   don   Opas,   dando   un   golpe   recio
       claimed Mr. O.   giving a   blow   hard
       '"It is annoying that I have such a savage nephew!" Mr. O. exclaimed forcefully'
       (A. Bello, *Leyendas españolas por José Joaquín de Mora*, 1840, CORDE).

   b. *¡Que   haya   yo   vivido   eso   y   venga*
       that   have$_{\text{subj}}$ I lived   that and come$_{\text{subj}}$
       ahora   un   cataplasma   a   sacarte   a   bailar!
       now   a bore   to invite-you$_{\text{ac}}$ to dance

---

10 The construction exhibited this temporal constraint in the 16th, 17th and 18th centuries too, as these examples show (see also fn. 5 above):

(i) *¡Que   haya   entregado   mi   libertad a   quien   no   sé   si la estimará*
   that   have$_{\text{1sg.subj}}$ given my freedom to   whom not know$_{\text{1sg}}$ if it appreciate$_{\text{fut}}$
   ¡Que   mire   yo   a   quien   ni   me   conoce   ni conozco,   y
   that   look I to whom neither me$_{\text{ac}}$ meet$_{\text{3sg}}$ normeet$_{\text{1sg}}$ and
   que   haya   de   rogar   quien jamás   admitió ruegos   de   nadie!
   that have$_{\text{1sg}}$ to pray   who never admittedpray of   nobody
   'That I have given my freedom to a person that will not appreciate it! That I look at a person who doesn't meet me and whom I don't meet! That I have to pray when I never admitted pray from anybody!'
   (V. Espinel, *Vida del escudero Marcos de Obregón*, 1618, CORDE)

(ii) *¡Valgame   el   cielo,   qué   pena! ¡Que   haya   de*
    help me the heaven what pity   that has   to
    haber   siempre   acasos,   que mis   fortunas   alteran!
    be   always accidents that my fortune change$_{\text{3p}}$
    'God help me! What a pity! That should always be accidents that change my fortune!'
    (N. Fernández de Moratín, *La petimetra*, 1762)

'After all I've done in my good life, here comes this awful person who invites you to dance'
(L. Landero, *Juegos de la edad tardía*, CREA)

c. *¡Que   pueda   pasar   esto   aún!*
that   can$_{3.sg.subj}$ happen   this   still
'It is annoying that this can still happen'
(Oral, grupo G 13, España, CREA)

d. *¡Que   tenga   que   ser   G. S.,   el   más   voraz*
that   must$_{subj}$ to   be   G.S.,   the   more   voracious
y   universal de   los   especuladores,   quien   denuncie   a
and   universal of   the   speculators   who   denounces   at
estas   alturas   la   falacia   del   laisser-faire   (...)!
this   point   the   deceit   of the   laisser-faire
'It is annoying that G. S., the most voracious and universal of the speculators, has to be who, at this point, denounces the deceit of the laisser-faire (...)!'
(El País, 8/5/1997, CREA)

Tense restrictions provide a strong argument for not considering <*que*+V$_{SUBJ}$> sentences as subordinated sentences that depend on a silent or elided evaluative verb. Subordinate sentences depending on both a verb of desire (6a) and an evaluative verb (6b) are compatible with past tenses, whereas main optative and evaluative sentences are not:

(6) a. *Yo quería   que   María {llegase   / hubiese   llegado} a mediodía*
I   wanted that   M   arrived$_{3sg.subj}$ had$_{3sg.subj.}$ arrived at noon
'I wished that María {arrived / had arrived} at noon'

b. *Es terrible   que   María {llegase   / hubiese   llegado} a mediodía*
is terrible that   M   arrived$_{3sg.subj}$ had$_{3sg.subj.}$ arrived at noon
'It is terrible that María {arrived / had arrived} at noon'

The main predicate deletion hypothesis wrongly predicts that the examples in (4b) ought to be grammatical with a past tense, unless a specific condition on tenses restricts the ellipsis of the matrix predicate when the subordinate verb displays past tense. As is obvious, such a condition would not be far from being an *ad hoc* stipulation.

In addition, declarative sentences introduced by *que* depending on volition verbs display an 'obviation effect': when the matrix subject and the subordinate subject are co-referent, the obviation effect blocks the use of a finite subjunctive verb and obliges the use of an infinitive (see the contrast in (7a)). In contrast, some evaluative predicates do not display the obviation effect and allow for a subjunctive sentence but reject an infinitive sentence, as shown in (7b).

(7) a. *Quiero {*que yo gane el premio/ ganar yo el premio}*
     want$_{1s}$ that I win$_{subj}$ the prize / win$_{inf}$ I the prize
     'I want to win the prize'

  b. *Es terrible {que yo gane el premio / *ganar yo el premio}*
     is terrifying that I win$_{subj}$ the prize / win$_{inf}$ I the prize
     'It annoys me that I win the prize'

Summarizing, <*que*+V$_{SUBJ}$> sentences are main clauses that have the complementizer *que*. A temporal constraint limits the tense features the verb can display: present temporal features (present and present perfect tenses) are admitted and past temporal features (past and pluperfect tenses) are excluded. These formal properties are common for both the optative reading and the evaluative reading.

2.2 The optative reading of <*que* + V$_{SUBJ}$> sentences

Two semantic properties are associated with the optative reading of <*que*+V$_{SUBJ}$> sentences: they express the vivid wish, desire or hope of the speaker about the realization of proposition, and they presuppose that the content of the proposition is not a fact.

In Sánchez López (2016a, 2017), I proposed that optatives are anti-factive. The optative meaning consists in expressing the speaker's vivid wish or desire that the propositional content of the sentence becomes a fact and, therefore, they convey the presupposition that the desired eventuality is not factual. They are not compatible with a context that contradicts the non-factual reading of the proposition. That is why the *que*-sentences in (8) would be acceptable with the evaluative reading but odd with the optative reading:

(8) a. *¡Que haya venido Pepe. ., como de hecho ha venido!*
     that has$_{subj}$ come Pepe, as of fact has come
     #'If only Pepe had come, as he in fact did'
     'It is annoying that Pepe had come, as he in fact did'

    b. *¡Que tengas   suerte..., y   de   hecho la   tienes!*
        that have2sg.$_{subj}$ luck   and of   fact it$_{ac}$ have$_{2.sg}$
        #'I hope you have good luck!... and actually you do'
        'It is annoying that you have good luck, and actually you do'

This means that the optative meaning is conventional and cannot be cancelled by context. This property makes a strong difference between optatives and declarative sentences depending on a verb of desire. Declarative sentences with a verb of desire or hope are compatible with a context in which the factual nature of the desired eventuality is expressed.

(9)   a. *Esperaba que él   hubiera venido, como de hecho ha   venido*
        hoped$_{1sg}$ that he   had$_{subj}$ come   as   of   fact   has   come
        'I was hoping Pepe had come, as he in fact did'

    b. Yo *deseo que tú   vengas, y   soy*
        I   wish that you   come$_{subj}$ and am
        feliz porque sé   que vienes
        happy because know$_{1sg}$ that come$_{2sg}$
        'I want you to come in, and I am happy because I know you are coming'

2.3 The evaluative reading of <*que* + V$_{SUBJ}$> sentences

Que-Eval sentences express the displeasure, unease or discontent of the speaker about the propositional content; in other words, the propositional content denoted by the utterance is evaluated negatively on the part of the speaker.[11]

---

11 Italian and Portuguese have evaluative sentences, which receive a negative evaluative reading as well:

(i) *Che Mario debba comportarsi così (dopo tutto quello che abbiamo fatto   per   lui)*
    that M.   must$_{subj}$ behave$_{inf}$ this way after all   that that   have$_{1.pl}$ done for
    'It is annoying that Mario has to behave this way after what we did for him!'
    (Benincà 1988)

(ii) *Que ele passe   a   vida a zangar-se connosco é   o   cúmulo!*
    that he   spends$_{subj}$ the   life kidding   with-us is the   top
    'That he spends his life kidding us is so annoying!'
    (Duarte 2003)

Benincà (1988: 133) describes the meaning of (i) in the following way: "the exclamative utterance introduced by *che* 'that' can be interpreted like the argument of a predicate such as *è*

Que-Eval sentences presuppose that the proposition is a factual situation that is contrary to the expectations or desires of the speaker. Since the proposition denotes a fact that contradicts the expectations or desires of the speaker, the propositional content is evaluated negatively and the utterance expresses the speaker's displeasure, unease or discontent (Sánchez López 2014, 2016b; Gras and Sansiñena 2017).

The evaluative reading is the only one possible when these sentences are followed by some phrases that make explicit the negative evaluation; those statements that express a positive evaluation are rejected, as shown in (10):

(10) ¡Que tenga   yo un sobrino tan salvaje! ¡{Terrible/ #fantástico}!
     that have_subj I a nephew so savage terrible/   fantastic
     'I have such a savage nephew! That's {terrible/fantastic}!'

In addition, the contrast above shows that the discursive context cannot cancel the interpretation of the sequence as a negative evaluation on the part of the speaker. This fact provides a strong argument for the conventional nature of this meaning. If the negative evaluation meaning of <*que*+V$_{SUBJ}$> sentences were the result of a generalized implicature, it could be cancelled by context, but this is not the case. So, we can conclude that the negative evaluation reading is a conventional meaning of the sentence. This fact provides a strong argument for considering *que*-Eval as insubordinate sentences, since, according to Evans's (2007) insubordination account insubordinate constructions have conventionalized independent meaning.

The negative evaluation, which is only a part of the wide range of evaluative attitudes that can be expressed by the speaker, crucially characterizes these types of statements. This property excludes a possible analysis of evaluatives as truncated subordinate clauses. that is, as subordinate clauses that are a complement of a silent or elided main predicate. This kind of analysis is proposed by Benincà (1988: 137), who affirms that the kind of exclamative

---

proprio inaudito 'it is incredible', *è proprio il colmo* 'it is an annoyance' ", («*La frase [esclamativa introdotta da che] può essere interpretata come argomento di un predicato del tipo è proprio inaudito, è proprio il colmo*» – author's translation). A similar description is provided by Duarte (2003) regarding (ii). The *Trésor de la Langue Française (s.v. que)* states that the conjunction *que* 'that' followed by a subjunctive verb expresses the wish, *the anger* or the surprise («*suivi d'un verbe au subj., exprimant le souhait, **l'indignation**, la surprise*», underlined is author's translation). Similar constructions exist also in Rumanian and French; see Sánchez López (2016b) regarding evaluatives in Romance languages. Insubordinate constructions with a negative evaluative meaning have been tested also in English and German (Evans 2007: 403–404) and Swedish and Danish (D'Hertefelt and Verstraete 2013).

exemplified by (1a) is *dipendente ellittica della principale*, or, 'dependent on the elided main clause' (see also Rivero 1977; Spaulding 1934).

A subordinate clause introduced by *que* with a subjunctive verb can be the argument of both predicates expressing a positive evaluation, as in (11a), and predicates expressing a negative evaluation, as in (11b). *Que* evaluatives only receive the second interpretation, which would not be the case if they were the result of the elision of the main predicate, since nothing prevents positive evaluation predicates from being elided under the same conditions that negative evaluation predicates are:

(11) a. *¡Es {fantástico / bueno}   que   tenga   yo este sobrino!*
      is   wonderful   good   that   had$_{subj}$ I   that nephew
      'It is wonderful / good having such a nephew!'

    b. *¡Es {terrible / malo} que tenga yo este sobrino!*
      is   terrible   good   that   had$_{subj}$ I   that nephew
      'It is terrible / bad having such a nephew'

The contrast between the example (10) above and the examples in (11) allows us to reject a potential main predicate elision analysis for evaluatives and to conclude that they are not truncated subordinated sentences but main sentences with a complex left periphery by which the speaker expresses his/her discontent or unease.

Evaluatives are compatible with the presupposition that the proposition is a real fact and this is why they are incompatible with a context that denies the factual presupposition, as in (12a):

(12) a. *#¡Que   tenga   yo   un   sobrino   tan   salvaje!...*
      that   had$_{subj}$ I   a   nephew   so   savage
      ¡Espero   que   eso   nunca   suceda!
      I hope   that   it   never   happens$_{subj}$
      'It is annoying that I have such a savage nephew, and I hope that never happens.'

    b. *¡Que   tenga   yo   un   sobrino   tan   salvaje!...*
      that   had$_{subj}$ I   a   nephew   so   savage
      ¡Lo   tengo,   ciertamente,   y   es   terrible!
      him$_{ac}$ have   certainly   and   is   terrible
      'I have such a savage nephew! I actually have one, and that's terrible!'

As pointed out above, *que*-Eval sentences express that the actual situation is contrary to the expectations of the speaker. Since the proposition denotes a fact that contradicts the expectations of the speaker, the propositional content is evaluated negatively and the utterance expresses the speaker's displeasure, unease or discontent. Some optative sentences can have a counter-expectation meaning as well; this is the case for optatives introduced by the conjunction *si* 'if' (13a) and the particle *ojalá*[12] (13b), when the verb is in a past tense:

(13) a. *¡Si al menos yo no tuviera un sobrino tan salvaje!*
If at least I not had$_{subj}$ a nephew so savage
'If only I did not have a nephew so savage!'

    b. *¡Ojalá yo no tuviera un sobrino tan salvaje!*
PART I not had$_{subj}$ a nephew so savage
'If only I had never had this nephew!'

Optatives in (13) express desires that are contrary to the real situation; the evaluatives express the factual situation that is bad for the speaker, and, therefore, contrary to his expectations as well.

2.4 Prosody

Main clauses with the form <*que*+V$_{SUB}$> have the intonational properties of exclamative sentences. They are prosodically marked by exaggerated acoustic intensity (wide ranging peaks and troughs) and can be orthographically indicated by exclamation marks "¡!". They have a fundamental frequency higher than declarative sentences associated to the expressive and pragmatic meaning of the utterance.

In European Spanish, the exclamative pattern differs according to what the interpretation of the sentence with the form <*que*+V$_{SUBJ}$> has: the optative reading is marked with a downward final intonation whereas the evaluative reading is marked with an upward final intonation.[13]

---

12 *Ojalá* comes from the Hispanic Arabic *law šá lláh* 'if God wants'. In current Spanish, it is a sentential particle that means 'I wish'; this word does not have a literal translation into English, so I use the generic term PART 'particle' in the glossa.
13 The prosodical analysis presented in this section refers to the variety of Spanish spoken in Spain. My analysis predicts that some differences must exist between the intonation of *que*-Eval and *que*-Opt in other varieties, but I do not have data to prove it. In despite of this fact,

The intonation of *que*-Opt sentences consists of a clear rising pitch in the first stressed syllable and a falling final intonation movement at the end of the sentence.[14] Figure 1 represents the intonation pattern of the sentence, *¡Que tengas suerte con tus sobrinos esta tarde!* 'I hope you have good luck with your nephews this afternoon!':

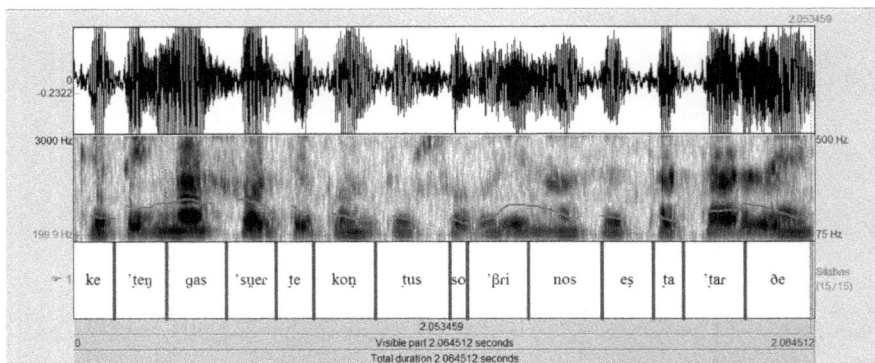

Figure 1: Intonation of a <*que*+V$_{SUBJ}$> sentence with optative reading.

Conversely, the intonation of *que*-Eval sentences consists of a clear rising pitch in the first stressed syllable and a rising intonation movement at the end of the sentence, which contrasts with the falling final intonation of *que*-Opt. Figure 2 bellow represents the intonation pattern of the sentence, ¡Que tenga yo un sobrino tan salvaje! 'It is annoying that I have such a savage nephew'.

The rising final intonation has been related to truncated utterances. Montolío (1999) explains how the suspended intonation marks the difference between optative sentences introduced by *si* 'if' and truncated conditionals, which must be considered semantically and syntactically subordinate. With this same reasoning, Gras (2011) considers that evaluative sentences introduced by *que* are not plain insubordinates, but suspended sentences that are not fully fixed.

The point of view I will adopt here is different. I will assume that the final rising intonation is not evidence of truncation, but a formal mark to induce

---

I consider that the empirical analysis presented here is a promising begining for the prosodical analysis of these sentences.

14 The analyzed utterances in Figure 1 and Figure 2 bellow were produced by an adult female speaker from Madrid. It has been analyzed with PRAAT (Boersma and Weenink 2015). I would like to thank the generous help of Professor Juana Gil, who did the phonetic analysis of these utterances.

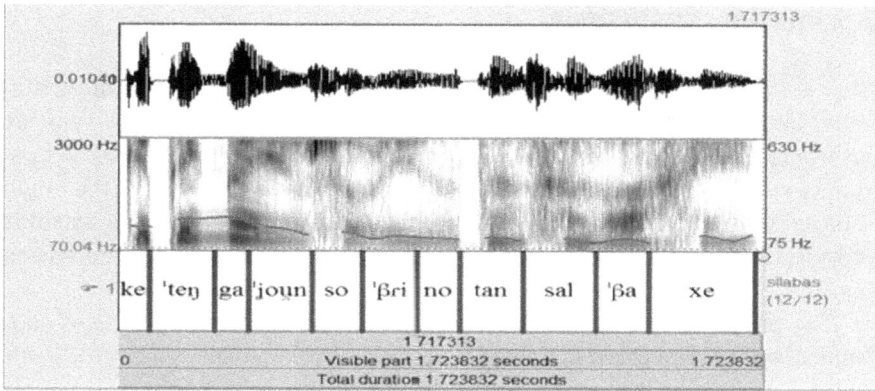

Figure 2: Intonation of a <*que*+V$_{SUBJ}$> sentence with evaluative reading.

a certain interpretation. The relationship between intonation and the expression of the speaker's negative attitude in Spanish was observed and cleverly described by Navarro Tomás (1974), who wrote:

> The rising inflection occurs in exclamations expressing amazement and surprise which involve, at the same time, the intention to make a reply, correction or protest. The amazement and surprise is often referred to facts, purposes or attitudes whose allocation is considered inappropriate [...]. Exclamative utterances with a sense of disconformity, censure or disapproval exhibit rising intonation as well.
> (Navarro Tomás 1974: 175ss, author's translation).[15]

The relationship between a rising final intonation and evaluation on the part of the speaker has been documented in Catalan in declarative and interrogative sentences.[16] Prieto (2014: 17) documents a pattern related to "disapproval statement", which consists in a low last tonic syllable followed by a rising final intonation to a medium level; anti-expectational (echo) questions also display a final rising intonation (Prieto 2014: 23–25; see also Rigau and Prieto 2008). Although more experimental research would be necessary, I will assume that a rising final intonation is related to meaning rather than truncation in these sentences.

---

15 "La inflexión ascendente ocurre en exclamaciones de extrañeza y sorpresa que envuelven al mismo tiempo intención de réplica, rectificación o protesta. La extrañeza y sorpresa se refieren de ordinario a hechos, propósitos o actitudes cuya atribución se considera injustificada. [...] Las proposiciones exclamativas con sentido de franca disconformidad, censura o reprobación ofrecen también inflexión ascendente" (Navarro Tomás 1974: 175ss).
16 I thank Elvira-García (p.c.) for bringing these data to my attention.

2.5 Interim conclusions

The data presented until here allows the formulation of some interim conclusions. Insubordinate Spanish sentences with *que* plus a subjunctive verb are not truncated subordinate clauses, but main sentences with a complex left periphery and specific semantic and syntactic properties. Regardless of the origin of these constructions, which is not the subject of this paper, there are semantic and formal properties that allow for exclusion of any main predicate elision analysis.

The principal formal, semantic, and prosodical properties of <*que*+V$_{SUBJ}$> sentences are summarized in Table 1.

Table 1: Properties of <*que*+V$_{SUBJ}$>.

		Optative reading	Evaluative reading
Formal properties	*Que* is obligatory	+	+
	Subjunctive mood	+	+
	Tense restrictions	+	+
Semantic import	Presupposition of the proposition		
	Factivity	–	+
	Anti-factivity	+	–
	Desirability of the proposition		
	Desirable	+	–
	Undesirable	–	+
	Assessment		
	Positive	+	–
	Negative	–	+
Prosody	Exclamative intonation	+	+
	Final toneme		
	Rising	–	+
	Falling	+	–

The formal properties of <*que*+V$_{SUBJ}$> sentences are the same, whether their interpretations are evaluative or optative. The presence of *que* is obligatory; the verb displays subjunctive mood and is compatible with present temporal features (present and present perfect tenses), but incompatible with past temporal features (past and pluperfect tenses).

The construction can receive two different readings. On the one hand, the optative reading is related to desirability (the proposition is desirable for the speaker) and antifactivity (the proposition is presupposed not to be a fact); in addition, the optative reading is most probably related to positive assessment, since the speaker would not desire something (s)he does not consider good for him/her. On the other hand, the evaluative reading is related to negative assessment (the proposition is negatively evaluated by the speaker) and is compatible with a factual presupposition; in addition, the evaluative reading is most probably related to undesirability, since the speaker would not consider the proposition bad for him/her if (s)he really hopes it happens.

Prosody of <*que*+V$_{SUBJ}$> is always expressive, that is, these sentences have a special intonation different from declarative sentences. The intonation, indeed, plays a central role in disambiguating these sentences: a falling final intonation corresponds to the optative reading, and a rising final intonation indicates an evaluative reading. Prosody is, indeed, the only formal difference between the optative reading and the evaluative reading.

3 Analysis: Syntax and semantics of optatives and evaluatives

In this section, I propose a formal and semantic analysis of <*que*+V$_{SUBJ}$> sentences as expressive utterances with a basically optative interpretation. According to this analysis, the formal similarities between *que*-Eval and *que*-Opt are due to the fact that they are both basically optative statements constructed with the same structural and semantic architecture. Their semantic differences come from the fact that they are interpreted according to different bouletic scales: optatives are interpreted with respect to a bouletic scale and express what the speaker desires, whereas evaluatives are interpreted with respect to an inverted bouletic scale and express what the speaker does not desire.

3.1 The illocutionary force of <*que*+V$_{SUBJ}$> sentences

My analysis of <*que*+V$_{SUBJ}$> sentences is based on the hypothesis that they are expressive, that is, sentences whose illocutionary force consists in expressing the speaker's emotion about a proposition. This differs from declarative, interrogative and jussive sentences. Expressive sentences convey the speaker's emotion about a proposition, rather than describe a situation. They differ from declaratives, which are descriptive utterances, in that expressive utterances serve to directly express an emotional or affective state. Expressives are subject to a sincerity condition, in that they can be sincere or insincere utterances, and they can be either felicitous or infelicitous in a given context, but they are not true or false. Descriptive statements, however, are truth functional, and are true or false.

I assume that the illocutionary force of an utterance is due to the presence of an operator in the functional layer Force Phrase. Expressive sentences contain a generalized exclamation operator *EX*, as proposed for exclamatives by Gutiérrez Rexach (1996, 2001), Castroviejo (2006), Jónsson (2010) and for optatives by Grosz (2011) and Sánchez López (2016a, 2016b). I am actually assuming that expressives include both optatives and exclamatives, in line with Grosz (2011, 2012). The illocutionary operator *EX* selects a truth conditional statement (a proposition) *p* and a scale *S* and quantifies over scalar alternatives to *p*. In <*que*+V$_{SUBJ}$> sentences, *S* is ordered according to the speaker's preferences, that is, the proposition *p* and its relevant alternatives are ordered according to the property 'more desirable for the speaker'. As a result, expressive utterances with an optative meaning are modalized propositions anchored to the world of the speaker's desires or preferences. The presence of *EX* explains the expressive nature of these sentences, since the operator combines with a proposition, and turns it into a felicity-conditional expression of an emotion. I take the formulations below from Grosz' (2011) hypothesis about optatives:

(14) i. An utterance of EX(*p*) conveys the information that the speaker at the point of utterance has an emotion (or at least an evaluative attitude) towards *p*. By uttering an utterance of EX(*p*), the speaker intends to express his/her emotion, rather than describe his/her emotion.

    ii. EX: For any scale *S* and proposition *p*, interpreted in relation to a context *c* and assignment function *g*, an utterance *EX(S)(p)* is felicitous if:
$$\forall q \, [\text{THRESHOLD}(c) >_s q \rightarrow p >_s q]$$

That is to say: *EX* expresses an emotion that captures the fact that *p* is higher on a (speaker-related) scale *S* than all contextually relevant alternatives *q* below a contextual threshold, where THRESHOLD (c) is a function from a context into a set of worlds/a proposition that counts as high with respect to a relevant scale *S*.

I propose that the analysis in (14) is valid for both the optative and the evaluative readings since, in both cases, *S* refers to a scale that models the speaker's preferences (i.e. a bouletic scale). The optative and the evaluative readings differ in the orientation of the scale: in the unmarked situation, the top of the bouletic scale is occupied by the most desirable proposition and the sentence has an optative reading; if S is inversely oriented, the top is occupied by the less desirable proposition and the sentence has an evaluative reading. Intonation marks an inverted orientation of the scale. The conditions in (15) are in order:

(15) Being an utterance of *EX(S)(p)*, S is a bouletic scale that orders *p* and the relevant alternatives to *p* according to the speaker's preferences,
   i. *EX(S)(p)* will have an optative meaning if Vq [THRESHOLD(c) $>_S q \to p >_S q$]
   ii. *EX(S)(p)* will have a negative evaluative meaning if Vq [THRESHOLD(c) $>_S q \to p <_S q$]

This account is consistent with the idea that desirability is the result of the comparison of a proposition and salient alternatives, which goes in line with Villalta's (2007, 2008) analysis. I propose that the negative evaluation of the proposition is the result of the desirability and, therefore, of the comparison of the proposition with its contextually relevant alternatives. The speaker evaluates the proposition negatively because the proposition is less desirable for him/her.

This analysis explains why the evaluative reading only expresses a negative attitude on the part of the speaker, that is, the evaluative reading only expresses a part of the wide range of evaluative attitudes that would be possible for subordinated sentences depending on a main verbal predicate (recall the contrasts in (10) and (11) above). The positive evaluative attitude, indeed, coincides with the optative reading.

It is important to note that the positive or negative evaluation of the proposition does not depend on the very meaning of the proposition itself but on the speaker's evaluative attitude. This is why the utterance *¡Que se muera!* 'I hope he dies!' can be considered an optative statement though its propositional content is intrinsically bad. The proposition 'he dies' is positively assessed by the speaker because it is desirable for him. On the other hand, the utterance *¡Que él haya ganado el premio!* 'It is annoying that he has won the prize!' can receive a negative evaluative meaning; although the fact that he won the prize looks good at first, the speaker can consider it less desirable than other alternatives, or even the least desirable at all.

The fact that the evaluative reading of <*que*+V$_{SUBJ}$> sentences involves an inverse bouletic scale explains why the negative form of an evaluative is equivalent to the corresponding affirmative optative. As noted by Salvá (1830: 221), Spanish negative exclamatives with *que* can express desire and be equivalent to affirmative optatives introduced by the particle *ojalá* 'I wish'; examples in (16) are his:

(16) a. *¡Que no pueda yo explicar todo lo que siento!*
That not can$_{subj}$ I explain all that feel$_{1sg}$
'It is annoying that I cannot explain what I feel!'

b. *¡Ojalá pudiera yo explicar todo lo que siento!*
PART could$_{subj}$ I explain all that feel$_{1sg}$
'If only I could explain what I feel!'

3.2 The syntactic structure and the role of Force and Mood

Associating the expressive interpretation of a sentence with an exclamatory operator means that there has to be a syntactic projection hosting this constituent expressing force. In line with the cartographic approach, which takes CPs as involving a fine-grained structure encoding topic, focus, and force constituents, I will assume that *EX* is syntactically merged into the specifier of ForceP (Rizzi 1997; Gutiérrez Rexach 2001; Sánchez López 2016a, 2016b). I propose that overt lexical material must merge in Force° to satisfy the mood feature entailed in evaluative sentences, and that in <*que*+V$_{SUBJ}$> sentences, the conjunction *que* 'that' merges in Force° to satisfy the requirement that lexical material is realized in Force° to ensure the right clause type marking. My analysis is consistent with the proposal by Rodríguez Ramalle (2008a, 2008b), who argues that *que* is located in the Force Phrase in subjunctive sentences, and differs from the analysis of Demonte & Fernández Soriano (2007, 2009), who argue that *que* is situated in the head of the Finiteness Phrase.[17]

Mood is a functional head between CP and IP (Giorgi and Pianesi 1997; Kempchinsky 1998). The suggested link between Mood head and C can be traced back to Kempchinsky's (1987) analysis of the Romance subjunctive (see also Rivero and Terzi 1995). In subjunctive sentences, Force° has an interpretable feature that attracts the uninterpretable feature [mood$_{subjunctive}$] in MoodP associated with the subjunctive morphology. The syntactic structure, then, is the following:

---

17 Both Demonte and Fernández Soriano (2007, 2009) and Rodríguez Ramalle (2008a, 2008b) propose that the conjunction *que* 'that' occupies a different position in indicative sentences: the former supposes that *que* is in the head of the Speech Act Phrase, and the latter suppose that *que* occupies either the head position in the Force Phrase whenever it precedes an interrogative element, or the head in the Evidentiality Phrase, when it functions as a reportative evidential (Demonte and Fernández Soriano 2013, 2014). Núñez Lagos (2005) proposes a unitary account of *que* as a marker of propositional subordination position.

(17)

ForceP

EX   Force'

Force   MoodP

                    Mood   TP

Que [i-MOD] ·········· *f* [u-MOD subjunctive]

This syntactic analysis relies on the idea that the subjunctive is selected by the *EX* operator. I assume Villalta's (2007, 2008) hypothesis about the subjunctive indicative alternation in main clauses. According to her, the selection of the subjunctive mood follows a general principle, according to which the predicates that require the subjunctive mood introduce an ordering relation between propositions by comparing the proposition to its contextually available alternatives. The realization of subjunctive features in Mood ensures that the evaluation of alternatives happens at the right place in the tree.

I propose that the analysis of Villalta can be extended to the selection of mood in main clauses: *EX* ensures an ordering relation between *p* and the salient alternatives according to a scale anchored by the speaker. Optative-*EX* orders *p* and its alternatives according to the speaker's preferences, such that the evaluation has to take place at the level of the proposition and, more precisely, in MoodP (Villalta, 2007, 2008).

In other words, *EX* ensures an ordering relation between alternatives according to a scale provided by the speaker. Subjunctive features in Mood ensure that the alternatives are evaluated at the level of the proposition, in MoodP. A deontic modal base associated with the desires of the speaker provides the alternatives; the proposition must be interpreted as the more salient proposition in a bouletic scale associated with the desires or wishes of the speaker. The evaluative reading is obtained when the proposition is evaluated with respect to an inverted bouletic scale.

Evaluatives are similar to factive emotive predicates (Kiparsky and Kiparsky 1970) in that they presuppose the truth of the proposition (factivity) and, nevertheless, require subjunctive Mood. As is known, a subjunctive under factive emotive predicates looks like *realis* subjunctive cases and clearly does not fit the traditional understanding of subjunctive as occurring in *irrealis* contexts (Givón 1994; Mithun 1995). They are neither clearly intentional (Farkas 1985, 1992) nor non-veridical (Giannakidou 1997), nor can they be considered old information in all cases and they are not negation/polarity-licensed (Guitart 1991).

Under the analysis proposed here, the negative evaluation of the proposition is the result of comparing the proposition with other salient alternatives according to a bouletic scale: the speaker expresses an emotion about his/her desires by saying that what happens is the less desirable situation in his/her scale of preferences. According to this analysis, no incompatibility between the factive nature of evaluatives and the subjunctive mood is predicted.

3.3 Tense restrictions and the (anti)-factive presupposition

In Section 2.1, I showed that $<que+V_{SUBJ}>$ sentences are constrained by a temporal criterion: they only admit a verb with present temporal features whether they receive an optative or an evaluative reading. The fact that both readings exhibit the same tense restrictions follows directly from the fact that they have the same syntactic structure and the same basic optative meaning. In this section, I will propose that these tense restrictions are due to the modal base the sentences are anchored in. Concretely, I propose that tense features under subjunctive mood are linked to the modal base the sentence must be interpreted in.

Following Laca (2010: 198), I argue that present and present perfect subjunctive are deictic tenses, always anchored to the time of utterance, which provides a not completely realistic modal base (Iatridou 2000), that is, a domain that contains a world or worlds of evaluation compatible with the real world $-w_0-$ in addition to other possible worlds. The $<que+V_{SUBJ}>$ sentences, with both evaluative and optative readings, display a subjunctive feature in Mood and present features in Tense, in that they are interpreted according to a not completely realistic modal base.

Two important consequences follow from this explanation: firstly, $<que+V_{subj}>$ sentences with an evaluative reading are compatible with the presupposition that the proposition in which the speaker expresses an evaluation denotes a fact. Since they are interpreted with respect to a not completely realistic modal base, that is a modal base containing some worlds of evaluation in addition to the actual world, the factivity presupposition is not ruled out.

Secondly, $<que+V_{subj}>$ sentences with an optative reading express wishes that are interpreted as feasible desires which are compatible with the actual state of affairs. That explains why these optatives are anomalous if the context determines that the desired situation is impossible, as in (18):

(18) #*Es*   *imposible*   *que*   *ella*   *venga*   *hoy,*
     is   impossible   that   she   comes$_{subj}$ today
     pero   *¡que*   *venga*   *solo*   *un*   *ratito!*
     but   that   comes$_{subj}$ only   a   while
     'It is not possible that she comes today, but I hope that she comes only for
     a little while'

The temporal constraint on <*que*+V$_{SUBJ}$> sentences is due to the modal base they are interpreted in, but it is not a general constraint on optatives. In Sánchez López (2017), I describe how the temporal restriction makes the difference between optatives headed by *que* and optatives introduced by *si* 'if' (see 20a), which display verbs with past and pluperfect tense, and optatives introduced by the particle *ojalá* (see 19b), which do not exhibit any temporal constraints at all:

(19) a. *¡Si*   *al menos*   *él*   *{*sea*   /   **haya*
       if   at least   he   is$_{subj}$ /   has$_{subj}$
       sido   /   *fuera*   /   *hubiese sido}*   *amable!*
       been   /   was$_{subj}$ /   had$_{subj}$ been   gentle
       'If only he was/had been gentle!'

     b. *¡Ojalá*   *él*   *{*sea*   /   **haya*   *sido*   /
       PART   he   is$_{subj}$ /   has$_{subj}$ been   /
       fuera   /   *hubiese*   *sido}*   *amable!*
       was$_{subj}$ /   had$_{subj}$ been   gentle
       'I hope he is/was/has been/had been gentle!'

4 Conclusions

I have proposed that <*que*+V$_{SUBJ}$> are expressive sentences that voice the speaker's emotion about a proposition. Their main formal properties (mood and tense restrictions) and semantic properties (presupposition of factivity and negative evaluation of the proposition) follow from an analysis that considers them as inverted optative statements.

     The description expands the inventory of Romance main expressive sentences and provides a new empirical base for the understanding of the relationship between the left periphery of the sentences, their illocutionary force, and the properties of Mood. The analysis proposed here supports the idea that the illocutionary force of statements has a syntactic correlate in the merge of the Force and Mood heads.

References

Alcina, Juan & José Manuel Blecua. 1975. *Gramática española*. Barcelona: Ariel.

Bello, Andrés. 1964 [1847]. *Gramática de la lengua castellana, con notas de Rufino José Cuervo y N.iceto Alcalá-Zamora*. Buenos Aires: Sopena.

Benincà, Paola. 1998. Il tipo esclamativo. In Lorenzi Renzi, Giampaolo Salvi & Anna Cardinaletti (eds.), *Grande grammatica italiana di consultazione*, vol. III, 127–152. Bologna: Il Mulino.

Boersma, Paul & David Weenink. 2015. *Praat: doing phonetics by computer [Computer program]*. Version 5. 4.08. http://www.praat.org/ (24 March 2015).

Bosque, Ignacio. 1980. Retrospective imperatives. *Linguistic Inquiry* 11 (2). 415–419.

Castroviejo, Elena. 2006. *Wh-Exclamatives in Catalan*. Barcelona: Universidad de Barcelona dissertation.

CORDE *Corpus diacrónico del español*. http://www.rae.es.

Corr, Alice V. 2016. *Ibero-Romance and the syntax of the utterance*. Cambridge: Cambridge University doctoral thesis.

CREA *Corpus de referencia del español actual*. http://www.rae.es.

D'Hertefelt, Sara & Jean Christophe Verstraete. 2013. Independent complement constructions in Swedish and Danish: Insubordination or dependency shift? *Journal of Pragmatics* 60. 98–102.

Demonte, Violeta & Olga Fernández-Soriano. 2007. La periferia izquierda oracional y los complementantes del español. In Juan Cuartero & Martine Emsel (eds.), *Vernetzungen: Kognition, Bedeutung, (kontrastive) Pragmatik*, 133–147. Frankfurt: Peter Lang.

Demonte, Violeta & Olga Fernández-Soriano. 2009. Force and finiteness in the Spanish complementizer system. *Probus* 21 (1). 23–49.

Demonte, Violeta & Olga Fernández-Soriano. 2013. El *que* citativo, otros elementos de la periferia izquierda oracional y la recomplementación: Variación inter e intralingüística. In Daniel Jakob & Katya Plooj (eds.), *Autour de que- El entorno de que*, 47–69. Frankfurt am Main: Peter Lang.

Demonte, Violeta & Olga Fernández-Soriano. 2014. Evidentiality and illocutionary force: Spanish matrix 'que' at the syntax-pragmatics interface. In Andreas Dufter & Álvaro S. Octavio de Toledo (eds.), *Left sentence peripheries in Spanish: Diachronic, variationist, and typological perspectives*, 217–252. Amsterdam: John Benjamins.

Elvira-García, Wendy. 2015. *La prosodia de las construcciones insubordinadas conectivo-argumentativas del español*. Barcelona: Univsersidad de Barcelona doctoral thesis.

Elvira-García, Wendy, Paolo Roseano & Ana María Fernández Planas. 2016. Prosody as a cue for syntactic dependency. Evidence from dependent and independent clauses with subordination marcks in Spanish. *Journal of Pragmatics* 109. 29–46.

Etxepare, Ricardo. 2008. On quotative constructions in Iberian Spanish. In Ritva Laury (ed.), *Crosslinguistic studies of clause combining: The multifunctionality of conjunctions*, 35–78. Amsterdam: John Benjamins.

Etxepare, Ricardo. 2010. From hearsay evidentiality to samesaying relations. *Lingua* 120 (3). 604–627.

Duarte, Inês. 2003. Estrutura da frase simples e tipos de frase. In Maria Helena Mira Mateus, Ana Maria Brito, Inês Duarte, Isabel Hub Faria (eds.), *Gramática da língua portuguesa*, chap. 12. Lisboa: Caminho.

Evans, Nicholas. 2007. Insubordination and its Uses. In Irina Nikolaeva (ed.), *Finitness. Theoretical and empirical foundations*, 366–431. Oxford, Oxford University Press.

Farkas, Dona F. 1985. *Intensional descriptions and the Romance subjunctive mood*. New York: Garland.

Farkas, Dona F. 1992. On the semantics of subjunctive complements. In Paul Hirschbühler, E.F. K. Koerner (eds.), *Romance languages and modern linguistic theory*, 69–104. Amsterdam & Philadelphia: John Benjamins.

Garrido Medina, Joaquín. 1998. Discourse structure in grammar. *Estudios Ingleses de la Universidad Complutense* 6. 49–63.

Garrido Medina, Joaquín. 1999. Los actos de habla: Las oraciones imperativas. In Ignacio Bosque & Violeta Demonte (ed.), *Gramática descriptiva de la lengua española*, vol. 3, 3879–3928. Madrid: Espasa Calpe.

Giannakidou, Anastasia. 1997. *The Landscape of polarity items*. Groningen: Rijksuniversiteit Groningen dissertation.

Gili Gaya, Samuel. 1943. *Curso superior de sintaxis española*. Barcelona: Bibliograph.

Giorgi, Alessandra & Fabio Pianesi. 1997. *Tense and aspect. From semantics to morphosyntax*. New York & Oxford: Oxford University Press.

Givón, Thomas. 1994. Irrealis and subjunctive. *Studies in Language* 18 (2). 265–337.

Gras, Pedro. 2011. *Gramática de construcciones en interacción: Propuesta de un modelo y aplicación al análisis de estructuras independientes con marcas de subordinación en español*. Barcelona: University of Barcelona dissertation.

Gras, Pedro. 2013. Entre la gramática y el discurso: Valores conectivos de *que* inicial átono en español. In Daniel Jacob & Katja Ploog (eds.), *Autour de que: El entorno de que*, 89–112. Frankfurt am Main: Peter Lang.

Gras, Pedro & María Sol Sansiñena. 2015. An interactional account of discourse-connective *que*-constructions in Spanish. *Text and Talk* 35 (4). 505–529.

Gras, Pedro & Sansiñena, María Sol. 2017. Exclamatives in the functional typology of insubordination: evidence from complement insubordinate constructions in Spanish. *Journal of Pragmatics* 115. 21–36.

Grosz, Patrick Georg. 2011. *On the grammar of optative constructions*. Massachusetts, Massachusetts Institute of Technology dissertation.

Guitart, Jorge M. 1991. The pragmatics of Spanish mood in complements of knowledge and acquisition-of-knowledge predicates. In: Suzanne Fleischman & Linda R. Waugh (eds.), *Discourse-Pragmatics and the verb*, 179–193. London: Routledge.

Gutiérrez Rexach, Javier. 1996. The semantics of exclamatives. In Edward Garret & F. Lee (eds.), *Syntax at Sunset. UCLA working papers in linguistics*, 146–162. Los Angeles: Dept. of Linguistics, UCLA.

Gutiérrez Rexach, Javier. 2001. Spanish exclamatives and the semantics of the left periphery. In Johan Rooryck; Yves D'hulst & Jan Schroten (eds.), *Selected papers from Going Romance* 99, 167–194. Amsterdam, John Benjamins.

Iatridou, Sabina. 2000. The grammatical ingredients of counterfactuality. *Linguistic Inquiry* 31 (2). 231–270.

Jónsson, Jóhannes Gísli. 2010. Icelandic exclamatives and the structure of the CP layer. *Studia Linguistica* 64 (1). 37–54.

Kempchinsky, Paula, 1987. The subjunctive disjoint reference effect. In: Carol Neidle & Rafael Nuñez Cedeño (eds.), *Studies in Romance Languages*, 123–140. Dordrecht: Foris Publications.

Kempchinsky, Paula. 1998. Mood phrase, case checking and obviation. In: Armin Schwegler, Bernard Tranel & Myriam Uribe-Etxebarria (eds.), *Linguistic Symposium on Romance Languages XXVII*, 143–154. Amsterdam: John Benjamins.

Kiparsky, Paul, Kiparsky, Carol, 1970. Fact. In: Manfred Bierwisch & Karl Erich Heidolph (eds.), *Progress in Linguistics*, 143–170. The Hague & Paris: Mouton de Gruyter.

Laca, Brenda 2010. Mood in Spanish. In Björn Rothstein & Rolf Thieroff (eds.), *Mood in the languages of Europe*, 198–220. Amsterdam: John Benjamins.

Mithun, Marianne. 1995. On the relativity of irreality. In Joan Bybee & Suzanne Fleischmann (eds.), *Modality in grammar and discourse*, 367–388. Amsterdam & Philadephia: John Benjamins.

Montolío Durán, Estrella. 1999. '¡Si nunca he dicho que estuviera enamorada de él! Sobre construcciones independientes introducidas por *si* con valor replicativo, *Oralia* 2. 37–69.

Navarro, Tomás. 1974. *Manual de Entonación Española*, Madrid: Guadarrama.

Núñez Lagos, Carmen. 2005. *Le signifiant espagnol* Que*: Quel signifié?* Paris: University Paris IV-Sorbonne dissertation.

Pons, Salvador. 2003. *Que* inicial átono como marca de modalidad. *Estudios Lingüísticos de la Universidad de Alicante* (ELUA) 17. 531–545.

Porroche Ballesteros, Margarita. 1998. Sobre los usos de *si, que* y *es que* como marcadores discursivos". In María Antonia Martín Zorraquino & Montolío Durán (eds.), *Los marcadores del discurso: teoría y análisis*, 229–242. Madrid: Arco Libros.

Prieto, Pilar. 2014. The intonational phonology of Catalan. *Prosodic typology* 2. 43–80.

RAE [Real Academia Española]. 1973. *Esbozo de una nueva gramática de la lengua española*. Madrid: Espasa Calpe.

RAE-ASALE [Real Academia Española/Asociación de Academias de la Lengua Española]. 2009. *Nueva gramática de la lengua española*. Madrid: Espasa Calpe.

Ridruejo, Emilio. 1983. Notas sobre las oraciones optativas. In Emilio Alarcos Llorach (ed.), *Serta Philologica F. Lázaro: natalem diem sexagesimum celebranti dicata*, vol. I, 511–520. Madrid, Cátedra.

Rigau, Gemma & Pilar Prieto. 2008. A typological approach to Catalan interrogative sentences headed by *que*. http://prosodia.upf.edu/cat_tobi/en/references/The_Intonational_Phonology_of_Catalan-july-2008.pdf.

Rivero, María Luisa & Terzi, Arhonto. 1995. Imperatives, V-movement and logical mood. *Journal of Linguistics* 31. 301–332.

Rivero, María Luisa. 1977. La concepción de los modos en la Gramática de A. Bello y los verbos abstractos en la gramática generativa. In María Luisa Rivero (ed.), *Estudios de Gramática Generativa del español*, 69–85. Madrid, Cátedra.

Rizzi, Luiggi. 1997. The Fine Structure of the Left Periphery. In Liliane Haegeman (ed.), *Elements of grammar. A handbook of generative syntax*, 282–337. Dordrech, Kluwer.

Rodríguez Ramalle, Teresa M. 2008a. Estudio sintáctico y discursivo de algunas estructuras enunciativas y citativas del español. *Revista Española De Lingüística Aplicada* 21. 269–288.

Rodríguez Ramalle, Teresa M. 2008b. Marcas enunciativas y evidenciales en el discurso periodístico. In Inés Olza, Manuel Casado Velarde & Ramón González Ruiz (eds.), *Actas del XXXVII simposio de la sociedad española de lingüística (SEL)*, 735–744. Pamplona: Servicio de Publicaciones de la Universidad de Navarra.

Salvá, Vicente. 1830. *Gramática de la lengua castellana*. Quoted from the 1852 edition, Madrid.

Sánchez López, Cristina. 2014. The mapping between semantics and prosody: Evidence from Spanish main sentences with the form <*que* +V~subj~>. Paper presented at the Linguisticae Societas Europea, Leiden, 2–5 September, 2014.

Sánchez López, Cristina. 2016a. Person features and functional heads. Evidence from an exceptional optative sentence in Ibero-Romance. In Ernestina Carrilho, Alexandra Fiéis, Maria Lobo & Sandra Pereira (eds.), *Romance languages and linguistic theory. Selected Papers from the Going Romance 28, Lisbon*, 259–278. Amsterdam: John Benjamins.

Sánchez López, Cristina. 2016b. Romance evaluative *que/che/să* sentences as inverted optatives. Paper presented at the 46 Linguistic Symposium on Romance Languages, Stony Brook University, New York, March 31 – April 3 2016.

Sánchez López, Cristina. 2017. Optative sentences in Spanish. In Ignacio Bosque (ed.), *Advances in the analysis of Spanish exclamatives*, 82–107. Ohio: The Ohio University Press.

Sansiñena, María Sol, Hendrik De Smet & Bert Cornillie. 2015a. Displaced directives: Subjunctive free-standing *que*-clauses vs. imperatives in Spanish. *Folia Lingüística* 49 (1). 257–285.

Sansiñena, María Sol; De Smet, Hendrik & Cornillie, Bert. 2015b. Between subordinate and insubordinate. Path toward complementizer-initial main clauses. *Journal of Pragmatics* 77. 3–19.

Sirbu-Dumitrescu, Domnita. 1994. Función pragma-discursiva de la interrogación ecoica usada como respuesta en español. In Henk Haverkate, Kees Hengeveld & Gijs Mulder (eds.), *Aproximaciones pragmalingüísticas al español*, 51–85. Amsterdam: Rodopi.

Sirbu-Dumitrescu, Domnita. 1998. Subordinación y recursividad en la conversación: Las secuencias integradas por intercambios ecoicos. In Henk Haverkate, Gijs Mulder & Carolina Fraile Maldonado (eds.), *Diálogos hispánicos*, vol. 22, 277–314. Amsterdam: Rodopi.

Sirbu-Dumitrescu, Domnita. 2004. La expresión de buenos deseos hacia nuestro prójimo: ¿un acto de habla cortés automático? In Diana Bravo & Antonio Briz (ed.), *Pragmática socio-cultural: Estudios sobre el discurso de cortesía en español*, 265–284. Barcelona: Ariel.

Spaulding, Robert. 1934. Two elliptical subjunctives in Spanish. *Hispania* 17. 355–360.

Villalta, Elisabeth. 2007. *Context dependence in the interpretation of questions and subjunctives*. Tübingen: Universität Tübingen dissertation.

Villalta, Elisabeth. 2008. Mood and gradability: An investigation of the subjunctive mood in Spanish. *Linguistics and Philosophy* 31. 467–522.

Volker Struckmeier and Sebastian Kaiser

10 When insubordination is an artefact (of sentence type theories)

Abstract: In this paper, we discuss the basic foundation of research on insubordination. We argue that some clause types should, in fact, not be classified as insubordinated which have been taken, in the literature, to constitute examples of insubordination. We argue that an *illusion* of subordination can be brought about by sentence type theories which define subordination on an empirical basis that is simply too narrow to do justice to the sentence type inventory of a language under discussion. Thus, the sentence type theory mislabels sentences as subordinated which are, demonstrably, not subordinated at all (and may never have been). Since non-subordinated sentences, of course, do not behave like subordinated clauses, the consecutive mistake in insubordination research then is to mislabel the *non*-subordinated sentences as *in*subordinated. As a consequence, typologically oriented descriptions of insubordination phenomena exist which, upon closer examination, turn out simply to be based on inadequate descriptions of individual languages. Given empirically adequate sentence type theories for the individual languages, the misanalysis of subordination and the consequential misanalysis of *in*subordination are avoided from the start. As an example of the problem at hand, we discuss the case of German, which according to Evans (2007) displays insubordinated sentences. We show that his analysis is misguided, in that the alleged subordination of the sentence types in question is an artefact of (well-established, but still empirically inadequate) sentence type theories, not a property of the clauses themselves. Note that we do not argue that insubordination does not exist. However, we submit that insubordination research must be carried out with extreme empirical caution and must involve the careful and delicate analysis of individual languages – not by making statements about languages the insubordination researcher simply has not investigated carefully enough.

1 Introduction

The term insubordination, as it is used by Evans, essentially describes a linguistic mismatch: Clausal structures are used autonomously which, "on prima facie

Volker Struckmeier, Ruhr-University Bochum
Sebastian Kaiser, University of Cologne

https://doi.org/10.1515/9783110638288-011

grounds, appear to be formally subordinate clauses" (Evans 2007: 367). This mismatch, it is claimed, points towards a potential partial disconnect between, e.g. compositional syntacto-semantic analyses of sentence types often found in theoretical publications (cf., e.g., Lohnstein 2000, 2007) on the one hand, and the usage of structures, which can be less predictable than the theoretical perspective would have us believe. In this paper, we point out a problem for this kind of research: If we cannot clearly define what we mean by "subordination", there is no way to define "insubordination" in a logically acceptable manner.

We feel that we must begin our endeavour by stressing, in the most explicit manner possible, that we do not intend to criticize the concept of insubordination as such, or the research that is devoted to it. The phenomenon of insubordination, we agree, is not only patently real, it also goes virtually without saying that the concept is fascinating and has spawned very many interesting research results. To name but a few, connections between the usage of structures and their grammaticization, or phenomena of diachronic reanalysis, or the observable directionality inherent in these processes (cf. Evans 2007; Mithun 2008; d'Hertefelt 2015 amongst many others), are extremely interesting as a matter of course.

However, we also observe that there may be a recurring problem that can be pointed out in the actual practice and practical implementation of this field of research which is worrisome, for empirical and methodological reasons. All research in this field must, we insist, be approached with extreme empirical caution and theoretical reflection when it comes to the description of individual languages for which insubordination phenomena are claimed to exist. Research in insubordination, we demonstrate below, requires great circumspection with regard to the definition of sentence type theories (henceforth STTs). We illustrate this concern on the basis of an analysis of German. Evans (2007) claims that German is a language that displays insubordination phenomena. While we agree that this may be the case, we cannot agree that the sentence types (henceforth STs) used as empirical evidence in this regard can indeed be described as "insubordinated" in any meaningful sense of the word. Rather, as we show, these cases of alleged insubordination concern STs that are, more simply, not subordinated in the first place. Therefore, without proper empirical scrutiny, and without a thorough understanding of the constitution of STs in a (single, specific) language, we run a risk of postulating insubordination phenomena where in fact there are none. We claim here that some sentence type theories (which are defined on too narrowly syntactic factors of ST formation) create the illusion of insubordination. Below, we will give examples for structures which have been misanalyzed as insubordinated – but which are actually not subordinated. Let us stress again, however, that we do not want to claim that insubordination could not or does not exist in other languages, or even in general: This conclusion could only be reached by dedicated research in other (single, specific) languages, and such a conclusion has in no way been argued as of today.

The paper proceeds as follows: Section 2 points out that we must be very careful to define criteria that we take to be constitutive of main and subordinate clauses, so that we can handle these superordinate groupings of STs reliably. As Section 2 shows, we risk creating insubordination *artefacts*, i.e. cases of alleged insubordination which, however, are caused purely as an artefact of our STT, and thus should not be counted towards the actual phenomenon of insubordination. Examples of STTs that may cause insubordination artefacts are given in Section 2.1, for traditional descriptive grammars of German, and in Section 2.2, for contemporary compositional analyses of German STs.

Section 3 then points out factors of ST formation that should be taken into account to avoid insubordination artefacts: STTs for German, we claim, need to take into account the range of modal particles found in this language (3.1), and the different prosodic implementations that different clause types may receive (3.2).

Section 4 summarizes what we take to be the theoretical and methodological desiderata that follow from our demonstration: STTs should, we argue, be designed in a certain way, as to avoid superficial and misleading ST descriptions.

Section 5 concludes.

2 Insubordination and insubordination artefacts

In order to be able to describe precisely what we mean by insubordination, we must first define what appear to be the formal criteria of subordination itself. It is only when these features are present that a clausal structure could appear to be used autonomously despite reliable formal indicators for subordination. Furthermore, we have to define precisely which attributes or properties of insurbordinated structures justify our assessment, i.e. that these structures are in fact, used autonomously. In other words, we have to define those aspects of usage that would appear to be definitely incompatible with their "formally subordinated" status. Both of these assessments and classifications hinge completely on our conception of STs and the uses they can be put to. Note, however, that STTs themselves may turn out to be at fault when artefacts arise: STTs consider some types of sentences as subordinated for some (potentially even unspecified) reasons – but upon closer inspection, the sentences in question appear in autonomous usage all the time, and show no properties that would reliably indicate that they are, in fact, subordinated in the first place. Therefore, these STTs would appear to be simply empirically false. It would consequently be a mistake to base a classification of a sentence as insubordinated on any such STT from the start.

STTs could also disregard certain types of sentences altogether, and thus only address a fragment of the sentences of language. They tend to propose subordination criteria that turn out to hold only for the subset of subordinated (and non-subordinated) sentences they describe (and would classify this fragment of sentences correctly). However, they would fail to classify sentences outside the fragment (e.g., more marginally used or less carefully investigated structures) correctly and reliably. These STTs we consider empirically incomplete.

As we will see in the following, both kinds of problems are attested for German STs.

2.1 Traditional grammar STTs can cause insubordination artefacts

Traditional German grammars often use some version of the *Topologisches Feldermodell* (cf. Drach 1937). In the Feldermodell, the two possible positions for verbs in this language define two "brackets", which open up three "fields" between the brackets, containing specifiable elements (arguments, adverbials, etc.) of the clause[1], as illustrated in Table 1:

Table 1: Sentence types recognized by most traditional grammars.

Sentence type	prefield	left bracket	middle field	right bracket
V2 declarative (matrix)	Peter *Peter*	hat *has*	den Kindern den Schnaps *to-the kids the booze*	gegeben *given*
	'Peter has given the booze to the children.'			
subordinated V-last declarative	–	dass *that*	Peter ihnen das *Peter to-them that*	gegeben hat *given has*
	'that Peter has given it to them'			
V2 wh-question (matrix)	Wer *who*	hat *has*	ihnen das *to-them that*	gegeben *given*
	"who has given it to them?'			

(continued)

---

1 The postfield will be ignored here and in the following discussion, since it does not contribute to the definition of sentence types in German.

Table 1: (continued)

Sentence type	prefield	left bracket	middle field	right bracket
V1	–	Hat	Peter es ihnen *Peter it to-*	gegeben?
yes/no-question		*has*	*them*	*given*

'Has Peter given it to them?'

Traditional grammars that employed the *Feldermodell* tried to come up with generalizations about these STs. Comparisons between STs like the ones above yielded generalizations which are often encountered in descriptive works on the language. Main clauses, it is argued, are characterized by the positioning of the finite verb in the left bracket. The verb morphology differentiates imperative clauses from other clauses. The materials in the prefield further differentiate (non-imperative) clause types: No prefield material is encountered in polar yes/no-questions, a wh-phrase occupies the prefield in a wh-question, and other (non-Wh) materials in the prefield yield the declarative. Importantly for our purposes here, the diagnosis of subordination is mostly pinned on the position of the verb. If the finite verb is *not* in the left bracket, but in the right bracket, sentences are claimed to be subordinated by many traditional grammars. The left bracket, in these sentences, is taken up by various subordinating conjunctions, which sub-differentiate types of embedded clauses. For example, ob_{+wh} 'whether' in the left bracket heads an embedded question, whereas $dass_{-wh}$ 'that' in the left bracket yields a subordinated declarative. In this way, STs were grouped on the basis of collections of descriptively observable features, and many clauses could be assigned STs on the basis of small sets of rules.

However, at a closer look, problems arise. According to the rules above, verb-last word orders, for example, were considered as indicative of subordination. This, however, turns out to be false in less central STs – and these make up a typical set of examples of alleged insubordination cases in the language. Consider the following examples:

(1) *Dass die aber auch den Peter küssen muss!*   (exclamative)
     that she MP[2] MP the Peter kiss must
     'Oh, (I am so disappointed) that she had to kiss Peter (of all people)!'

---

2 MP = modal particle

(2) *Dass Du aber BLOß die Katze fütterst!* (autonomous, strong command)[3]
    that you MP MP the cat feed
    'Make absolutely sure you feed the cat!'

In both examples, we find what appears to be a subordinating conjunction at the beginning of the clause, and the verb indeed occupies the right bracket position. Still, these sentences should not be considered subordinated; they are simply used autonomously, and no matrix clause is ever required to accompany them, in any discourse, given any common ground, or in fact any background information. Therefore, they can be formally distinguished from elliptical clauses, since German ellipsis requires (minimally) the discourse givenness of materials that ellide (cf., e.g. Merchant 2001; Reich 2007; Ott and Struckmeier 2016, 2018).

Attempts to consider these sentences as subordinated under matrix clauses that ellide optionally (leaving only the subordinated material) fail for semantic reasons, too. The potential set of embedding matrix clauses is invariably very large. However, the resulting semantics of the allegedly elliptical clauses is never as wide-ranging as the ellipsis approach would have to predict. It seems, then, that the specialized semantics of these structures is in no way predicted by ellipsis approaches (see below, and cf., especially, Gutzmann 2011 for a convincing discussion).

In sum, we see that some allegedly insubordinated sentences are, in fact, best not analyzed as subordinated in the first place. With these examples, we simply witness empirical problems for the traditional STT – rather than plausible examples of insubordination. However, problems of this kind never really bothered old school grammars. Marginal sentences were derided ("bad German!"), or simply ignored altogether ("marginal!"). To this day, some descriptive works continue to make false predictions regarding the non- or insubordinated sentences we have just seen.[4] As we will see in the next subsection, however, similar mismatches also did not bother modern-day compositional analyses, either.

---

3 Note that this type of strong, positive command is impossible in *prima facie* comparable *dat* clauses in Dutch (cf. Verstraete et al. 2012).
4 Even when exceptions such as exclamatives and Vlast commands are added to more elaborate traditional grammars, these typically do not prevent the use of terms like *Nebensatzwortstellung* for Vlast orders, etc.

2.2 Contemporary, compositional STTs can also cause insubordination artefacts

Over the last 20 years or so, there has been a renewed interest in STTs in German. Many approaches attempt to derive ST properties from a small set of ST criteria, such as word order, choice of left bracket materials, etc. One of the most successful (and widely cited) attempts along these lines was proposed by Lohnstein (2000, 2007, based on Groenendijk and Stokhof 1982, 1984, and Higginbotham 1996). Rather than define STs extensionally (as lists of properties like the ones we have seen above), Lohnstein proposes criteria that define STs intensionally and derive them compositionally. Approaches of this type propose that the syntactic positioning of crucial elements (e.g., verbs, conjunctions, etc.) cause certain abstract semantic effects. Taken together, these semantic effects explain the overall semantics of various clause types, and these semantic properties, in turn, explain the aptitude of the clause types for certain pragmatic usages. To describe (a subset[5] of) the ST criteria by Lohnstein (2000, 2007), consider the following cases:

If the verb remains in the right bracket,[6] the proposition denoted by the sentence is not evaluated against an extra-linguistic world under discussion, but only in the linguistic context of the matrix clause:

(3) *Peter glaubt, dass die Welt eine Scheibe ist.*
     Peter believes that the world a disc is
     'Peter believes that the world is flat.'

This sentence is true if Peter holds a certain belief. The truth of the subordinated proposition ("the world is flat") itself, however, is irrelevant for the truth value of the overall sentence, since the proposition of the subordinated clause is not evaluated against extra-linguistic facts. Therefore, even if the world is, in fact, not flat, the sentence in (3) can still be true – since it can, of course, be true that Peter entertains a false belief in this matter.

Placing the verb in the left bracket derives a semantic object that conforms to a bi-partition of possible worlds, i.e. in yes/no-questions: The set of worlds where the denoted proposition p is true, and the set of worlds where the denoted proposition p is false. Consider for the proposition *p= believe (Peter, story)*:

---

5 We ignore verbal morphology here, which Lohnstein's model represents accurately.
6 Lohnstein uses generative terms, e.g. "verbs move to C°", "phrases move to SpecCP". For ease of comparison with the traditional grammar STTs, we will stick with the traditional terms here.

(4) *Glaubt   Peter die Geschichte?*
     believes Peter the story?
     'Does Peter believe the story?'   (Possible answers:{yes= p; no= ¬p})

A yes/no-question is a semantic object that can therefore be used to indicate that the speaker has no knowledge about the truth or falsity of the proposition expressed in the clause vis-a-vis some situation currently discussed in the discourse.

If a [-wh] phrase occupies the prefield, the bi-partition reduces to the set of worlds where the denoted proposition is true – yielding a declarative sentence type:

(5) *Peter glaubt   die Geschichte.*
     Peter believes the story
     'Peter believes the story.'   (p is true)

Since filling the prefield reduces the semantic partition expressed by the yes/no-question to the set of worlds where the proposition is true, the declarative sentence containing the proposition can now be used by a speaker to assert the truth of that proposition.

If, on the other hand, a [+wh] phrase occupies the prefield, the derived semantic object consists of the partition of all possible worlds into a set of sets of worlds for which the set of conceivable answers is true – yielding the wh-question:

(6) *Was glaubt   Peter?*
     what believes Peter
     'What does Peter   (an unspecified subset of propositions taken from
     believe?'   {Peter believes that p, Peter believes that q, . . .})

Given that all propositions from the set include as their common denominator some abstract proposition of the type 'there exists an x, such that Peter believes x', the presupposition of the clause, and its use for asking for the subset of true propositions, both fall out without further ado. In sum, Lohnstein's treatment is able to define the compositional semantics of the STs covered by the analysis successfully (and rather elegantly). However, its treatment of the allegedly insubordinated STs, we saw above, is actually not all too different from the traditional grammars discussed already – since the compositional analysis bases the derivation of STs on the position (and inflection) of verbs, too. Note that sentence types that have a word-to-world fit (unlike directives, i.e.) require that the finite verb moves to C in order for the proposition to be evaluated against a world under discussion. All STs that have either nothing or a conjunction in their left bracket must therefore be anchored in a (linguistically encoded) matrix context, Lohnstein claims (cf. 2000, et seq.). They are therefore predicted to be "subordinated" in this (functional) sense of the word, since they cannot refer to worlds under discussion themselves (and only the respective matrix clauses, with V in C, can). Lohnstein acknowledges the existence of ST-related prosody and ST-related modal particles, but crucially does not give them any formal status in his compositional ST model – which thus remains a syntactically defined one in this respect.[7]

This narrow choice of syntactic STT criteria makes the STT incomplete, we believe: V1 questions, V2 wh-questions and V2 declaratives are captured adequately, as are truly subordinated verb-last sentence types.[8] However, sentence types that do *not* couple verb-last word orders with subordination are simply not in the fragment Lohnstein considers, making the STT empirically incomplete, we believe. Not surprisingly, then, we can point out mismatches between the ST predicted on the basis of syntactic forms and actual functions of STs, as e.g. the ones in the following paragraphs.

[-Wh] V2 sentences only assert their proposition when uttered with a falling intonation, with a low final boundary tone (L%). With a rising intonation, they do not commit the speaker to the truth of the proposition (cf. the argument in Gunlogson 2003):

(7) [Judge to defendant:] *Ladendiebstahl macht Spaß?*
                   shoplifting   makes fun?
                   'Shoplifting is fun?'

V1 sentences in German can be questions like in (8a). However, they can also be parts of conditional complexes, as in (8b), or autonomous exclamative assertions, as in (8c) and (8d):

(8) a. *Füttert Justus das Nilpferd?*
          feeds   Justus the rhinoceros
          'Does Justus feed the rhinoceros?'

---

7 Recall that Lohnstein also takes into account verb morphology, however.
8 Relative clauses are not considered, but can be subsumed under a wider compatible typology (cf. Struckmeier 2007)

b. *Füttert Justus das Nilpferd,*   *(geht es dem Tier gut)*
   feeds   Justus the   rhinoceros (goes it   the   animal good)
   'If Justus feeds the rhinoceros, (the animal is fine)'

c. *Hat   DIE   Beine!*   (exclamative commits S to
   has   she   legs   extraordinary nature of legs,
   'Oooh, what legs she has!'   and an attitude of surprise)

d. *IST   der   doof!*   (exclamative commits S to
   is   he   stupid   truth of p and an attitude of
   'Gosh, how stupid he is!'   surprise or incredulity)

Verb-last orders with conjunctions in the left bracket do not need matrix clauses, as we already saw above. To discuss more specific examples, consider the following:

(9)   *Ob   er   wohl   kommt?*
     whether he   MP   comes
     'Will he come? (You may not know)'   (deliberative, autonomous question)[9]

Last, but not least: V-last word order is not only not a sufficient condition for subordination, it is not a necessary one either, since V2 embedded clauses exist in the language, too (cf. Truckenbrodt 2006a, 2006b for some examples).

It seems to us that structures of this kind warrant the assumption that we are not witnessing spontaneous uses of truly subordinated clauses as autonomous utterances. Rather, we are faced with the boundaries at which the compositional STTs discussed here start to break down. These STTs simply make false predictions about subordination in the cases discussed. Now, it may appear difficult to identify insubordination artefacts in many cases. However, we believe that some observations can help illuminate the issue.

---

9 Note that deliberative questions complete a veritable paradigm of verb-last structures: Propositions can be expressed to be true by autonomous verb-last exclamatives (1), can be the basis for autonomous verb-last directives (2), and can be used for autonomous (deliberative) questions (11). As it turns out, verb-last word orders seem to have hardly any connection to "subordination" in any clearly definable sense of the word. Conversely, clearly subordinated clauses *can* be verb-second in the language (e.g. with *weil* and *denn*). This, we believe, is a central problem for Evans (2007) and publications that (seem to) assume that subordination is formally and clearly tied to verb-last orders in German (cf., e.g., d'Hertefelt 2015: 158, 173, 195).

The semantics of all allegedly subordinated clauses mentioned above is very specialized. Note, for example, that the exclamative clauses we have seen above are clearly restricted to definable propositional attitudes. This, however, is hard to reconcile with the idea that these clauses are actually embedded clauses – under some ellided matrix clause: The huge range of potential matrix clauses that could embed these structures would predict that we find an equally wide range of semantic functions expressed by the elliptical structures (cf. Gutzmann 2011). Note, however, that we can, in fact, embed the above sentences only under very few matrix clauses and maintain their semantics at all, e.g. for (1) above:

(10) *Ich bin   so   erbost und   verblüfft, dass*
     I   am   so   angry and   surprised that
     die (??aber) auch den   Peter küssen   muss!
     she (MP)   MP   the   Peter kiss   must
     'I am so angry and surprised that she had to kiss Peter, of all people!'

(11)?? *Ich   finde es   völlig   normal, dass die*
       I   find it   completely normal that she
       (??aber) auch den   Peter   küssen muss!
       (MP)   MP   the   Peter   kiss   must
       'I consider it completely normal that she had to kiss Peter, too.'
                                                             (intended)

Note, moreover, that the semantic restrictions probably cannot be derived from general compositional semantics. There seems to be no good reason that in German, only these interpretations are possible, and furthermore, even a language as closely related as Dutch seems to make different choices in this regard (cf., e.g., Verstraete et al. 2012: 145 on clauses introduced by Dutch *dat* vs. German *dass* and compare Example (6) above, and d'Hertefelt 2015 for more general comparisons).

The prosody of the allegedly insubordinated sentences must be executed in a very specific manner – which is often completely different from the prosody of truly subordinated clauses. For example, compare the example in (9) above with the structures in:

(12) *Ich frage mich, ob   er wohl kommt.*   L% (low boundary tone
     I   ask   myself whether he MP   comes   adequate)
     'I wonder whether he will come.'

(13) * Ob er wohl kommt.   L% (same contour not
                                                  adequate)

Any analysis that postulates elided matrix clauses would therefore face
enormous challenges in determining which matrix clause an addressee
should reconstruct, and why. In some cases, it is extremely unlikely that
certain prosodic implementations of allegedly subordinated clauses could
ever be found in truly subordinated clauses, i.e. clauses that surface together with their (overt) matrix clauses. Not only would these special rules
for the elliptical cases seem to complicate our theories of ST properties –
they would furthermore make it more difficult for children to acquire an adequate understanding of these virtually undetectable properties of grammar.
It would clearly be preferable for a child's language acquisition process if
the observable properties of actual utterances guide the acquisition process
of the child. However, with the STTs above, the restricted semantics of exclamatives remains, at the very least, unpredicted. In fact, the properties
the child is required to learn are completely at odds with the observable
properties in other cases, e.g., when the prosody of exclamatives is different
from subordinated clauses, yet the child is supposed to learn that they are
"underlyingly" the same. Note, moreover, that there seem to exist no transparent reasons as to why verb-last orders should, in fact, be logically linked
to "subordination" (however defined) in the first place. No typological generalization exists to the effect that languages with more than one position
for the verb always reserve one position for subordination transparently,
and it is the structurally lower one. Even less likely is any (plausible)
argument to the effect that structurally low verb placement (e.g., in the
V position in German) would have to constitute subordination obligatorily,
for compositional semantic reasons. In sum, no cogent reason seems to
link (main) verb positions to sentence types in German from a logical perspective at all.

   We would therefore very much prefer for STTs with such incongruous results to simply turn out to be wrong, or incomplete. Once STTs are re-
defined, language acquisition should not be a problem anymore – since
insubordination artefacts would simply cease to arise. The sentence types
that an empirically more complete STT would have to cover include (minimally)
the following overview in Table 2:

Table 2: Sentence types that minimally need to be added to German STs[10].

Sentence type	prefield	left bracket	middle field	right bracket
V1 declarative	–	Kommt	ein Pferd zum Arzt	–
		comes	*a horse to-the doctor*	
	'A horse comes to the doctor, and...'			
V1 protasis	–	Kommt	ein Pferd zum Arzt, ...	–
	'If a horse comes to a doctor, ... (then...)'			
V1 exclamative	–	Kommt	der aber schnell daher!	–
		comes	*he MP quickly along*	
	'Boy, is he moving fast!'			
V2 Wh exclamative	Was	HAT	die Beine!	–
	what	*has*	*she legs*	
	'Wow, what legs she has!'			
Vlast Wh-exlamative	Was	–	die BEINe	hat!
	what		*she legs*	*has*
	'Wow, what legs she has!'			
Vlast deliberativequestion	–	Ob	er wohl	kommt?
		whether	*he MP*	*comes*
	'(I'm wondering:) Will he come' (You may not know)			
Vlast strongcommand	–	Dass	Du JA die Katze	fütterst
		that	*you MP the cat*	*feed!*
	'Make absolutely sure you feed the cat, y'hear me!'			

We will see in the next section that we can show how STTs could potentially be defined to meet these requirements.

---

10 Note with regard to this set of sentence types, that the problematic cases of STs are not all exclamative in nature, and seem to us not to fit completely the semantic classes that have been proposed for insubordinate clauses, e.g. in d'Hertefelt (2015): Rather, deliberative questions (*ob er wohl kommt?*), strong commands (*dass Du aber bloß die Katze fütterst!*), optatives (*wenn ich doch noch mal 20 wäre!*) as well as exclamatives are problematic for the assumption of "prima facie" subordination in German (defined as verb-last, mostly).

3 Additional factors empirically viable STTs of German need to consider

As we have seen, STTs can cause insubordination artefacts. In this section, we point out two factors of ST constitution which, we think, have been underrepresented in previous STTs. If these factors are taken into account for the definition of STs, we show, the insubordination artefacts we witnessed above simply vanish. Therefore, mismatches between forms and functions do not arise anymore for the cases that we have discussed above.[11]

3.1 Modal particles in the middle field: Another structural position to watch

For the longest time, German modal particles were disregarded in the literature. Over the last years, a renewed interest has centered on these miraculous elements (cf., e.g. Bayer and Struckmeier 2017, for a compilation of new findings). In one of the proposals, Struckmeier (2014) assumes that MPs should technically be considered partial spellouts of sentence-type related features (cf., similarly, Zimmermann 2004). While the proposal is still obviously syntactic in nature, it enlarges the *Feldermodell* in a way that makes an additional position – located smack in the middle of the middle field – a decisive position to consider for ST formation (cf. Struckmeier 2014 for a more detailed analysis):

(14) $[XP_{prefield} [C^0 [_{TP} \ldots YP_{left\ middle\ field} \ldots [_{MP} \textit{particles} [_{vP} \ldots ZP_{right\ middle\ field} \ldots V^0 v^0]T^0]]]]$

In generative theories, sentence type features are often associated with a structurally "high" position, e.g. in the so-called left periphery of clauses (cf., similarly, Katz and Postal 1964; Rizzi 1997 Grohmann 2003). However, we see no reason that elements that contribute to ST formation should, in fact, be so limited in their distribution. Note specifically in this regard that MPs take scope over complete extended propositions in German, from the positions where they are

---

11 However, let us remind the reader that we do not claim that there could be no true cases of insubordination in German – the following discussion represents only what we consider the artefacts caused by STTs, and says nothing whatsoever about true cases, wherever they may arise. In order not to beat around the bush, however, let us state here that we would be hard-pressed to point out cases of true insubordination in German ourselves, once all non-subordinated clauses (and elliptical structures) are taken care of.

located (Struckmeier 2014). Therefore, MPs could easily be tied to propositional attitudes – as in fact they often are. This would seem to hold regardless of whether MPs move to higher positions (in some covert manner, cf. Zimmermann 2004) or not (Struckmeier 2014). In order to point out their significance for ST formation in German, we can point out some facts about MPs in the following paragraphs.

MPs can only occur in certain sentence types in German. As Struckmeier (2014) shows, the distribution of MPs can be restricted on the basis of formal properties of the prefield and the left bracket. For example, *doch* is restricted to the feature specification of C^0 (as $[-Wh]^{12}$), rather than the pragmatic function of the clause (as erotetic or directive[13]):

(15) *Ich mach noch ein bisschen Kaffee...*
    I   make another a   bit   coffee
    'I'm making some more coffee...'

  a. *Ihr trinkt doch auch noch ein Tässchen?* (erotetic, [-wh])
     you drink MP   also another a   cup
     '... you'll have another cup, too, won't you?'

  b. **Trinkt ihr doch auch noch ein Tässchen?* (*erotetic, [+wh])
     drink you MP   also another a   cup
     'Do you also drink another cup?' *(intended)*

  c. **Wer trinkt doch auch noch ein Tässchen?* (*erotetic, [+wh])
     who drinks MP   also another a   cup
     'Who drinks another cup?' *(intended)*

  d. *Trinkt Ihr doch auch noch ein Tässchen!* (directive, [-wh])
     drink you MP   also another a   cup
     'Go ahead, have another cup!'

---

12 The [wh] feature specifies whether the structures are questions from a formal point of view. (15b) and (15c) are undoubtedly questions, given their syntax and lexical constitution, justifying the classification as [+wh]. Also, (15d) is clearly a directive, not a question ([-wh]). The specification of (15a) may be a contentious choice, but see Gunlogson (2003) for a very convincing argument that rising declaratives are, in fact, declaratives, not questions.

13 By erotetic, we simply mean that these sentences can be used to elicit a (verbal) response on the part of the hearer, as a true question would. Directives, on the other hand, (claim to) aim to elicit an action by the hearer, as an imperative, e.g., normally would. Obviously, indirect speech acts complicate this simple picture, which is still assumed by some linguistic works, and in some philosophical investigations of questions.

However, properties of the left bracket and prefield are not sufficient to make deterministic predictions as to which MPs are used in a specific sentence type. Quite on the contrary: It rather seems as though the presence or absence of certain MPs, for some STs, is a necessary part of the very constitution of those sentence types. We can demonstrate this by pointing out that seemingly "optional" MPs can in fact *change* the ST of the clause they appear in:

(16) a. *Ob   er   wohl   kommt?*
whether   he   MP   comes
'Will he come? (You may not know)' (deliberative, autonomous question)

   b. *Ob er ___ kommt?*   (embedded question, elided matrix[14])

(17) a. *Wäre ich ___ Millionär...*
were   I   Millionaire
'If I were a millionaire...'   (protasis, elided apodosis)

   b. *Wäre ich doch Millionär!*
were   I   MP   millionaire
'If only I were a millionaire!'   (autonomous exclamative)

In formal syntactic terms, we can show here that MPs seem to constitute interveners for higher sentence-type related heads. Given common assumptions about relativized minimality (Rizzi 1990), this would seem to indicate that MPs and C heads share at least parts of their feature make-up. More precisely, modal particles intervene between features of matrix C heads, and subordinated C heads, while adverbials that are semantically near-identical do not (18d)[15]:

(18) a. *Es ist so,   dass es immer regnet.*
it   is   such   that it always rains
'It's the case that it always rains'

---

14 One anonymous reviewer has indicated to us that he could use (16b) as a deliberative question. We still maintain that (16a) would minimally be the strongly preferred choice for such usage – in fact, we maintain our original intuition: (16b), for us, is virtually unusable as a deliberative question, even if the embedded question reading is, of course, substitutable for precisely that reading in many cases: *We don't know, after all... whether he comes?*

15 As is well known, German does not have sequence-of-tense phenomena like English does. We simply report here that some tense combinations of matrix/sub clauses are distinctly odd. More general claims are not intended.

b.?? *Es ist so,   dass es immer   regnete.*
   it is such that it always rained
   'It's the case that it always rained.'   (intended,
                                                       but tenses conflict)

c.   *Es ist wohl so,   dass es immer   regnete*
   it is MP such that it always rained
   'It's the case that it always rained, I assume.'   (MP waives
                                                         tense conflict)

d.?? *Es ist wie ich annehme so,*
   it is as I assume such

   dass   es   immer   regnete
   that   it   always   rained
   'It's the case that it always rained, I assume.'   (adverbial:
                                                    conflict persists[16])

As we see, then, arguments can be pointed out at various levels of linguistic description for the assumption that MPs are constitutive for STs, rather than just sensitive to them. Distributionally, MPs display properties very much like the "sentence bracket" positions: Whereas the left and right bracket delimit the outer boundaries of the middle field in an unchanging way, MPs split the middle field in an equally "fixed" way. This is noteworthy in that the normally rather free word order of German does not apply to the bracketing positions and MPs – but virtually no other elements of German clauses. Semantically, MPs display properties that fit in well with ST properties in general – and demonstrably contribute to ST formation in more specific ways, too. Morphosyntactically, MP seem to interfere with structural relations between sentence-typing heads, underlining again that they are intimately related to the latter.

As far as the lexical material in syntactic structures is concerned, we therefore submit that MPs should be considered as factors for ST definitions as well. In the next subsection, we will now argue the case for completely extrasyntactic ST factors.

---

16 One anonymous reviewer disagrees with us on this judgement. However, the contrast indicated in this example seems to be quite robust to us, certainly in our variety of German. Note, moreover, that we are simply sampling some of the arguments for the syntactic status of particles as C heads. For the complete argument, please refer to the analysis in Struckmeier (2014).

3.2 Clausal prosody: Another dimension for ST formation

As we have already seen above, prosody can influence the formation of STs as well. However, prosodic factors have only recently begun to make inroads into STTs. We assume that this state of affairs is often connected to the kinds of syntacto-semantic backgrounds that previous STTs relied on. Lohnstein, for example, employs a generative syntactic theory. Given that Phonological Form (PF) is an extra-syntactic interface, and given furthermore that in generative approaches, syntax must not *look ahead* to PF, it seems hard to implement prosodic factors in generative syntactic theories: Given their undeniable semantic impact, ST factors should rather be syntactic, not phonological in nature. What would seem to be necessary in these cases, are syntactic features which cause both the semantic ST effects, as well as trigger certain prosodic implementations that reflect the choice of ST. In the following, we will remain agnostic as to the formulation of such a generative-syntactic theory. Our goal here is to establish the empirical importance of prosodic ST factors – not their integration into any specific syntactic theory.

In order to demonstrate that prosody is an important factor for ST constitution, we can point out minimal pairs of sentences. The only properties that differentiate these clauses are prosodic in nature. Kaiser (2014), for example, assumes that the interpretation of autonomous clauses is in part determined by their prosody, so that the syntactic positions of elements, in turn, also can make only partial contributions to the constitution of STs: In V2 sentences, [-wh] material in the prefield will lead to a potential correspondence between the proposition of the sentence, and a state of affairs in the discourse world. In this regard, then, his theory does not differ from the established theories (e.g. Lohnstein 2000) in fundamental ways.

However, as Kaiser demonstrates verb-first structures are not necessarily questions or imperatives, as Lohnstein is forced to predict. Rather, empty prefields seem to denote a more abstract semanto-pragmatic property (cf., similarly, Reis and Wöllstein 2010 and their discussion of V1-questions and V1-conditionals): Yes/no-questions do not assert the truth of the proposition they contain. Imperatives, too, do not assert, since their semantic direction of fit seeks to make the world change according to the sentence, rather than change the sentence to fit the facts, as in assertions (cf. also the assumptions in Altmann 1993 and Wunderlich 1984). Therefore, neither yes/no-questions nor imperative clauses are designed to have their truth value evaluated *vis-a-vis* a discourse world by the interlocutors. Additionally, the more abstract description also accords well with those sentence types that lie outside the fragment that Lohnstein derives: Verb-first sentences that form the conditional protasis of a complex sentence do not evaluate their proposition *vis-a-vis* a specific world. Rather, they state that the conclusion (the apodosis) is true in every world in which the protasis is true (cf. the semantic interpretation of conditionals developed by Bhatt and Pancheva 2006). Therefore, no reference to specific worlds is made and consequently no evaluation of the facts of these worlds is required for the interpretation of the protasis clause.

Verb-first declaratives used e.g. in joke contexts cannot refer to a specific world under discussion. The addressee evaluates the proposition in an unspecified world in which the proposition is true by definition. Therefore, the addressee interprets the proposition as a description of an alternative world that is certainly not the world under discussion (but most likely some fictional one).[17] Given that the speaker can define an imaginary world any way s/he likes, the proposition is, by definition, true:

(19) Kommt ein Pferd in   die Kneipe. ...
    comes   a   horse into the   pub
    'A horse walks into a pub. ...'

Verb-first exclamatives also do not *assert* the truth of the proposition they contain – despite the fact that they certainly *express* that truth.[18] However, note that exclamatives are constitutionally unable to move the common ground forward, i.e. answer to a question under discussion (see (20a) and (20b)). Rather, they inform the hearer of speaker-internal thought processes (see (20c) and (20d)), which are informative to the addressee independently of the propositions in the common ground that already describe speaker-external states of affairs:

(20) a. A: Does   he   have normal legs?
         B: #Was HAT der   Beine!   (intended:
                                                    'He has extraordinary legs.')
     b. A: How   clever is   she?
         B: #Wie KLUG   sie   ist!
            how   clever she is   (intended:
                                                    She is extraordinarily clever)

---

17 Note, for example, that this particular V1 declarative cannot be used to answer to a question under discussion such as *What is coming into the pub?* This holds not only for questions regarding the real world, but also for, e.g. aspects of a fictional story: V1 declaratives obviously cannot refer to *any* specific world. Cf. the discussion in Reis (2000).
18 While the use of an exclamative expresses that the speaker believes that p is true, exclamatives cannot be used as answers to yes/no-questions regarding p, which would be entirely inexplicable if they could assert the truth of p: *Hast Du die Katze ungewöhnlich gut gepflegt? – */#Ja, HAbe ich die Katze ungewöhnlich gut gepflegt!*

c. A: I have known Bob for years
now, and know every little
detail about him.
Oh, look, there he is, with his
long legs!
B: Was HAT der Beine! (look of legs not informative for A)
d. A: I have known Kim for years now, and I
know exactly what an extremely smart
person she is. Take a look at her great
new STT!
B: IST die clever! (not informative regarding cleverness)

Last, but not least, there are verb-first clauses in German which employ conjunctive verb mood. These clauses do not report (or inquire about) a fact regarding a world under discussion. For example, they cannot answer information-seeking questions (see (21a)). Rather than assert that the proposition p contained in them is true in some world under discussion, they define a world where the proposition is true. Since this world is, by definition, not necessarily the current world under discussion (in fact, any *single* world), p's truth value can also be changed by semantically incompatible claims at any time without contradiction (see (21b)):

(21) a. A: Is it true that Darwin considers biological evolution to be non-
teleological?
B: *#Sei die darwin'sche Evolution nicht-teleologisch.*
be the Darwinian evolution non-teleological
'Let the Darwinian evolution be non-teleological'
(intended: 'Yes, he does')

b. A: We do not know whether X is a prime number or not. However will
we solve the equation?
B: *Sei X eine Primzahl.   Dann gilt die Vermutung.*
be X a prime-number then holds the assumption
'Let X be a prime number. In that case, the assumption holds.'
Sei X eine gerade Zahl.   Auch dann gilt die Vermutung.
be X an even number also then holds the case
'Let X be an even number. In that case, too, the assumption holds.'

Autonomous verb-last structures are used in optative sentences, exclamatives or deliberative questions. All of these clauses have empty prefields – and all of them cannot be used to assert the truth of the proposition they contain. Of course, the lexical semantic (and verbal mood) of the finite verb plays an important role as well (compare e.g. *dass* (not interrogative) vs. *ob* (interrogative)):

(22) a. *Hätte ich doch bloß nichts gesagt!*   (optative)
      had   I   MP   MP   nothing said
      'If only I could not say anything.'

    b. *Wenn ich doch noch mal 20 wär!*   (optative)
      if   I   MP   once again 20 were
      'If only I could 20 again!'

    c. *Dass er immer zu SPÄT kommt!*   (exclamative)
      that   he always too late   comes
      'That he is always coming too late!'

    d. *Ob er wohl kommt?*   (deliberative question)
      whether he MP   comes
      'Will he come? You may not know'

Even for autonomous wh-sentences, it could be worthwhile to rethink established STTs: While most STTs (at least since Katz and Postal 1964) assume some kind of wh-feature in C^0 to trigger interrogative interpretations (and attracting wh-words syntactically), non-interrogative sentences with wh-prefields seem to exist as well. These appear to be formally interrogative – but in fact, it turns out they are not. We submit that it could prove worth our while to investigate the option that the syntactic position of wh-elements again only contributes some basic meaning aspects of the overall interpretation of STs with wh-prefields. Again, it seems to us that prosody takes the lead, often coupled with the appearance of modal particles:

(23) a. Was hat DIE für Beine! L% (Wh-exclamative)
    b. Was die für BEIne hat! L% (VL-wh-exclamative, not embedded)

Given this very abstract definition of the semantic contribution of verb-first orders, a lot of semantic questions remain open, we openly admit. With respect to the difference between (25a) and (25b), e.g., it becomes obvious that the difference in forms (verb-first versus verb-last) does not seem to cause a clear-cut difference in meaning at all – and certainly not along the lines proposed, e.g., by Lohnstein (2000). Both clauses are exclamatives, with very similar usage patterns and (almost?) indistinguishable meaning.[19] As we can see, then, the verb placement here does not seem to answer semantic questions – but rather to pose one. Some of these questions can be resolved by inspecting MP choices, as we have seen above. However, other undecided options may not depend on word order properties or the presence of certain lexical elements altogether. Rather, prosodic markers could add meaning aspects of (at least some) STs, as some authors have claimed (e.g., Peters 2006; Truckenbrodt 2013; Kaiser 2014). As of today, a complete theory of all semantic contributions seems far out of reach. However, to demonstrate our point, we can point out those prosodic factors here for which it has already been established that they figure prominently as ST formation factors. Since the seminal work of Pierrehumbert (1980), the prosody of sentences can be represented via accent tones (e.g. L*, H*) and boundary tones (e.g. L%, H%). In this article, we follow the GToBI (German Tones and Break Indices) guidelines for labelling aspects of the intonation of Standard German within the autosegmental-metrical framework (c.f. Grice and Baumann 2002). As Baumann (2006) shows, the information status of lexical elements in sentences correlates with the choice of accent tones: Given information, which is presented by the speaker as recoverable from the discourse context, is preferentially deaccented or marked by a low accent tone (e.g. L*). New information, which is presented by the speaker as not recoverable from the discourse context, in contrast, is preferentially marked by a high accent tone (e.g. H*). The so called "early peak-accent" (H+L*) is appropriate for cases of semi-active information. Particularly new information is usually marked by a "late peak accent" (L+H*) (cf., e.g., Baumann and Riester 2013). Taking these observations as a basis, intonation is also associated with the relation of the sentence proposition to the Common Ground (cf. the concept of the CG developed by Stalnaker 1978). Peters (2006) and Truckenbrodt (2013) claim that a high (nuclear) accent tone (H*) signals, that the proposition should be added to the Common Ground. With a low (nuclear) accent tone (L*), the speaker signals that the proposition should not be added to the Common Ground. In (24a) the proposition is presented as new information and thus should be added to the CG. In (24b), the proposition is part of the CG already and thus need not be added to the CG as a matter of course:

---

19 Some authors have actually proposed that the choice between these two forms is completely free (see Altmann 1993; d'Avis 2013). Other proposals envision a very subtle semantic effect that is completely *unlike* the compositional effect Lohnstein proposes (cf. Repp 2016).

(24) a. Justus füttert (*ja) das NAShorn. L% (H* on NAShorn: p new
     information?)
   b. Justus füttert (ja) das NAshorn. L% (with a H+L* on NAShorn,
     p is given)

A high boundary tone (H%), on the other hand, signals that S does not commit
to the truth of p. A low boundary tone (L%) signals that S commits to the truth
of p. Below we show how syntactic and intonational factors contribute to the
interpretation of different V1 sentences as well as modal particles:

(25) ø Füttert Justus das Nashorn?   *(yes/no question)*
     feeds   Justus   the   rhinoceros
     'Does Justus feed the rhinoceros?'
     Prosody L* H-^H% interpretation

L*	H should not add p to the CG (unclear whether p is true)
H%	S does not commit to p

(26) *ø Füttert Justus wohl das Nashorn?*
     L* H-^H%, as in (25).
     Modal particle *wohl* signals H need not fully commit to p or ¬p.

(27) *ø Füttert Justus das Nashorn...*   (protasis of conditional: if Justus feeds rhino)
     Prosody L+H* H-%   interpretation

H*	Add p to CG: In every world, where p is true...
H%	... but S does not commit to p's truth...

(Note: prosodic contour slightly different from (25) and (26), see Kaiser and
Baumann 2013)

(28) *HAT die Beine!*   (V1 exclamative)
     has   she   legs
     'Wow, the legs she has!'
     Prosody L+H* L-%   interpretation

H*	Add p to CG
L%	S commited to p

Let us stress again that these observations do not amount to a full-fledged description of all prosodic ST factors. However, these facts show that minimal
pairs of clauses which are only differentiated by prosody can differ with regard
to those factors that would have to be recognized by STTs. Thus, the examples

above, we claim, suffice to show that prosodic properties must be taken into account in STTs, since they obviously serve as ST factors.

4 First steps towards more robust, multi-factorial STTs

As we have seen at the beginning of this paper, some STTs only employ a very limited subset of grammatical dimensions and lexical properties as ST factors. These theories, we showed, are capable of assigning plausible STs to a subset of clauses. However, the same theories clearly have empirical problems with clauses outside of the fragment they describe. They can easily be set up to assign STs to some clauses which, upon even only superficial scrutiny, do not conform to empirically coherent sets of sentences: Verb-first clauses with finite verbs are not uniformly used as "questions" that would bring the truth value of the proposition they contain on the table, e.g. as the current question under discussion of the discourse (instead, they could be V1 exclamatives or declaratives, e.g.). Verb-second clauses with finite verbs, likewise, do not necessarily assert a proposition (but could be, e.g., V2 questions, exclamatives, etc.). Given the rather general trouble with these clauses, it seems unreasonable to assume that some specific uses of them should warrant the assumption that insubordination occurs with these STs.[20] It seems, rather, that narrowly syntactic STTs remain empirically incomplete to begin with. The STT we envision would be, we hope, more robust in its definitions – and, at the same time, cover more empirical ground.

In a more circumspect STT, the compositional properties would hold in exceptionless, and empirically demonstrable manners. With the addition of lexical

---

20 An anonymous reviewer warns us that the sentence types under discussion here could be the end result of a diachronic development instigated by former insubordination scenarios. While we acknowledge the possibility in principle, we do not agree that there is any historical evidence that modern German could have had such a development: Most modal particles are a very late addition to the German lexicon: Only four particles can be demonstrated to even exist in Middle High German. All other particles appear as late as the 16th, 18th, or even 19th century (Burckhardt 1994:139f.). As regards the older particles, it is far from clear that their function resembled their modern-day counter parts at all (cf., e.g., Petrova 2017). From the relatively recent genesis of (contemporary) modal particles to the present day, however, no major changes at all have occurred in the German sentence type system, as far as the historical record suggests. Therefore, the assumption that the sentence type system could have changed (e.g., as a reaction to the emergence of modal particles as a new class of heads) is simply not justified for this language, as best as we can tell.

materials and prosody to the picture, the compositional meaning aspects of the overall structure should (hopefully) be more transparent.[21] As far as we can see, the way to arrive at properties of this kind would require a fresh start for STTs. We should not restrict the combinations of properties we expect by a priori assumptions about "sentence types" that need to be "reconstructed" via our compositional analyses. On the contrary, we propose to define as large an option space as seems possible given the lexical, morphological, syntactic and prosodic vectors that span that option space – and only then investigate which combinations of properties are actually attested in the world's languages. If indeed cross-linguistically robust gaps in the option space can be identified (given a large enough sample of languages to actually warrant the postulation of the gap), these gaps would serve as important entry points to a deeper understanding of ST formation. Within these gaps, formal and/or functional properties may be identifiable which really cannot combine – pointing out the limits of free property combination, and *ipso facto* the actual subdivisions of the option space (which may be completely unlike the preordained "sentence types" of traditional grammars). The generalizations pointed out above regarding prosody and modal particles in German are intended as a proof of concept for such an approach to STTs, and we hope that our findings stimulate attempts in this general direction. However, let us stress again here that we do not claim to offer a complete STT of this type (a massive undertaking, obviously).

5 In lieu of a conclusion: Whither STTs, and whither insubordination?

After all is said and done, this article does not offer a new STT in any detail. Rather, it wants to point out that ST properties from some of our best and most well-established STTs (most notably, syntactic properties) can be placed in

---

21 Note that, for STTs in historic developments, prosodic properties themselves could, of course, be (partially) obscure, since diachronic sources are written texts – and these often do not reflect the array of prosodic options available in spoken language (cf. Fodor 2002). Note also that the specific (exclamative) prosodic markers we describe here are especially hard to track in written texts in German, our paradigm case: Exclamative prosody cannot be found – but nor can tell-tale punctuation, as far as we can tell: The exclamation mark especially (which would be used today to signal exclamative prosody in writing) is not known to have been in use before the 17th century – and its wide-spread use dates much later than even that (cf. Kirchhoff 2016, Bredel 2007). Again, this takes the time span discussed safely into modern German times, where no changes to STs are known. As for exclamative sentences before that time period, very subtle judgments seem to us to be required to even point out how, e.g., an exclamative could be defined grammatically in those older stages.

a larger context of many more multi-factorial ST criteria. We will probably see a lot clearer with regard to sentence types after the narrow preconceptions handed down to us from older grammars are cast aside.

Only after the definition of STTs is handled with sufficient empirical care and theoretical circumspection, however, can the question of insubordination be addressed in more definitive terms. We expect that changes to our conception of STTs would lead to at least the following changes for insubordination research:

Some of the alleged cases of insubordination may not appear to be insubordinated after all. Rather, clauses which displayed properties that formerly lead to their classification as subordinated "on prima facie grounds" (Evans 2007:367) will then be classified differently, i.e. in ways that seem empirically more sensible, and theoretically better argued. Some cases of alleged insubordination, we have shown, are insubordination artefacts, caused only by unsuccessful (false or incomplete) STTs.

Of course, other cases of insubordination will remain, or even be found anew. We would hope that none of those insubordination phenomena would have to be tied, again, to poorly defined STTs. For as long as the factors that underlie ST-related effects are defined well enough to truly hold across the board, we can hope to escape the artefacts that older theories incurred. In the new STT, sentences do not have to fit into preconceived notions of STs – and therefore, the notions may combine in any and all ways that are empirically attested.

Of course, as we have stressed throughout, no exceptionless and complete STT of this highly desirable type exists as of right now. Therefore, for the investigation of insubordination phenomena, we will have to make do with the STTs available to us. In closing, therefore, we would like to point out some precautions we think are necessary to avoid research into phenomena that will later turn out to be insubordination artefacts.

German is probably not an under-investigated language overall. However, the question of ST formation in this language is still a contested issue, as we have seen. Phenomena that turn out to be insubordination artefacts even only under one STT, we think, should be handled with extreme caution. It is far from clear, obviously, that some formal definitions of subordination are reliable enough in these cases, for the affected clauses to support insubordination analyses. More generally, we caution against a careless use of the term (in-)subordination based on superficial STTs of individual languages. If dubious STs are defined by those STTs, for those individual languages, there simply is no scientifically viable way to use these (potentially false or incomplete) STTs for insubordination research at all.

Cross-linguistically, it is simply not enough to point towards some descriptive grammar (or, worse, to the unavailability of such grammars) for some language L, and then go on to claim that given that grammar (or some hunch), certain clauses should probably count as insubordinated in L. Even for a relatively well-studied language like German, there is a real danger to fall for insubordination artefacts, as we have seen. In languages where even less facts are known empirically, these dangers are probably just about incalculable. Therefore, a thorough investigation of individual languages and their STs is required to be able to begin talking about valid cases of insubordination.

The individual analysis of individual structures from individual languages will be a central concern for the study of true insubordination across languages. The definition of an empirically robust and theoretically viable STT for languages under investigation will likewise have to precede any preconceptions of what clauses should count as insubordinated in the world's languages – given merely "prima facie" appearances.

References

Altmann, Hans. 1993. Satzmodus. In Joachim Jacobs (ed.), *Syntax: Ein internationalesHandbuch zeitgenössischer Forschung*, vol. 1, 1006–1029. Berlin: de Gruyter.

Baumann, Stefan. 2006. *The Intonation of Givenness – Evidence from German*. Tübingen: Niemeyer.

Baumann, Stefan & Arndt Riester. 2013. Coreference, lexical givenness and prosody in German. *Lingua* 136. 16–37.

Bayer, Josef & Volker Struckmeier (eds.). 2017. *Discourse Particles: formal approaches to their syntax and semantics*. Berlin: de Gruyter.

Bhatt, Rajesh & Roumyana Pancheva. 2006. Conditionals. In Martin Everaert & Henk. vanRiemsdijk (eds.), *The Blackwell Companion to Syntax*, 638–687. Oxford: Blackwell.

Bredel, Ursula. 2007. Interpunktionszeichen: Form-Geschichte-Funktion. In Dieter Boschung & Hansgerd Hellenkemper (eds.), *Kosmos der Zeichen: Schriftbild und Bildformel in Antike und Mittelalter*, 67–86. Wiesbaden: Reichert.

Burckhardt, Armin. 1994. Abtönungspartikel im Deutschen: Bedeutung und Genese.*Zeitschrift für germanistische Linguistik* 22. 129–151.

d'Avis, F.-J. 2013. Exklamativsatz. In Jörg Meibauer, Markus Steinbach & Hans Altmann (eds.), *Satztypen des Deutschen*, 171–201. Berlin: de Gruyter.

D'Hertefelt, Sarah. 2015: Insubordination in Germanic: A typology of complement and conditional constructions. Leuven: Katholieke Universiteit Leuven dissertation.

Drach, Erich. 1937. *Grundgedanken der deutschen Satzlehre*. Frankfurt a. M.: Diesterweg.

Evans, Nicholas. 2007. Insubordination and its uses. In Irina Nikolaeva (ed.), *Finiteness: Theoretical and Empirical Foundations*, 366–431. Oxford: Oxford University Press.

Fodor, Janet Dean. 2002: Prosodic disambiguation in silent reading. In Masako Hirotani(ed.), *Proceedings of the North East linguistics society* 32, 112–132. Amherst: GSLA.

Grice, Martine & Stefan Baumann. 2002. Deutsche Intonation und GToBI. *LinguistischeBerichte* 191. 267–298.

Groenendijk, Jeroen & Martin Stokhof. 1982. Semantic Analysis of wh-complements. *Linguistics & Philosophy* 5. 175–233.

Groenendijk, Jeroen & Martin Stokhof. 1984. On the semantics of questions and thepragmatics of answers. In Fred Landmann & Frank Veltmann (eds.), *Varieties of Formal Semantics*, 143–170. Dordrecht: Foris.

Grohmann, K leanthes. 2003. *Prolific peripheries: A radical view from the left.* Ann Arbor,MI: ProQuest UMI.

Gunlogson, Christine. 2003. *True to form: Rising and falling declaratives as questions in English.* New York: Routledge.

Gutzmann, Daniel. 2011. Ob einer wohl recht hat? Zwei Satzmodustheorien für das Deutsche im Vergleich. *Deutsche Sprache* 39 (1). 65–84.

Higginbotham, James. 1996. The semantics of questions. In Shalom Lappin (ed.), *The handbook of contemporary semantic theory.* Oxford: Blackwell.

Katz, Jerrold J. & Paul M. Postal. 1964. *An Integrated Theory of Linguistic Descriptions.* Cambridge, MA: MIT Press.

Kaiser, Stefan & Stefan Baumann. 2013. Satzmodus und die Diskurspartikel hm:Intonation und Interpretation. *Linguistische Berichte* 236. 473–496.

Kaiser, Stefan. 2014. *Interpretation selbständiger Sätze im Diskurs. Syntax und Intonationin Interaktion.* Frankfurt, a.M.: Peter Lang Verlag.

Kirchhoff, Frank. 2016. *Von der Virgel zum Komma: Die Entwicklung der Interpunktion im Deutschen.* Cologne: University of Cologne PhD thesis.

Lohnstein, Horst. 2000. *Satzmodus – kompositionell: Zur Parametrisierung der Modusphrase im Deutschen.* Berlin & New York: Akademie Verlag.

Lohnstein, Horst. 2007. On clause types and sentential force. *Linguistische Berichte* 209. 63–86.

Merchant, Jason. 2001. *The syntax of silence.* Oxford: Oxford University Press.

Mithun, Marianne. 2008. The extension of dependency beyond the sentence. *Language* 83. 69–119

Ott, Dennis & Volker Struckmeier. 2016. Deletion in clausal ellipsis: remnants in the middle field. *University of Pennsylvania Working Papers in Linguistics* 22. 225–234.

Ott, Dennis & Volker Struckmeier, to appear: L nguistic Inquiry, Volume 49, Number 2, Spring 2018 393–407

Peters, Jörg. 2006. Intonation. In Cathrine Fabricius-Hanse, Peter Gallmann, Peter Eisenberg, Reinhard Fiehler & Jörg Peters Duden, . *Die Grammatik*, Bd. 4, 7,95–128. Mannheim: Dudenverlag, 95–128.

Petrova, Svetlana. 2017. On the status and the interpretation of the left-peripheral sentence particles inu and ia in Old High German. In Josef Bayer & Volker Struckmeier (ed.), *Discourse particles: Formal approaches to their syntax and semantics*, 304–331. Berlin: deGruyter.

Pierrehumbert, Janet. B. 1980. *The phonology cnd phonetics of English intonation.*Cambridge, MA: Massachusetts Institute of Technology dissertation.

Reich, Ingo. 2007. Toward a uniform analysis of short answers and gapping. In Kerstin Schwabe & Susanne Winkler (eds.), *On Information Structure, Meaning and Form*, 467–484. Amsterdam: John Benjamins, 467–484.

Reis, Marga. 2000. Anmerkungen zu Verb-erst-Satz-Typen im Deutschen. In Rolf Thieroff, Matthias Ramrat, Nanna Fuhrhop & Oliver Teuber (eds.), *Deutsche Grammatik in Theorie und Praxis*, 215–227. Tübingen: Niemeyer.

Reis, Marga & Angelika Wöllstein. 2010. Zur Grammatik (vor allem) konditionaler V1-Gefüge im Deutschen. *Zeitschrift für Sprachwissenschaft* 29(1). 111–179.

Repp, Sophie. 2016: Semantic restrictions in verb-second vs. non-verb-second wh-exclamatives. Paper presented at the Deutsche Gesellschaft für Sprachwissenschaft conference 2016, Konstanz.

Rizzi, Luigi. 1990. Relativized Minimality. Cambridge, MA: MIT Press.

Rizzi, Luigi. 1997. The fine structure of the left periphery. In Liliane Haegeman (ed.),*Elements of Grammar. A Handbook in Generative Syntax*, 281–337. Dordrecht Boston & London: Kluwer Academic Publishers.,

Stalnaker, Robert. 1978. Assertion. In Peter Cole (ed.), *Syntax and Semantics 9:Pragmatics*, 315–332. New York: Academic Press.

Struckmeier, Volker. 2007. *Attribute im Deutschen*. Berlin: Akademie Verlag.

Struckmeier, Volker. 2014. Ja doch wohl C? Modal Particles in German as C-related elements. *Studia Linguistica* 68. 16–48.

Truckenbrodt, Hubert. 2006a. On the semantic motivation of syntactic verb movement to C in German. *Theoretical Linguistics* 32. 257–306.

Truckenbrodt, Hubert. 2006b. Replies to the comments by Gärtner, Plunze, and Zimmermann, Portner, Potts, Reis, and Zaefferer. *Theoretical Linguistics* 32. 387–410.

Truckenbrodt, Hubert. 2013. Satztyp, Prosodie und Intonation. In: Jörg Meibauer, Markus Steinbach & Hans Altmann (eds.), *Satztypen des Deutschen*, 570–601. Berlin: de Gruyter.

Verstraete, Jean-Christophe, Sarah D'Hertefelt & An Van linden. 2012. A typology of complement insubordination in Dutch. *Studies in Language* 36 (1). 123–153.

Wunderlich, Dieter. 1984. Was sind Aufforderungssätze? In Gerhard Stickel (ed.),*Pragmatik in der Grammatik: Jahrbuch 1983 des IdS*, 92–117. Düsseldorf:Schwann.

Zimmermann, Malte. 2004. Zum 'Wohl': Diskurspartikeln als Satztypmodifikatoren. *Linguistische Berichte* 199. 253–286.

Jeanne-Marie Debaisieux, Philippe Martin
and Henri-José Deulofeu

11 Apparent insubordination as discourse patterns in French

Abstract: In current syntactic literature, two empirical situations are typically earmarked as cases of "insubordination". Their common trait is that, despite formal features that should technically define them as subordinate clauses (they are preceded by subordinators – a subordinating conjunction or some other appropriate morpheme), they behave in discourse like "independent sentences". This description takes into account both formally subordinate clauses functioning as independent discourse units (Evans 2007) and peripheral subordinate clauses which display "main clause features" (Debaisieux 2013: chap 2). Our stance is that, in both cases, the concept of "insubordination" is an artefact of sentence type theory (Struckmeier and Kaiser 2015). Committed to the pioneering model of Claire Blanche-Benveniste (1990), which posits a fundamental distinction between *grammatical syntax* on the one hand and *discourse syntax* on the other, Desbaisieux (2016) has conclusively shown that, in actual fact, neither of the structures identified in the macrosyntactic paradigm as candidates for "insubordination" – peripheral clauses with main clauses features – are in any way governed by the so-called "main clauses" with which they are combined. In this paper we deal with two types of apparent exclamative insubordinates in French introduced respectively by the subordinating conjunctions *si* and *quand*. We argue by extending syntactic dependency to discourse that both are regular syntactic patterns.

1 Introduction

In linguistic literature, two different "sets of facts" have been identified as cases of insubordination. What they have in common is that, according to the mainstream paradigm in linguistic research, a clause formally marked as subordinate (by a conjunction or a dedicated verbal morpheme) behaves in the discourse as a main clause. This definition subsumes, on one side, the case of a formally subordinate clause behaving as an independent discourse unit (Evans 2007), and, on the other side, a peripheral subordinate clause

Jeanne-Marie Debaisieux, Université Sorbonne Nouvelle Paris3, LATTICE
Philippe Martin, Université Paris 7 Paris Diderot, LLF
Henri-José Deulofeu, Université d'Aix-Marseille

https://doi.org/10.1515/9783110638288-012

displaying "main clause phenomena" (Debaisieux 2013: chap 2). Our contention is that in both cases the descriptive tool of insubordination is an artifact. Following the pioneering work of Blanche-Benveniste (1990), Debaisieux (2016) shows that within a paradigm that distinguishes between grammatical and discourse syntax, the macrosyntactic paradigm, peripheral clauses with main clause phenomena are autonomous discourse units pragmatically and not grammatically dependent on the "main" clause they are combined with.

In this paper we will focus on clauses at first sight pertaining to more prototypical cases of insubordinate structures along the lines of Evans (2007). After a detailed description, we will conclude that they can be explained with descriptive devices other than insubordination. To reach such a result, we will take advantage of a general hypothesis put forward by our paradigm: subordinating conjunctions as well as other so called subordination markers are polyfunctional units involved in grammatical dependency as well as in discourse or pragmatic dependency. Let us give an example of the structures we are to deal with.

Spontaneous spoken French corpora provide various examples of utterances that could formally be considered as main clause free subordinates:

(1) *la tante avec le petit chapeau et le panier dans le bras / il a fallu qu'elle range tout ça qu'elle nettoie tout ça / elle était pas très contente /* **mais si tu savais ce que moi j'étais contente**
'my aunt with her little hat and basket in her arms she had to put all this stuff in order she had to clean up all that she was not very happy **but if you imagine how happy I was**' [CRFP]

(2) *quand tu penses que euh en 1978 + 80 / 82 l' agneau on le vendait 34 francs le kilo à la carcasse*
'when you think that in 1978 80 82 lamb was sold for 34 francs per kilo by the carcass' [CRFP]

These examples, according to standard analyses, display structures that should formally be connected to a main clause, but which behave here as autonomous statements. These constructions can be considered formally subordinate, as they are introduced by a subordinating conjunction. However, they stand as isolated discourse units that are impossible to link syntactically to what precedes or follows. No main clause can be found in the context that could govern the subordinate clause. They also form independent prosodic units.

The main goal of this paper is to show that it is possible to account for these constructions not as irregular instances of syntactic structures but as an expected result of the way grammar and discourse interact in licensing linguistic forms.

To do so, we will organize our paper by confronting the analysis proposed by Evans (2007) in terms of insubordination, i.e. "the conventionalized main clause use of what, on prima facie grounds, appear to be formally subordinate clauses" with an alternative analysis based on the framework of the Approche Pronominale (Blanche-Benveniste 1990; Debaisieux 2007, 2013: chap 3, 2016; Deulofeu 2008, 2010, 2014 among others.) which, instead of resorting to the problematic device of ellipsis, proceeds by extending the scope of syntactic description to the wider domain of discourse units.

The paper is organized as follows. In Section 2, we give a detailed corpus-based analysis of the prosodic, syntactic, semantic, and pragmatic properties of the apparent insubordinates in (1) and (2). This description highlights that both constructions share many common properties but that they additionally obey specific constraints that we deal with separately in Section 3. Example (1) can be analyzed as a construction that associates a *si*-clause functioning as a pragmatic marker with a main clause of the exclamative type. Example (2) is closer to prototypical cases of insubordination in as much as it involves a complex clause introduced by the subordinating conjunction *quand* without a possible main clause. Nevertheless we will show that this clause does not display the internal properties of a prototypical subordinate, being closer to clauses fulfilling a meta-discursive function within a discourse pattern. In Section 4, we show that an analysis following the steps of Evans' insubordination model faces serious difficulties in dealing with both constructs.

Finally, we show in Section 5 how the descriptive generalizations can be captured within the Approche Pronominale framework, which assumes that grammatical and discursive relations combine to build up utterances and, consequently, that the apparent insubordinates are instances of regular syntactic patterns. The spoken data used in this analysis are extracted from two corpora: the TCOF Corpus, collected in the French city of Nancy and the corpus CRFP compiled at Aix-en-Provence University. The size of the whole data base is about 1 million words representing several spoken genres. The spoken examples are edited without punctuation marks according to the source conventions. The written data are extracted from the Frantext database, a resource containing more than 1500 texts of French fiction. (editing conventions and references in the Appendix section).

2 Characteristic properties of the patterns *si tu savais*... and *quand je pense*...

From an overview of the observed properties, we can provisionally regroup (1) with (2). Broadly speaking, both share many properties with independent exclamative clauses. In order to take sufficient relevant data into account, we will expand our corpus of spontaneous spoken French findings with examples from the Internet and written fiction.

2.1 Prosodic properties

In example (1), *si tu savais ce que moi j'étais contente*[1] ends with a conclusive prosodic contour characterizing independent declarative clauses in French. As shown in Figure 1, we observe a falling melody (fundamental frequency F0) on the second occurrence of the word *contente*:

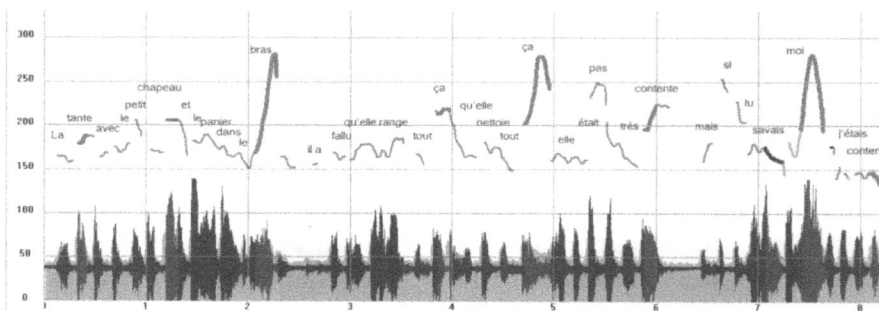

Figure 1: Prosodic analysis of example (1).

(1′)   *La tante avec le petit chapeau et le panier dans le bras il a fallu qu'elle range tout ça qu'elle nettoie tout ça elle était pas très contente **mais si tu savais ce que moi j'étais contente***
'my aunt with her little hat and basket in her arms she had to put all this stuff in order she had to clean up all that she was not very happy **but if you imagine how happy I was**' [CRFP]

---

1 Our prosodic analysis relies on the tools and models of French spontaneous speech prosodic structure set out in Martin (2009, 2014)

We can also observe on the word *moi* a specific prosodic contour with a contrastive focus interpretation, which is found only in main clauses.

In (3), we find again the conclusive prosodic contour of an autonomous statement with an exclamatory value in the insubordinate *si* clause, as can be seen in Figure 2 which displays a subpart of the clause[2]:

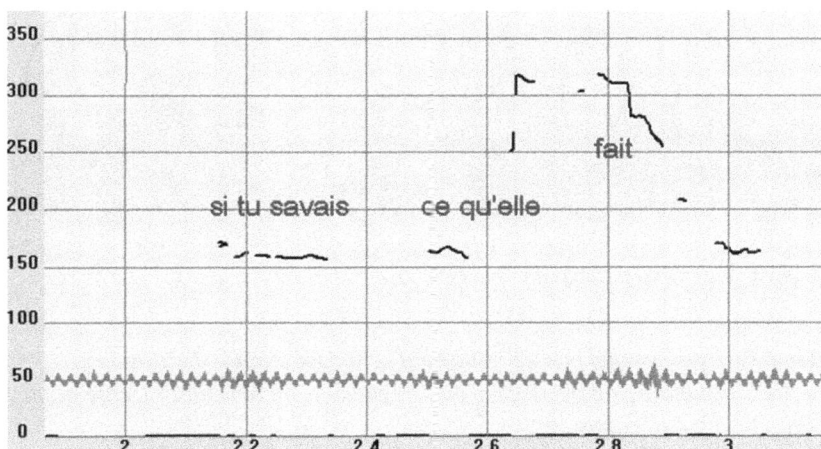

Figure 2: Prosodic analysis of subpart of example (1).

(3) *bon ben ils font des trucs // **si tu savais ce qu'elle fait** / elle fait plein de stages / elle fait euh assistante de metteur en scène*
'well they do stuff // **if you knew what she does** / she does a lot of internships / she uh is assistant director' [CRFP]

(3′) *si tu savais ce qu'elle fait*   'if you knew what she does'

Figure 2 shows the characteristic property of conclusive contours: F0 falling on the last syllable. The exclamative conclusive contour can be distinguished from a mere assertive contour by the presence of a hump on *elle* before the falling melody.

As regards *quand (je/tu) penses que* clauses, many occurrences found in our corpus show an assertive conclusive contour instead of the expected exclamative one. This is observed in Figure 3, in which the excerpt from example (2) shows the lack of a hump before the falling F0 on *carcasse*.

---

2 Notice that this terminal contour instead of a continuative contour undermines the analysis of *the si clause as subordinated to "elle fait plein de stages"*.

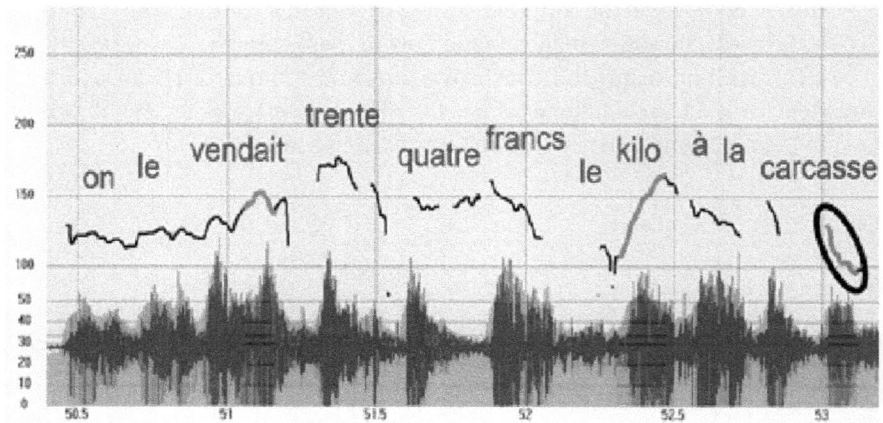

Figure 3: Prosodic analysis of subpart of example (2).

(2′)   *quand tu + penses que euh en mille neuf cent soixante-dix-huit (hum)*
    quatre-vingt quatre-vingt- deux + euh l'agneau + on le vendait trente-quatre
    francs le kilo à la carcasse
    'when you think that in 1978 80 82 lamb was sold for 34 francs per kilo by
    the carcass' [CRFP]

The prosody of the examples confirms their status as independent clauses.
Furthermore, if isolated from the context with a sound editor, they appear prosodically complete (i.e. no further sequel is expected by listeners to complete
the sentence).

2.2 Syntactic properties

Numerous formal cues support the independent clause status of these constructions. As regards the external links, the following examples show that they cannot be involved in any kind of dependency. In example (4), we note a feedback
discourse particle *hein* "isn't it" that never appears between a subordinate and
a main clause.

(4)   speakers are referring to the stand-off between students and the Government
    about plans to institute non-binding work contracts for first-time under
    26 year-olds.

moi je pense qu'ils [les étudiants] sont .assez euh + assez mordus et assez dans le coup pour pas se laisser faire / **quand tu penses que déjà euh il [le gouvernement] a reculé hein** *oh non ça c'était pour te dire*
'But as for me I think that they are involved enough and aware enough not to accept things passively / when you think that he has already backed down isn't it oh no this was just to say' [TCOF]

Furthermore, the non-clausal fragment *oh non* could not provide a possible governor for the *quand* clause. Notice that, even if these clauses are followed by a plain declarative clause, it is often impossible to consider the following clauses as main clauses to which the *si* or *quand* clauses could be subordinate. Consider example (3), repeated here as (5):

(5) *bon ben ils font des trucs // si tu savais ce qu'elle fait / elle fait plein de stages / elle fait euh assistante de metteur en scène //*
'well they do stuff // if you knew what she does / she does a lot of internships / she uh is assistant director' [CRFP]

The autonomous status of the clause is, independently of the prosody, highlighted by the incorrect semantic interpretation which would result from considering *elle fait plein de stages* as the main clause of the *si* clause as shown in (5'):

(5') *??si tu savais ce qu'elle fait / elle fait plein de stages*
'if you knew what she does / she does a lot of internships'

However the semantic interpretation becomes perfect if we assume that *si tu savais ce qu'elle fait* is a main exclamative clause in which the *ce que* pronoun has an intensive value "what an amount of things is she doing". The following clause *elle fait plein de stages* may be analyzed as an independent assertive clause justifying the 'exclamative' stance conveyed by the insubordinate.

As far as their internal structure is concerned, we can point out the presence of 'main clause phenomena' related to message organization, that is main clause phenomena of type 2, according to Verstraete's (2007) classification,[3] such structural remodelings are predominantly found in main clauses. We note for instance the topicalized *moi* in (1) *moi j'étais contente* conveying a narrow

---

3 Verstraete (2007: 179): "The second category of main clause phenomena relates to the organization of the message in the secondary clause: preposing of the VP, negative adverbial or negative NP marks discursive prominence for the element in Question".

focus effect, or the topicalisation of *agneau* in (2) combined with a detached fo-
cussed adjunct *à la carcasse*.

Similar phenomena are found in examples from written fiction. For example, (6) displays a complex information structure organization: a topicalized
constituent *de nous deux* combined with a focalisation on *moi* by means of
a cleft sentence:

(6) **Quand je pense** que, de nous deux, **c'est moi qui** passe pour un sale
caractère!
'To think that, out of the two of us, it's me who is considered the bad-
tempered guy!'
[COLETTE, Sept dialogues de bêtes, 1905]

These constructions must be analyzed as stand-alone clauses. As for their
clause type, we will follow the proposition of Marandin (2008), who posits for
French an exclamative clause type characterized by a set of criteria that distinguish it from declarative and interrogative ones. We will show that the constructions we are analyzing meet these criteria and therefore are instances of
the exclamative clause type. Thus, like other exclamative clauses, they cannot
combine with evidential adverbs:

(7) **à mon avis si tu savais ce qu'il m'a dit!* 'in my opinion if you knew
what he told me!'

(8) **à mon avis quand je pense que. . .!* 'in my opinion when you
think that. . .!'

(9) **à mon avis qu'il est beau !* 'in my opinion how handsome
he is!'

Indeed if we follow the evidential approach of Marandin (2008: 446) which
"captures the expressive flavor of exclamatives without arbitrarily assuming
that they have to express an emotive attitude, and in particular, surprise" we
can understand that they "are incompatible with overt perspective markers"
that could be redundant with the "ego-evidentiality" (speaker based) force
characteristic of exclamative illocution (Garrett 2001). As well, ego-evidentiality
entails that the addressee cannot be directly called on. Hence the incompatibility of exclamatives with tags like *tu sais* 'you know', whose function is to call
upon the addressee for collaboration:

(10) *??ce qu'il est beau **tu sais***   'how beautiful it is you know'

(11) **quand je pense que... **tu sais***   'when you think that... you know!'

As exclamative main clauses, these constructions cannot serve as answer or reply to questions:

(12) A: *Paul est-il intelligent?*   'is Paul smart? '
       B: *si tu savais ce qu'il est intelligent 'if you knew how smart he is!'

We can also point out that we find mainly evaluative vocabulary, such as subjective adjectives like *contente* 'happy' inside the copular construction in (1), the verb *reculer* 'back down' in (4) that here does not refer to an actual movement but is an expressive way to signal a defeat, and the word *chantier* in (15), which literally means 'warehouse', but here does not refer to an actual works site and instead has the evaluative meaning of 'mess'. We find also scalar expressions, forming the basis of judgments of high degree, as the scale of price of the lamb is easily inferable in (2).

Now it is important to point out that even as these exclamative clauses meet the characteristic properties of clauses used in exclamative utterances, they display additional ones that make them a specific subtype. These clauses *si tu savais/avais vu* show only instances of main verbs of cognition and perception (*savoir, voir*) with *si*. With *quand* we likewise find, first and foremost, verbs expressing belief or opinion: *savoir, penser* or perceptual verbs such as *voir* or *entendre*.

These restrictions can be related to "the fact that exclamatives are selected by verbs describing an experience of the content, be it perceptual or mental" (Marandin 2008: 444). As for their grammar, the tense must convey an irrealis meaning (*Si* + anperfect with *voir*, imperfect with *savoir*), (*Quand* + only imperfect and present tense). Subjects are restricted to the clitic pronouns *je, tu* or *on* – and bear in mind that the 'indefinite clitic' *on*, generally interpreted as a first person plural, can include the point of view of the speaker. These restrictions may be linked to the fact that in standard exclamatives the evidentiality source is the direct knowledge or perception of the speaker. Third person subjects, as in (1'), shift the meaning towards a suspended interpretation:

(1') *??si les gens savaient ce qu'elle fait!*   'if people knew what she is doing!'

Likewise (13), with a lexical subject, is not a possible exclamative and can only be taken as a suspended temporal *quand* clause:

(13) *??quand les gens pensent!*   'when people know this!'

These lexical and person constraints combine with more subtle syntactic ones. In these constructions the verb cannot be modified by an adjunct phrase. In (14), excerpted from (4) above, inserting adjuncts, as in (13′), renders the utterance quite unacceptable:

(14) *mais moi je pense qu'ils sont assez mordus et assez dans le coup pour pas se laisser faire **quand tu penses que déjà il a reculé hein***
'when you think that has already backed down' [TCOF]

(14′) *??quand tu penses **sérieusement / un instant** que déjà euh il a reculé hein*
'when you think **seriously / for a moment** that'

A similar example is (15). Again, inserting an adjunct, as in (15′), severely degrades its acceptability:

(15) *ah ben il a bouché toutes les voies hein tous les wagons se sont achevalés l'un sur l'autre **si tu avais vu le chantier***
'well it (the train involved in the accident) blocked all the tracks isn't it all the carriages ended one over the other **if you could have seen that mess**'
[TCOF]

(15′) *??ah ben il a bouché toutes les voies hein tous les wagons se sont achevalés l'un sur l'autre si tu avais vu **précisément / en compagnie de Jean le** chantier*
'if you could have seen **precisely / with John** that mess'

These facts suggest that in these clauses the verbs do not fulfill the function of full-fledged governors and are devoid of denotative meaning, such as we find in their uses as parentheticals. There is additional evidence that the clauses following *si tu savais* are not in fact governed by the verb. First, *savoir* in insubordinates combines with exclamative clause types that are not possible complements in other contexts:

(16) *C'est pour lui que j'ai quitté la France... car si tu savais qu' il est beau que son regard est enivrant et que sa voix a de charme!*
'It is for him that I left France... because if you knew how handsome he is, how intoxicating his eyes are and how charming is his voice!'
[*forum.aufeminin.com › ... › Ruptures et deceptions amoureuses*]

The apparently embedded exclamative *que sa voix a de charme*, is normally found only as a free-standing exclamative clause. *Savoir* without *si* cannot take these clauses as complements as shown in (17):

(17) *Pierre sait que ma voix a de charme*
    'Peter knows how much my voice is charming'

Insubordinated *savoir* conditionals can also combine with clauses that Milner (1978: 259) calls "indirect exclamatives", as in (18) excerpted from (1) above:

(18) *si tu savais ce que moi j'étais contente*
    'if you imagine how happy I was'

But all indirect exclamatives can function as direct ones, except the one introduced by the degree complementizer *que*. If we take into account example (16), the following descriptive generalization emerges: *si tu savais* exclamative insubordinates can combine with all types of direct exclamatives, including those that are not embeddable under *savoir*. The logical conclusion that we can draw is that there is no grammatical dependency relationship between *si tu savais* and the associated clauses. As a consequence, we may propose that the construction consists of two independent clauses with a kind of paratactic link between the two.

Another important conclusion is that only exclamative clauses combine with *si tu savais* in this construct, whereas *savoir* regularly subcategorizes other sentence types. This conclusion is in keeping with our analysis of *savoir* as a verb deprived of a governing function. Indeed the verb *savoir* in the insubordinate does not display the full range of its possible clausal complements. For instance, in main clauses, *savoir* takes a declarative (and non-exclamative) clause introduced by the complementizer *que* as in (19):

(19) *tu savais qu'il est revenu*
    'you knew that he returned'

But with such complements the insubordinate cannot get the exclamative interpretation as shown in (19'):

(19') ??*si tu savais qu'il est revenu!*
    'if you knew he returned!'

All these puzzling facts become clear if we split the insubordinate into two subparts: a main exclamative clause combined with a reduced *si tu savais* clause, fulfilling the function of a pragmatic marker. In the case of *quand* clauses, there are also specific syntactic structures, which partly depart from the pattern of the *si* clauses. What they have in common with the *si tu savais* clauses is that the insubordinating *quand* combines with clauses that are not possible complements of the apparent main verb, in particular with indirect exclamatives:

(20) *quand je pense ce qu' ils vont se mettre sur la gueule partout ailleurs*
       'when I think they will fight everywhere else'
       [https://fr.wikiquote.org/wiki/Kaamelott/Arthur]

(21) *quand je pense comme c'est tellement génial quand c' est lui qui decide*
       'when I think how it's so great when it's he who decides'
       [forum.aufeminin.com › . . . › Sexualité › Couple – Sexualité & technique]

This combination of clauses is impossible in other syntactic contexts as shown in (20′)

(20′) **Pierre pense ce qu'ils vont se mettre sur la gueule partout ailleurs*
        'Peter thinks they will fight everywhere else'

However, in contrast to *si* insubordinates, *quand* insubordinates accept regular *que* declarative complement clauses of *penser*, as in (22) excerpted from (4):

(22) *quand tu penses que déjà il a reculé hein*
       'when you think that has already backed down, right'

The conclusion is that insubordinates in *quandi je/tu pense(s)* split into two distinct structures: one, very similar to the *si tu savais* construct, in which the *ce que* introduces a main exclamative and *quand je pense* is a parenthetical. And another one with *quand* introducing what looks like an "insubordinate" complex clause in which the *que*-clause seems to be the embedded complement of *pense*. We should add that this second type is in fact a construction of its own, in so far as the verb *penser* does not display the properties of a full-fledged governor, as we will show in the next section. These results raise the following issue: are these constructions merely instances of two entrenched exclamative constructions, or can we derive them from more regular patterns? In order to address this issue, in the next section we will deepen the description of both constructions.

3 Two structures for the apparent "insubordinate" exclamatives

3.1 The *si tu savais* clause

Additional evidence supports the hypothesis that the *si tu savais* clause is not integrated within the grammar of the exclamative clause. A search through the Frantext database brings to light examples in which the chunks *si tu savais/ si tu avais vu* can appear alone without the exclamative clause and followed by marks of omission or exclamation:

(23) | **Si** | **tu** | **savais**... | *mon* | *Dieu*... | **si** | **tu** | **savais**... |
if	you	knew	my	god	if	you	knew
mon	*Dieu*...	**si**	**tu**	**savais!**			
my	god	if	you	knew			

'If you only knew ... my God ... if you only knew ... my God ... if you only knew!'
[SUE Eugène. Le Juif errant.1845]

In (24), the chunk behaves as an autonomous utterance linked to the following one by the coordinator *car*, which forbids any grammatical dependency:

(24) *Ah! – **si tu savais!** car tu m' as prise!*
'Ah! – If you only knew! because you took me!'
[LAFORGUE Jules/ Les Complaintes / 1885]

When grouped with a main utterance, many cues show that the two are not integrated in their grammatical structure. In (25), the clause appears just inserted as a parenthetical inside a noun phrase between the head and a detached adjunct:

(25) *c' était d' un curieux... il y avait une vitrine de bijoux... un collier de perles noires entre autres... **si tu avais vu!** ... à trois rangs...*
'It was so strange ... there was a jewelry shop window ... a black pearl necklace among others ... if you had seen! with three rows ...'
[Edmond de GONCOURT Jules de, *Renée Mauperin*, 1864]

In (26) it appears as an appended parenthetical chunk after the main clause:

(26) *J' ai le coeur si plein de toi, **si tu savais!***
   'I 've my heart so full of you, if you only knew!'
   [SAMAIN Albert / Le Chariot d'or /1900]

The grammatical independence of the chunk is underlined by the fact that it is not necessarily associated with a main verb. Consider for instance example (27), in which the topical non clausal fragment cannot be a governor:

(27) *oh! Les autres, **si tu savais!***
   'oh! The others, if you only knew'
   [ZOLA Émile / La Bête humaine / 1890]

We could easily use this pattern to modify example (15):

(15′) *mais le chantier si tu avais vu*

In the front position, the idiosyncratic status of the chunk is highlighted by a high degree of variation in the punctuation marks separating it from the accompanying clauses. Besides the marks of omission or exclamation noted before, we find a comma in (28):

(28) ***Si tu savais**, je t'aime!*
   'If you only knew, I love you!'
   [HUGO Victor / Théâtre en liberté : Mangeront-ils ?/1867]

And strangely enough a colon in (29):

(29) *O mon vieux Brèchemain, **si tu savais**: il arrive! il arrive!*
   'O my old Brèchemain, if you only knew: he arrives! he arrives!'
   [DAUDET Alphonse / Les Absents]

This variation in punctuation shows that the writers are struggling with the challenge of expressing what they feel to be an unusual relationship between the constructions.

   All these facts support a syntactic analysis that does not require an "insubordination" framework. Its *si tu savais* part can be analyzed as a construction of its own. As it is emancipated from syntactic dependency, it behaves as a mobile autonomous phrase available for pragmatic functions that we will specify later. In sum, it shares many properties with members of the syntactic category of discourse parentheticals including marked clauses like *si tu veux* 'if you like', *si je peux* 'if I may', as well as 'bare' ones like *tu vois* 'you see', *tu sais* 'you know', *je veux dire* 'I mean', fulfilling the same pragmatic functions as epistemic and evidential adverbs. This parenthetical is combined with a regular exclamative main clause.

3.2 The *quand je pense* clauses

For the *quand* clause, an analysis as a segment not integrated in the grammar of the associated clause fits in very well with examples such as (30):

(30) *Bon de toutes façons, c'est de l'histoire ancienne maintenant le Tb1*[4]...
Quand je pense ce que ça a coûté à certains ! Ils ont vraiment gaspillé leur argent
'Well anyway, that's ancient history now the Tb1... When I think of what it has cost some people! They really wasted their money'
[www.photoetmac.com/2014/06/du-raid0-en-thunderbolt-2-aller-vite/]

In (30), the associated clause cannot be analyzed as a complement of *penser* as shown in (30'):

(30') *Pierre pense ce que ça a coûté à certains*
'Pierre thinks of what it has cost some people!'

Neither can the whole insubordinate be analyzed as subordinate to *ils ont vraiment gaspillé leur argent*. The same syntactic autonomy can be observed in the following examples in which the lack of the complementizer *que* reveals a paratactic link, in French literary style (31) or modern French (32):

(31) **Quand je pense** *il n' y a pas six mois nous dansions de si bon coeur à la Vote de Cassis!*
'When I think about it not six months ago we danced so heartily at the Vote in Cassis!'
[DAUDET Alphonse, *Lise Tavernier*, 1872]

---

4 Thunderbolt One (Computer technology).

(32) ***Quand je pense*** *il y a juste 3 semaines j' ai encore fait un aller retour en*
avion Bruxelles Nice sans présenter une seule fois une pièce d'identité!
'When I think about it just three weeks ago I made another round trip
flight Brussels Nice without showing an ID once'
[www.instinct-voyageur.fr/8-facons-de-rater-lavion-et-son-voyage-mes-c.]

The construction *quand je pense* can even appear as an isolated unit as in (33):

(33) *Quelles maîtresses, mon Dieu!... Et Jenkins pour seul protecteur...Oh!*
quand je pense... Quand je pense...
'What mistresses, my God... And Jenkins as sole protector ... Oh! When
I think...When I think ...'
[DAUDET Alphonse, *Le Nabab*, 1877]

Nevertheless, the *quand je pense* clause shows a lesser degree of independence
than observed with *si tu savais*. It never appears inserted or postposed to the
associated clause and its uses as an isolated clause are in fact not very numerous: 16 occurrences out of 1315 "insubordinates" were returned in our search,
whereas we get 126 occurrences of isolated *si tu savais* out of 804 "insubordinates" in Frantext.

In any case, even if the main clause + parenthetical analysis is suitable for
to the examples with *quand je pense* combined with overt exclamative clauses,
it cannot be used for the *quand je pense que* + declarative case. For this case,
the most frequent in oral style, an insubordination analysis could be supported
by the strong links between the insubordinate *quand je pense que* and the use
of the clause in plain subordinates. In order to specify this link, we must distinguish two types of apparently subordinate *quand* clauses.

We certainly find examples in which the construction *quand je pense que*
can be analyzed as a regular adjunct integrated into the syntactic structure of
a following main clause as a dependent of the main verb[5]:

(34) *Quand je pense que vous m' aymez, je ne dors pas*
'When I think that you love me, I can't sleep'
[VOITURE Vincent, Lettres, 1648]

---

5 The usual semantic interpretation of this adjunct is as a time modifier, but other interpretations of this syntactic structure are possible, for instance a conditional one.

Such an adjunct can be postponed to the main clause, as shown in (35):

(35) *Je me porte bien quand je pense que vous vous préparez à me venir voir.*
'I feel well when I think that you are preparing to come and see me'
[SÉVIGNÉ Mme de, Correspondance, 1680]

Another syntactic test can confirm the adjunct status of the construct: it can be used as an answer to a clause containing the time *wh-* interrogative pronoun *quand*[6]:

(34′) *Quand est-ce que je ne dors pas? Quand je pense que vous m'aimez*
'When is that I do not sleep? When I think that you love me'

(35′) *Quand est-ce que je me porte bien? Quand je pense que vous vous préparez à me venir voir.*
'When is it that I am well? When I think that you are preparing to come and see me.'

But in numerous examples, an analysis of the construction as an adjunct integrated in the grammatical structure of the main clause is impossible, either in contemporaneous speech:

(36) *Et quand on pense aux progrès de la médecine depuis 10 ans évidemment c'est merveilleux*
'And when you consider the advances in medicine for 10 years, of course it's wonderful'
[CRFP]

or in classical French literary style:

(37) *Quand je pense et parle sur ce sujet, ce sont mes véritables affaires, je n' en connais point d'autr es.*
'When I think and speak on this subject, it is my genuine business, I don't know of any others.'
[SÉVIGNÉ Mme de, Correspondance, 1696]

---

6 A wider set of criteria to distinguish between grammatical and discourse dependency has been addressed in an abundant literature within the framework of the *Approche Pronominale*, Debaisieux (2016: chap. 3), Deulofeu (2017) among others.

In both cases the morpheme *quand* is disconnected from its grammatical status of conjunction introducing a phrase modifiying the propositional content of the associated bare clause. A compositional interpretation assuming that the *quand* clause is a canonical time adjunct would lead to an odd meaning (e.g. for (35), the advances of medical science are wonderful at the very moment when you think of them). The necessary non-compositional semantic analysis of these ex- amples is corroborated by a syntactic test: the *quand* clause cannot be an an- swer to the interrogative pronoun *quand* as shown in (37'):

(37') *??Quand est-ce que ce sont mes véritables affaires quand je pense et parle sur ce sujet. . . .*
'When is it the real business when I think and speak on this subject'

These facts undermine an analysis of the *quand* clause as a dependent time ad- junct in (36) and (37). The specific syntactic status of these *quand* clauses is also supported by their information structure. In (38), it is the clause following the verb *penser* that has preeminent informational status, in that its content is referred to by the pronoun *cela* in the 'main clause':

(38) *quand je pense que je ne me separe de vous que pour rendre à la nymphe un service extremément important, cela me sert d' une espece de soulagement*
'when I think I am separating you from me to give to the nymph an ex- tremely important service, it serves me as a sort of relief.'
[BARO Balthazar, La Conclusion et dernière partie d'Astrée, 1628]

Consider also that (36) could be paraphrased by a dislocated pattern skipping the verb *penser*:

(36') *les progrès de la médecine depuis dix ans c'est merveilleux*
'the advances in medicine for 10 years it's wonderful'

These facts are properly accounted for if we consider that *quand* introduces a metadiscursive clause fulfilling the pragmatic function of establishing a new topic, the commentary on which is provided by the main clause. Insubordinated *quand je pense que* is clearly related to these metadiscursive peripheral clauses, with which they share the property that the verb is not a full verb, contrary to time adverbial clauses in *quand*. Another common property is an additional re- striction that bears on the subordinating morpheme *quand*. We could expect that the clause might have been introduced by the literary equivalent of *quand*, i.e. *lorsque,* as both can be used interchangeably in canonical integrated temporal subordinates. But this is not the case for the constructions under study here. That is, the lexical constraints are not limited to the main verb but extend to the linking morpheme. From (39) in which *quand on pense que* is clearly a time adjunct, we can derive (39′):

(39) *Quand on pense que le bonheur dépend beaucoup du caractère, on a raison*
'When we think that happiness depends a lot on one's character, we are right'
[VAUVENARGUES, *Des lois de l'esprit : florilège philosophique*, 1747]

(39′) *Lorsqu'on pense que le bonheur dépend beaucoup du caractère, on a raison*
'When we think that happiness depends a lot on one's character, we are right'

The same test applied to the "insubordinate" in (40) excerpted from (4) above, gives the unacceptable (40′):

(40) ***quand** tu penses que déjà euh il a reculé hein*
'to think that it has already backed down'

(40′) ***??lorsque** tu penses que déjà euh il a reculé hein*
'to think that it has already backed down'

Nor can *lorsque* introduce a metadiscursive "subordinate":

(36") *??lorsque je pense aux progrès de la médecine c'est merveilleux*
'when I think of medical advances. . .'

Taken together, these facts suggest that the insubordinate *quand je pense que* does not function as a canonical temporal adjunct and must be considered as a specific entrenched construction in a synchronic description of French.

3.3 Interim conclusion

So far we have brought to light two different syntactic patterns for the apparent insubordinates (1) and (2). One pattern encompasses all the cases of *si tu savais* occurrences and minor cases of *quand je pense* clauses. Under close examination, this pattern does not seem to be related to insubordination. Rather, it consists indeed of an exclamative main clause associated with a *si tu savais* clause not integrated into the grammatical structure of the main clause. The standard embedding pattern is restricted to *quand je pense que* clauses, which therefore remain candidates for an insubordination analysis. But there is still to be addressed the issue of what type of subordinate underlies the insubordinate: are there former adjuncts or metadiscursive peripherals, and what is exactly meant by "peripheral"? We will see in the next section that the interpretative properties of the patterns support the distinction made on syntactic grounds.

3.4 Semantic interpretation

In the exclamative main clause pattern, neither reconstruction nor added material is needed to get a full interpretation. The example in (1) has the meaning of a self-contained exclamatory utterance. This meaning is mainly conveyed by the syntactic main clause: *'mais ce que moi j'étais contente!'* 'How happy I was!' As for the *si tu savais* clause, it does not contribute to the propositional content of the whole utterance but adds an interactive evidential value to the meaning of the exclamative clause. It is indeed expected for syntactically emancipated clauses that they fulfill pragmatic or discourse functions (Verstraete 2007). The pragmatic function of *si tu savais* is to encode a special type of evidentiality. *'si tu savais'* invites the addressee to share the ego-evidentiality that is the source of the exclamative interpretation of the main clause. Consider the following two examples:

(41) .. *tes yeux ! . . . si tu savais, tes yeux ! . . .*
'your eyes! . . . if you knew your eyes'
[BATAILLE Henry/ Maman Colibri / 1904]

(42) *Quelle tête ! . . . si tu avais vu sa tête ! . . .*
'What a head! . . . If you saw her head'
[MAUPASSANT Guy de/Contes et nouvelles, 1885]

In both cases the function of *si tu savais/si tu avais vu* is to create by means of the irrealis imperfect a possible world in which the addressee could have directly experienced the situation triggering the exclamation, so that he could be in a position to share the ego-evidential stance of the speaker.

As for *quand je pense que, quand on voit que* etc it is also the case that the clause as a whole gets an independent exclamative interpretation. Consider example (43):

(43) ***quand on voit la place qu' on a fait devant la mairie*** *– c'est une place où il y a plus personne / avant il y avait des un parking il y avait des voitures – donc il y avait une vie quand même avec euh les voitures – maintenant ils ont enlevé toutes les voitures – il y a une belle place – ah ça elle est belle – mais il y a rien dessus – c'est un trou à courant d'air -*
'when you see the square that was built in front of the town hall – it's a square where there is nobody left / before there was a parking lot there were cars – so there was still a life with the uh cars – now they have re-moved all the cars – there is a beautiful square – oh it is beautiful – But there is nothing on it – it's a hole for a draft of air' [CRFP]

The semantic interpretation is perfect if we assume that *quand on voit la place qu'on a fait devant la mairie* is a main exclamative clause conveying a negative subjective stance to the situation: how outrageous it is to see the square in front of the Town Hall. The following clause justifies the negative stance con-veyed by the insubordinate, just as it would have done with regard to a mere fragment bearing an exclamative contour: *Alors, la place qu'on a fait devant la Mairie !* 'Then (look at) the square they have built in front of the Town Hall'. The exclamative stance can be positive as well as negative, as in standard ex-clamatives. Here, the following context shifts towards a negative stance, since the speaker criticizes the urban policy of the town council, contrasting it with a positive appraisal of the former condition of the square: *il y avait une vie quand même* ('so there was still a life') which opposes the negative metaphor used to describe the current site: *c'est un trou à courant d'air* ('it's an airstream hole').

But there is a major difference compared to the main clause + parentheti-cal patterns. Here it is the *quand je pense* fragment that triggers the exclama-tive meaning. The clause introduced by *que* is a plain declarative clause and in general the prosodic pattern of the whole clause is not exclamative. The *quand je pense* fragment as a whole has the function of marking the type of the clause as exclamative. The verb *penser* displays properties similar to those by which Tomasello (2005: 251) defines the 'clausal operators': "the subject is in first/second person, the verb is active [...] without auxiliaries or other ac-coutrements; the matrix clause is shorter than the dependent clause and can occur in various positions." That amounts to saying that *penser* is not a full-fledged main verb and can be analyzed as a subcase of clausal operators giv-ing intersubjective or evidential modulation. The verb *je pense* may alternate with another stance indicator *je vois* in the insubordinate exclamatives: it gives the perceptual source triggering the exclamative interpretation of the clause introduced by *que*.

4 Analysis: Insubordinated structures or discourse patterns?

Looking for the best way to give an integrated description of these structures, we will compare two hypotheses within two theoretical frameworks. The first hypothesis claims that the idiosyncratic properties of the two structures result from a diachronic process of reanalysis of canonical sentential structures leading to the emancipation of the formally subordinate clauses: these clauses with properties of independent clauses"have diachronic origins as a subordinate clause" (Evans 2007: 370). The second hypothesis is that the constructions with *si* and *quand* do not result from the emancipation of a former subordinate clause but are genuine pragmatic routines. In the first one, a pragmatic marker *si tu savais / quand je pense* is combined with a free-standing exclamative. For the *quand je pense que* clause, we will propose an analysis inspired by the insubordination hypothesis but working at a discourse level

4.1 The insubordination framework

Evans (2007: 366) uses the term *insubordination* to refer to "the conventionalized main clause use of what, on prima facie grounds, appear to be formally subordinate clauses." This historical process follows four steps which we have set out in the figure 4 below excerpted from Evans and Wanatabe (2016: 3):

Subordination	Ellipsis	Conventionalized ellipsis	Reanalysis as main clause structure
A	B	C	D
Biclausal construction with subordinate construction	Ellipsis of main clause, any contextually appropriate material can be recovered	Restriction of interpretation of ellipsis material	Conventionalized main clause use of formally subordinate clause (Constructionalization)

Figure 4: Historical trajectory of insubordinated clause (Evans and Wanatabe 2016).

Within this framework, examples (1) and (2), which have been described as autonomous speech acts whose interpretation does not rely on context, would belong to the final stage of insubordination.[7] Prima facie, they look like the constructions that Lombardi (2004: 206) calls "free conditionals", in which the

---

7 See the analysis of Patard (2014) on *si* and Saez (2014) on *quand*.

semantico-pragmatic function of the former main clause has been by convention incorporated into the former subordinate.[8] However we will see in the next section that the reconstruction of the process leading to this final step raises some problems.

4.2 Reconstruction problems

4.2.1 The *si tu savais* clause

We argued in the preceding sections that we have good synchronic reasons to prefer a split analysis of the construct rather than a protasis for a missing apodosis. In this section we will present additional evidence against a diachronic analysis of the *si* insubordinate as the reanalyzed protasis of an understood apodosis. The only semantically and syntactically possible apodosis would be a declarative clause like *tu serais étonné* 'you'd be surprised':

(44) *Si tu savais ce que moi j'étais contente tu serais étonné*
     'If you knew how I was glad you'd be surprised'

This will result in unexpected differences between the full construction with the apodosis, and the reduced insubordinate pattern that has been analyzed as an instance of an exclamative clause by applying the tag test. Indeed the full pattern reacts as a declarative clause type with respect to the same test, as in (45–46), in contrast to the reduced pattern, as in (7) - (11).

(45) ***à mon avis*** *si tu savais ce que j'étais contente tu serais étonnée*
     '**in my opinion** if you knew how happy I was you would be amazed'

(46) *si tu savais ce qu'il m'a dit tu serais étonnée **tu sais***
     'if you knew what he said to me you would be amazed **you know**'

It would not be easy to explain how the integration of a declarative clause in the subordinate clause results in a shift of illocutionary force from assertive to exclamative, including a change in prosodic contour. Moreover, even if we could succeed in building such an explanation, we would still have to face the problem of the outcome of a free-standing exclamative after the insubordination process.

---

8 We had also presented this analysis in Debaisieux, Deulofeu and Martin (2008).

Both problematic issues disappear if we posit that the construction has involved stance framing, with no apodosis, from the beginning. This hypothesis is supported by the existence of such a construction with *voir* as early as the end of the 12th century written style as noticed by Buridant (2000):

(47) *Se voiez oere le palés principel*
      comme il est hauz et tot entor fermé!

Si	*vous*	*voyiez*	*le*	*palais*	*principal*
if	you	see	the	palace	main

comme	*il*	*est*	*haut*	*et*	*fortifié*	*de*	*tout*	*côté!*
as	it	is	high	and	fortified	on	all	sides

'If you could see what the main palace is like, high and fortified on all sides!'
[la prise d'Orange, late 12th – early 13th century]

It is perfectly possible to apply a parenthetical + main clause analysis to the construct, since *le palés principel comme il est hauz et tot entor fermé !* 'the main palace as it is high and fortified on all sides' is a possible exclamative main clause and *Se voiez oere* 'If you see' a possible evaluative frame.

From synchronic as well as diachronic evidence we are led to conclude that it is more economical to consider the construction as a genuine exclamative main clause and not resulting from the emancipation of a former subordinate clause. The situation may be different for the *quand je pense* insubordinates, which are dealt with in the following section.

4.2.2 The *quand je pense* clause

In order to trace the path of the insubordination process of *quand je pense* clauses, two types of events in Old French are useful to consider. The first concerns the status of temporal constructions, the second, the role of *quand*. On the first point, the properties of segments that were analyzed lead us to link them to the comment of Combettes (2013: 112) who emphasizes the independence of constructions introduced by *quand* with simultaneity value in Old French: "This loose dependency [of the time clause] allows us to consider the link between the clauses as a paratactic one." As evidence, he adduces a set of facts that undermine an analysis of the clause as an integrated adjunct: the lack of subject-verb inversion, and the fronted position with insertions of root constituents before the main clause, as we can see in this example from the 15th century translated into modern French:

(48) *Quant je pense, lasse au bon temps,*
 Que me regarde toute nue
 Quelle fuz quelle devenue
 Et je me voy si tres changee,
 Povre, seiche, maigre, menue,
 Je suis presque toute enraigee.
 Quand je pense hélas au bon temps
 'When I think alas about the good time
 Et que je me regarde toute nue
 And when I look at myself naked
 Comment étais–je, que suis-je devenue
 How I was, how I became
 Et je me vois si changée
 And I see myself so changed
 Pauvre, sèche, maigre, menue,
 Poor, dry, thin, shrivelled'
 [VILLON, *LE TESTAMENT*, 1461]

We can indeed notice after the subordinate clause, the interjection *lasse !* 'alas!' the direct discourse *quelle fuz, quelle devenue* 'what was I, how (ugly) have I become' and above all the coordination conjunction *et* 'and' before the main clause. All these facts highlight "the autonomous status of the *quant* clause, assuming, from the point of view of information structure, the role of a topic setting a discourse frame". As regards the status of *quant*, Combettes (2013: 116) signals: "What occurs can be considered as a weakening of the subordinating nature of *quant* towards various discursive functions; in argumentative discourse, *quant* loses its temporal value to take the function of a topic marker; in narratives, it no longer conveys a temporal modification of the predicate, but signals a new step in the narrative line".

 This comment nicely applies to the grammatical status and to the discourse orientation of the construction *quand je pense* in contemporary French. We noticed above that it syntactically introduces a grammatically independent clause and that the clause, emancipated from grammatical integration, becomes free to fulfill a range of pragmatic functions depending on the discourse context. In a narrative context, the clause sets a transition frame between two different steps in the main line of the narrative. In an argumentative sequence, it is used to shift to a new discourse topic. The shift to a new topic, achieved by means of a metadiscursive use of *quand* is explicitly assumed by the speaker via the epistemic *je pense*, (while I am saying P, it occurs to my mind that Q). This move brings out a subjective contrast between the situation evoked by the *quand je pense* clause and the one described in the preceding context. This contrast triggers a positive or negative emotion from the speaker, which is frequently expressed by an exclamative clause like "I can't believe it!" Such association can be a step towards the integration of the 'exclamative' stance into the *quand je pense* clause itself. *Quand je pense que* becomes a conventionalized way to project an exclamative meaning.

Nevertheless, the looseness of the link between the "subordinates" and the following clauses cast doubt on the claim that the construction is the result of the integration of the exclamative meaning of a former main clause in the *quand* clause and that it is "a subordinate clause that has been nativized as main clause" (Evans 2007: 375). To make it plausible, we have to imagine a step previous to the reanalysis as a main clause in which the link between the two constructions strengthens from pragmatic dependency to grammatical subordination. Such a transformation may indeed have occurred according to the following comment of Combettes (2013: 123). "During the transition between middle and preclassical French, clauses whose former status was close to parataxis became involved in the network of grammatical dependency between subordinate and main clause, subject more to syntactic rules than to loose discourse patterns."

This step would provide the suitable starting point for the regular process of insubordination: *quand* subordinate + main clause. We could then revise the insubordination path like this, inserting a new Stage 0 and modifying Stage A from that given in Figure 5:

	Gramaticalization Subordination	Ellipsis	Conventionalized ellipsis	Reanalysis as main clause structure
Stage 0	Stage A	Stage B	Stage C	Stage D
Weak dependence	Process of grammaticalisation leading to Subordinate construction	Ellipsis of main clause	Restriction of interpretation of ellipsis material	Conventionalized main clause use of formally subordinate clause (Constructionalization)

Figure 5: A new historical trajectory for insubordinate clause.

But this revision is undermined by the fact that the exclamative stance does not need to be expressed by means of a clausal syntactic frame. We indeed find examples starting from Middle French such as:

(49) *Quand je pense à vos jambes nues, le matin, deux et trois heures pendant*
    que vous écrivez, mon dieu! Ma bonne, que cela est mauvais!
    'When I think of your bare legs in the morning, two and three hours while
    you are writing, my God! My dear, how bad is this!'
    [SÉVIGNÉ Mme de, *Correspondance*, 1680]

up to contemporary French, through Classical French:

(50) *Quand je pense qu' il était possible que cet argent m' eût été redemandé!*
    Au lieu de venir à son secours, il eût fallu lui annoncer... Ah ! Dieux !..
    'When I think that it was possible that this money would have been asked
    again of me! Instead of coming to his aid, he would have had to tell
    him ... Ah! Ye Gods!'
    [BEAUMARCHAIS Pierre-Augustin Caron de, *Les Deux amis ou le Négociant
    de Lyon*, 1770]

In those examples there is no possible governor for the subordinate. A better
way to properly capture all these facts is to assume that the basis for the process of integration is not a canonical sentence pattern, comprising adjunct
clause + main clause, but a pragmatic routine relying on the following discourse pattern: sudden subjective awareness of a strong contrast between two
situations, plus entailed exclamation (whatever its syntactic frame might be).

    Within this approach, we must anyway assume a further step to deal with
the facts that depart from the ongoing analysis: those in which *quand je pense*
or *si tu savais* combines with a main exclamative clause and those in which
quand je pense is an isolated clause, as in (51):

(51) *Quelles maîtresses, mon Dieu !... Et Jenkins pour seul protecteur... Oh!*
    quand je pense... Quand je pense...
    'What mistresses, my God ... And Jenkins as sole protector ... Oh! When
    I think... When I think'
    [DAUDET Alphonse, *Le Nabab*, 1877]

To deal with these facts, we can resort to a further emancipation of the segment
quand je pense as an interactive discourse marker endowed with exclamative
function, inviting the addressee to infer from the context the source of the exclamation. There is however a caveat: this use needs a deeper corpus investigation both to clarify its formal status – since, from our limited set of examples, it
appears more constrained than *si tu savais* – and to specify its usage scope.

4.3 Interim conclusion

A synchronic analysis, possibly complemented by a diachronic insubordination analysis, may contribute to a better understanding of the difference between the uses of *si tu savais* and the *quand je pense* clauses. These overall syntactic analyses can be matched with different plausible pragmatic organizations: the first clause of the paratactic *si tu savais* and *quand je pense* patterns is used as a pragmatic marker transferring to the addressee the attitude expressed in an associated exclamative cause. In the insubordinate pattern, *quand je pense que* functions as a marker of the exclamative force of the clause.

The pragmatic analysis of the grammatically independent "subordinates" is possible along these lines. But there remains an important syntactic issue to address: the relationship between the 'dependent clause' and the main clause in both patterns have till now been defined only negatively as "pragmatically" dependent clauses which are not integrated in the grammatical structure of the main clause. Is there something positive that we can say about this kind of loose dependency in syntactic terms? In order to give a positive answer to this question, we must address a more general one: what exactly is the relationship between syntactic entities and the text units into which we can segment the discourse?

5 The maximal syntactic unit: Sentence or utterance?

The analysis in Evans (2007) aims at regularizing the apparently irregular syntactic patterns of insubordinate clauses by resorting to the assumption that at some point in the language development all the formally subordinate clauses were also subordinate in syntactic structure that is governed by the "main" verb. Due to diachronic processing of pragmatic routines guided by a principle of economy the subordinate clauses appear presently as main clauses.

A first problem for this analysis is that on empirical grounds it is impossible to maintain that the subordinating use and the grammatically independent use were not coexistent in spontaneous speech at an early stage of language development. Indeed, Indoeuropeanists take the opposite stance when they argue that subordination is derived from paratactic uses of clauses. The Classical Latin subordinator *si* is said (Meillet and Vendryès 1924: §803) to have evolved from what was in early Latin a free adverbial to an integrated conjunction.[9] But it is simply impossible to choose on empirical grounds between the two hypotheses. A diachronic explanation, which is necessarily based only on written evidence, is undermined by the lack of early-stage spontaneous speech evidence. We all know that written styles are far from giving a direct access to all possible structures of contemporary languages. This lack of evidence is a fortiori true for earlier stages. The first consequence of this limitation of the data to written styles is the assumption that the sentence is the maximal unit for syntactic description. But this assumption cannot satisfy those who describe spontaneous spoken corpora. As pointed out by Mithun (2005: 180):

> If our syntactic analyses are based uniquely on single sentences constructed or elicited in isolation, we may miss some of the subtleties of the syntactic structures we are trying to understand, even in languages with literary traditions.

On theoretical grounds, Halliday (1985: 193) points out the need of new units in order to overcome the shortcomings of a sentence-based approach:

> The clause complex will be the only grammatical unit which we shall recognize above the clause. Hence there will be no need to bring in the term 'sentence' as a distinct grammatical category. We can use it simply to refer to the orthographic unit that is contained between two stops.

Following this line is the criticism of Mithun (2005), who insists on the fact that it is impossible to segment folk narratives into sentences. The clause complexes that emerge are better considered as paragraphs.

The need for text units distinct from the sentence pattern is empirically confirmed by the findings of the C-Oral Rom project (Cresti and Moneglia 1996). A manual segmentation of 400,000 words based on explicit prosodic and pragmatic criteria reveals that only 66% of the resulting units fit the canonical sentence model centered on a main clause. The remaining text units are built on many kinds of phrases, each of them with its specific illocutionary force. Similar results emerge from Chapter 14 'Grammar of conversation' in Biber et al. (1999): the so-called non-clausal text-units constitute one third of the segmented utterances in the sample corpus.

The text units correspond indeed to one of the uses of the term 'utterance', i.e. roughly stretches of discourse that are syntactically independent and prosodically and semantically autonomous. The notion of utterance as a synonym of text unit is widely accepted to designate a turn made up of non-clausal

---

9 See Deulofeu (2003) for a more detailed presentation.

material, because it signals that a non-clausal syntactic phrase (e.g. the adverb *forward*) 'unexpectedly' plays the part of a main clause (*Forward!*) instead of being a mere constituent integrated in a clause as in *I am moving forward* (Culicover and Jackendoff 2005: 236–8). But if the text unit is clause-like, it is useful to make the distinction between a clause as a pure syntactic frame and an utterance that is a clausal syntactic frame endowed with illocutionary force. Yet the difference can be still related to a clear formal property: a clause is a syntactic unit integrated into a construction without an independent prosodic contour, an utterance is a syntactic unit endowed with an autonomous prosodic contour.

Yet it is possible to adopt descriptive frameworks in which text units or utterances may appear to be built upon non-clausal as well as clausal frames. Here descriptive linguists would replace the assumption of the sentence as the maximal syntactic unit by an alternative one: (almost) any word or phrase or combination of phrases can form a syntactic frame for building a text unit with the appropriate prosodic contour. A main clause, on this account, is just one type of text unit among many possible ones, namely the one that is based on a construction headed by a finite verb. We will now elaborate on this new perspective to show precisely how a model constructed on these assumptions can deal with the examples analyzed in this chapter. However, first we need to make one more step to capture the syntactic structure of spontaneous discourse: we must go beyond text units and move on to discourse units.

5.1 From text units to discourse units

Discourse is usually reduced to a concatenation of utterances, which amounts to saying that the building blocks of discourse, in other words utterances, are necessarily formed by means of a syntactic unit, be it clausal or non-clausal. But the actual units that speakers use to convey messages to their addressees go far beyond these forms. Addressees also accept messages without syntactic units. Some of them retain phonetic segments, such as interjections, or onomatopoeias. They certainly have phonetic substance, but are not integrated into the grammatical system of the language. Other messages have no phonetic content and consist of what we may call communicative behaviors: mimics or gestures. The last step is to include discourse units with no symbolic form at all. They consist of pieces of meaning derived by inferences from what has been said by the speaker.

Berrendonner and Groupe de Fribourg (2013), Blanche-Benveniste (1990), Deulofeu (2008), and Debaisieux (2013) claim that it is possible and necessary to capture the combinatorial regularities of discourse units in a separate component of the linguistic description (macro-syntax) and to articulate these regularities with the rules of syntax in the narrow sense (micro-syntax) in order to properly describe the way in which messages are processed. At the microsyntactic level syntactic units (phrases and clauses) combine into larger units according to grammatical dependency rules. At the macrosyntactic level, discourse units, i.e. utterances (syntactic frames endowed with prosodic contours) and communicative behaviors, combine according to the regularities of what Mithun (2005) calls pragmatic dependency. We will focus on the easiest combinations to capture, that is, those between discourse units based on symbolic frames, and especially relevant to our argument here, clause frames.

5.2 Typology of discourse units

It is indeed possible to define two types of clauses based on utterances according to their internal structure as well as their combinatorial possibilities: free units ('Nuclei') and discourse dependent units ('Satellites'). A nucleus can stand by itself as an autonomous free-standing message. As for its internal composition, the nucleus is by default a construction endowed with illocutionary force. This property that we code by the feature [+illoc] may be assigned to the various clause types (declarative, interrogative and exclamative) to the extent that they bear a range of conclusive prosodic contours. The combination of clause types and conclusive contours yields various types of nuclei, whose illocutionary force (assertive, interrogative injunctive. . .) is coded here by punctuation marks:

(52) *Il est arrivé / Il est arrivé ? / il est arrivé !*
'He arrived' / 'has he arrived ?' he has arrived!'

(53) *Ce que c'est beau ! quand je pense qu'il devait venir!'*
'That is beautiful! When I think he was coming!'

(54) *Est-ce qu'il est arrivé?*
'Did he arrive?'

To sum up, the nucleus is essential for the processing of discourse: it may constitute a complete message, acknowledged as such by the addressee, and can assume various speech functions (Verstraete 2007) according to its specific terminal prosodic contour. This central unit may be accompanied by one or several satellites, which can be considered as discursively or pragmatically dependent on the nucleus, since they cannot by themselves form a free standing message but need to be grouped with a nucleus to be properly interpreted. As regards their internal composition, the satellite bears the feature [-illoc] irrespective of whether it is realized before or after the Nucleus. The [-illoc] feature codes the fact that the construction displays a non terminal contour and that, in case of a satellite introduced by a conjunction, no sentence type variation is possible (55'):

(55)   *Comme il était là je ne suis pas venu* 'As he was there I didn't come'

(55')   **Comme est-ce qu'il était là, je suis pas venu* *'As was he there I didn't come'

If we take the default option of a weakly constrained interface between syntactic entities and discourse units we predict that there is no one-to-one correspondence between the types at the respective levels. (52) shows that a declarative clause type can be endowed with all the major speech functions, (53) that syntactic units introduced by a conjunction such as *quand* can function as main clauses, and (54) that some syntactic frames are specialized in conveying specific speech functions.

The clear cut distinction we make between microsyntax as the domain of grammatical dependency and macrosyntax as the domain of discourse dependency is a radical answer to the issue of the grammatical status of so called extra-clausal constituents (Kaltenböck 2016).

Within this framework, we propose to analyze examples like *si tu savais ce que moi j'étais contente* as a macrosyntactic combination of the satellite *si tu savais* pertaining to the subclass of stance markers such as *tu vois, tu imagines. . . .* and a nucleus *ce que moi j'étais contente*. This nucleus is an instance of a subclass of exclamative nuclei introduced by *ce que, comme, que. . .*). Examples like (2) *quand tu penses que euh en 1978 + 80 / 82 l' agneau on le vendait 34 francs le kilo à la carcasse* are analyzed as a macrosyntactic nucleus based on a construction introduced by a complex marker (Verb + Que complementizer). This configuration groups together a relevant number of members formed by the association of an entrenched verb phrase and a complementizer (*est-ce que* 'is it that', *c'est que* 'it is that ',*dire que* 'to say that', *c'est à dire que* 'that is to say that', *ça veut dire que* 'it means that. . .'* The complex marker is in turn embedded into a metadiscursive non-integrated *quand* clause. Indeed *quand* is just one among several conjunctions able to introduce clauses performing metadiscursive functions, such as *parce que* 'because', *bien que* 'although', *puisque* 'since' (Debaisieux 2007).

To account for the switch from metadiscursive satellite to nucleus status, we propose to extend the insubordination model by allowing the incorporated material to be an exclamative nucleus (macrosyntactic unit), instead of a main clause (grammatical unit). In this specific case, the basis of the process is a discourse pattern that can be traced back to a pragmatic routine. *Quand je pense* behaves as an instructional marker to reconstruct an exclamative stance about the propositional content of the clause, without reference to a particular "main" syntactic frame. Our claim is that such an extension is the best way of capturing the descriptive generalizations.

6 Conclusion

In Section 2, we provided a detailed corpus-based analysis of the prosodic, syntactic, semantic, and pragmatic properties of *si* clauses and the *quand* "insubordinate" clauses in French. In Section 3, we showed that the two constructions differ in various ways. The type of constructions as in example (1) with a *si* clause and some cases with *quand je pense* clauses can be analyzed as a configuration which associates a main exclamative clause with a parenthetical clause functioning as a pragmatic marker. The type of construction as in example (2) with a complex *quand je pense que* clause is related to metadiscursive clauses fulfilling the pragmatic function of establishing a new topic. In Section 4, we compared Evans' solution to our own analysis. In Section 5, we presented our framework and showed that the apparent "insubordinates" are instances of regular syntactic patterns. For the *si tu savais* clause, it seems more economical to consider that the whole construction does not result from the emancipation of a former subordinate clause. As for the case with *quand je pense que*, the insubordination model helps to reach explanatory adequacy but needs to be extended to conventionalization of discourse patterns instead of resorting to reduction of grammatical structures.

We have been providing a tentative typology of the syntax of discourse relations based on explicit criteria that allow us to challenge the descriptions couched in terms of the standard insubordination model. But we are aware that for the specific problem of insubordination the choice of a solution should not be a matter of theoretical preference. It should be defended both on empirical grounds and on the basis of its comparative complexity. We hope we have outlined the solution that best captures the descriptive generalizations presented in earlier sections.

Acknowledgements: We thank N. Evans and H. Watanabe for their relevant comments on a preliminary version of our work. We are grateful to the editors and two anonymous reviewers for their help in improving a first version of this chapter.

References

Berrendonner, Alain & Groupe de Fribourg. 2013. *Grammaire de la période*. Berlin, Bruxelles: Peter Lang.

Biber, Douglas, Stig Johansson, Geoffrey Leech, Susan Conrad & Edwin Finegan. 1999. *Longman grammar of spoken and written English*. London: Longman.

Blanche-Benveniste, Claire. 1990. *Le français parlé, études grammaticales*. Paris: Editions du CNRS. Coll. Sciences du langage.

Buridant, Claude. 2000. *Grammaire nouvelle de l'ancien français*. Paris: SEDES.

Combettes, Bernard. 2013. Quelques aspects de la *subordination* en ancien et moyen français. In Jeanne-Marie Debaisieux (ed.), *Analyses linguistiques sur corpus*, 99–140. Paris: Hermes Lavoisier.

Cresti, Emanuella & Massimo Moneglia (eds.). 1996. *C-ORAL-ROM: Integrated reference corpora for spoken Romance Languages*. Amsterdam & Philadelphia: John Benjamins Publishing Company.

CRFP : Corpus *de référence du français parlé*.http://www.up.univmrs.fr/delic/corpus/index. html

Culicover Peter & Ray Jackendoff. 2005. *Simpler syntax*. Oxford: Oxford University Press.

Debaisieux, Jeanne-Marie. 2007. La distinction entre dépendance grammaticale et dépendance macrosyntaxique comme moyen de résoudre les paradoxes de la subordination. *Faits de Langue* 28. 119–132.

Debaisieux, Jeanne-Marie (ed.). 2013. *Analyses linguistiques sur corpus*. Paris: Hermès Lavoisier.

Debaisieux, Jeanne-Marie. 2016. Toward a global approach to discourse uses of conjunctions in spoken French. *Language Sciences* 58. 79–94.

Debaisieux, Jeanne-Marie, José Deulofeu & Martin Philippe. 2008. Pour une syntaxe sans ellipse. In Jean Christophe Pitavy & Michelle Bigot (eds.), *Ellipse et effacement*, 225–247. Saint Etienne: P.U.

Deulofeu, José. 2003. L'approche macrosyntaxique en syntaxe: un nouveau modèle de rasoir d'Occam contre les notions inutiles. *Scolia* 16. 47–62.

Deulofeu, José. 2008. Peripheral constituents as generalized hanging topics. In Robert Kawajima, Gilles Philippe & Thelma Sowley (eds.), *Phantom sentences: essays in linguistics and literature presented to Ann Banfield*, 227–257. Berne: Peter Lang.

Deulofeu, José. 2010. La greffe d'un énoncé sur une construction: une combinaison originale de parataxe et de rection. In Marie-José Beguelin, Mathieu Avanzi & Gilles, Corminboeuf (eds.), *La Parataxe Tome 1: Entre dépendance et intégration*, 175–208. Berne: Peter Lang.

Deulofeu, José 2014. La problématique de la liaison entre prédications à la lumière de la distinction entre construction et énoncé: intégration versus insertion. *Langue Française* 182. 59–73.

Deulofeu, José 2017. La macrosyntaxe comme moyen de tracer la limite entre organisation grammaticale et organisation du discours. *Modèles Linguistiques* 2016. 135–166.

Evans, Nicholas. 2007. Insubordination and its uses. In Irina Nikolaeva (ed.), *Finiteness: theoretical and empirical foundations*, 356–431. Oxford: Oxford University Press.

Evans, Nicholas & Wanatabe Honore (eds.). 2016. *Insubordination*. Amsterdam & Philadelphia: John Benjamins Publishing Company.

FRANTEXT. http://www.frantext.fr/

Garrett, Edward 2001. *Evidentiality and assertion in Tibetan*. Los Angeles: University of California Los Angeles dissertation.

Halliday, M.A.K. 1985. *Introduction to Functional Grammar*. London: Edward Arnold.

Lombardi Vallauri, Edoardo. 2004. Grammaticalization of syntactic incompleteness: free conditionals in italian and other languages. *Sky Journal of Linguistics* 17. 189–215.

Kaltenböck, Gunther. 2016. On the grammatical status of insubordinate *if*-clauses. In Kaltenböck, Gunther, Evelien Keizer & Arne Lohmann (eds.), *Outside the clause: Form and function of extra-clausal constituents*, 341–378. Amsterdam: John Benjamins Publishing Company.

Marandin, Jean-Marie. 2008. The exclamative clause type in French. In Stefan Müller (ed.), *Proceedings of the 15th international conference on head-driven phrase structure grammar*, 436–456. http://cslipublications.stanford.edu/HPSG/9/toc.shtml.

Martin, Philippe. 2009. *L'intonation du français*. Paris: Armand Colin.

Martin, Philippe. 2014. Spontaneous speech corpus data validates prosodic constraints. In Nick Campbell, Dafydd Gibbon & Daniel First (eds.), *Proceedings of the 6th conference on speech prosody*, 525–529. http://fastnet.netsoc.ie/sp7/sp7book.pdf.

Meillet, Antoine & Jules Vendryès. 1924. *Traité de grammaire comparée des langues classiques*. Paris: Champion.

Milner, Jean-Claude. 1978. *De la syntaxe à l'interprétation: quantités, insultes, exclamations*. Paris: Editions du Seuil.

Mithun, Marianne. 2005. On the assumption of the sentences as the basic unit of syntactic structures. In Zygmunt Frayzingier (ed.), *Linguistic diversity and language theory*, 169–183. Amsterdam & Philadelphia: John Benjamins Publishing Company.

Patard, Adeline. 2014. Réflexions sur l'origine de l'insubordination: Le cas de trois insubordonnées hypothétiques du français. *Langages* 4. 109–130.

Saez, Frédérique. 2014. Découplage de constructions en *quand*. *Verbum* 36 (1). 207–233.

Struckmeier, Volker & Sebastian Kaiser. 2015. When *insubordination* is an *artefact* (of sentence type theories). Presentation at workshop (Semi-)independent subordinate constructions, 48th Annual Meeting of the Societas Linguistica Europaea, Leiden University Centre for Linguistics 2–5 September 2015.

TCOF: *Traitement de Corpus Oraux en Français*. http://www.cnrtl.fr/corpus/tcof/

Tomasello, Michael. 2005. *Constructing a language*. Cambridge: Harvard University Press.

Verstraete Jean Christophe. 2007. *Rethinking the coordinate-subordinate dichotomy. Interpersonal Grammar and the analysis of adverbial clauses in English*. Berlin & New York: Mouton de Gruyter.

Index

https://doi.org/10.1515/9783110638288-013